An Intervening Love

An Intervening Love

The Mystery of God's Providence
and the Paradox of His Grace

THOMAS M. STALLTER

Foreword by Christine Hill

WIPF & STOCK · Eugene, Oregon

AN INTERVENING LOVE
The Mystery of God's Providence and the Paradox of His Grace

Copyright © 2025 Thomas M. Stallter. All rights reserved. Except for brief quotations in critical publications or reviews, no part of this book may be reproduced in any manner without prior written permission from the publisher. Write: Permissions, Wipf and Stock Publishers, 199 W. 8th Ave., Suite 3, Eugene, OR 97401.

Wipf & Stock
An Imprint of Wipf and Stock Publishers
199 W. 8th Ave., Suite 3
Eugene, OR 97401

www.wipfandstock.com

PAPERBACK ISBN: 979-8-3852-4341-9
HARDCOVER ISBN: 979-8-3852-4342-6
EBOOK ISBN: 979-8-3852-4343-3

VERSION NUMBER 042925

Scripture quotations are taken from the Holy Bible, New International Version®, NIV®. Copyright © 1973, 1978, 1984, 2011 by Biblica, Inc.™ Used by permission of Zondervan. All rights reserved worldwide. www.zondervan.com The "NIV" and "New International Version" are trademarks registered in the United States Patent and Trademark Office by Biblica, Inc.™

To Annabella, Madeleine, George, and Charlie,
the young ones of our clan.

May their lives be filled with the awe of God's goodness and mercy as they open their hearts to the intervention of this love, the mystery of his providence, and the paradox of his grace.

Often, when we need him most, he seems farthest away . . . gone on ahead, leaving only the faint print of his feet on the path to follow. And the world blows leaves across the path. And branches fall. And darkness falls. . . . We all must live in faith. . . . [For] Christ is there with us on our way as surely as the way itself is there that has brought us to this place. It has brought us. We are here. He is with us . . . but only in unseen ways, as subtle and pervasive as air.

—*Fredrick Buechner*

I am the way the truth and the truth and the life.
Blessed are those who have not seen and yet believed.

—*Jesus*

Contents

Foreword | xv
Introduction | xix

1. Spiritual Fog | 1
2. The Truthful Way | 4
3. Moral Society | 6
4. Asceticism or Freedom in Christ | 8
5. Christianity or Religion | 10
6. Misplaced Loyalty | 13
7. The Proud Heart | 15
8. Moral Law Forgotten | 17
9. Divided Loyalty | 19
10. Service and Loyalty | 21
11. Trusting the God of Grace | 23
12. Justice in Society | 25
13. Beliefs Must Result in Behavior | 27
14. Differences Between People Matter | 30
15. Imperfect but Forgiven | 32
16. The Information Stalker | 34
17. Social Roles | 36
18. People Are Not Equal | 38
19. Social Idols | 40
20. Some Are Further Along than Others | 42
21. Free Will in a Broken World | 44
22. God Chose to Use Us | 47
23. Religion or Relationship | 49

24. Resolve or Rest | 51
25. God's Will Achieved? | 53
26. How Much Do You Matter? | 55
27. Playing Our Part Well | 57
28. Determination | 59
29. Choosing God | 61
30. Self-Assertion or Service | 63
31. Dangerous Virtues and Dark Disciplines | 65
32. Perfectionism | 67
33. The Paradox of God's Gift of Freedom | 69
34. Lost Values in a Broken World | 71
35. Not Alone in His Plan | 73
36. What Kind of Fool | 75
37. The Friends We Keep | 77
38. To Do Good or to Be Good? | 79
39. The Seeing and the Blind | 81
40. Honor, Grace, and Humility | 83
41. The Pure in Heart | 85
42. Ritual Behavior | 88
43. He Comes | 90
44. Here but Wanting to Be There | 92
45. What I Want | 94
46. Free Will | 96
47. Cultural Filters and the Bible | 98
48. Personal Barriers | 100
49. God, So Different from Us | 102
50. God Chooses Some | 104
51. "Biblical" Doctrine | 106
52. God at Work in You | 108
53. I Believe It | 110
54. Unreliable Feelings | 112
55. Explaining God | 114
56. Good People | 117
57. The "Ordinary" Christian Life | 120
58. The Ultimate Identity | 122

59. Our Cultural Lens | 124
60. Learning Is Not for the Faint of Heart | 126
61. Truth | 128
62. Reaction | 130
63. Failings | 132
64. The Mystery of God's Ways | 134
65. The Justice of Man and God | 136
66. In the Ordinary Things | 138
67. Quiet People | 140
68. Why Go to Church? | 142
69. Reminders of Sin and Grace | 144
70. God Speaks with Purpose | 146
71. Meaning and Purpose | 148
72. Worldview Gone Wrong | 150
73. Social Authority | 153
74. Security | 155
75. Good Things Made Bad | 158
76. Cultures of the Bible | 160
77. Walking Worthy of the Gospel | 163
78. Our Part in Making Disciples | 165
79. Information About God | 167
80. Fatal Mixture | 169
81. Perfect Christians | 171
82. Never Good Enough | 173
83. Maybe God Doesn't Mind | 174
84. A Lifetime | 176
85. The Nature of Worship | 178
86. Commanded to Worship? | 180
87. Glorify God | 182
88. To Do or Not to Do | 184
89. Heaven or Hell? | 186
90. Encouraging Popular Christianity | 188
91. Life as a Christian | 190
92. Sustaining Faith | 192
93. Biblical Christians in Ordinary Life | 194

94. For the Love of God | 196
95. Freedom from Cultural Conscience | 198
96. Early Impressions | 200
97. In the Stillness | 202
98. Miracles | 204
99. Improvements to Worship | 206
100. Glorify (?) God in Our Lives | 208
101. What Is Your Name? | 209
102. The Fear of God | 211
103. Religion or Righteousness | 213
104. Beauty with Tremors | 215
105. God's Work | 217
106. Bargaining with God | 219
107. God's Sovereignty | 221
108. Good Is Evil, Evil Is Good? | 223
109. Look at Me | 225
110. Hard Times | 227
111. I Have Been Wronged | 229
112. The Power of Darkness Undone | 231
113. Culture and Conversion | 233
114. God's Goodness and Our Freedom | 235
115. God's Help | 237
116. Human Religion | 239
117. Doing Good | 241
118. Faith | 243
119. Quiet Loyalty in Times of Trouble | 245
120. The Builder at Work | 247
121. Independence Has Its Dangers | 249
122. Confusion in the Church | 251
123. What We Don't Know | 253
124. The Pride of the Self | 255
125. Knowing or Not Knowing | 257
126. I Don't Feel Like It | 259
127. Taking Others Seriously | 261
128. Roadblocks to Knowing the Truth | 263

129. To Be Free of Anxiety | 265
130. The Value of Weakness | 268
131. Personal Peace | 270
132. A Broken World | 272
133. The Power of Culture | 274
134. Problems Reading the Bible | 277
135. The Barrier of Culture | 278
136. Satan Makes No Friends | 280
137. The Journey | 282
138. The Importance of Names | 284
139. Different from Each Other | 286
140. Truth and Experience | 288
141. Approaching God | 290
142. Beginnings of a Life with God | 292
143. What Is It to Be Spiritual? | 294
144. The Simplicity or Complexity of Faith | 296
145. Spiritual Disciplines | 298
146. Missionaries? | 300
147. Motives and Ritual Behavior | 302
148. The Human Jesus | 304
149. Behavior and Freedom in Christ | 306
150. God's Ways Are Not Our Ways | 308
151. The Good and Evil of Humankind | 310
152. Personal and Social Choices | 312
153. Human "Justice" Judged | 314
154. The Human Heart | 316
155. Theologians and Everybody Else | 318
156. The Kingdom of Heaven First | 320
157. Bad Maps to Knowing God | 322
158. Love | 324
159. Common Sense | 326
160. Confusion in Difficult Times | 328
161. Never Alone | 330
162. Doubt | 332
163. Remember | 334

164. Get Busy | 336
165. Simple Faith | 338
166. Knowing God and His Purposes | 340
167. The Fall of Humankind | 342
168. Creatures of Habit | 344
169. The Ways of God | 346
170. The Grace of God in Christ | 348
171. Confidence in Being Right | 350
172. The Weakness of Wealth | 352
173. Feeling Saved | 354
174. Theological Maps | 356
175. Human Culture in the Church? | 358
176. Our Part in God's Plan | 360
177. God Uses the Most Unlikely People | 362
178. God's Providence at Work | 364
179. The Real Me | 366
180. Born Again—A New Beginning | 368
181. The Mirror Doesn't Lie | 370
182. The Demands of Culture | 372
183. Weakness and Walking Worthy | 374
184. The Essentials of God's Word | 376
185. Connecting with the Message of the Bible | 379
186. Sovereignty with Grace | 381
187. Knowing Heads and Anxious Hearts | 383
188. Self-Centered | 385
189. Is God Angry? | 387
190. Satan at Your Side in the World | 389
191. Nature Speaks | 391
192. To Love or Not to Love | 393
193. Opinions or Wisdom | 395
194. Mask and Ego | 397
195. Fear of Hell | 399
196. Blind Leaders | 400
197. Human Weakness, God's Strength | 402
198. Loving Others | 404

199. Impatience | 406
200. Envy | 408
201. Starved for Grace | 410
202. Making Disciples | 412
203. Fixing Things | 414
204. The Paradox of God's Ways | 416
205. The Irony of God | 418
206. Seeing God | 420
207. God Among Gods | 422
208. Risking the Local Church | 424
209. The Sweet Poison of Legalism | 426
210. The Other Side of the Door | 428
211. The Nature of God's Word | 430
212. The Church Today | 432
213. Time on Our Hands | 434
214. Unreasoned Death | 436
215. Unending Hope | 438
216. Poor in Spirit and Pure in Heart | 440
217. Obedience | 442
218. A Selfless Person Who Can Find? | 444
219. Forgiving Others | 446
220. Trouble in the Church | 448
221. Jesus and Social Justice | 450
222. Biblical Thinking | 452
223. To Forget God | 454
224. Freedom in Christ That Honors God | 456
225. Religion Is Not the Cure | 458
226. God's Great Disappointment | 460
227. Those Who Are Well | 462
228. Years Go By | 464
229. God's Providence Matters | 466
230. Dread and Anxiety | 468
231. The Disintegration of a Culture | 470
232. The Power of God Today and Tomorrow | 472
233. Adam, Eve, and Sin Today | 474

234. Doing Good and Evil | 476
235. The Ordinary | 478
236. The Cross | 480
237. Jesus Gives Hope | 482
238. Suffering, Difficulties, and Sorrows | 484
239. Better for Having Suffered | 486
240. The End of All Things | 488
241. God's Message and Human Culture | 490
242. The Way of Wisdom | 492
243. Achieving Wisdom | 495
244. Unsettling Change | 497
245. The Dull Ache of Conscience | 499
246. Choosing God's Way in a Broken World | 501
247. Responding to an Intervening Love | 503

Foreword

Every once in a while a book speaks with gripping relevance to nuances of the Christian life, which provides clarity in the midst of confusing times and conflicting messages. The book *An Intervening Love*, focusing on relational Christianity, is among them. Dr. Tom Stallter expertly delivers words of wisdom that undermine a false form of the Christian life steeped in performance, pride, and self-reliance. The subtle spiritual syncretism that pervades the American church and Western mindsets is exposed so readers can learn a more biblical way of life in Christ. This way is not a formula or a map; it's a relationship with a person, God himself.

The reality of the good news is that we are fully loved and accepted, even in our messiness and slowness in the progressive sanctification process. The unconditional love of God allows our hearts to feel safe with God and to take off our masks of performance, legalism, and perfectionism so that we can internalize a sense of secure attachment to him. His love intervenes in our lives so we can experience healing from the broken patterns of trying to meet our need for security and significance outside God's shalom. The relational disconnect from God is what drives sinful attitudes, motives, and choices. So it makes sense that the healing from sin must necessarily come in the form of God's intervening love: the restoration of that relationship. The real work of God is on the inside of our hearts, where he desires to bring freedom and life that is truly life.

This book helps readers move from a formulaic posture with God (I do A, so God has to do B, so that I get C) in order to discover the God of the Bible. He is worthy of our trust and surrender, even if we do all the right things and don't get the "good" results that we desire in this life. Tom's gentle but firm words invite the reader to move out from under a subtle but deadly motive of trying to use God to get what one wants to letting God use us to get what he wants out of our life with him. And can we trust that when God gets what he wants, it will also be what we really wanted as well? This is the essence of a true relationship. When God's intervening love invades our hearts, we are caught up in the larger story of God's redemptive work in our lives and through our lives. The natural by-product of living life loved by God will free us up to move towards others in sacrificial and God-honoring ways. We will have the fruit of the Holy Spirit's work in our lives, which is not enforced by external mechanisms but comes from the internal reality that our identity is in Christ.

As you read these pages, you will be engaging in what spiritual authors have recognized as the foundation for spiritual maturity: growing in double knowledge. Double knowledge is defined as knowing God and knowing self. Both of these aspects of knowledge are necessary for the spiritual journey. This book will equip you in both types of knowledge.

In terms of knowing God, you will encounter a sovereign, gracious, and pursuing Lord, who is "bringing his plan to its completion in history" (chap. 43). We find that "there is nothing this broken world can do to us that cancels his love for his own" (chap. 110). His motive for how he runs the world is fueled by love, wisdom, and goodness. He is the type of God who doesn't just want our begrudging compliance; he actually wants our hearts, which includes our deep-seated trust and loyalty. As we get to know the God of the Bible in the pages of this book, we are also confronted with false notions of God, what I like to call the "god of our imagination." Tom expertly points out the subtle but misguided versions of God that have been shaped in us by the values of Western culture and popular religion, such as a God who primarily just wants us to be happy over being holy, a God who is dedicated to giving me what I want when I ask in faith, a God who basically serves my will. We will experience spiritual growth as we exchange the god of our imagination for the God who is—the Great I AM of the Bible.

In terms of knowing self, you will be confronted with truth about your motives, values, knee-jerk reactions, and often unquestioned assumptions about life. You might not like this aspect of the book. Like any good medicine, though, it might be unpleasant to our palate but it is necessary for the healing of our misshapen soul. *An Intervening Love* uncovers aspects of the self, enculturated in Western individualism, that have been built on shifting sand instead of the solid foundation of life in Christ. For example, the self is exposed as deeply performance-driven, insatiably craving approval horizontally, and burdened with the immense task of constructing an identity on one's own merit. Immature relating patterns with God and others assume that I am at the center of the universe and that God is my helper to achieve the significance I need to quell the fears and insecurities of life outside of Eden. *An Intervening Love* invites us to move into the deep with God, relinquishing the illusion of control we thought we had over outcomes, repenting of trusting in false formulas, recognizing idols of the heart, and confessing our neediness before a God who is not overwhelmed with our brokenness. This really is good news for the weary pilgrim.

As you open up the pages of *An Intervening Love*, you will find yourself with a seasoned trail guide in the spiritual journey. He has experienced heartaches that have refined his assumptions about God and have tested his loyalty to the God of the Bible. I have seen Tom's attachment to and trust in God on display in times of great adversity and immense pain, which has inspired me deeply. I can attest that God's intervening love has not made his life comfortable or easy, but it has made him a trusted guide for the walk of faith. You'll be in good company for your own journey of faith.

—Christine Hill
Professor of Women's Ministries and Spiritual Formation
Grace College and Grace Theological Seminary
Winona Lake, Indiana

Introduction

WHAT? ANOTHER BOOK OF musings about God at work in our lives and the world around us? Yes, it is a continuation: a second book intended to help longtime believers, as well as those at a distance or disenchanted with what they have seen in Christianity, to know God better and from the inside. The first volume, *Finding Freedom and Grace in a Broken World: A Journey in the Purposes and Providence of God*, emphasized the way we think about God.

> Sometimes, "knowing God" is reduced to a cold, rational, informational domain that limits God to the extreme of naked intelligence. Other times, knowing him is cheapened at the extremes of sentimental simplicity or mystical secrets. But there is a correct use of our minds that results in understanding and faith, producing gratefulness, humility, loyalty, worship, and wonder [reaching deep into the heart]. This way of thinking nurtures love for the Creator-God of the universe [and for one another].[1]

The themes here are intended to help us who know or want to know God to become what he wants us to be in a broken world that is trying to shape us into something else. Trusting God's work in us to this end, that we might fulfill his purposes and help others to do so, should be the outcome of our relationship of grace with him. Of course, for one who does not know him, the Bible introduces the Creator-God of the universe, full of grace, and reveals what he wants us to know about his purposes, providence, and plan for the world. He has indeed intervened in the history of humankind. Mystery and paradox are not removed in this revelation, so trust and freedom are, once again, central to the readings here, helping us achieve our intention of living within the design of God. As with the first book, I am writing for people who want to move from Christian routines, rituals, and information about God to flourishing faith and trust, enveloping an ongoing,

---

1. Thomas M. Stallter, *Finding Freedom and Grace in a Broken World: A Journey in the Purposes and Providence of God* (Eugene, OR: Wipf and Stock, 2024), 1.

INTRODUCTION

intimate relationship with him in our broken world. I want to clarify here that God's word is the foundation for my books. It is the frame of reference for the freedom he gives us, as well as for his intervening love, the mystery of his providence, and the paradox of his grace.

I hope people read introductions. I know of no other way the reader will understand my intentions and "strange" approach than for me to tell them what they may expect. The expanded introduction to the first volume and shorter one here are essential if the reader is to "feel at home" with such an approach. God's word is given to us. But, once again, you are in a readers' theater, dealing with the interpretation and application of my comments here in your own mind and heart. It is a foundational principle of human communication theory that meaning is not in words but in people. People make associations with words, culling up meaning for them from their own experience. Since I cannot know yours, I am leaving the application to you.

Some who read the first book thought that adding my personal experiences would be helpful, and I believe it would be for some. But I am following the present format because, for others, our journeys are very different. You may be only on the edge of believing in God. And for the seasoned believer, I may, indeed, be one of the strangest Christians you have ever met. So, though I regret it for some, stories are mostly absent and applications are few, as I do not want to assume the reader's needs and skew the application in an unhelpful direction. I do encourage reading stories of the journeys of others, and there is a plethora of excellent ones available.

Of course, this leaves some work for the reader in a day when we are used to having it done for us. We grew up in the age of entertainment and convenience. I, too, am in love with my microwave, TV remote, laptop, and motorized recliner. I apologize in advance, but if you are one who pores over your reading, looking for latent inspiration and all the potential applications, I hope I have met your expectations and, in some paradoxical way, that God will use something here to help and encourage you on your journey. Take it slow and easy, a little at a time. Let it get under your skin before you react or turn the page. If a reading does not touch you where you are in your life today, go on to another and come back to it later—months later, and read it again before you toss it out.

This book will also deal with how the cultural and social values of individualism, personal achievement, and self-assertion cause problems in our daily desire to know, love, and honor God. This may, at first, raise feelings of defensiveness since these are the tools given to us by our culture for personal survival, and they are not easily evaluated or replaced by biblical values. Not everything in our culture is bad; much of it is very helpful. However, we must approach the Bible with an open heart and mind. We will be reminded to let God speak for himself and asked to weigh the truth about ourselves, the influence of our culture, and God's will for us. Ultimately, our cultural frame of reference must be replaced by a biblical understanding of reality. We must see things as they are, not as our culture shapes them. My concerns about this are more detailed in my book *The Gap Between God and Christianity: The Turbulence of Western Culture* (Eugene, OR: Wipf and Stock, 2022).

Other prominent themes are freedom in Christ as opposed to legalism, trusting God instead of ourselves, God's sacred gift of free will to make love and loyalty possible, and his providence and continued work in us for his purposes. As I said in the previous volume, I am aiming at the Christian who knows they need to move ahead in their faith, the person who has grown tired of only popular ideas about God in his or her life, those who want to think carefully and understand where they are and how to move ahead on their journey to maturity in Christ. Some of us are damaged goods with deep scars from dysfunctional homes and churches. There is no better time than today to move beyond crippling insecurities to a resilient faith. There are none of us without the need to grow in our loyalty to Christ, our trust in God's providence, and our progress toward wisdom. All this may sound like I think I have arrived and see you as needing advice, but let me assure you, I am, with all my weaknesses, faults, and failures, just like you in many ways. We are people up to our knees in imperfection, with a perfect standing before God in Christ, but on a journey toward reflecting that grace in our everyday lives and the perfection that lies ahead. Writing this book has, once again, brought me face-to-face with myself and helped and encouraged me on that journey. I hope it will in some way encourage you.

Emotions, rituals, and traditions will not take us very far on the journey. They may point to the destination but do not provide safe conduct to our journey's end. It will take humility, gratefulness, and trust. I am writing to tired Christians and to those tired of Christianity—to Christians who have yet to trust God completely and to those who have tried Christianity but never met God. I want us to know God's grace, providence, and purposes in a way that changes our lives and experiences in this broken world from this day on.

In both volumes of this work, some disclaimers must be made about the intentions and completeness of each entry and the reasons I use this format. I repeat/paraphrase here from the Introduction to *Finding Freedom and Grace in a Broken World: A Journey in the Purposes and Providence of God*.[2]

---

2. See Stallter, *Finding Freedom*, 8–10.

INTRODUCTION

Some concepts may seem repeated several times, but each time I add to or develop that idea, showing some additional angle or perspective from which to view that truth, or connecting it to some new concept or experience in our lives. Again, you may profit by giving certain thoughts here some time, coming back to them later. We grow in our perspective as we go along in the Christian life. In the spring of our lives, we see things one way, then we go through the summer, and in the autumn we are surprised at how we have changed. These thoughts are reflections during the autumn of my life as I look back at years of God's providence and grace along the way.

Each topic is followed by "Scripture References" that stand behind the comments, so you may go to the Bible directly for help. There, you can go deeper on your journey and see those verses in the larger context of the original, God-inspired author. I have used the 1986 New International Version to select these verses. You may find another version or a modern paraphrase helpful. The number of verses mentioned at the end of each theme is not exhaustive, and the ones listed may not always be those you expect. Some directly relate to the paragraph's themes, while others are indirect or add more context. Some are slightly tangential and touch on a lateral meaning. These may suit the more inquisitive reader. But in each case, go to the source. Like the Bereans, examine the Scriptures yourself to see what is true.

Some passages from the Bible come up over and over as basic themes over broad areas of life and apply to differing scenarios. This will benefit those who read these thoughts topically rather than in sequence. Some verses come from a context in the Bible that seems quite different from the subject of the paragraph, but they also show us something about God that is true for that topic. Some concepts have more verses than others, depending on the nature of the subject matter, and some passages are longer than you might expect to provide more context for better understanding.

I hope you will see new applications of old and familiar verses that have lost their impact in our day. You may see the connection later as you go along and then look back. You may spend a week considering the verses given for one paragraph. Please note the verses are listed in their biblical order, not in the order of the concepts they accompany in the paragraph. In no way are these paragraphs and the verses cited a complete commentary on the subject. They are not intended as such. Neither is every topic of the Bible represented. There is much more in God's word than mentioned here. My purpose is to make an impression on us in our day of need, to help us reflect on what kind of people God purposes for us to be, to help us turn our personal thoughts to God and his ways, to see ourselves in the light of his word, and, finally, to further reflect his image in a desperate world. These

INTRODUCTION

comments are only a beginning. They may take shape in your life in ways only you and God can understand.

I did not intend a one-sitting reading of these comments. At least I did not design them to be read that way. I expected the reader to take them in small doses. Give yourself time to digest each topic a few pages at a time, noting your thoughts and additional Bible verses in the margins or in your journal. For those of us ordinary people, too much of a book in this format at one time blurs our vision as ideas run together, and we forget individual points we might do well to remember. My great inspiration is God's word itself, and I hope my efforts here will lead you to pore over the Bible more often, more deeply. Allow yourself to explore your mind and heart in the shadow of the greatness of our God.

Do not accept the paragraphs in this book as complete or final for you. Though they are statements of what I believe God's word says to us, I cannot, as I have said, apply them specifically to you. Only you can do that. These are broad strokes. Make your own observations that touch you where you are in your life. Each of us has his or her own journey with God. But God's providence is at work in all of us and can be trusted completely. I sincerely hope some of these comments will be helpful to you on your journey.

I have one more suggestion. Though some of us read alone, reading these entries with a friend or spouse might be more meaningful for others. Also, studying the Scripture references for their connection with the paragraphs is a good way to stimulate thinking with a friend or in a small group as you reflect together. God's word is our starting place for a growing commitment to him. We must give it thoughtful attention. The stakes are too high and our lives are too short to do otherwise.

Yes, God's love has intervened in our situation as he did in the lives of wealthy and educated Nicodemus, the five-times-divorced Samaritan woman, blind and poor Bartimaeus, the woman taken in adultery, Zacchaeus, the gouging tax collector, and so many others. These lives were changed by that love. Many today who read this page have accepted that love through faith in Christ. They began a journey of living for God, as have you. I pray this book will be helpful to you along the way. For others of you, God is waiting to intervene in your life with love and grace, bringing forgiveness, purpose, and meaning. Read on.

1. Spiritual Fog

The goal . . . is love, which comes from a pure heart and good conscience and a sincere faith. Some have wandered away from these and turned to meaningless talk.

—1 Tim 1:5–6

SOME PEOPLE MAKE THE Christian life an out of reach, overwhelming fog of spiritual activity and elusive power, clouding it with sensations and signs that Paul never mentioned to young pastors he was mentoring. As important as they are, the work of the Holy Spirit and prayer, God's calling, spiritual gifts, and even obedience can become issues of burdensome confusion in many teachings of popular or legalistic "Christianity." God intends in his word that our "ordinary" lives, our everyday experience, would be characterized by trust, gratefulness, freedom, and confidence in his good providence. In this way of life, all the important concerns mentioned above take on their proper place and emphasis. There is plenty of mystery in God himself, but his purpose for our lives is pretty straightforward. Don't be intimidated by those who leave our walk with God in the clouds of spiritual obscurity. Come in out of the fog and open your heart and mind to God in his word; open yourself to humility, trust, and loyalty to him. Trust the Spirit who leads you to this uncomplicated and essential, even "simple," faith. Our lives in Christ begin there. The two aims of these paragraphs are to encourage tired Christians to trust God and walk this path of freedom in Christ and to help those tired of Christianity to know God as he is, the grace he offers, and the peace he gives.

    The Spirit brings things to our minds and hearts as we read God's word, and uses our conscience to convince us of truth as well as our sin, pride, and double motives. Sometimes we do not hear what he wants because we want to hear something else. But if we listen to his word and turn from the negative values and clutter of the world around us, we can renew our minds and let God become the center of our worldview. We can begin to think differently, setting our minds and hearts on things above and doing the good works that are its fruit. But the Spirit does not override us and do for us what he is showing *us* to do. We will have to decide whether to follow his lead or not, to trust God or not, to humble ourselves or not, and to move ahead in a way that honors him or not.

Neither is there mysterious power in prayer. All the power for God's intervention is in himself—our great God of unlimited grace and powerful providence—not in our prayers. We do not get points or advantages from God for praying. Instead, we get closer to God and he to us, whether we cry out to him in need or worship his goodness, grace, and power. Praying on and on when we have already given him our needs, requests, and praise, or to meet some quota, to "get on his good side," or just because we have to check that off our list is very close to the babbling of pagans Jesus speaks of. We may be close to worshiping the spiritual disciplines themselves instead of letting them shape our hearts and lives.

God is not more inclined to listen if we spend more time praying than another, ask for something many times, or pray at the same time each day. He is not interested in novelty or gimmicks. He hears the honest heart the first time, intently values the shortest plea or groan, and gives little attention to clocks and calendars, for he is always there, anytime, anywhere. Particular positions, special activities, or spiritual language do not incline God to help us more than the simple, often silent, prayer of the humble soul, for he looks at the heart and longs to help us. Power is not in prayer, however extraordinary, but in the God with whom we speak—the God who hears.

In the New Testament, God tells us to live lives worthy of the gospel that show the world his goodness and mercy. Mysterious power over sin or Christ living the obedient life through us are not New Testament themes. Enablement is found in the Holy Spirit's use of God's word to lead us to a deeper understanding of God's grace, providence, and power to do the impossible. This leads the honest heart away from selfish grasping to humility and submission. This fruit of the Spirit begins to take root in us as we allow it. Instead of a tingling sensation, he becomes our guide, motivating us to choose a different path for our lives. The intended result is a pattern of good works in our everyday lives. These become the light desperately needed in a dark and broken world so people might see the truth of the gospel.

Scripture References: Pss 25:9, 91:14–16, 145:13b–14a; Prov 20:27, 22:4, 30:5–6; Isa 32:17; Matt 5:3–10, 14–16; 6:5–8; Luke 1:37, 18:9–14; John 13:34–35, 14:25–27, 16:12–13, 17:15–23; Rom 12:1–2; 1 Cor 2:14–15,

1. SPIRITUAL FOG

6:19–20; 2 Cor 4:4–6; Gal 5:16–26; Eph 2:10, 4:1–6, 5:15–18; Phil 1:27; Col 3:1–17; 1 Thess 4:11–12; 1 Tim 1:3–7, 2:1–6; 2 Tim 3:17; Titus 3:1, 8, 14; Heb 13:15–16; Jas 1:13–15; 1 John 2:15–17.

2. The Truthful Way

Jesus answered, "I am the way and the truth and the life. No one comes to the Father except through me."

—*John 14:6*

I ONCE HEARD A presentation by "slow art" Christian artist Makoto Fujimura. It was impressive how he expressed his faith through his art and honored God in his purpose. Here was a man with a name deeply infused with Shinto beliefs, living for Christ. *Makoto* in Japanese means the way of truth that combines the virtues of love, loyalty, and faithfulness needed to maintain harmony throughout creation and as part of our lives. Though it is a commendable ideal, Shinto people believe this can only be accomplished through the *musubi*, the mysterious power, of the *kami*, the gods and spirits of nature. Before us that day was a highly gifted man showing us these qualities come through a relationship with God alone—an invalidating of the *kami* of the religious culture of his birth—and giving glory to God. Culture-care for him puts God at the center, giving us the truthful way.

Truth, like humility, is becoming hard to find in our day. Our American or Japanese culture leads us in the opposite direction and is a powerful influence in our lives. But truth is still there in the person and works of God for those willing to look for it, those seeking it in honesty and humility. Though many try to deny them, the "old stories" of God in the world seeking those who would give their hearts to him are confirmed over and over. Though he uses different letters than our cultural alphabet allows, and it is written too large for many habitually close to it to see, his message of grace is there for all who realize their desperate need for it.

Those who have found this truth have found a treasure worth more than anything the world can offer—meaning and purpose in God's lasting

2. THE TRUTHFUL WAY

love and grace. While the world would like to shape us into something opposed to any resemblance of God's truth, his intervening love seeks to make us his children through Christ. Jesus *is* the way, the truth, and the life he calls us to—the "*makoto*" of God. There we find the undeserved paradox of his grace and forgiveness, releasing us to know freedom from the social rules and cultural expectations of a world without him.

Scripture References: Prov 16:25, 21:2; Jer 29:12-14; Matt 7:7-14, 13:44-46; Luke 9:23-25, 19:1-10; John 1:12; 4:23-24; 8:12, 31-32; 10:10; 14:6; 16:12-15, 17:17; Rom 8:38-39; 2 Cor 4:4, 11:13-15; Eph 2:1-10; Col 3:1-4; 1 Tim 1:7-9, 2:5-6; 1 John 2:15-17.

3. Moral Society

Do not love the world or anything in the world.... The world and its desires pass away, but the man who does the will of God lives forever.

—*1 John 2:15–17*

MANY HUMAN POLITICAL AND social systems have existed throughout the history of our world. Each has its own story with a beginning—and an end. Some have been better than others for a time, but all have failed to rule societies peacefully and provide for their flourishing for long. The reason for this is the source of these systems. They are man-made systems ruling human behavior in a broken world that has removed God from the arrangement, and their members are left without a moral compass. Some Western countries are involved in experiments in democratic socialism and democratic capitalism. The ideals may be commendable. But we also see the results of this democracy and freedom in the hands of human beings without virtue, who desperately seek personal happiness on their own terms.

We are approaching a precipice in Western societies today, all warning signs ignored. But no wonder. Leading voices in the society believe life began in a pond, and mud cannot have virtue or honor; it cannot think. Neither can the finely tuned order of the universe, the exact properties of life support on Earth itself, or the wonders of the human body come out of an explosion followed by millions of years of chance. "Survival of the fittest," as they call it, is, in fact, going backward at the human level. An individualist society without God becomes each person's extermination of everything that does not add to their personal happiness or neurotic pleasure on their terms. The theory is the beginning of the end for human societies—the natural outcome of the old philosophy of nihilism that nothing matters, all is arbitrary, and there is no God.

3. MORAL SOCIETY

But God is not unaware. He can, and often does, restrain this downward spiral so that his purposes are carried out, for and through his people, and his plan accomplished in the world, broken as it is. Those in Christ have the answer to the struggle for survival; their peace and contentment come from loyalty in a relationship with the Prince of peace, the God of grace, and the Spirit of intercession on our behalf, our counselor. They have read ahead in the book with eyes of faith and know how the story ends.

In a perfect world—a moral, ethical world of personal and social justice and selfless behavior—any political system would work. In a world without these virtues and values, no system can endure. For men love darkness rather than light. Certain basic principles have to be in place. Reliable, ethical behaviors must be intact for leadership, and virtue must bear fruit in society for it to thrive, even for it to survive. God's purpose for human government is to maintain justice, peace, and freedom in society, to punish harmful behavior, and to reward good. These principles are given to mankind by our Creator-God. When they weaken or are replaced with human appetites for power, wealth, recognition, or pleasure, when corruption is condoned and the righteous persecuted, society perishes. For there is a point of no return. In the past, when the people of a nation became engrossed in their rebellion against God, he gave them over to their way ... and their inevitable end. But where humans fail, God succeeds. He gives peace and contentment to his own in this fragmented world, and, one day, he will set things right again and put a kingdom in place that will be ruled perfectly.

Scripture References: Gen 6:5–9, 19:12–13; 2 Chr 7:14; Pss 11:1–7, 14:1, 15:1–5, 33:11, 91:14–16, 99:4–7; Prov 6:12–19, 21:3; Eccl 5:8–12; Isa 9:6; 11:1–4a; 24:1–23; 26:3–4, 12–13; 43:1; Mic 6:8; John 3:16–21, 14:15–18 with 25 and 27 with 16:33; Rom 1:18–32, 2:1–11, 5:1–2, 13:1–7; 2 Thess 2:7; 1 Tim 1:14–17; 2 Tim 3:1–5; 1 Pet 2:13–15, 4:1–2, 7–11; 2 Pet 3:1–9; Rev 21:1–4.

4. Asceticism or Freedom in Christ

To the pure, all things are pure, but to those who are corrupted and do not believe, nothing is pure.

—*Titus 1:15*

SOME HAVE GIVEN US asceticism—complete self-denial—as the way to know God. You may have given up on such a God's existence, and you should. This is not the God of the Bible. Though we seek the kingdom of God first, he has given believers all good things to enjoy with thankful hearts and love for those around them. Paul tells Timothy to instruct the wealthy "to put their hope in God" and, in the context of that commitment, goes on to say, "who richly provides us with everything for our enjoyment" (1 Tim 6:17). With the priority of God and his boundaries first, all the good things he provides—all of creation—are to be enjoyed: the wonders of nature, joy of relationships, and provisions for our bodies. Using asceticism and sacrifice to earn God's favor is not his way. It becomes a system of legalism from which we have been delivered by Christ's sacrifice and the rich generosity of God's grace. The injurious severity of this legalistic asceticism is focused on fleshly denial, but, as Jesus said, "The Spirit gives life; the flesh counts for nothing" (John 6:33).

Our salvation is by God's grace, through the Spirit, and achievements in the flesh accomplish nothing to this end. We can make no amount of sacrifice in our bodies that will persuade God to favor us, to gain access to his grace, to know his forgiveness. We already have it all through faith in the perfect sacrifice of Christ on our behalf. To add our imperfect, perhaps selfish, even prideful "good" works—we may even call them "spiritual disciplines"—to the work of Christ to earn God's approval contradicts his word and denies all he has told us about his grace. It is legalism disguised

4. ASCETICISM OR FREEDOM IN CHRIST

as spiritual commitment. We become his sons and daughters and know the freedom Jesus talks about by God's unmerited favor alone. Any good work we do as his child is a result of that relationship, not a cause.

No, asceticism is not the way. God wants our hearts, not our physical self-denial or sterile obedience. If our hearts are right with him—if he has them—the question of physical asceticism is moot. Over time, if we remain in him and with the help of his Spirit, all else will become more and more what it ought to be to honor him. We are reminded of the Pharisee and the tax collector in the temple, where we see religious works compared to humble dependence on God. Even under the law of Moses, God sought people's hearts. Spiritual disciplines may greatly help us if we are not in love with the practice or our achievement. We must realize they are only the maps that point us to God, strengthen our relationship with him, and remind us of his grace in our lives.

Yes, we can become wrongly attached to material things and physical pleasures, and these attachments, in place of the good things God gave us rightly enjoyed, become suffering for us and lead us away from our relationship with him. Wrong attachments come between us and our love for others as well. But our attention to his more excellent gifts, his all-embracing grace, providential goodness, and prevailing love, however little we deserve them, is the remedy we need. It is the foundation of a relationship with him of humble loyalty, however imperfect, in return for all he has done. To die to self is to die to the wrong attachments of selfish loyalties and loves. To find life is to know his grace and trust him for our well-being while enjoying all he has given us. It is, and always has been, a matter of the heart.

Scripture References: Ps 51:16–17; Prov 21:2–3; Isa 58:6–12; Hos 6:6; Mic 6:8; Matt 5:8, 6:33, 23:11–12; Luke 9:23–25, 18:1–14; John 1:12, 4:23–24, 6:64, 8:31–32, 15:5–8, 17:3; 2 Cor 3:12–18; Col 3:17 with 1 Tim 4:4–5 with 6:17b and Titus 1:15–16; Jas 1:17; 1 John 2:15–17.

5. Christianity or Religion

Now this is eternal life: that they may know you, the only true God, and Jesus Christ whom you have sent.

—*John 17:3*

BIBLICAL CHRISTIANITY IS MADE up of the group of those whose loyalty belongs to God in an undeserved relationship with him through Christ, those who are committed to his word for instruction, encouragement, and strength, with lives motivated by worship, prayer, good works, and the message of hope in a broken world. But before we go too far in listing the qualities and values believers should be known for, let me say, without delay, that they are each a work in progress. Despite their best intentions, they are in need of God's grace each day in the ordinary or extraordinary events of life, and they know it better than anyone. To desire and intend to live out the values and intentions that God is concerned about is to be pure in heart. The Bible calls people like this "righteous," perhaps with a small *r* since they are never perfect. In God's plan, perfection for us is yet to come. In the meantime, we live and act in a relationship with God through the perfect righteousness (we might use a capital *R* here) of Christ given to us by his sacrifice on our behalf. We can know this perfection only by seeing and knowing our imperfection and desperate need for God's grace, in a word, humility. Yes, it is too good to be true for us, but not for God to give it to us. That is his grace, generous and bountiful.

This biblical Christianity is *the* church. But it loses its authenticity and contradicts this relationship with God when it becomes overinstitutionalized, ritual-bound, laden with social politics, overcome with concerns for self-survival, and attendance becomes only a respectable habit. Yes, Christianity can be superficial. It can become one of the many man-made religions

5. CHRISTIANITY OR RELIGION

through our abuse of it for our own ends. The more materialistic, legalistic, sentimental, or syncretized with culture it gets, the more it serves our purposes rather than God's. Some Christians leave a church when it loses its life-giving commitment to God's intentions and plan for them. And if those on the inside are repelled by this popular kind of Christianity, how must the world around us see it? This is no longer biblical Christianity. It is the effects of the broken world inside the church.

It may cause us embarrassment and regret to recall times when we have been part of this human substitute for the church. But, though willful in our choices, we are not alone in the self-deception Satan encourages. Adam and Eve were good people. They had every need met, were given every good thing, and were invited to enjoy creation's beauties and pleasures. They were also warned of the danger of a particular tree, that its fruit would spoil their lives and bring death. But they were told by God's enemy that he had not told them all, that he was withholding something good from them in that tree. They fell for the appealing deception that there was more they could have to improve their situation, something that would give them more knowledge leading to power. They were lured away from trusting God's word. At first the poison was sweet, but it had a bitter end, and they had nothing to get the bitterness out of their mouths. How could they face God now? His eye sees all. He would know. The knowledge of good and evil caused a gap between them and God's desire for them. Thus, they tasted spiritual death while physical death waited for them.

Satan encourages the misrepresentation of God and his will and then uses it against us and against God's purposes in the world. He does not necessarily tell us that God has lied to us in his word, but that he is not telling us everything. Many of us are deceived, thinking that if we do things God's way, we will miss out on material gain, an identity of importance and social worth, or pleasures that could be ours. We think God is withholding something from us, so, swallowing the bait, hook, and all, we set about creating our own security and well-being by adding our preferences to what he has given us. The outcome is to miss God's purposes for us and the church, to have religion without a trusting relationship with God. Jesus was not kind to the Pharisees of his day, who added to God's law for their own social status and financial benefit. He tells us instead to seek the kingdom of God first and that all else we need will be given to us.

God's grace is held out to us, and the church must rest on that foundation with trust and humility, or it ceases to be the church. No, he has not withheld anything good from us. Every word he has spoken is true; every promise is ours. The knowledge of that truth leads to godliness and freedom. But we can accept or reject it, take it or leave it. It may look like too much risk, but life itself is at stake. The seed must die to bring forth life; all the world offers cannot save the soul. Many blessings of a faithful life are not immediate here on earth. But contentment with God *is* ours now. Patience. Christianity is not a religion; it is knowing God, the Creator and Savior of the world, the lover of our souls.

Scripture References: Gen 3:2–7; Pss 16:1–4, 51:16–17, 63:3–5, 84:10–12, 34:8–10; Prov 21:2–3; Isa 66:1–2; Hos 6:6; Mic 6:8; Mal 1:10–13a; Matt 6:31–34, 7:13–23; 15:7–9, 23:1–39; Mark 12:32–34; Luke 9:23–25, 18:9–14; John 4:13–14; 8:12, 31–32; 11:25–26; 12:23–26; 14:6; 17:3; Rom 8:32; Eph 2:8–10; Phil 2:12–13; 1 Tim 4:1–8; Titus 1:1–3, 2:11–14; Heb 6:10–12; Jas 1:17–18; 1 John 2:15–17.

6. Misplaced Loyalty

Yet I hold this against you: You have forsaken your first love.
—*Rev 2:4*

FALLING IN LOVE WITH Christianity or a theological system is a dangerous business. When we belong to a church or denomination for the social identity and feelings of self-worth it gives, making us "somebody," we identify with a group or theological position for the wrong reasons. It is turning away from God himself—misplaced loyalty—a wrongful attraction to the map instead of the destination to which it should guide us. At its worst, it is an illicit love affair—unfaithfulness to God out of love for another. God calls idolatry a spirit of prostitution in the prophecy of Hosea, leading God's people away from him. It may sound too strong to our sensitive ears, but is there spiritual adultery among us? Can a church or a system of theology become an idol? Only too easily. Instead of our theology serving us, we end up serving our theology, and members can become more loyal, more attached, to a church or ministry than to God himself—allegiances that belong to God alone.

The church has a purpose in God's plan, and it is not that it should come between him and us. It is for instruction in God's word, corporate worship, and encouragement to walk with him and be salt and light in a dark world. Your culture has given you solutions for feelings of security and self-worth, and sometimes we carry these with us into the church when we become Christians. But God intends the rich fulfillment of these needs to be found in him, his grace and love, the merits of Jesus Christ in your stead, and his providence in all things. Churches and theologies should move you to this end, not take its place in your life. They are both human and subject to error, even heresy. Some of them are enemies of God himself instead of the bride's maids leading the bride to her groom. God's word stands above them; we must always let him speak for himself through it. His word will accomplish what he desires in us, his providence the impossible, if we allow it.

Scripture References: Exod 20:3; Pss 23:1–6, 37:28; Isa 55:10–11; Hos 4:1 with 12 and 5:4; Matt 5:13–16, 6:1–8, 7:24–27; Luke 1:37; John 12:42–43; Rom 2:22, 8:28; 2 Cor 11:1–4; Gal 5:1, 6, 13–15; Eph 5:8, 25–27; Phil 1:6 with 2:12–13 and 1 Thess 5:24; Titus 2:11–14; Jas 1:22–25; 1 Pet 5:7; 1 John 1:5–7; Rev 2:1–7, 19:6–8.

7. The Proud Heart

The fear of the Lord teaches a man wisdom, and humility comes before honor.
—*Prov 15:33*

TRUSTING OURSELVES WHEN THINGS seem to be going well is to court the danger of pride in our lives. We can become addicted to feelings of success, control, and self-confidence. The deceptive thing is that the results may not be evident until much later. By the time we realize pride has had its way with us, things may be pretty bad. It may be too late to repair much of the damage in our lives and the pain we have caused others. A career may be lost, a family ruined, our health in tatters, and the shame unbearable. The dragon of pride has made ashes and cinders of everything. But it is *never too late* to trust God and grasp life as he wants us to have it. He will help us through the wreckage we have made of our lives, and, from that day forward, we can live with purpose and meaning we have never had. God gives us one life to trust him, be loyal to his ways, and love others with empathy and compassion. We must put the self in its place to know his blessings and be part of his plan in the world. His providential help is there, but we make the choice to know its blessing. He will not make it for us.

Unlike Nebuchadnezzar, whose pride brought him seven years of suffering, or Haman, who, for his pride, was hanged on the gallows he built for Mordecai, Solomon tells us to "remember your Creator . . . before the silver cord is severed" (Eccl 12:1, 6). If we are serious about him, we will learn, as the Proverbs tell us, to acknowledge him in all we do, seek to depend on his strength, grace, and goodness, and humble ourselves before him. It is the only reasonable response. Time is not on our side. The gift of life here only lasts so long, and the hours soon vanish; the pitcher is soon shattered. Many of us live divided lives, proud people in church pews. We have yet to decide where our true loyalty lies. He waits for us to trust him.

The room of our life becomes barren with pride. There is one rigid chair and a small table where we sit to design our greatness while God longs to fill the room "with rare and beautiful treasures" (Prov 24:3–4) that it can only accommodate with the wisdom of acknowledging the Master Craftsman who built it and what it cost him. In this wisdom is hope that never ends and a room of treasures with which nothing, *nothing*, you desire can compare.

Scripture References: 2 Chr 7:14; Esth 5:10b–11 with 7:8c–10; Pss 10:4; 16:2 with 18; 20:7; 51:16–17; 56:3–4; 147:3 with 6a and 11; Prov 3:5–7, 13–17; 11:2; 15:33; 16:18–19; 22:4; 24:3 and 14; 26:12; 28:26; Eccl 9:17–18, 12:1–7; Jer 9:23–24; Dan 4:28–33; Matt 23:11–12; Luke 1:51–52, 12:13–21, 18:9–14; Gal 6:14; Jas 4:10; 1 Pet 5:5–7.

8. Moral Law Forgotten

The world and its desires pass away, but the man who does the will of God lives forever.

—*1 John 2:17*

THE FREEDOM OF DEMOCRACY is often the envy of those in countries that do not have its benefits. But they do not take into account human nature. Individual rights and an elected government seem to be the highest good society could have. But without people of virtue at its base and in its daily affairs, the institution weakens, and human values replace God's. We in the West have not spread the essential principles of morality, integrity, and justice around the world with our idea of freedom, and it does not last long without these virtues. The two messages have been kept quite separate over the centuries. Yet unless the Lord builds the house, its builders labor in vain.

The freedoms of democracy in the hands of human beings where corruption, injustice, greed, and immorality reign, run aground. Those in authority soon turn away from God's purpose for them and the good they might do. Deep in the human heart, selfish ambition comes to the surface when there is freedom but no moral standard. Freedom itself is then weaponized against those who oppose the godless ways of social influencers. It is indeed the blind leading the blind. There can be no long-term survival of society in any system that is not built on knowledge and fear of God from where that moral law, that standard of ethical and just behavior, emanates.

If a human social system *is* put in place by those who seek to honor God, later generations tend to move away from the biblical values of its foundation, the virtues that made it possible, leaving a vacuum to be filled. In the book of Judges, the Israelites forgot God seven times and turned to the gods of the people around them. The same sickness plagues our societies today. People try to erase true Christianity and, often, history itself. Weaponizing "justice," race, crime, murder, and sexual confusion, they imprison the masses and blackmail those who sleep in numbness. But we must wake up, for they annihilate society in the act. As Eve listened to Satan and Israelites turned their backs on God, these today worship the great deceiver while deceiving and destroying themselves and taking everyone they can with them.

It is not new for men to love darkness instead of light. But God is our help and strength. Though society may fail, we can know God's way, his providence, and freedom in Christ. He is the light for our way as we "trust in the name of the Lord" and rely on our God (Isa 50:10–11). Those who have taken his way can build their lives on the foundation of the work of Christ and live forever while institutions, societies, even civilizations, come and go. We who have taken God's way by his grace look forward to a lasting place he has created for us elsewhere. We will soon join him there. We are not perfect, but we are his children, not of this world, and no one can take us out of his hand. Though the time is not yet complete for us to leave, we who know him in this way will be finished with human suffering on that day. Our world today makes us look forward to our true home. Until that day, we are to be salt and light, showing love for our neighbor and holding out the truth and grace of God to a lost world.

Scripture References: Judg 2:6–15, 10:6–10, 13:1; Pss 9:7–10, 14:2–3, 20:7, 33:10–22, 37:39–40, 46:1–11, 62:1–2, 127:1 with Prov 24:1–2; Ps 146:3–5; Prov 3:5–7, 6:12–19, 17:20, 26:12, 28:26; Eccl 5:8–9; Isa 50:10–11; Jer 17:9–10; Matt 5:13–16, 6:13–14 with John 14:6; Matt 7:24–27; Mark 12:28–34; John 3:19; 6:35–40; 8:12 with 12:35–36; 10:28–30; 14:1–4; 17:13–19; Rom 1:18–23, 13:1–4; 1 Cor 2:9; Eph 2:1–5 with 11–12; 5:8; Phil 3:17–21; 1 Tim 2:5–6; Heb 11:6; 1 John 2:15–17; Rev 21:1–4.

9. Divided Loyalty

To the pure, all things are pure, but to those who are corrupted and do not believe, nothing is pure.

—*Titus 1:15*

Paul says, "To the pure, all things are pure." Purity speaks of things set apart from contamination. When we say we have a hobby purely for enjoyment, we mean it is not for other things like income or reputation. But it is hard to keep things pure. This is especially true of our spiritual lives. Many distractions in the world, maybe especially in our Western individualist world, can contaminate our endeavors to serve and honor God and to serve and love others. We can sometimes become too busy to notice that our insecurities and appetites, our Western values, or our selfish intentions have crept into our best intentions to live for God. Perhaps we are telling ourselves that we seek to glorify God, but on the side we are counting how much more money, ease, popularity, or personal security we will gain in a particular endeavor. Yes, our hearts can have secret motives for other outcomes, so secret we sometimes are not aware of them ourselves. Paul says all things are pure to those with pure motives. Even though they sometimes fail, they desire to honor God; for that, Jesus calls them "the pure in heart" (Matt 5:8).

Yes, even with good motives, we sometimes fail to honor God in thought or action. God is not unaware of this. But he is very interested in our motives, looking at our hearts. It is not that the pure in heart do not sin but that they do not intend to sin, and deal with it as soon as they are aware of it. This is a heart for God. This is walking in the Spirit. All Christians fight this battle in one way or another, from those doing the simplest act of Christian service to those leading the largest church in town. It is the fundamental decision between loyalty to God or to self in the small things of life as well as the big things. We make that decision every day, and sometimes several times a day. That is why so much of the Bible is written to encourage us to have pure intentions and not to allow other influences in our lives to pollute our faith, good works, and public ministries. This does not mean we do not reason out the best uses of our time, what will provide well for our families, or what may not be worth doing in our vocations. But it does mean that all these thoughts are moderated by our desire to glorify God—make him and his ways known through our lives.

In our culture of success and attainment, we are at risk of combining personal achievement with service to others. Irrational fears and insecurities concerning our social survival and preferences for personal ease and independence drive these values and move us to dual loyalties. But these mixed motives do not necessarily come from insincerity. Most of us want to glorify God, but we also want to fix our situation and prefer that it happens sooner rather than later. If we are not careful, an inordinate amount of energy can go into the survival of self and little into honoring God or love for others.

Our dilemma is fixed by the simplicity of acknowledging God in all we do and trusting him for the outcomes. Of course, it is more easily said than done, and will never be our perfect state of being. But for it to become our guiding value, our survival must depend on God and our desire for his purposes to be fulfilled in us and in the world. That is having one loyalty, singleness of heart and mind, desiring to honor God. This is the purity Paul speaks of, the goal of the Christian life.

Scripture References: Ps 9:10 with 91:14–16 and John 12:26; Prov 3:5–7, 28:26 with Jer 17:5–11; Prov 16:2, 20:27; 21:31; Matt 5:8 with Titus 1:15; Matt 6:19–21 with 24; John 12:24–26; Rom 12:1–2; 1 Cor 10:31; Eph 2:10 with 2 Tim 3:17 and Titus 2:14 and 3:14; Phil 2:1–11; Col 3:1–4, 12–17; 1 Tim 6:17–19; Heb 13:15–16.

10. Service and Loyalty

Do not love the world or anything in the world.
—*1 John 2:15*

WHEN MONEY, STATUS, OR power overshadows the ministry of the church, mixed motives are at work like a slow poison. Though it may look impressive on the outside, it is dying on the inside, on its way to becoming a cold sarcophagus for those who come to hear a life-giving message. Church leaders and people of position often risk this dangerous mixture of ministry with self-assertion, pride, or greed. Unfortunately, people can serve themselves while appearing to help others flourish in their faith, and a position of service to others becomes a personal matter of social achievement and material gain. Singular loyalty is hard to come by in our society because it demands the humility of dependence on God, which independent individualists find hard to accept.

The answer to our situation is both simple to understand and hard to practice, but it gives us the peace and the rest Jesus promised. As I said earlier, it is to *acknowledge* God's providence in all we do and *trust him* for our well-being and the outcomes of our efforts. This will not be done and finished with a simple resolution; it will mean ongoing monitoring of our intentionality and entrusting our needs and desires to his care. It is the answer to our Christian lives in every realm, but it is sometimes more difficult for those whose vocation is to teach others the truths of God's word.

To be a Christian leader demands a strenuous, even fierce, loyalty to God's ways. Yet we spend little, if any, time in seminaries cultivating the necessary integrity of character that comes with humility. It seems counterintuitive in a culture that values self-assertion and achievement, with its goals of social status and successful leadership. It will take a daily renewal of the mind and heart that looks to God instead of at the values of our broken world. Christian leaders will have to be aware of their motives and desires and, in humility, fuel an intentional passion for God if they are to help those they lead and incarnate God's pattern for us. It will take the wisdom that comes from above. Some have given themselves to God and their ministry this way, and we are forever changed as he uses them in our lives.

Scripture References: Pss 9:9–10; 62:1–2, 5–8; 91:14–16; Prov 3:5–6, 22:4; Isa 26:3–4, 66:1–2; Hos 6:6; Mic 6:8; Matt 6:19–21 with 24; 7:15–23; Luke 9:23–25; John 12:24–26, 14:27; Rom 5:1–2, 12:1–2; Phil 4:4–9; Col 3:1–4; 1 Tim 6:1–11; Jas 3:1–2, 13–18; 4:4–6; 1 John 2:15–17 with 4:4–6.

11. Trusting the God of Grace

But I am like an olive tree flourishing in the house of God; I trust in God's unfailing love for ever and ever.

—Ps 52:8

IN THE OLD TESTAMENT, God revealed himself in powerful displays of his sovereignty and transcendence so that the people would remember and trust him in the face of temptations, dangers, suffering, and the human inclination for doubt. This remembrance and trust, this ultimate respect for him as God, was called the fear of the LORD. In the book of Proverbs, it is connected with humility and knowing him. One cannot know him without fearing him or fear him, with this kind of fear, without knowing him. This knowledge and fear of God comes with humility and leads to understanding and wisdom (in John 17:3, it is eternal life). But the people of Israel, who had every reason to know his greatness and grace, did not allow it to lead to the fear of the LORD. As astonishing as it seems to us, they forgot God and went after the stone and wooden idols of the people around them. They committed spiritual adultery. But God knows; he sees.

Human will and determination are weak, but that does not change God and his intentions for his people. We also are to trust God in our New Testament age. Strange as it may seem, we are to fear him because of the depth of his grace in sending Jesus and allowing him to die in our stead to give us his righteousness before the God of the universe. The fear of God for us in Christ is not of his stern justice as a consuming fire. Though that description is accurate for all who reject him, we must have a deep humility and a recognition of being created humans before our Creator-God of justice, who has chosen to show us immeasurable grace. That humility should result in a life of loyalty, trust in his love, and rest in his providence. We who fear the LORD today must continually recognize his unfathomable grace and unlimited forgiveness of us in Christ and his care, power, and providence at work in our varied situations.

We know this, and yet, similar to the people of Israel in the wilderness or in the days of the judges, we often fail to trust the God who cares for us. We forget his power, providence, and grace in our worry and anxiety, continued guilt over sins forgiven, fear of losing our independence, or, like Demas, our love for the world. Because of this, we forfeit his peace and rest for us. We must turn from our wrongheaded willfulness and come back to him. We must remember what he has done. He has given us every reason to trust him. He waits for us as a father waits for a wayward son or daughter to return, never wavering in his love for us, always ready to bathe us in his grace again.

Scripture References: Exod 6:1–8 and 19:16–22; Judg 2:16–19; Pss 19:9, 33:18–19, 52:7–9, 56:3–4, 62:5, 77:11–20, 78:34–39, 147:3 with 6a and 11; Prov 1:7 with 29 and 2:5–6 and 9:10; 3:5–7; 5:21; 16:2; 20:27; 22:4; Isa 50:10–11; Jer 23:13–14 with 24; Nah 1:2–8; Matt 11:28–30 with John 14:27; Matt 23:11–12, 26:40; Luke 15:11–31; John 3:16–21; Rom 3:22–26, 7:14–25, 8:31–32; 1 Cor 2:7–10a; 2 Cor 5:21, 9:8, 12:7–10; Eph 2:1–10; Phil 2:1–11; 1 Tim 1:12–15; 2 Tim 4:9–10; Heb 12:28–29; 1 Pet 5:6–7; 1 John 2:15–17.

12. Justice in Society

He does not bear the sword for nothing. He is God's servant, an agent of wrath to bring punishment on the wrongdoer.

—Rom 13:4

CHRISTIANS OFTEN CONFUSE "love your neighbor as yourself," "turn the other cheek," or "love your enemies as yourself," or the many times we are told to "forgive that we might be forgiven" as statements against judicial process—the punishment of wrongdoing and the stopping of evil in society. Are we to forgive or not? Yes, we are to forgive, but we are not told to be part of allowing evil to hurt and destroy others. Without justice, people suffer deeply and are ruled by the selfish ambition of blind leaders. There is no community and, for many, only terrorism and desperation for survival. Thus, though the situation is a result of rejecting him, to keep mankind from annihilating itself, God gives the sword to the governing power to accomplish a human sort of peace, imperfect as that is. We are told to cooperate to the fullest extent possible. But while society must detain and punish the wrongdoers, they, too, must hear the gospel.

We are told to love even those who do us wrong, not in terms of having affectionate feelings or being attracted to them but out of a desire for their ultimate good. Though they must be stopped and kept from hurting others, we are to seek their humility and repentance and the salvation that would follow. We cannot allow the aggression of one man against another, for it is hardly loving our neighbor to allow others to destroy them if we can stop it. And, in the end, we may best share our faith with the lawless when they are behind bars. They may be our enemies today, but not necessarily forever. God waits for them to turn to him.

In a democracy, we are all given a part in that judicial system, imperfect as it is. It falls to us to vote for those we feel will uphold justice, and perhaps serve on a jury. This is responsible and follows God's own desire for justice in society. He criticized the people of Israel many times for their lack of justice toward the poor and oppressed and their lack of care for widows and orphans among them. Justice must be carried out in society, or it will perish. One day, it will be the rule rather than the exception.

Scripture References: Pss 96:11–13, 97:1–6; Prov 21:15, 29:7; Isa 9:6–7; 10:1–4; 32:5–8, 16–20; 42:1–4a; Jer 17:11; Mic 6:8; Matt 5:43–48, 12:15–21, 22:34–40, 23:23; Luke 18:1–8; Acts 17:31; Rom 13; Heb 1:8–9; Rev 19:11–16.

13. Beliefs Must Result in Behavior

Dear children, let us not love with words or tongue but with actions and in truth.

—*1 John 3:8*

WE MAY AGREE WITH God's truth about ourselves once we are open to seeing it in his word. But it is very much in our nature to forget what we learned a few minutes later, "like a man who looks at his face in a mirror . . . forgets what he looks like" (Jas 1:23–24). The competition for our minds and loyalties is everywhere in our day, and a moment's quietness to think about our own direction in life is hard to find. While life is speeded up, progress toward becoming more like Christ seems slower for many of us. The longer we are at it, the more we realize how far we have to go. We still do things we regret and must come to him often for his forgiveness and healing. But God looks at the heart. He knows our loyalty, intentions, and potential, as well as our weaknesses, and he is patient in his love for us. He reminds us of his grace and that we are his very own. In his providence and patience, he gives us opportunities to love and serve him, to grow out of our weak conditions, and we must be sensitive to them.

The narrow way is one of disciplining the old man to behave like the new one, a job that is never quite finished. Some have taken comfort in saying that you must let go and let God do this through you. Yes, he is always with us to help and encourage us, to give us the time, resources, and energy needed, motivate us, and make the way straight before us; however, he does not do in our stead what he tells *us* to do. But his grace is sufficient if we lean on it, and his providence is at work in and through us even on our worst days when we are his. To walk worthy of the gospel is to walk humbly in the grace of his forgiveness and ownership, knowing full well how much we need him, and then to do the good works he planned for us (Eph 2:10), purposed for the church (4:12), for which he equips us with his word (2 Tim 3:17), and redeemed us to do (Titus 2:14)—the works that should be the result of his work in us (Jas 3:1, 17–18), *our* works for him.

We don't like thinking we could be better Christians if we were more willing. We would prefer God take care of that. But his grace is enough to humble and stimulate us to good works if our hearts are set on honoring him. The goal is not to become recognized as a "spiritual giant," a "Christian celebrity," but to set social rewards, reputation, feeling good about ourselves, and substitutes for God aside and practice the care and consideration for others needed in the routines of life. Listening to and understanding those around us, practicing humility, mercy, and justice, and showing the kindness so rare in our world reveals God's grace in our lives. It is the love we are to be known for.

Kindness is a good example. It is to be central to the life of a Christian. Patience and kindness are Paul's first words in his description of love, the identifying mark of the Christian. He talks about sustained selfless attention, compassion, and generosity toward one another in Philippians, chapter 2—the opposite of selfish ambition. These values and attitudes result in good works to help others. Though some personalities are more generally kind, all are called to honor God in this way. We learn about kindness in God's word, and, like all behavior, we learn to express it from the influence of parents we trust, examples of others, and personal experience. The greatest example and encouragement we have is God showing us the kindness of his grace while we were his enemies at immeasurable cost to himself. This grace goes beyond human kindness and can replace the lack of kindness we have experienced with people.

We also have the example of the life and ministry of Jesus, who gave us the range and extent of that love and its kindness. Our challenge is to choose kindness toward others when our society emphasizes self-assertion for "success" and "survival." In summary, kindness is learned, intentional, and largely countercultural. Its expression in love and good deeds toward others is central to our faith. The encouragement of one another in this way is not just a formal affair on Sunday mornings but the meeting of other believers anytime—"where two or three come together in my name." This kindness is not based on the goodness of its object but on the act and presence of God's grace in our lives.

Scripture References: Prov 3:6a; 16:2; 17:3 with 15:26; 20:27; 27:19; Isa 32:17, 43:1; Mic 6:8; Matt 5:16, 7:13–14, 12:20, 18:20; John 13:34–35; Rom 12:9–12; 1 Cor 13:4–7; 2 Cor 12:9; Gal 5:22–23; Eph 2:1–10, 4:12; Phil 1:6; 2:1–4, 12–13; 1 Thess 1:2–3, 2:12; 1 Tim 4:7–8, 6:18–19; 2 Tim 2:21,

13. BELIEFS MUST RESULT IN BEHAVIOR

3:16–17; Titus 1:8; 2:7, 11–15; 3:1, 8, 14; Heb 4:12–13, 6:9–11, 10:24–25, 13:15–16; Jas 1:22–25; 2:18–24; 3:1, 17–18; 1 Pet 2:11–17, 3:8–17; 2 Pet 1:3–9; 1 John 3:18.

14. Differences Between People Matter

For God so loved the world that he gave his one and only Son, that whoever believes in him shall not perish but have everlasting life.

—John 3:16

CULTURAL SYSTEMS VARY SIGNIFICANTLY between people groups. Each group lives by a different frame of reference based on various values, beliefs, and understandings. Each has differences in personal and collective experiences and current social situations. Culture gives people the frame of reference for formulating meaning in communication, interpreting their experience, and choosing appropriate or advantageous social behavior. Most of us think culture is only about what people do, but behavior is actually the result of the cultural system behind it.

It is too simplistic to say that Japanese behavior differs from American behavior on the streets, at the workplace, or at home. Culture is much more than the superficial observations and social categories we maintain in our stereotypical thinking. Most of it is unseen, and these invisible influences cause the differences in behavior we see. Even cultures that look similar to outsiders, such as South Korean, Chinese, Vietnamese, and Japanese, are all *very* different, although they have a common thread of influential Confucianism in the background.

God relates to people who seek him in spirit and in truth. This has to do with the intentions of the heart and can be expressed in many ways. But culture can get in the way and influence our desires and motives away from God's purposes. We have too long held on to *our* way of social and personal survival as the only way. For example, Jesus did not go after high-profile people in his cultural situation, but we tend to think they are beneficial to building a ministry in our culture. What we call a "successful" ministry

14. DIFFERENCES BETWEEN PEOPLE MATTER

by getting high-profile people into the pews is culturally encouraged, not scripturally prescribed. It is like Samuel looking among the sons of Jesse for the person God wanted to anoint as the next king in Saul's place. His cultural value on physical stature was getting in the way. Culture can have too much control over our decisions and evaluations. If we let it, it enters into our preferences, motives, and activities as Christians. If we do not manage it, it manages us.

Cultural differences are important, but personal differences—lifestyle, social status, giftedness, experience, and personality—are also critical. To be understandable and relevant, we must approach each culture and each person differently with the gospel. Jesus spoke differently to Nicodemus, the woman at the well, the rich young man, and Zacchaeus. Each had their own frame of reference: the influential, high-status leadership position of a Pharisee; the low status of an untouchable run-around woman; the wealthy, confident life of ease of a rich young man or ruler; and the greedy and gouging tax collector. Each needed a new wineskin. Each needed to accept Jesus. But these were not one-size-fits-all conversations.

Instead of assuming people are like us except for superficial differences, we must realize they are only outwardly like us, and the deeper differences are significant. We must take the time to learn about the cultural and personal frames of reference of the people we want to reach or teach. It will take time and work, perhaps finances. But it is highly worth the investment. Unfortunately, it is not given much thought when our cultural values are romantic feelings, quick results, or larger churches rather than a relevant incarnation and personal communication of the life-changing gospel—a message of hope for every person.

Scripture References: 1 Sam 16:1–13; Pss 51:6, 145:18–19; Matt 9:16–17, 19:16–22; Luke 5:27–32, 36–39; 18:18–30; 19:1–10; John 3:1–15, 4:7–26; Acts 17:16–34; Rom 12:2; 1 Cor 1:20; Eph 4:22–24; Phil 1:9–11; 1 John 2:15–17.

15. Imperfect but Forgiven

If we claim to be without sin, we deceive ourselves and the truth is not in us.

—*1 John 1:8*

CHOOSING GOD AND HIS way over our own or our culture's way is continually a choice before us. God's desire from the beginning was that his created beings would choose to trust him. Having already fallen from God's ideal, Satan presented an alternative to Eve that seemed sweeter, even wiser, raising doubt where only trust should have been. Once Adam and Eve chose to know good and evil over loyalty to God, they were faced with the consequences of such a choice. The context of deception and the results of that fatal choice continue, and the choice of our loyalties and behaviors remain before us in a damaged world. Do we fall short at times in our Christian lives? We do. That's the point—we do not always choose the best behavior or have the best motive. Old survival habits go deep and often show up again after we become Christians.

So how do we live a life pleasing to God? We do it by his grace. Considering this grace gives us encouragement and humility, the desire to serve him and trust his providence. It brings out loyalty to his purposes and gives us the courage to move in the right direction. His presence with us in unending grace and overpowering providence strengthens us to move ahead. Yes, we stumble at times, but the God who created the universe from nothing has the power and supreme right to forgive us and keep us in his hands all the way to our eternal destiny. He can do this on the scale of divine justice. When we come to Christ fully, recognizing and repenting of our sins, we are declared righteous by God himself based on the sacrifice of his perfect Son, Jesus Christ. We are given Jesus' righteousness. No one can

15. IMPERFECT BUT FORGIVEN

undo this declaration. It stands for all time, written in an eternal book, freeing us from all condemnation. His providence is at work for all we cannot do or change in our ongoing lives for him. We will still make mistakes. But when we sin, recognize it, and repent, the grace of his forgiveness is at work to keep us from the guilt that destroys. This is walking in the Spirit. Not recognizing that we sin is a rejection of God's word. It may be a sign that we are not his after all.

Scripture References: Gen 3:1–24; Pss 34:22; 91:1, 14–16; Prov 3:6, 24:16; John 5:24, 10:27–30; Rom 3:21–24, 8:1; 2 Cor 5:21; Gal 4:4–7, 5:4–6 with 16–18 and 22–26; Eph 2:4–10, 6:10–18; Col 1:22, 2:6–15; 1 Pet 3:18; 1 John 1:8–10; Rev 20:11–15.

16. The Information Stalker

A gossip betrays a confidence; so avoid a man who talks too much.
—*Prov 20:19*

FOR THE PREDATOR, EVERYONE else's business is their business. The solitude of others is an irritation, an annoyance because they feel they have a right to know what is happening with them and how they live their lives. In their quietness, they must be hiding something. They have no right to such privacy. The pursuer notices every reserved person in the organization or neighborhood. Sometimes small groups in the church can become their vehicle. Driven by a competitive spirit, they attack with questions, bombarding their target at every opportunity, trying to dig deeper into their lives to satisfy their need to know. What they learn then becomes gossip or ammunition. The person minding their own business hardly has a chance. Despite all the verses in Proverbs telling us to guard our words and James's teaching to be slow to speak, pursuers often talk about keeping to oneself as a sin. They must find some shortcoming that proves the prey is no better than the pursuer. Some feel it is their calling to expose a quiet person's weakness. Other pursuers are simply busybodies. Some shoot darts from the shadows, hoping to cause their prey to stumble. Such is their resentment that secrets are being kept from them. The Proverbs tell us to avoid such people.

None of this searching out of others fits the biblical pattern. If a woman doesn't talk much or a man is "of few words," it does not mean they think they are better than someone who talks a lot or are trying to hide things from others. They live in the same world and have struggles to deal with like anyone else. God is at work in their lives in ways that fit his purposes, doing different things than he might be doing in the extrovert. He calls disturbers of the peace to become peacemakers.

16. THE INFORMATION STALKER

After the resurrection, Peter was concerned that Jesus was hard on him and not John. Jesus simply told Peter that what he would do in John's life was none of Peter's business. Jesus told him that he was to be concerned about his own life before God, and John was to be concerned about his. God's plan and providence are not the same for each person. Watch out for yourself and let other Christians do the same.

Scripture References: Prov 11:13; 17:27; 18:8; 20:19; 26:20, 22, 23–26, 28; Matt 5:9; John 21:17–23; Rom 12:9–18; Gal 5:13–15; Phil 2:3–4; 1 Thess 4:11–12; 2 Thess 3:11–12; 1 Tim 2:1–4, 3:11, 5:13; Jas 1:19–25; 1 Pet 3:8–11; 3 John 9–10.

17. Social Roles

A wife of noble character who can find? She is worth far more than rubies. Her husband has full confidence in her and lacks nothing of value.

—*Prov 31:10-11*

IN A WESTERN CULTURE heavily based on individualism, the theme of all men and women being created equal is central. This, however, leads to an emphasis on comparison and statements that others are no different or no better than we are. Indeed, those in traditionally respectable positions and influencers of our society are not always worthy people such that respecting everyone equally has become respecting no one at all. This seems normal to its advocates, and has become a social expectation resulting in our culture's lack of ways to show respect for anyone as they are eradicated by the doctrine of egalitarianism. This attitude tries to erase the roles God designed and society has traditionally given to people in different positions, such as to parents for their children, spouses in marriage, social authorities for maintaining the community, or roles and differences associated with gender. The institutions of government, economics, education, and family, under God's grace and providence, have responsibilities as well as boundaries. So there are consequences if, for example, government or education interferes with parents to indoctrinate children or a social movement decides to do away with the police. There are limits to what society can withstand regarding this social confusion and dysfunction. However, the answer is not to erase the functions of social institutions or personal positions. God's intention for communities from the beginning was for each person to have and do their part faithfully and with integrity, all being equal before God but different in

17. SOCIAL ROLES

their social roles—the behavior that should go with the position one holds in society.

The attempt to level the playing field, allowing any institution or person to have any role, to have every role, or not to have any role, ends somewhere. No one can say it will be good for society. We are driven by our short-term orientation, self-centered need for control, desire for immediate gratification, and thirst for personal advancement. The results are only beginning to be felt and are not encouraging. Such was Habakkuk's complaint to God about the Jews in Judah around 605 BC, where the law was paralyzed and there was no justice. He prophesied about the disaster to come upon them, as did Isaiah before him. But as societies disintegrate, God and his purposes remain unchanged. He is the hope of his people. Though they may suffer in this world of malfunction, their ultimate well-being is in him.

Scripture References: Pss 37:1–11, 146:1–10; Prov 31:10–31; Isa 10:1–4; Lam 3:22–26; Mic 6:8; Hab 1:1–4; Matt 22:15–11; John 14:25–31, 16:33; Rom 5:1–6, 13:1–5; Eph 4:11–16, 5:22—6:9; 1 Thess 4:11–12; 1 Tim 2:1–4; Titus 2:1–15; 1 Pet 1:3–7, 3:8–18.

18. People Are Not Equal

He who walks with the wise grows wise, but a companion of fools suffers harm.

—*Prov 13:20*

ALL PEOPLE ARE CREATED in God's image and of equal importance to him, objects of his love and longing, and, though he works differently in each life, all are equally affected by his grace as they allow him into their lives. But outside this essential, legal, and spiritual standing before God in Christ, people are not equal. They are all very different. If they were equal, a woman would marry any man instead of a particular man. We would not interview people for a job or position within a company or institution. Anyone could join the orchestra. We would not have courts of law to adjudicate antisocial behavior. We would not say one presidential candidate for the country was better than another. We would have no need to vote at all.

People differ in abilities, character, expertise, giftedness, ethnic group, religion, habits, physique, or popularity. Though everyone should be valued as a person with rights and privileges and, in that sense, respected, they have not all earned the same respect. Some have earned the highest regard, some none at all, and others have forfeited their rights and freedoms by refusing to respect others. Many do not get social appreciation who deserve it; others get far more than they deserve; some deserve none.

The book of Proverbs details the characteristics of those worthy of attention and those we should avoid, such as the "easily angered" (22:4), the "gossip" (20:19), or the "fool" (23:9). Psalm 1 advises us to stay away from the proud "mockers" (1:1). Even Paul tells us to avoid certain people, some of whom may call themselves Christians. Of course, though we are to be salt and light in the world, achieving social recognition or praise is not

18. PEOPLE ARE NOT EQUAL

part of God's way. Those seeking the kingdom of heaven will not often be respected in our society today. We should not expect it. One might think that constitutional freedom of religion and speech would allow Christians to speak about God's grace and their faith wherever they go. But the liberal doctrine of equity and inclusion that all should be respected the same does not extend to Christians. However, our standing in God's eyes, even in our weaknesses, is very different. In Christ, we have an essential, legal, and spiritual standing before God with all other true Christians, and the powers of darkness cannot change that.

Scripture References: Pss 1:1–6, 37:1–11; Prov 3:33–35, 6:9–11, 9:7–9, 12:1, 14:14–18, 20:19, 22:24, 23:9, 28:26; Isa 29:13 with Jer 12:1–2; Matt 5:3–10, 13–16; 7:6; 15:8–9; John 16:33; Rom 1:18, 16:17–19; 1 Cor 15:33, 16:17–20; 2 Thess 3:6–10; 1 Pet 2:9–12 with 3:13–18.

19. Social Idols

Do not put your trust in princes, in mortal men, who cannot save. When their spirit departs, they return to the ground; on that very day their plans come to nothing.

—Ps 146:3–4

OUR SOCIETY IS NOT very particular about who should be recognized in public life—not particularly judicious about who gets our approval. We have beauty pageant winners, the extremely wealthy, sports stars, Hollywood celebrities, and political figures filling the virtual headlines, not to mention self-made "experts" proliferating from one end of the internet to the other, saturating our lives with their unfounded advice. We often welcome these people into our lives because society has made them celebrities without a thought for the quality of their character, which in many cases falls short of the most superficial standards. Some of them become such popular idols of our times they draw the loyalty and worship that should be God's alone.

We are criticized in an egalitarian society if we do not respect everyone the same, then we move those who least merit it to the top of the social order. Political correctness shades our judgment and removes the right to critical thought about the values of these social idols. But God's word tells us to look beyond the superficial to the things that matter. He looks at the heart, and appearance, position, or words are often false indications of what is there.

People who trust God may not be popular and don't seek it. They may avoid attention and recognition, giving thought instead to their personal lives, fully aware that any accomplishment in their lives is owing to him, who gave them life and any abilities they have, that the results of their efforts in life are in his hands. They are not afraid of using their gifts for him

19. SOCIAL IDOLS

and feel satisfaction for a job well done, but never forget he is behind it all, and tomorrow they and their accomplishments may be gone. But there is meaning and purpose for them in today's work because they seek to honor God with their effort and hope to attract others to him through it. This is what Jesus means by seeking the kingdom of heaven first; then all else we need will be provided. Though the light of our hope in Christ must shine out to the world, anxiety or pride about our achievements has no place, applause no purpose, in the life of the believer.

Scripture References: 1 Sam 16:6–7; Pss 37:16, 56:3–4, 84:10–12, 146:1–10; Prov 3:3–10; 15:16 and 26 with 17:3; 16:2, 8; 20:27; 27:19; Isa 2:22, 40:23–24, 66:2b; Matt 5:3–16, 6:33; Rom 12:17–18; 1 Cor 1:20–31; Gal 5:22, 6:3–4; 2 Thess 4:11–12; 1 Tim 2:1–4; 2 Pet 1:3–9.

20. Some Are Further Along than Others

We continually remember before our God and Father your work produced by faith, your labor prompted by love, and your endurance inspired by hope in our Lord Jesus Christ.

—*1 Thess 1:3*

CHRISTIANS ARE NOT WITHOUT their faults. When we pick on someone else's behavior, we may be overlooking our own weaknesses. We like to think we are above certain levels of motive and intent, which we think we see in another, and perhaps we are right concerning that particular offense. But as I have expressed in comments about egalitarianism, we are not all equal. Each person has their own weaknesses, and some are further along in dealing with them and living in the freedom of Christ than others. In our shortcomings, we are all on a journey to become more mature in Christ. Knowing this makes a huge difference in our attitude toward others. We all make choices, and they are not always good ones. If we ever think we have reached total maturity in Christ and can judge others, we are in the danger zone of arrogance, leading us further away from the very core of God's truth and the humility it requires.

Are there some people that we can honestly say are good people? Yes. We don't know them all, but many are called righteous in the Bible, setting them apart from others. Under the law, none were perfect, but these are examples and teachers for the rest of us. Since Jesus' sacrifice on our behalf, all those who believe are given the righteousness of Christ before God. We are immensely grateful for this, which we could never attain on our own. And yet some of us are weaker and others stronger in our faith and faithfulness to him. And, strange as it may seem, those stronger in the faith may often have the feeling of being weaker. Feeling spiritual is not necessarily

20. SOME ARE FURTHER ALONG THAN OTHERS

part of a growing maturity in Christ. Sometimes it gives you the feeling of being the worst of sinners. But this keeps us from numbly taking for granted what ought to be humbly received with deepest gratitude—God's plentiful and lavish grace.

Barnabas is called a "good man" in Acts 11:24. It is not that good people have no faults or never make mistakes but they have a measure of humility, love, and honesty in their character and loyalty in their purpose of serving God, even if they are not perfect at it. They have chosen a trusting relationship with God, and he has honored that choice. He may use them to lead and influence the rest of us. Their faults are not controlling or competing with others, but they, like all of us, still deal with the self and opposing desires. They still need God's grace and know it more than others.

Scripture References: Pss 51:1–6 with 16–17; 91:14–16; 103:10–18; Prov 15:8–9, 22:4; Isa 32:17, 66:1–2; Mic 6:8; Matt 1:19, 7:1–5; Luke 1:5–6, 26–30; 2:25; John 4:23–24; 8:31b–32, 36; Acts 11:19–24, 13:22–23; Rom 3:21–24, 14:1—15:13; 2 Cor 5:21, 12:7–10; Phil 2:1–11; 1 Pet 5:5–11; 1 John 1:7–10.

21. Free Will in a Broken World

Now choose life.

—*Deut 30:19*

THE LINE BETWEEN THE free will God gives us and his sovereignty in the universe can be difficult to find because we are not looking in the right places and are leaning on our own understanding. We do not get to make every decision. We do not get to choose the family or ethnic group into which we are born. We do not choose our gender or a physical handicap we carry with us. We do not get to choose to be free of living in a broken world. Sometimes we do not get to make life choices because someone else has made them for us. Many of our circumstances are outside our control, but God is not unaware of all of this. His providence is active when we do not realize it: in the things that happen to us, in situations we do not choose, and in whatever we cannot change about ourselves. He can use any events and circumstances in our lives for his purposes.

The mystery of God's providence does not negate the sacred gift of free will he has given to his creatures, and, though he controls the circumstances and situations, he allows us to make many decisions in life. God gives us direction so we may choose the good things he provides, and sometimes we regret the results of our choices when we do not follow his advice, experiencing the consequences of our selfishness or greed. But he can be quite persuasive in his leading at times, and other times overrule the outcomes of our decisions for his purposes. He sometimes uses what we choose without much thought—or later regret—to great advantage in his purpose for us.

He directs our lives, meets our needs, and answers our prayers, although often in ways we do not expect or may not recognize until much later. Then there are things he does not change; many circumstances are his

21. FREE WILL IN A BROKEN WORLD

plan for us, and we must lean on his grace. Isaac finds himself on an altar, Joseph in Egypt, Jeremiah in a deep, muddy cistern, Daniel in a lions' den, Paul with a "thorn in his flesh" he called a messenger of Satan, and Jesus on a cross, but God carried out his purpose in each case. Many of our present circumstances and weaknesses are God's way of calling attention to his help and lovingkindness in our lives as he uses us for his purposes. Many other events and circumstances are simply the result of living in a fallen world and remind us of a coming, perfect world.

Then there are the situations and incidents in our behavior against God and others in our past that we greatly regret and wish so much we could change. Can it really be true that "in all things God works for the good of those who love him" (Rom 8:28)? Yes, it is true, but not always how we expect it to be. God wants us to know that when we were at our worst, his grace awaited us; he longed to redeem us. And when we came to him for that emancipation through Christ, he washed us of every evil deed we may have done, showing even the worst of us his intervening love, his all-embracing grace, and his far-reaching forgiveness. We may still remember those things with regret, but God does not intend for us to forget. He wants us to be reminded of his lavish and undeserved mercy and grace, his "unlimited patience" (1 Tim 1:16) with us, his complete, undistracted attention to us in our greatest need, for it is all still there and at work in us and our situation.

We need him. He tells us to pray for his help in all these things, for strength and wisdom, and for him to provide opportunities through which to honor or serve him. And he says, "I will answer him" who loves me and acknowledges my name (Ps 91:14–16). He is at work in everything to shape us into what he wants us to be for his reasons, for his part for us in his plan. That is the mystery of his providence in our lives and the paradox of his grace.

God's sovereignty does not contradict his answers to our prayers. We need not be surprised. We should instead expect God to be beyond our logic, controlling the entire universe, yet being very personal and concerned about our needs and requests. Our prayer does not interrupt his plan any more than our sin throws him off course. He answers, and he forgives. Such is the dignity God has given man—the free will to choose his destiny—to refuse God and condemn himself, or accept God's forgiveness and become part of what he is doing in the world.

So even the damaged parts of the creation, though he did not make them that way, are used by God in his plan and purpose for us. We choose how we will respond to our situation in life, how we will deal with our human thoughts and desires, and how we will respond to God's grace and his ownership of our lives. That people would choose to love and trust him is not just what he wants; these virtues are impossible unless there is a choice, and there is no choice unless there are alternatives to that love and trust. Ambiguity and uncertainty can lead to anxiety and fear, but for us they are opportunities to trust God. We create confusion when we expect him to be like us. He is not. There is much we do not know, but we can trust his way with us fully in humility and gratefulness. The choice to do so is ours.

Scripture References: Gen 45:4-8 with 50:19-21; Deut 30:11-20; Josh 24:14-15; Pss 37:23-24 with 28 and 34; 84:10-12; 91:1-2, 14-16; 138:8; 147:11; Prov 3:5-7, 24:16; Isa 41:10; Matt 7:13-14; John 3:36, 9:1-5, 17:15-19; Rom 8:28-29, 11:33-36; 2 Cor 12:7-10; Eph 1:7-14; Phil 1:6, 2:12-16; Heb 13:20-21; Jas 1:2-8; 1 Pet 5:6-7.

22. God Chose to Use Us

The grace of our Lord was poured out on me abundantly.... Christ Jesus came into the world to save sinners—of whom I am the worst.

—*1 Tim 1:14–15*

It is a great paradox of God's grace that, in his wisdom, he has chosen to use human beings to accomplish his plan in the world—we who often fail to trust him and can be selfish in our ways are to be his hands and feet in the world. He could accomplish everything perfectly and efficiently by his own power or even send angels—far above us in perfection—to effect his will on earth. But he has elected to use us, imperfect, sometimes oblivious to our weaknesses, inefficient, and worried about ourselves, our possessions, or our reputation. Why would God do such a thing? It is insightful that when Jesus chose the twelve, he was not looking for perfect people. They were very much like you and me in these ways.

We are often disappointing as his people in the world, yet he has his heart set on us. We cannot entirely escape the mud on our feet from the damaged and polluted world we walk in and our selfish inclinations, yet he poured out his grace on us in Christ and continues to wash our feet each day in forgiveness and lovingkindness. He wants *us* to be his disciples, his messengers, and lights in the world. It does not surprise me that Peter did not want Jesus to wash his feet. C. S. Lewis called it an "intolerable compliment."[1] Peter says, "Don't touch me," and Jesus says, "I want to, and I must in order to use you." What he must go through to use us in his work! The paradox of his choice!

But that is the point. God does not use perfect people because there aren't any. We are his sheep, and sheep do not always go in the right

---

1. C. S. Lewis, *The Problem of Pain* (New York: Macmillan, 1953), 29.

direction. They need a shepherd. We know him, and he knows us and is intensely concerned for our welfare and that we fulfill his calling for us. God gives us the high and holy privilege of serving him here. He is at work in our lives as much as in the world. While he uses us to represent him in the world, he uses his word and the events and circumstances that come our way to shape us for his will and bring us closer to him. Jesus said he was born to bear witness to the truth, and so were we. As the Father sent him with truth and grace, he now sends us to be his message to the world.

Once forgiven, our past, whatever it may have been, cannot negate our being witnesses to the truth today, this hour. Though it has left scars, we now belong to him. We are "his very own" (Titus 2:14). He knows our struggles and cares for us in our weaknesses. Whatever ways we can serve him—teaching, preaching, writing, serving others, helping others serve him, encouraging, contributing, showing hospitality, etc.—are examples of the great commission for us who know him; it is his calling in our lives. As we go about life, wherever we go, we can bear witness to the truth in the ways he has given us. It is the point of our lives at this time to work for the honor of the one who sent us. Never is our greed, self-seeking, or self-righteousness set in higher relief than when we realize we are his chosen representatives; never do we want more to honor him with our lives than when we recognize our imperfections and weaknesses and respond to him in humility and gratefulness.

So he has work in the world to carry out, and work in our lives, which he is accomplishing. It is true for those who know him: we don't need a bath, but we will have to let him wash our feet daily to show the truth of the gospel to the world. As we grow in our faith, we will see more mud to be washed off each day and become stronger through his continuing grace.

Scripture References: Pss 95:6–7, 100:3; Prov 3:5–6, 15:33, 28:26, 91:1; Isa 40:28–31 with 41:10 and 42:1–4 and 43:1–3; Mic 6:8; Matt 12:20, 28:18–20; John 7:18; 10:2–4, 14–15; 13:1–17 with 15:1–17; 18:36; 20:21; 28:18–20; Rom 8:1, 12:1–21; 2 Cor 12:7–10; Eph 2:10; Phil 1:6 with 2:12–13; Col 3:1–4; 1 Tim 1:12–17; 2 Tim 3:17; Titus 1:14 with Isa 43:1b; Jas 3:13–18; 1 Pet 2:11–12 with 15; 1 John 1:8–10, 2:15–17.

23. Religion or Relationship

Now this is eternal life: that they may know you, the only true God, and Jesus Christ, whom you have sent.

—John 17:3

My neighbor once told his noisy relatives camping on his property to keep the vulgarity down: "My neighbors have religion," he said. Maybe that is what it looks like to others, that we who know God have ascribed to religion. But it shouldn't. Ritual religion is unrelated to authentic Christianity. Our loyalties, allegiance, and attachment to God make a relationship, not a code of ritual behaviors like that of the religions. Genuine relationships are, first of all, based on trust and loyalty. This kind of relationship results in natural behaviors reflecting its commitment in everyday life. Ritual behaviors based on rules and regulations at certain times and places have little part in such a relationship. Though we may repeat some activities in our Christian lives over and over, certain spiritual disciplines that are good for our souls, their regularity must not become an empty ritual. Telling your spouse you love him or her because it's three o'clock on Tuesday again is not the same as telling them because you cannot keep silent.

I do not mean that we should pray or read God's word or journal our spiritual journey only when we feel like it, but that we should do it knowing how important it is for us in our relationship with God. We must train ourselves for godliness, as Paul told Timothy, for the value of our relationship with God, our service and love for others, and our part in his purposes in the world. We train the family dog to be a more enjoyable pet; how much more we should train ourselves to honor God! However, when it becomes a ritual without life, it becomes legalism—a straining to meet what we imagine are God's demands to earn his approval. To habitually do something needed is different than having a rigid discipline for its own sake, being able to say we did it, or having a strict and harsh practice that overrides our love for others. Regularity is safer when it is not punctual, but each person has their way of maintaining their relationship with God and their growth in Christ. Even Christians must beware of the inclinations of their hearts, for there are dragons in the land, and legalism is their prince.

Our natural behaviors, as opposed to ritual behaviors, demonstrate that our commitment exists. We are human, and our natural behavior will not be perfect. It must, from time to time, be confessed, forgiven, and corrected. We regret our weaknesses and wish we trusted God more. But all this is evidence of loyalty, chosen allegiance, commitment, and dependence at the core of our relationship with him. Those in a true relationship are faithful to each other through thick and thin, the good times and the bad times. When things go wrong between them, they seek forgiveness and reestablish the commitment and loyalty that was there before the problem. Our relationship with God is even stronger. His love is enduring, and his forgiveness is real and consistent, repairing our daily inadequacies and strengthening our faith where it is weak. It is not religion, for religion cannot save. God wants our hearts. What we do in the ordinary things of life (if there are any) are the results of that relationship and signs of its reality.

Scripture References: 1 Sam 13:13–14 with 16:6–7; Pss 21:7, 51:16–17; Prov 15:11, 16:2, 21:2–3; Isa 58:6–12; Hos 6:6; Mic 6:8; Mal 1:10 with 12b; Matt 15:8–9, 25:40; Luke 18:9–14; John 3:16–17 with 36 and 5:24 and 8:12; 4:23–24; 10:28–30; 13:34–35; 17:3; 20–23; Gal 3:22–25, 5:4–6; 1 Tim 4:7; Jas 1:26–27, 2:14–17; 1 John 1:8–9.

24. Resolve or Rest

For I desire mercy, not sacrifice, and acknowledgment of God rather than burnt offerings.

—Hos 6:6

THE WAY TO A life of trusting God and resting in his providence is not a direct one, and, though the principles are the same, no one's journey looks like anyone else's. It seems we have to learn the same lessons repeatedly, fail time and again, and only gradually progress to a life of wisdom, of trust in God's providence in our lives, in the lives of those we love, and in the world around us. Sometimes it seems our heads are too thick. We see how much we need his grace and encouragement. But it usually takes more time than expected to become even imperfect examples of that grace, and we are impatient and distracted. Some of us may be determined to make something of ourselves, but determination and resolve do not always end well. Instead they can become an end in themselves and result in our own achievement of something outside his ideal for us. We might resolve not to miss a single church service in a year while ignoring the needs of our neighbors. We might discipline ourselves to read the Bible at a particular time each morning while the needs of our spouse or children are essential just at that time. Determination and resolve are not primarily what God is looking for in us. He wants our hearts and our sensitivity to him and his ways. As good as our disciplines may be, he wants our trust in him to override our grit, and love for others to become our pattern. He wants us to listen to him.

Accomplishing self-discipline in itself is not our goal. Resolve and achievement serve habits of survival our individualist culture has given us and can reflect legalistic or popular Christianity, canceling out God's grace and our freedom in Christ. Becoming a person of God will not mean to forsake spiritual disciplines, but it will mean learning to rest in him. It is a difference in our motives. Trusting God is a way of looking at life and seeing ourselves. Reading God's word, prayer, and worship have new meaning on this journey. Their frequency is important, but their irregularity may actually make them more significant in our lives. We must stop our activity and notice his words, aim to trust his ways, be grateful for his providence, and be humbled by his attentions instead of proud of our achievements.

Scripture References: Pss 138:8, 51:16–17, 62:5–8, 91:14–16; Prov 3:5–7, 20:27, 21:3; Hos 6:6; Mic 6:8; Matt 11:25–30, 25:40; Luke 10:41–42; John 8:31–32; 10:1–10, especially 10b; 13:9–10a; 17:3; Rom 715:13; Gal 5:3–6; Phil 1:6, 2:12–13, 4:6–7; 1 Thess 5:23–24; 1 John 1:8–10, 5:11.

25. God's Will Achieved?

Be transformed by the renewing of your mind. Then you will be able to test and approve what God's will is—his good, pleasing, and perfect will.

—*Rom 12:2*

KNOWING GOD'S WILL FOR our lives does not always look like we think it should. It might be pretty shocking. Our cultural values and personal needs give us expectations that do not always fit his intentions for us. We may think he will provide us with a final revelation of what he wants us to do, where he wants us to go, or an ultimate understanding of the way things are. Will he not show us the exact person to marry, university to attend, house to buy, or vocation to take on? We are practical and want to know precise information about these things. We always want to know something else, something new from him.

But it turns out, upon closer inspection, God's will revolves around something old. The priority of his will for us is not so tangible. He is seeking faithfulness to things we have known for a long time. Trust, gratefulness, humility, and love are central to his desires for us. But knowing about them is not enough. They must get under our skin—get planted deeper in the soil of our lives. We need to give our attention to them, understand them, and remember them. The things we have read over and over in his word must become part of us. The process is ongoing. Any serious person seeking to know God's will finds more and more of their own will standing in the way. And when we get around one barrier, another crops up. We are humans wanting the things of God; for that, we will need the humility that our humanness resists while amply displaying its need. Nevertheless, we must "seek first his kingdom and his righteousness" (Matt 6:33).

God's will is, first of all, about being rather than doing. As we become more and more what he wants us to be, it resolves a lot of questions about what he wants us to do. And what he wants us to do is not so specific as we may prefer but rather a choice between options within the boundaries of honoring him, gratefulness, humility, and loving our neighbor. These values can be true of us in any honest vocation, marrying any of several well-suited, Christian people with a true heart for him, living in any neighborhood, or choosing one of many Christian universities to prepare us to serve him in a vocation with our lives. His word gives us both these boundaries and the freedom to choose within them. Unlike the law of Moses, it is a way of love, wisdom, and freedom rather than specific signposts.

Do not get discouraged by failure on the journey. Acknowledge your humanness, your feeble ability to walk in God's way. He knows you better than you know yourself. Look at each failure as a tool for shaping your heart to want his way more, each disappointment as an opportunity to renew your trust in him. Don't look for perfection where it is not to be found, but where it has always resided—in him. Despite our weakness, God sees us through the work of Christ on our behalf. He lays out the way before us; our goal is to stay on that path. Our ultimate trust is not in ourselves or our achievements but in his grace, providence, and purposes. There, we can learn to walk in the spirit and live in the freedom of Christ with wisdom.

We must also remember that God's will for our lives may well include a journey to Egypt. Joseph, in the book of Genesis, was sent there to save his people. The Joseph of the early verses of the Gospel of Matthew, after all the angels' promises of what the Messiah would do, also found God's will would include a long, dry, dusty trudge to Egypt to avoid Herod's sword. Can you imagine his thoughts halfway there? Tired, sore feet, grit in the sweat on his face, chapped lips, and all he could see ahead was more sand and rocks. But God was bringing salvation to the world. It does not always look or feel like it could be God's providence in our lives. Patience. Wait on the LORD.

Scripture References: Gen 37:28 with 45:5; Pss 25:1–15, 37:7, 23–24, 103:10–18; Prov 3:5–7, 20:9, 24:16, 26:12, 28:26; Lam 3:23–26; Matt 2:13; John 15:1–8; Rom 3:21–24, 8:1–8, 12:1–2; 1 Cor 3:18–23; 2 Cor 3:15–18, 4:7, 5:15–17; Phil 2:3–4, 3:12—4:1; Col 3:1–4, 9b–17; Jas 3:13–18; 1 John 1:5–10, 2:15–17.

26. How Much Do You Matter?

Let us run with perseverance the race marked out for us.
—Heb 12:1

A PERSON'S LIFETIME CAN seem very long to the young, but older people know it is not a long time to accomplish the many meaningful things God puts before us. Each day matters. The Japanese think about life as a *"yo."* A *yo* is the growth span between two joints on a bamboo cane. Each *yo* connects what has preceded with what comes after it, and each is vitally important to the bamboo tree. If a *yo* is unhealthy or incomplete, the plant stops growing at that point. It is similar for Christians. Our lives connect with the faith of those who have gone before and influenced us. We, in turn, impact those around us and those who will follow us. These connections will not be perfect, but they must be enduring. We must be willing to play our part. Your opportunity to be a spouse, a parent, or a friend can be a deep connection of one life to another that God has given you for his purposes. We don't know how far it will go as one life touches another, as one person is changed by our interaction, one kindness, one deed of love passed on. God told Israel to remember his laws and make them part of their daily lives, passing them on to their children. Today, we must remember his grace and truth in the same way. Ongoing knowledge of that grace and truth, the hope of each generation, is at stake.

The author of Hebrews tells us of the "great cloud of witnesses" from the past that should challenge us on our journey to "run with perseverance the race marked out for us"(12:1), to grab the baton from those who went before us, and continue the race we share with them. We, too, should leave an example, however human it will be, that will influence those around us and those who come after us to set their eyes on Jesus' example, their hearts on the expansive grace of God in him, and their trust on God's prevailing providence in all things "for the good of those who love him" (Rom 8:28) and the accomplishment of his plan.

Scripture References: Deut 64-9 and 11:18-21 with John 1:14-18 and Matt 28:18-20; Pss 115:3 with 135:6; Prov 22:6; Matt 25:40; Rom 8:28-39, 12:9-13; Eph 5:22—6:9; Phil 2:1-4, 3:17; 1 Thess 10:2-10; 1 Tim 4:12-16; 2 Tim 1:5-6, 15-17; Titus 1:1-3, 2:1-8; Heb 11:1—12:3; 1 Pet 2:16-17.

27. Playing Our Part Well

Let us not become weary in doing good, for at the proper time we will reap a harvest if we do not give up.

—*Gal 6:9*

WE HAVE TALKED ABOUT our part in the lives of others as a spouse, a parent, or a friend. The opportunity to be a teacher, nurse, fireman, homemaker, electrician, or faithful employee in any job is equally important. By touching lives, encouraging, and offering deep and enduring hope in God for those around us, we each become a meaningful connection between the past and the future, between people and God. It is our part today in the history of tomorrow. You may never become well known or recognized for your faithfulness, good works, or words, but these are your personal, unique, God-given opportunities in the lives of those around you today and those who will follow. The Japanese call it *naka'ima*, the middle present. It is seeing today as the center of time. It is where the past meets the future.

Let me mention again how most Christians today do not notice that good works are to be the end result and evidence of our salvation (Eph 2:10), and are the purpose of God's inspired word (2 Tim 3:17) and the church (Eph 4:12). They are the evidence and outcome of wisdom from God (Jas 3:13), and central to the message of grace and hope in Christ for the world (Matt 5:16; 1 Pet 2:12 and 15; 1 John 3:18). Jesus takes them personally and as evidence of our faith at the judgment (Matt 25:34–40).

Contentment comes to those who see today's opportunities of their short lives as God-given and faithfulness to others as faithfulness to him. These opportunities come to us through the family, vocations, and communities God has provided us. Things will not go perfectly every day. On the job, coworkers may be cranky and unkind, we may be out of sorts and grumpy ourselves, and there may be frustrations in the family, but stop! Stop feeling sorry for yourself, and think of all you have from God for which to be grateful. Slay the demon of self-pity and straighten out your crumpled faith. It is our day to live for him and express his grace as he has expressed it to us. He never forgets our faithfulness, good works, or kind words.

Scripture References: Ps 37:1–6; Isa 32:17; Lam 3:25; Matt 5:13–16, 25:34–41, 28:18–20; 1 Cor 1:26–31; Gal 6:7–10; Eph 4:11–13; Phil 2:1–4; Col 3:12–14, 4:5–6; 1 Thess 4:11–12; 1 Tim 2:1–4; 2 Tim 3:17; Titus 2:11–14; 3:1, 8, 14; Heb 6:10, 10:23–24, 12:1–3, 13:15–16; Jas 1:17–18 with 22; 3:13; 1 Pet 2:12, 15; 2 Pet 1:5–9.

28. Determination

Let us throw off everything that hinders and the sin that so easily entangles, and let us run with perseverance the race marked out for us.

—*Heb 12:1*

You do not have enough determination, and what you have can never go far enough. Self-assertion, resolve, and control to achieve your personal goals, regardless of who gets hurt, go in the wrong direction altogether, whatever your culture and society may tell you. In the end, knowing God is beyond this kind of grit. It is more than information, ambition, and determination. It is preceded by humility and surrender. But we often get the cart ahead of the horse. A culture of achievement leaves humility out of the picture. In fact, it is considered counterproductive, a weakness or flaw, a liability in a person who will never accomplish the goal of life: the satisfaction of self-fulfillment. No wonder humility is hard to find in Western cultures, even among Christians.

Truth be known, pride is the corrosive flaw, and self-assertion the distressing weakness of humankind that needs to be overcome and tossed aside for a relationship with God and others that fulfills our deepest needs. As the Proverbs put it, "He who trusts in himself is a fool" (Prov 28:26). That does not mean there is no need for discipline and determination. But they must be framed by humility, grace, and truth. Culture's influence can be blinding, but God can open our eyes to his way. Most Evangelicals do not recognize that we are not saved by faith. What??!! It is true. We are saved by the humility required for genuine faith in God's grace. Faith begins with humility and ends with good deeds, or it is not faith at all. No humility, no faith.

We may have to step back from organized Christianity to see it, for it is written in such large letters in the New Testament that we may not see the woods for the trees. It is often the biggest, most obvious, and common sense thing we do not see while we give our undivided attention to the minutia of an issue or question. Yet humility is central. We also have an aversion to paradox while it is in God's very nature and works everywhere in the Bible. Jesus tells us it is the humble and the meek who inherit heaven and earth while we celebrate the "success" and achievement of our churches. But the gate is narrow and small. We will have to bend down to get in. Let him who has ears to hear . . .

In our day, we lack a mental, emotional, and practical grasp of humility, and we do so at our own loss, at the risk of our well-being and peace, even to our ruin and, finally, our demise. Our pride stands between us and God, shutting the door to salvation and wisdom. The proud and arrogant have no resources for survival when things fall apart in life; pride does indeed go before the fall. Pride is a parasite that kills its host, self-assertion a cancer that ravages the body. We will have to acknowledge God's hand in our lives—his intervention of love, the paradox of his grace, and the mystery of his providence. We will have to let go of self-assertion and bend the knee, for the challenges before us in the spiritual universe are immeasurably greater than we are, and no amount of self-determination can rescue our souls from the powers of darkness. The spiritual forces against us are too strong, the deceptions of the dragon too great, his angels too numerous. We will stand or fall depending on humility or pride, for the battle hinges on the grace and power of God.

Scripture References: Pss 15:2, 18:27, 25:1–5, 31:19, 139:11–12, 145:14; Prov 9:10, 11:2, 14:12, 15:33, 16:18, 18:12, 22:4; Isa 66:1–2; Jer 9:23–24; Matt 5:3–10, 7:13–14, 12:24–16, 16:24–26, 19:30, 20:26, 23:12; Luke 1:47–53, 9:23–25, 18:9–14; John 8:12, 12:24; Rom 12:9–13; 2 Cor 4:4; Gal 6:9; Eph 2:1–5, 4:1–3, 6:12; Phil 2:3; Col 1:13–14 with Eph 5:8–9, 6:10–18; Heb 12:1 with 4:14–16; Jas 3:13–18; Rev 12:7 with 20:2.

29. Choosing God

But if serving the Lord seems undesirable to you, then choose for yourselves this day whom you will serve.... But as for me and my household, we will serve the Lord.

—*Josh 24:15*

In our individualism and independence, we dislike the demands of others thrown upon us against our will. We prefer control, if possible, over our situation for our satisfaction and contentment. We want to do things *our* way. It is part of Western culture to think like this, the normal way of survival for human beings. Is not the pursuit of happiness a right we have in our society? However, the results of such a pursuit by individualists who have pushed aside the necessary virtues are not of God. Duty gives way to inclination, humility to personal pride, and concern for others to self-assertion. Happiness is not an achievement; it is the choice of a gift from God.

Our culture gives us reasons that help us rationalize that we are doing what is right and necessary for our well-being, and, though we may often have to leave the chips fall where they may, in many cases, we can better our situation. But whatever we accomplish to subdue our insecurities is only temporary and is more fragile than we realize. It is the most serious mistake we can make to trust ourselves and not recognize that God wants us to be part of *his* plan, not become part of *ours*. Many mistakes are forgotten or can be put behind us, but not this one; it follows us wherever we go, relentlessly reminding us that, in reality, we are not in control. In various ways, he continually calls for our submission to his grace and providence while we rationalize away his pursuit of our hearts.

We have our reasons for putting him off. We are reluctant because we do not think our self-needs will be met. God is okay in his place at church, but we don't want him messing with our lives; we each want to be our own master. The idea of his providence seems dismal, canceling what we want in life. The last thing a strong individualist wants is to lose control. Our culture teaches us that we may lose everything if we do not assert ourselves. And, indeed, many self-interested people are ready to grab what could be yours, even what is already yours. It makes us afraid to trust God.

We are right to think this one through. It entails the risk of many things we depend on, things we have in place that give us some small feeling of security. What will happen if we let God into our lives, all on a promise from him we have never seen? And that's not all. This one is for all time. We'll be burning our ships. There is no turning back. These reluctant thoughts are because we do not know him; we do not understand his far-reaching grace, penetrating love, powerful providence, and ultimate truth. Our culture has baited us with the idea that we can do it on our own. But there is a sharp hook in that bait, and it goes deep. By the time we realize we're caught, it may be too late. We must come to realize that our culture is often a false teacher. It is blackmailing us with conformity for survival. But the truth about God could not be more certain.

It will take humility to accept Jesus as the only one who makes authentic survival possible, and welcome God's way in our lives. It does not seem possible or even necessary from our finite perspective, but we *can* know God's truth, embrace his lavish grace, and experience freedom in Christ. Then we can become what he intended and relax in the security of his powerful providence, "in the shadow of the Almighty" (Ps 91:1). Genuine meaning and purpose are found nowhere else in our temporary lives. True engagement in a meaningful life now and for eternity begins with knowing and trusting him, the way, the truth, and the life.

Scripture References: Pss 10:4, 14:1, 16:11, 20:7, 37:1–4, 91:1 with 14–16; Prov 14:12, 28:26; Matt 7:13–14, 11:28–30, 19:16–26; Luke 9:23–25, 12:13–21; John 1:4–5, 10–12; 3:16–21; 8:12; 10:11–15; 14:6, 27; 16:33; 2 Cor 11:13–15; 1 Tim 2:5–6; 1 John 2:15–17.

30. Self-Assertion or Service

Whatever you did for one of the least of these brothers of mine, you did for me.

—*Matt 25:40*

WHILE SOME PEOPLE MAY be naturally at ease in our Western society, most individualists have characteristic ways of hiding their insecurities. Certain options for emotional survival are more common among us than in other cultures. At the center of our individualist value system, self-assertion can give us a defensive posture against anything that might expose our vulnerability. Some of these attempts to defend ourselves are more benign than others. However, particularly malignant is the need to control our situation and the people around us to feel good about ourselves. There can be a certain arrogant independence about this kind of person. (We recall the Pharisee in the temple with the tax collector.)

While critical of any who turn to artificial means to escape emotional pain, the controller is free to roam, leaving devastation in their wake as they plow through anyone who gets in their way to achieve feelings of security and self-worth. We might think there are fewer people like this in the church, and especially in ministry, but, harsh as it may seem, the ratio looks to be nearly that of our society in general. The same individualism from our culture is at work in both situations, but it is far more lamentable among Christians. Syncretizing individualism with Christianity is the opposite of the message of the gospel. We are blind to our culture's influence and have let the enemy in the door.

When we add the personal value of perfectionism to the values of individualism and independence, we have an even more potent formula for self-assertion, leading people away from trusting God. We must begin by examining our own lives. We have been told to be self-assertive to survive in our Western culture, but God tells us to love one another in the body of Christ. These two values are mutually exclusive. We cannot be perfect in our love, but that does not change the goal, which is to pursue harmony (Phil 2:1–4), unity (John 17:20–23), and love (13:34–35) among ourselves. To love others takes empathy with kindness, and is usually an effort in the everyday things of life, rarely an exceptional behavior; it may not even be remarkable. It is usually an "ordinary" effort that serves others regarding their needs. And may I remind us that we only have today to do it?

In loving others in this way, we also love and serve God. To love God also means to step away from self-assertion. We must be humble and honest before him and desire to honor him with our lives. It is more about loyalty than affection, more about gratefulness for his grace and trust in his providence. It is a relationship full of security, peace, and freedom.

Scripture References: Pss 25:9, 91:1 with 14–16; Prov 16:18–19; Matt 25:31–40; Luke 10:25–37, 18:9–14; John 13:34–35; Rom 6:5–7; 12:3, 9–13; 2 Cor 5:15–18; Gal 5:16—6:10; Phil 2:3–4; Col 3:1–10; Jas 3:13–18; 1 Pet 4:1–2; 1 John 2:9–11, 15–17; 3:18; 4:4–6, 19–21.

31. Dangerous Virtues and Dark Disciplines

God, I thank you that I am not like other men. I fast twice a week and give a tenth of all I get.

—*Luke 18:11–12*

WE DO NOT USUALLY think about spiritual disciplines as dangerous. There is a strong biblical emphasis on disciplining ourselves, which is extremely valuable for our lives. Through it, we can make the most of our days on earth, apply ourselves to gain wisdom, and serve God with our lives. But there is also potential for grave abuse. Those taken up by self-discipline as an end in itself think of it as a virtue that others lack and are therefore inferior for their weakness. This is a trap of individualist achievement culture bleeding through what we call our faith. Dangerous "virtues" and dark disciplines can lead to deadly arrogance. Are there people who need more self-discipline? Of course. There is one writing this paragraph. But our achievements can never be ends in themselves—especially our spiritual disciplines. The grim legalism and selfish gossip that can accompany this pride are truly dangerous, dark, and deadly.

Our self-control cannot become the master, leading to a dependence on human achievement. It may be a salve on the raw insecurities created by our perception of God as a father like we had, one we can never please, never earn his approval, but it will not do. We must put aside the memories and our need for the missing human affirmation to know God. We cannot and do not have to earn his approval. Jesus has earned it for us. We can only accept his mercy for not giving us what we deserve and his grace for giving us what we do not. No one is exempt. An honest view of our heart is required for personal pride is the very opposite of knowing him in a relationship. It is challenging for the Western Christian, but we must realize all our personal "righteousness" is undone in his presence. Only humility will do. It is the ultimate requirement, for we are in need of a righteousness not our own, that of Christ Jesus.

Though how we think about our achievements is important, the Bible also emphasizes our words in the book of Proverbs and the letter of James. Our pride is often revealed in the gestures, facial expressions, and paralinguistic cues that accompany our words. Words of love guarded by the restraint of wisdom and humility bring healing, encouragement, and life. But the words, as well as the thoughts, of the proud, bring death. Not physical death, an unwelcome visitor who comes sometime, calling on us all, but the great enemy, spiritual death, who destroys them even while they live, separates them from the giver of true life, now and forever.

Scripture References: Ps 12:3 with Prov 10:31–32, 12:18, 16:18–19; Pss 15:4; 19:14; 59:12; 90:4 with 10 and 12; 141:3; Prov 10:8–11; 14:12; 16:18; 17:27; 18:4–8, 20–21; 20:9, 27; 21:23; 28:26; Isa 58:6–12; Hos 6:6; Luke 18:9–14; John 10:10, 11:25–26, 17:1–3; Rom 3:21–24, 5:15–19, 8:35–39, 10:1–4, 12:9–19; 2 Cor 5:21; Eph 2:8–9; Phil 1:9–11, 2:1–8; 1 Tim 3:6; Jas 1:26; 3:1–13, 17–18; 1 Pet 5:6–11; 1 John 3:18.

32. Perfectionism

There is a way that seems right to a man, but in the end it leads to death.

—*Prov 14:12*

WE WILL FIND IT hard to organize or manage social relationships in our perfectionism. Under its influence, we may tend to avoid closeness with some and seek to exert control and micromanage others. Agendas, budgets, planning, and organizing have a place, but they can strangle friendship and love; these are jewels too precious to lose. Spouses, children, friends, and neighbors are our world to be cared for. But our monochronic time orientation (desiring only one thing at a time and systematic order) and obsessive value on accomplishment can get in the way. People do not fit schedules very well. Our attempt to control too much of life with calendars and agendas will eventually hurt the very ones we say we love but have no time to give to them. Yes, there are things we need to accomplish, but we must be careful that, if we do not get them all checked off, we do not push our loved ones aside, neglecting the more important for the lesser. Ultimately, our relationships will fall apart, or *we* will. The need for control eventually hurts its owner. This is especially true when God is scheduled in where we think he might fit and made to wait his turn.

At its worst, when obsessive perfectionism is combined with selfish ambition, the control of others becomes a severe compulsion for self-survival. Things only go well when the individual gets *what* they want or need from those around them *when* they want it. They plan and scheme to control outcomes to their advantage. Their skillfulness at this tactic can become exceptional. They have learned how to get what they want and use the good nature of others to their advantage. They see them as gullible and naive.

Most will fall for the scheme, not realizing they have been exploited. Others will feel powerless to do anything about it. No one, it seems, dares confront the sharply assertive or the smooth and smiling kinds of controllers.

God wants us to love others as we do ourselves. When we do, we make time for them and listen to them. When differences are not essential, we respect their opinions. We should seek their best with kindness and loyalty. You will notice that sentiment is not on this list. That is because, though feelings of affection often accompany it, they are not the purpose or central point of this love. So it is with our love for God and his people, all the while remembering that the people we love are not perfect, and we should not expect it. Neither are we, and we should accept it. We all need God's grace, and we can be part of showing it to others.

Scripture References: Ps 15:1–2 with Mic 6:8; Matt 5:8 and John 4:23–24; Prov 6:12–19, 14:12, 17:17, 18:24, 21:2–3, 27:6; Mic 6:8; Matt 22:34–40; John 13:34–35, 15:12; Luke 10:25–37, 38–42; Rom 3:22–24, 12:9–13; 1 Cor 13:1–13; Phil 2:1–4; 1 Pet 5:5b–7; 1 John 1:8–10, 4:7–16.

33. The Paradox of God's Gift of Freedom

And whatever you do, whether in word or deed, do it all in the name of the Lord Jesus, giving thanks to God the Father through him.
—Col 3:17

As dear as we may hold our freedoms granted by a democratic government, a great deal of abuse, neglect, and corruption enters the situation with numbing regularity. God also grants freedom to his individual created beings, and the same neglect and abuse can accompany it. Outside life itself, free will is the most sacred gift God has given to humankind. He wants us to have the peace and security of a relationship with him but allows us to ignore or refuse him. Such a paradox is necessary so the choice to follow him can be genuine. He knew that most of those he created would turn their backs on him, and even his chosen people would abuse the prophets and eventually kill his Son. From the first couple, humankind has been easily tempted to trust themselves more than God, and that self-assertion continues today. Social influencers try to erase the memory of God from the people so that they can have their own way. God was willing to take that risk with humankind and sacrificed his Son to open the door to himself. We who know him seek to be salt to preserve his ways and light to show the way to him in this regrettably broken world, but it is not so unlike the world Jesus walked in or the world Paul faced in his ministries. Humankind has always resisted God to have its own way.

Our freedom of choice does not end when we choose God through Christ. There is still the risk of our human inclination to satisfy the self—love and loyalty can only be voluntary. Even when we see the truth about God, we may tend not to trust him entirely. Our allegiance and loyalty to him are sometimes thin and weak. We often grant them with several disclaimers. Yet he does not reject us. He continues to love and forgive. We may even temporarily forget that our sin made necessary the tragic death of his Son. He does not. And yet he pours out his mercy and grace on us, who sometimes choose to be disloyal to his purposes. It is all the more reason to value the freedom he has given us, along with grace and truth, and realize the profound gift that it is.

God gives us freedom in how we express our love and loyalty to him, our worship and obedience, and our service in his kingdom. For this reason, we cannot criticize another who expresses his or her faith or serves God differently than we do. He looks at our hearts for faithful attachment to him and his ways—our desire to honor him in whatever way we choose to live for him. For this freedom, he gave us boundaries around acceptable alternatives that we might exercise it with caution. Without these boundaries, our freedom as individuals would destroy love in the body of Christ and its expression in our community, just as people who stretch and redefine the limits of their constitutional freedoms hurt others and cause society to disintegrate. Neither political nor Christian freedom exists without responsibility. Abused, freedom becomes the death of its owner and the disintegration of the church or society.

So Christians who are insensitive to those around them can abuse the freedom God has given them. We may indulge in what our conscience approves for us without considering the weaker faith of those around us. We are all maturing in Christ, and the stronger must help and encourage the weaker. Though we can decide otherwise, God has given us the only way to succeed in life and, therefore, in our communities. That is to choose to love and honor him with grateful hearts and to love those around us—the boundaries of his gift of freedom. Jesus came as the way, the truth, and the life. Justice, mercy, and humility are the virtues of his way for our lives and for a church or a society to flourish. We must be generous in their exercise.

Scripture References: Pss 1:1–6, 15:1–5, 24:1–6, 91:14–16; Prov 3:5–10; 4:20–27; 8:12–21; 21:21 with 22:4; 25:4–5; 26:12; 28:26; 29:4; Isa 66:2b; Mic 6:8; Matt 5:13–16, 22:34–40; John 3:16–21; 8:31–32, 36; 13:34–35; 14:6; Rom 14:5–8 and 16–23 with 1 Cor 6:12 and 8:4–13, 9:19–23; Gal 5:1 with 6 and 13–15; Col 2:16–23; Titus 1:15 with Matt 5:8; 1 Pet 2:16–17.

34. Lost Values in a Broken World

You must understand that in the last days scoffers will come, scoffing and following their evil desires.

—*2 Pet 3:3*

THE WEAKENING OF THE family in our Western societies has produced generations with no foundation for their lives. Liberal views of life have invaded this vacuum with meaninglessness—a sensual but unhappy, angry, desperate, and only temporary way of surviving. The followers of these views are self-deceived and without moral reasoning, indeed without reasoning at all. This worldly wisdom says that all the past must be erased, and commitment, duty, and responsibility in life canceled, so the people can be controlled by the new philosophy (which is not new at all, and has failed everywhere it has been propagated). It tells us, "There is no wrong decision, no wrong destination." To accomplish this manipulation of society, the central strategy is to deny God's existence and invent a theory of how we came to be here, erasing any basis for meaning, self-worth, respect for others, value of relationships, or moral or ethical behavior. Valor and virtue are left behind; courage and character wane. The defense of morality is considered an outrage unless it serves a political advantage. The deception in the garden goes on, as does the death and suffering it brought.

This situation has increased the level of narcissism, desperation, rage, and racialism in society. People are left grasping at anything that momentarily brings relief and, often, clinging to others doing the same for a thin sense of identity. Moral duty has been canceled, and the ability to think smothered, as good becomes evil and evil, good. People born into a world of this kind are numb to its underlying philosophy. They try to make sense of what is left of society but are at a loss. The answer is not hidden or secret, but their minds have been closed to its reality.

Christians do not escape the effects of this movement in the world as the family weakens. All around them, attachments of love and trust are severed, and children search for security elsewhere. The hedonistic disease of the worship of human independence and pleasure infects public education and shapes young minds. Christians are sometimes influenced away from clear thinking to nonsense, as opposite as that is from God's intentions for us. Weakened in the truth, hope, meaning, and peace found in God and his grace alone, Christians lose their ability to be salt and light in that world and can fail to create the necessary environment of security for their children. But we must remember we are different. We belong to a kingdom that is not of this world. We know God's mercy, for he *has not* given us what we deserve, and we know God's grace, for he *has* given us what we do not deserve, and it can never be taken from us. We are his, and his way is one of forgiveness, hope, freedom, peace, and meaning. We walk in the way he gives us and rest in the shadow of El Shaddai, the Almighty, in the blistering heat of a world gone wrong. We matter to him.

We who have humbled ourselves to accept Christ as our substitute can stand tall in loyalty to the King. His good providence works *for* us, his lovingkindness *surrounds* us, and his power *overshadows* us. We are safe and secure in his faithfulness because we acknowledge his name above all names. He does not change. His steadfast love for us endures forever. In this world, we may have trouble; we may suffer, and our bodies fail, but even in our weakest moments, this trouble cannot touch our souls if given to him. His light floods our darkness. We belong to the King, who will bring us deliverance from all trouble and pain for eternity.

Scripture References: Gen 1:1–5; 1 Sam 12:20–22; Pss 1:1–6; 9:9–10; 14:1; 23:1–6; 37:3–8; 62:5–8; 71:19–21; 91:1, 4, 14–16; 100:1–5; 102:25–28; 118:1–9; 136:1; 139:11–12; 145:14; 147:11; Prov 9:13–18, 16:5–6; Eccl 1:9; Isa 5:20–23; 26:3–4, 12–13; 43:1; Lam 3:25–26; Matt 5:13–16, 6:33, 24:4–14, 25:31–40; John 8:12, 16:33, 18:36 with 1 John 2:15–17; Rom 1:18–23, 28–32; 5:1–5; 8:28; 2 Cor 4:4–6; Eph 2:1–5; Phil 3:17–21; Col 1:13–14; 1 Thess 5:21; 1 Tim 4:1–10; 2 Tim 3:1–5, 4:1–2; Titus 2:14; Heb 4:14–16, 10:23–24; 1 Pet 3:18; 2 Pet 2:1–3, 3:3–7.

35. Not Alone in His Plan

Finally, be strong in the Lord and in his mighty power.
—*Eph 6:10*

Fight the good fight of the faith.
—*1 Tim 6:12*

Put on the full armor of God so that you can take your stand against the devil's schemes.
—*Eph 6:11*

WE CANNOT FIND MEANING in life on our own. But, then, we are not alone. Silently in waiting is the God of the universe, at our door, in all his grace and power. We can find our identity and worth in his love and grace for us, making us one of his own. No sin is too great, no scar too deep, no barrier too high that he cannot reach us with his love and bathe us in his forgiveness through the righteousness of his Son, Jesus. He has a purpose for each of us in his plan for creation. Our existence takes on meaning in that plan—our lives matter. We become significant parts of what he is doing in the world.

When we come to him, we will realize the extent of resistance to his movement in the world. Being a part of his activity takes courage in the face of criticism. But as we put self behind us and live in allegiance and loyalty to God, trusting his providence in each situation, we will know his peace. The need for recognition is over, the search for significance is ended, the emptiness is gone, and the need to be accepted and loved unconditionally is fully met in him. Though our trouble and suffering in the world may increase, though his way may take us "through the mighty waters" (Ps 77:19–20), our trust in his providence will give us stillness we cannot find elsewhere. He waited for us to look in his direction. He wanted us in his design for all things and holds our happiness in his hands. He waits now for others, and may use us to help them come to know him or know him in deeper ways.

We all have a part, large or small, in his work in the world. But we are not alone. We may only have one arrow to shoot in the great war for the minds and hearts of men. But God already knows that. It is what he asks us to shoot. We must take careful aim, with that one arrow, at the false ideologies that are the weapons of Satan in the world. But we do not shoot it alone. God will use our efforts. For some, it will be encouraging others, a life of faithfulness in the home, or supporting those on the front lines, and for others, engaging Satan's deception in the public square. It may be helping just one other person through life. But none of us are alone. The Creator-God of the universe is with us.

Scripture References: Deut 31:6–8; Josh 1:9; Pss 9:10; 23:4; 27:13–14; 34:4–8; 37:48; 46:1–3 with 10–11; 77:10–20; 91:14–16; 103:11; 107:12–16; Isa 26:3–4, 12–13; 43:1; Matt 28:18b with 20b; John 10:28–30; 14:1–6, 18–27; 15:1–8; 16:33; 17:20–23; Rom 5:1–11, 8:28–30, 15:13; 2 Cor 5:17, 21; Eph 6:10–18; Phil 4:6–7; Col 1:9–14; 1 Tim 6:11–14; Titus 2:11–14; 2 Pet 3:8–9.

36. What Kind of Fool

The heart of the wise inclines to the right, but the heart of the fool to the left.

—*Eccl 10:2*

CHRISTIANS ARE FAR FROM perfect people. We, too, can be foolish in our actions and words. We can all improve in considered and measured responses to life's twists and turns, embarrassing incidents, unpredictable outcomes, offensive people, and frustrating events. The book of Proverbs emphasizes wisdom and escaping the consequences of this carelessness. We must pursue this wisdom with God at the center—life as God intended—and avoid the fool's path, which leads to death. In the book of Proverbs, the fool is given all sorts of descriptions. Sometimes people are simpletons, not using common sense, and full of empty chatter and reckless words. Other times they are lazy, with plenty of opportunities to help others but not inclined, and have no concern for getting involved. They are not interested in the effort it takes to be the friend of another. Yet other times people are arrogant in their foolishness, mocking even the wise. Some are stubborn and unreasoning, refusing even the obvious solutions to their problems. This, too, is foolishness.

God wants us to seek his wisdom and do so at any cost. He calls it finding life as it should be; the alternative is death even while we live. Walking in his wisdom grants honor and grace outside our world of thin and superficial values. It is living a life of loyalty to God's purposes, gratefulness for his mercy, and humbly acknowledging his presence in every aspect of our lives. We will recognize his providence, proclaim his attributes, worship his majesty, realize his mystery, and accept the paradox of his ways. This is what it means to fear the LORD. In his way of wisdom, we will see ourselves as the sheep of his pasture, the objects of his love, and his light in a dark world.

Wisdom calls to everyone to seek her and grasp her counsel. And it is not just for the educated theologian in his office. It is for people from all walks of life, in the mundane things of everyday living, common vocations, and family matters. Wisdom is a way of looking at life with God at the center, giving us insight into the best responses to its ups and downs, and helping us make good decisions. This house of wisdom "filled with rare and beautiful treasures" (Prov 24:3–4) can only be built on a foundation of humility and trust in a relationship with God. Only a fool says there is no such God, and unless they turn toward him, the consequences are inevitable. Death awaits the simple, destruction, the fool.

Scripture References: Pss 1:1–6, 14:1, 91:14–16, 95:6–7, 100:1–5; Prov 1:7, 28–33; 3:5–7, 13–18; 4:5–13; 8:10–11 with 17; 9:1–6, 10; 12:13–19; 14:12, 15–19; 16:2, 5; 17:27; 18:6–8, 13; 21:4, 23–26; 22:4; 23:9; 24:3–4; 28:26; Eccl 5:1–7, 7:8–9, 9:17–18, 10:3; Isa 33:6; Matt 5:14–16 with John 8:12; John 10:4; 1 Cor 15:33; Eph 5:8; 2 Tim 2:14–16; Jas 1:19–20, 3:13–18, 4:6.

37. The Friends We Keep

Above all else, guard your heart, for it is the wellspring of life.
—*Prov 4:23*

CONTINUING WITH THE THEME of wisdom, there is also advice in Psalms and Proverbs about the people we associate with. We are not to be the companion of any of the many kinds of fools. Being friends with an angry person will turn out bad for us as we allow ourselves to take on his habits, negative outlook, injustice, and intolerance. Hanging out with the malicious, spiteful, cruel, or those who mock good can influence our character to become like them. Hanging out with a gossip will not turn out well. Just talking to a fool can end badly for us. There are some people in life who must be avoided if we are to guard our hearts and take care of our souls.

Some come in among those in the church but are not of God and must be avoided so that association with them does not contaminate our hearts and minds, keeping them from being transformed by God's word and his people, keeping them from being set on things above. Some nonbelievers are always present, but those who intend disruption, display selfish ambition, or assert themselves to cause division are to be stopped. Believers must display unity. Once pride and selfish ambition take root, they bear the bitter fruit of division and a conceited independence from God, the very opposite of God's purpose for us. To know him is eternal life, and separation from him leads to death. Divisions in the body of Christ deny this truth. Yet these masquerade among us as "friends" of the gospel. Paul warns the Ephesians, and Jesus, the disciples, that we are often sheep among wolves. We must be careful not to let worldly values contaminate the church.

The principle of taking on the values of those we associate with is what some have called the social proximity effect. As social beings, we tend to take on the values, habits, and outlook of those we spend time with. We will have to rub shoulders with nonbelievers in the world if we are to influence them with the gospel, but we must use caution. We are to be friendly, patient, and kind to everyone we can, but we must be on our guard that they do not disturb our desires for God.

Scripture References: Pss 1:1–6, 14:1, 26:4–5; Prov 4:20–27; 12:15; 13:20; 20:19; 21:2; 22:24–25; 23:6–8, 9; 26:4–5; Eccl 7:8–9; Matt 10:16, 28:18–20; John 17:3, 20–23; Acts 20:28–31; Rom 12:3–8, 16:17–18; 1 Cor 1:10, 13:4–7; 2 Cor 11:13–15; Gal 1:6–9; Eph 5:15–17; Phil 2:1–4; 1 Tim 1:3–7; 2 Tim 4:9–10; Titus 1:10–16; 1 John 2:15–17, 4:1–6; Jude 3–4, 12–13, 17–21.

38. To Do Good or to Be Good?

He does not treat us as our sins deserve or repay us according to our iniquities. For as high as the heavens are above the earth, so great is his love for those who fear him.

—Ps 103:10–11

WE OFTEN VIEW THE behavior of other Christians as good or bad, right or wrong, honoring or dishonoring God, without knowing their hearts. Other times we evaluate the outward actions of others using values shaped by our society and personal experiences when the Bible does not speak of them. Finally, we have difficulty recognizing God's paradoxical ways of using the unexpected, apparent contradictions, and what *we* do not allow for his work in people and the world. Of all the things God asks us to do, correcting our brother is only a thin slice of it and one that demands care, humility, and the evaluation of our own hearts first. We are not often aware of the causes of behavior in others, or even ourselves, and we must allow for the freedom each has in Christ to express and live out their faith.

At the root of honoring God is what we want to *be* for him. Out of that will come what we want and try, with his help, to do for him and others. Jesus' Sermon on the Mount is intended to contrast mere obedience to the law with the kind of people God wants us to be. But that frame of mind is often overcome by other less helpful inclinations. The most aggravating of all is selfishness. When we are self-centered, we tend toward those behaviors that feed the self: pleasure, gain, power, reputation, popularity, distractions from anxiety and insecurity, etc. We are individualists at heart, and become competitive for what is advantageous to us more quickly than we think.

Then there is pride, which can motivate many of the behaviors that, in our better moments, we want to avoid. Perhaps a person is good at something. Their pride can turn this into the desire to do it better than anyone else or become well known for it. This can lead to competition with others or using them to accomplish selfish ambitions. People who do not boast of their "significance and worth" become objects of resentment to be discredited. Selfish ambition and pride are enemies of one's life, Christian or not. These self-centered attitudes and their resulting behaviors characterize the lives of many people.

Everyone has some level of selfishness and pride in their hearts. I, the writer of this paragraph, and you, the reader, know that only too well. But God intends that we become people who live for a greater purpose. So, once again, we come to the question of what we want to *be* for him and then do for him. He does not make us into good people against our will but provides every encouragement and opportunity to that end. Telling us of his great love and sacrifice, the unconditional forgiveness we have in Christ, the meaning his purposes give to life, and the enduring peace that can be ours gives us every reason and discredits every reluctance to trust him. Humility and gratefulness help us choose well and desire to honor him, to become more sensitive to our straying, and to love those around us even on a bad day. That path has a rugged incline and may have many rocks to navigate. But with the wisdom and encouragement God gives us, by his strength and grace, we can take that way. Though we will never be perfect in ourselves, we will know perfection in Christ's sacrifice and God's forgiveness for us. We are not perfectly good, but we know who is.

Scripture References: Pss 34:4, 8, 17–19; 103:10–18; 106:1; Prov 14:12, 16:18, 29:23; Jer 17:5 with 7 but also 9; Matt 12:33–35, 15:17–20; Luke 6:41–42; John 13:34–35, 16:33; Rom 7:14–25, 12:1–2; 2 Cor 5:15–17; Gal 5:19–26, 6:1–5; Eph 2:1–10; Phil 2:1–4; Col 1:9–14 with 3:1–4; 2 Tim 3:16–17; Jas 1:2–8 with 3:13–18 and 2 Cor 12:7–10; 1 Pet 3:18 with 4:1–2; 1 John 1:5–10.

39. The Seeing and the Blind

The god of this age has blinded the minds of unbelievers, so that they cannot see the light of the gospel of the glory of Christ, who is the image of God.

—2 Cor 4:4

THE CREATION OF HUMAN beings is an astounding miracle. Their complexity is overwhelming. Everything they are and can do is a gift from God. Their bodies and all their attributes and abilities are given to them so that they can fully engage in all of life. The eye alone is beyond the tiniest scrap of any evolutionary theory of its development, and those who say it came from chance brandish the swords of their irrational human arguments only by the hands God gave them. In all their "learning," unbelievers have decided by their "own" reasoning that God did not make them—using the mind and will God gave them to deny him. It is the most desperate of all religions to fight against God so one can worship the self. They teach their children to reject the old stories and ignore the rumors of a Creator-God of the universe. But their eyes do not see. Like the ruthless in Israel before their deportation, whose "foolish hearts were darkened" (Isa 5:20–21; 29:16, 20–21 with Rom 1:21–22), they, too, follow a path of darkness.

Even a moment's reflection is enough for the simple but honest heart to see that every day is a miracle, as is every movement, every action performed, every word spoken, every heartbeat. They see the hand of an intentional God who moves with purpose throughout his creation as he has revealed himself. The heavens and the earth belong to the humble and pure in heart and echo the story of God's power, grace, and faithfulness. Gratefulness and humility swell when we see his attention to us, small as we are, in his vast universe. And where we fall short in honoring him, his patience and grace are abundant, his providence in our lives a blessing.

But the proud and spiritually blind cannot see him. Torches ablaze, they lead the masses in the darkness away from the true light. But their fire will go out suddenly, and the darkness will devour them, every hope extinguished. Jesus alone is the way, the truth, and the life, the light of the world, offering hope to those in the grip of the dark powers of spiritual death. For those who know they are lost, the anxious, the broken and discouraged, those wounded by life's disappointments, he has open arms of compassion and grace. He never fails the humble of heart who seek him. Even if they are physically blind, they will indeed see God.

Scripture References: Pss 8:1–9, 10:4, 14:1, 19:1–6, 24:1–6, 34:17–22, 53:1, 145:13–14; Prov 26:12, 28:26; Isa 5:20–21 with 29:13–16, 20–21; 45:9; 50:10–11; Matt 5:3–10, 11:28–30, 12:20, 15:12–14; Luke 6:39, 17:1–2; John 1:1–5, 3:19–21, 8:12, 12:37–41, 14:6; Rom 1:18–21; 2 Cor 4:4–6; Eph 6:12; Phil 3:17—4:1; Col 1:13–14; Titus 1:15, 16; Jas 1:17; 1 Pet 5:8; 2 Pet 3:3–10.

40. Honor, Grace, and Humility

So God created man in his own image, . . . male and female he created them.

—*Gen 1:27*

It is an honor to have a life, but there is no reason you or I should. We have not earned it. Human beings were created in God's image, by his power, and with his love, and, though it should humble us, we often live as though we had something to do with it. But God, who could have brought anyone into the world, brought the likes of you and me. Before we come to know him, it is an honor ill repaid. His gift of life should call for our loyalty to him and encourage our hearts, but without a knowledge of God we use it as if it was of our choice and making, ours to do with as we please without thought of a creator.

Then into this mixture of blessing and abuse comes God's invitation to know his grace. He intervenes through the sacrifice of Jesus on our behalf. He offers to come between us and the ruin of our lives. It is a second gift, an intervening love, and, once acknowledged and welcomed, his lavish and undeserved kindness removes the shame our willfulness has caused and puts us on the firm footing of perfect honor before him, that of Christ himself. Once again, we have done nothing to deserve it. It is all of him, and this honor upon honor calls for a deep humility of heart. As incredible as it sounds, each of us who know him stands before the Creator in righteousness given to us at great cost by him, no more deserving than anyone else.

Some know of God, but only superficially. They are popular Christians who love Christianity and the feelings of worth and belonging they find there. They do not know an intimate relationship with God. Others know of him but have not really trusted him with their lives. These are unhappy

Christians who are caught in a loyalty battle between trusting him and trying to manage on their own—knowing his providence and love or the misery and loneliness of trying to live without him at the center of their lives. Popular and unhappy Christians have yet to know the depth of God's grace or realize the honor of its offer to them. They have not experienced the humility of faith or freedom of trusting him and do not yet know gratefulness for such a gift and the peace it brings.

Scripture References: Gen 1:1; Ps 100:3 with 79:13; Prov 18:33; Isa 64:8; John 1:1–3 with 10–14; 3:16–18; Rom 3:23–24, 8:1, 11:33–36; 1 Cor 6:18–20; 2 Cor 5:21; Eph 1:3–8, especially 6; 2:4–10; Col 1:9–14; 2 Tim 1:8–10; Titus 2:11–14, 3:3–7; 1 Pet 3:18, 5:5b–7.

41. The Pure in Heart

Blessed are the pure in heart, for they will see God.

—Matt 5:8

JESUS TALKS ABOUT THE pure in heart in Matthew chapter 5. We in the West take statements like this to infer that some people sin in their hearts and others do not. Then we talk about having power from God over sin, or freedom from sin, confusing people even more as they ponder how people get this power or freedom and why they don't seem to have it themselves. But we are missing the point of God's word with this categorical, dualistic thinking. The qualities in Jesus' teaching here exist, but not in the ways our Western logic requires. We prefer to talk about a person as pure or impure, usually in terms of their behavior. But Jesus is talking about the motives and intentions of the heart. These attitudes and values we cannot see, measure, or categorize neatly might result in behavior we do not expect or may not allow for ourselves. Mutually exclusive categories, precision, logic, and directness are preferences our culture gives us, and we bring them to the Bible. But here, God's ways override them. As he often does, he gives us the truth in a paradox. The pure in heart are not perfect. That is not the requirement for knowing and seeing God.

When speaking about the character of human beings and their attachment to God and his ways, the Bible often gives us understandings of the heart that are not black and white, stone-cold, logical categories. These understandings are matters of wisdom concerning spiritual qualities and virtues. In one context, God can say that no one is righteous, and elsewhere people are described as righteous throughout the Old and New Testaments. Being righteous in character does not mean perfect. That perfection before God is only achieved through the righteousness of Christ.

The pure in heart do not grow past the ability and inclination to sin. Yes, some legalistic people disagree, saying they have not done this or that sin while disregarding that God is looking at the heart. It has even led to a doctrine teaching that some individuals arrive at a place where they no longer sin at all. However, John clarifies in his first Epistle that this is not the case. On the opposite side of the debate, others speak of "total depravity" in such a way that it excludes the possibility of the pure in heart, the humble, the merciful, or the peacemakers altogether. But Jesus affirms and encourages the very people with these virtues and values.

Though the sacrifice of Jesus was yet to be accomplished, under the law, where you might least expect it, what he says is true: the pure in heart would see God. But he does not say they are perfect people without the potential and even inclination to sin. He is saying the pure in heart do not want or intend to sin but desire to honor God, and in that motive *are* pure in heart. The tax collector in the temple, behind the Pharisee, went home *justified*. How far along anyone is in their spiritual journey is a matter for God, but the pure in heart *are* among us today. Paul can later say, "To the pure, all things are pure" (Titus 1:15). Does he mean they never sin? No. But they know that sin is not in things God created, but first of all in the heart, and then in the misuse and abuse of those things. The pure in heart are those who do not want to sin. It does not mean that they don't, but that the purpose in their hearts is not to do what dishonors God.

We may be uncomfortable with this, but God's word speaks to us in generalizations that include these qualities and the people who own them. The mature person in Christ, the man or woman of wisdom, the righteous, the pure in heart, know very well they are not perfect, and their humility (being "poor in spirit") is part of their purity. The more mature they become in Christ, the more they realize their shortcomings. They are called righteous people in the Bible because they know and trust God, not because they feel spiritual. They know they have nothing God has not given them, and their acceptance before him is only possible through his mercy and grace in the work of Christ on their behalf. And having the Spirit of God, they live in this grace with freedom because they trust his purposes and providence. They realize that good or evil are, first of all, matters of the heart.

Yes, the pure in heart will indeed see God. That is, they will see his good and powerful providence at work on their behalf, know his grace, comfort, and care in difficulties, and, one day, live in his presence forever. Those who are not pure in heart, no matter how good their record of achievements, are not spoken of so well. The Pharisee in the temple with the tax collector is an example. Worshiping God and serving others are to

41. THE PURE IN HEART

be done in spirit and truth—with humility and a pure heart. This worship and these good works come from people we will know by their wholesome values (wisdom from above, fruit of the Spirit, and love for one another) in circumstances, relationships, and social interaction.

Scripture References: Gen 6:9; 1 Sam 16:7; Ps 34:17–19; Prov 9:9; 12:14, 18; 16:2; 15:11; 17:3; 20:27; 21:2; 24:16; Isa 3:10, 32:16–17, 66:2b; Matt 1:19, 5:3–10, 7:15–23, 23:1–7 with 25–28; Luke 1:5–6, 26–28; 2:25; 18:9–14; 23:50; John 4:23–24 with 1 John 3:16–20; John 8:31–36; Rom 3:9–24; 2 Cor 3:17; Phil 2:12–13 with Rom 8:28; 1 Tim 6:11, 17; Titus 1:15–16; Heb 13:15–16; Jas 3:13–18.

42. Ritual Behavior

These people honor me with their lips, but their hearts are far from me. They worship me in vain; their teachings are but rules taught by men.

—Matt 15:8–9

RITUAL BEHAVIOR IS PLANNED and calculated to achieve something. If it is Christian, it is hoped it would be done with a pure heart and that its goal is to honor God through strengthening our faith, growing in our knowledge of him and his will, and better expressing the results of his grace in our lives. Spiritual disciplines of Bible study, devotional reading, and prayer are good and essential for us. However, ritual behavior is highly capable of the opposite. It can easily be used to hide selfish intentions: to impress others, to achieve a record, or to assuage our guilt and hide our true selves, none of which honors God. For many in our world, ritual is used to achieve "good karma," fill a favor bank with gods and ancestors, or avoid harm from nature spirits, all of which is useless. But for Christians, ritual behavior depends on the heart for its help in living our lives for God. This is why we cannot know its value for others. And it is unlikely that anyone would see another's true spiritual disciplines since they are practiced in secret.

Natural behavior is different. I do not mean to confuse it with worldly or ungodly behavior but refer here to the everyday behavior of responding to life's responsibilities, frustrations, challenges, and blessings. Our natural behavior reveals our true outlook on life, our values, intentions, and desires. It is what we do in ordinary circumstances or during unusual events in our broken world. Our reactions to the inconveniences and interruptions, the embarrassments and downturns, or the joy or popularity of others show us for what we are. None of us is perfect, but all of us should be humble.

42. RITUAL BEHAVIOR

Devotions, church attendance, and Scripture memory programs, for all the help they can be to us on our journey, can also become misguided rituals or achievements used to bolster our feelings of worth or gain God's approval. But if that is where our worth comes from, we are depending on our own works instead of on God, on our legalism instead of on his grace. We must let go of our accomplishments and do whatever we do for his glory instead of our own. Setting our minds on things above, we now live for him, and what we do is a result of his grace in our lives, not its cause; it demonstrates our faith, not our ability.

Scripture References: Matt 6:1, 5-8, 16-18; 15:8-9 with Isa 29:13, 58:6-7; Matt 19:30 with 23:11-12; John 7:18; Rom 6:8-11; 1 Cor 10:23-24 with 31; 13:4-7; 2 Cor 5:15; Gal 2:15-21; Eph 2:8-10, 4:1-6, 5:15-18; Phil 1:20-21, 27; 2:1-4; Col 1:9-14, 2:20-23, 3:1-4; 1 Pet 4:1-2.

43. He Comes

He is patient with you, not wanting anyone to perish.

—2 Pet 3:9

IN A WORLD THAT seems to be falling apart, where thinking gets criticized and good is called evil and evil, good, in our own culture, we need more than ever to realize God's overpowering providence in everything. Though people everywhere have abused the freedom and good gifts God has given them, loved darkness instead of light, and rejected him as their creator, God is still bringing his plan to its completion in history. Rejection does not impede him. As the Western mind becomes unable to think, it is not a time for anxiety but for trusting God and encouraging other believers. The world may look out of control to us, but, in his patience, he is at work to his own ends, and no one can stop his hand. We who know him can be confident in our relationship with him. No one can undo his grace on our behalf, our position in Christ. He is far above this world, and we may not expect or understand what he is doing or why, for his ways are not ours. But his Spirit stirs over the darkness; he moves in the world while waiting for more people to turn to him and know his grace. However, he will not wait forever. He comes.

The world plummets toward that hour of judgment; the sins of the Jews of Israel and Judah before judgment fell on them are repeated, Sodom and Gomorrah have been rebuilt, the arrogance and hypocrisy of the Pharisees are among us, and callousness, bribery, and injustice characterize the wealthy and powerful of our day. But the walking sleepers will stumble over their sins. During the events of the coming days, many will be placed on the left of Christ, but we who are in Christ now, who have sought to honor him with our lives despite our weaknesses, will be placed on his right to enter his

43. HE COMES

kingdom and receive the inheritance prepared for us since the creation of the world. Yes, we will be overcomers if we trust his sacrificial work on our behalf. Today, we can and must stand firm in our loyalty to him and seek, in whatever way we can, to honor his name and encourage others in the faith.

Scripture References: Gen 19:23–29; Pss 9:10, 46:1–11, 91:14–16, 95:6–7; Prov 28:26; Isa 5:20–23 with 59:14–15 and 64:4–5; 29:17–21; Ezek 33:11; Amos 5:14–15, 6:4–6; Matt 23:11–15, 24:1–51, 25:34; John 3:36, 8:12, 10:27–30, 14:1–4; Rom 1:18–20, 8:28–39, 13:8–14; 1 Cor 15:20–28, 50–58; Phil 3:20; 1 Thess 1:9b, 5:9–11; 1 Pet 4:7; 2 Pet 3:1–15; Rev 22:7, 12, 20.

44. Here but Wanting to Be There

No eye has seen, nor ear has heard, no mind has conceived what God has prepared for those who love him.

—*1 Cor 2:9*

WE ARE SOJOURNERS IN a physical universe, but it rests inside a larger one, the spiritual universe. As children, we must grow in our physical, emotional, and mental dimensions, but also in our spiritual dimensions. A deficit in any one of the four leaves us handicapped and unable to navigate our lives in this world as we were designed to. The first three mentioned here get a lot of attention. If we lack in any of them, it results from being in this broken world, but it is not a circumstance that keeps God from using us to represent, serve, or honor him in a particular way. However, if we lack in the spiritual dimension through unbelief, we will be blind to his love and grace, cannot know his purposes, and life will be meaningless. Though created in his image, his gift of life will not flourish in us. We will be on our own to manage in a damaged and hurting world, something God never meant for us.

It is not that way for we who know God through Christ. Elisha saw a glimpse of the spiritual universe in the horses and chariots of fire around him and his servant in Dothan. Zechariah and Mary were visited by its messengers. The shepherds were shocked by it on the day of Jesus' birth. Saul (Paul) was struck by it on the road to Damascus. We, who are in Christ, have become part of it; we have a particular aspect of eternity in our hearts—the Holy Spirit. We know where we came from and why we are here; his love and grace give this meaning and purpose to life. We see God's providence in our lives and the world around us. In the turbulence of life's ups and

44. HERE BUT WANTING TO BE THERE

downs, in a world that has rejected him, we know the peace he gives. It is the paradox of his grace that the undeserving can know God, and such we are.

We also know God has more for us. We cannot clearly define it, but we long for something outside ourselves that he saves for us. We see his fingerprints and shadow here and there in his providential care of us. We know we are in his attention, but we are just outside his eternal destiny for us. There are mysteries he has reserved for us, so great we cannot comprehend them here: sights and sensations of wonder and matters outside our present reasoning we will only understand and experience in his presence. So we wait for untold treasures of heaven, and, in that waiting, we humbly enjoy the peace he gives us, the grace that has been lavished on us while yet in this physical universe, the goodness of his providence in our lives. In our waiting, we serve him and his purposes for us here.

We must encourage fellow sojourners in this world, helping them with their needs while showing them God's love, grace, purpose, and destiny for us. They must "taste and see that the Lord is good" (Ps 34:8), that "his love endures forever" (107:1), that life here is temporary and our days "quickly pass" (90:10) with their trials and blessings. It is not how much time we have but whether we believe and trust him during what he gives us. In the coming days, warm joys God grants now will be magnified, and pain and suffering, relentless and intense though some of it is, will be eliminated. His presence will be experienced in the deepest way. We are here, wanting to be there. But Jesus will not delay long. He is coming soon to take us home.

Scripture References: 2 Kgs 6:15–17; Pss 34:8; 42:1–2, 8; 46:1; 130:5–6; 139:1–12; 145:17–19; Eccl 3:11–14; Isa 26:3–4, 12–13; Jer 23:24; Lam 3:25–26; Jonah 1:1–12; Mic 6:8; Matt 5:8, 28:20b; Luke 1:8–13, 26–33; 2:8–12; John 14:1–4, 15–17; 16:33 with 14:27; 17:20–21; Acts 9:1–6; Rom 5:1–2; 1 Cor 2:9; Eph 1:3–8; Phil 4:4–9; 1 Tim 1:15; Jas 1:27 with Matt 25:31–40; 1 Pet 5:10–11; Rev 21:1–5.

45. What I Want

Watch out! Be on your guard against all kinds of greed; a man's life does not consist in the abundance of his possessions.

—Luke 12:15

WHAT IS IT THAT we really want? Some of us have basic and legitimate physical needs, but others have everything they need for sustenance yet desire persists. Would more money, achievement, popularity, or becoming a leader bring the fulfillment and happiness we seek? It seems like it would. But these have been tried by many, and they have failed. Some things might make life easier, but they leave the happiness they promise just outside our reach. We need meaning, purpose, and peace in our lives no matter what else we have. These can only be had in our relationship with God, with the motive of entering into *his* purposes for our lives. It is the use of all we already have to honor and serve the Creator-God outside ourselves.

We must become preoccupied with *gratefulness* for his grace and providence in our lives. Jesus said the way is narrow, and the gate is small, so we must humble ourselves and bend low to enter and become his sheep. This *humility* is required for true faith. Then, as much as possible, we must *trust* him in all the events and turns and encounters in life. Gratefulness, humility, and trust lead us into *love, good works,* and *making him known* (glorifying him), which are the outcomes he desires for us. All this comes together to give us the meaning and purpose we need for our lives.

Our problem is that the self often stands in the way of our search for true fulfillment. Sometimes we *know* the truth, but we *want* something else to be true. We may know what the Bible says about riches, fame, and status not bringing ultimate happiness, but we don't think it would be true of us. At least we would like to try it, maybe prove this verity wrong in our case.

45. WHAT I WANT

And, anyway, we would still be Christians, which we think would change the outcome. But we forget that for those who know the truth but push it aside, it is often worse than for those who love the world not knowing God. We have stepped away from the wisdom that knowing God through Christ offers us and embraced a pragmatic, human approach to "happiness." We have our ladder up against the wrong wall, and when we reach the top, the other side will not be what we expected.

We must stop and take inventory of our heart's desires. Jesus is the way, the truth, and the life. Fulfillment is found in no other direction. Faith and wisdom pay attention to the truth and trust the Creator. We will never be completely free of a battle with the self and its human inclinations and desires; our liberal culture, media, and "progressive" government have seen to that by instilling their version of self-survival and happiness deep in our values and thinking. But the important thing is to allow God's word to have the upper hand, to want and purpose to honor him more than anything else. He looks at the heart. Remembering our indebtedness to God, we must humbly honor him and serve and help others do the same. In time, with maturity in Christ, it will become more habitual, more of an inclination for us by his grace and providence. There it is, what we need: life with purpose, promise, and peace, and eternity with even more.

Scripture References: Ps 33:11; Prov 14:12 with 16:2 and 17:3; Luke 12:15–21, 18:9–14 with Prov 3:5–10; John 10:1–15; 14:1–6, 27; Rom 5:1–11, 15:13; 2 Cor 5:15–18; Gal 2:20; Phil 4:4–9, 19; Col 1:3–6; Heb 6:13–20; 11:1, 6; 13:20–21; 1 Pet 4:2; 2 Pet 2:20–22; 1 John 2:15–17.

46. Free Will

Choose for yourselves this day whom you will serve.

—*Josh 24:15*

IN GOD'S WISDOM, HE gave humankind the free will to deliberate, choose, and make decisions. For this to be genuine, there had to be options from which to choose. We are given the simple statement of the complex concept of these options as good and evil. This dichotomy is shown in the garden of Eden as being about trusting or not trusting God. In a world of freedom, not everyone chooses the same actions or goals. In our individualist cultures, people have a natural inclination toward self-gratification. So a person decides on "what is good for me." It may sound harsh, but the Bible says that, without God, people "love darkness rather than light" (John 3:19) and that "the god of this world has blinded their minds" (2 Cor 4:4) so that they do not choose what is ultimately good. They must surrender, unbolt the door long closed to God, and welcome his grace into their lives to finally understand that "every good and perfect gift is from above, coming down from the Father" (Jas 1:17), and he has not forgotten anything.

Evil is deceptive. Satan impersonates an "angel of light," and his servants disguise themselves as "servants of righteousness" (2 Cor 11:14), though they are all from the dark world. He can make evil look good. He tempts with sweet poison that becomes bitter in the stomach. Falling into his snare results in suffering and emptiness. If we do not turn to God, it leads to more evil and, finally, death. Many can suffer from the selfish choices of one person. Why such a world? If God gave free will to humans, knowing they would choose so much evil resulting in so much suffering, what was his purpose? The ironic answer is "because he wanted a place where there could be love, loyalty, grace, virtue, patience, and compassion."

46. FREE WILL

The paradox of God is outside our logical reasoning, but, in *his* wisdom, these virtues cannot exist where their opposites do not—where there is no choice to own them in the face of rejecting them. Yes, they only exist where they are voluntary—willfully chosen from among the alternatives. Any of them coerced is no longer a virtue. Compulsory love is not love. In his wisdom, he provides a way for us to know peace and contentment amid the adversity of humans choosing evil. We can and must decide to trust him.

One cannot imagine light if there is no darkness or warmth if there is no cold. To imagine an empty space, we must know something of a crowded one, and to desire silence, we must be exposed to the aggravation of noise. To long for compassion is to know something of the devastation of indifference; love is in contrast to hatred, and we can think about perfection on a future day only compared to the imperfections we know today. But God does not force people to choose good or evil; they choose freely as both possibilities make themselves known. As did our ancestors, we naturally want to serve ourselves and our pride. Not knowing God, one sin leads to another. But in Christ we know his lavish grace on our behalf, his forgiveness and unconditional love in the highest contrast to life without him. We know the true light in a world of darkness, the water of life in a desert of thirst, true life only through death; it is the paradox of his grace. When we follow Christ, freedom from serving only self becomes a reality. We desire to undo our natural habits out of love for him instead of ourselves, to be loyal to his purposes rather than our inclinations.

God has given each person the sacred gift of free will, but the stakes are high. With it comes the dignity he will not remove of allowing each to decide their destiny. Such a gift! We will one day experience an existence entirely free of evil and suffering, or we will know what not choosing him means for eternity. Light or darkness is before us.

Scripture References: Gen 1:3–5, 2:15–17, 3:1–7; Deut 29:19–20; Josh 24:14–15; Lam 3:33; Matt 13:24–30 with 36–43; John 1:1–5 with 3:16–21 and 8:12; 4:4–14; 8:31–36; 12:24–26; 16:33 with 14:27; Rom 5:1–5, 7:14–25; 2 Cor 4:4–6, 5:15, 11:13–15; Eph 1:7–8; 2:1–5 with Col 1:9–14, 2:13–15; Eph 5:8–18, 6:10–13; Phil 2:1–4, 4:4–9; Col 3:1–17; 1 Tim 1:12–17; Jas 1:13–18, 3:13–18; 1 Pet 3:18 with 4:1–2; 2:16–17; 1 John 1:5–10, 2:15–17; Rev 21:1–8.

47. Cultural Filters and the Bible

Do not conform any longer to the pattern of this world, but be transformed by the renewing of your mind.

—*Rom 12:1-2*

THE CULTURE OF A people shapes their values, beliefs, understandings, and, therefore, their behavior. Along with experience, it provides a frame of reference, giving meaning to relationships, events, and communication in each situation. Because it works this way, each culture will function as a filter when its people encounter those of another culture. The new frame of reference for meaning causes confusion. The outsider cannot experience the social situation the way insiders do. It is the primary barrier to understanding the communication and behavior of people in another cultural context, either of those in the world around us or those of the Bible. To understand and empathize with others, we must know a good deal about them and their cultural values so we can enter their world with them. If we do not, we will use *our* cultural frame of reference in *their* situation, causing misunderstanding and hindering relationships and trust.

Given that we are entering a world of people very different from us when we read the Bible, we must be cautious about our culture's interference in understanding the text written within theirs. Our independent individualism blinds us to this need. When we go to school to learn what the Bible says, we should also study the cultural frames of reference, ours and theirs, to know more of what those words meant to the people in that time and place and what they mean for us today. If we know something about our own culture, we will be more sensitive to differences in the culture of the biblical message. We will also be better prepared to let God speak for himself without reading our cultural preferences into the text. Strapping

47. CULTURAL FILTERS AND THE BIBLE

God with our Western rational logic, casual informality, inclination toward legalism, or dislike for mystery and paradox shapes him into a God of our own making. We are not free to do so.

Just as it takes time to learn how to read and write or to play the piano, we must also take the time to learn how culture works and to understand how it affects the people we see in other societies, such as those in the Bible. We must grasp that their experience gives them mental and emotional associations with the words of their language that differ from ours. Unless we step into their collective and hierarchical world of honor and shame with them, we will try to pull them into our individualist and egalitarian world of guilt and innocence. Language does not equal communication without a shared cultural frame of reference and a sensitivity to the influence of social and personal experience that gives words their intended meaning for the speaker and their actual meaning for the listener.

Thus, the work of a pastor/teacher is to lead his flock to the best understanding of the Bible with an eye to the cultural context God used to reveal his will to us. God speaks, and we must hear him on his terms. We are to look intently into what he says in its context and then apply it to our lives in today's world. This is called contextualization. The result will necessarily be somewhat countercultural for us as it was for the original audience. As the biblical truth enters our modern lives, it will change our loyalties, values, and inclinations. The new wine must be put into a new wineskin. When our cultural values play less of a role in the process, our expression of faith in God may look different than our society expects, but it will be more what God intends. It is the practical side of the spiritual renewing of our minds Paul speaks of in Rom 12:1-2.

Scripture References: Prov 3:5-7, 30:5-6; Isa 40:13-14, 55:8-9; Hab 2:20; Matt 9:16-17; John 3:3; Rom 12:1-2; 1 Cor 10:31; Eph 5:15-17; Phil 1:6 with 2:12-13; 4:8-9; Col 1:9-14, 3:1-4, 17; 2 Tim 2:15 with 3:16-17; Jas 1:22-25; 1 John 2:15-17 with 4:4-6 and John 15:19.

48. Personal Barriers

Do not be anxious about anything, but in everything... present your requests to God. And the peace of God, which transcends all understanding, will guard your hearts and minds in Christ Jesus.

—Phil 4:6–7

SMALL THINGS OFTEN SEPARATE us from God: the distraction of some trouble, the anger at some loss, the frustration of some plan thwarted, some pleasure delayed, or some perfect arrangement spoiled. Other things are not so small, such as anxiety about tomorrow and emotional pain from events past or present. But often the real foes are the three basic struggles of selfish ambition, insecurity, and pride in our Western world of independent individualism. Statements like "I am going to *have* what I want, and I will get it *my* way," "I'm going to manage my *own* life," "I *have* to do this to survive," or "I'll show *them*" reveal our concerns.

These are not small things. They are our greatest barriers to intimacy with God, living for him, trusting him, and loving others. The psalmist often cries out to God about his enemies who are seeking to devour him. These barriers, great or small, are *our* enemies. The three basic struggles are the roots of every sin in our lives and nearly always hurt those around us. They are reflected in the smaller distractions and the cause behind them. But small or large, the barriers must come down, the enemies, subdued, if we are to engage with God's purposes, trust his providence, reflect his grace, and love our neighbor. It will take humility, submission, and time to allow his desires and purposes to become causes for our behavior toward him and others. If we trust him instead of ourselves, he will make that way clear before us.

48. PERSONAL BARRIERS

This is a tall order for Western individualists who are in love with their independence. The paradox that we must lose our lives to save them is not popular among us. But as we progress in Christ, the expression of our faith will become less of a religious ritual and more of a natural inclination. His ways are not our ways, but our ways can change to display his grace. The first step will be humility. No movement toward God's ideals for us can occur without it. But it also demands some resolve. As the treasure discovered in the field took determination to get hold of, it will take intentional effort to move toward this maturity in Christ. As a pearl of great price is searched for and found, it is worth every effort for us to grow into this way of the kingdom of heaven.

But our progress in knowing, trusting, and living for God will be impeded if we let worries, irritations, and frustrations fueled by selfish ambition, insecurity, and pride come between God and us. Maybe we are discouraged, thinking God does not know our situation or care about us, that waiting on God doesn't work, and that we have to manage on our own. But we are dead wrong. Our independence makes us impatient—another obstacle in our path. We must deal with these barriers causing the dark clouds of anxiety, and live in the light of the freedom Christ gives us in his Spirit. The truth of who he is, gratefulness for what he has done for us, and trusting him, always trusting him, for what he continues to do for us and in us, will set us free. Patience. Fretting and anxiety lead to more of the same and lock us in a prison. The key to that prison door is two-sided. It has humility cut on the top edge and trust on the bottom. It is always within reach but at the cost of turning from self to God.

We have often confused entering the kingdom with joining a church. We must enter the kingdom of heaven with our hearts, in spirit and truth, an honest and inward spiritual loyalty to God. Church attendance is outward activity that can lead us to the gate we must enter and help us understand the cost, but we must believe and decide our loyalty to the King, and then determine to bear the fruit of its reality. Weak as we may feel and imperfect as we are, he knows when our hearts are set on his kingdom. We are "the kind of worshipers the Father seeks" (John 4:23).

Scripture References: Gen 50:15–21; 1 Sam 17:45–50; Job 42:2; Pss 37:1–11 with 28 and 34; 51:17; 56:3–4; Prov 3:5–7, 28:26; Lam 3:22–26; Matt 6:19–34; 7:15–23, 24–27; 13:44–46; Luke 10:38–42; John 4:21–26, 8:31–32; Rom 6:5–10, 8:28–39; 2 Cor 5:15, 12:7–10; Gal 2:20, 5:16–26 with Eph 5:17–18; Phil 4:4–7; Col 3:1–4 with 12; Jas 4:7–10; 1 Pet 4:1–2, 5:6–9.

49. God, So Different from Us

Our God is in heaven; he does whatever pleases him.
—Ps 115:3

THE BIBLE TEACHES BOTH the election of actors in God's story and the hope of salvation given to all who choose it. Regarding God's sovereignty, nothing could be more central to the mystery of God's hand in the world and illustrate our misunderstanding of his ways more acutely than his promise to answer prayer, offer his grace to all, and elect all who accept Christ, no matter how bad they have been, to become his children and receive eternal salvation. All men and women are savable but free to accept or refuse God. Only the humble who accept God's grace become his own.

However, our cultural and personal preferences often take over. We are uncomfortable with the paradox, irony, and mystery we encounter in God's ways in the Bible. In our anxious need to resolve apparent difficulties and avoid uncertainty, we may lean on systems of logic, legalism, or mysticism. We may simply drift into a sentimental and superficial romanticism, or we may fall into syncretism with the culture around us to make "sense" of God in our situation, our cultural frame of reference, and our personal needs. But he regrets our efforts to box him up, as Jesus did Jerusalem's. While we are busy with our personal theories, God is looking for faith in our hearts.

We may not be comfortable with it, but God will continue to be beyond our cultural expectations and limits; his ways will continue to be different from our ways, his thoughts higher than our thoughts, and his purposes outside our logic—his answers to our prayers other than we might expect. We must live with him in a relationship of unconditional trust in his goodness, providence, and love for us. It is his way, his purposes, not ours, for we seek *his* kingdom.

49. GOD, SO DIFFERENT FROM US

Scripture References: Deut 32:4; Pss 25:9, 91:14–16, 111:10; Prov 3:5–7, 4:7, 9:10, 17:3, 24:3–4, 28:26; Isa 55:8–9; Matt 6:33; 7:13–14, 21; Luke 13:34–35; John 1:10–13; 3:16–21 and 16 with 8:12; 14:12–14, 21; 15:7, 16–17; Rom 1:16–17; 3:21–26, 11:33–36; 2 Cor 5:15; 2 Pet 3:8–9.

50. God Chooses Some

And now, do not be distressed and do not be angry with yourselves for selling me here, because it was to save lives that God sent me ahead of you.

—Gen 45:5

OUR INDIVIDUALISM AND ITS corollaries of informality and egalitarianism can push us to reject the possibility of God electing anyone for his special purposes. It seems against human nature to remove absolute freedom of choice from human beings. How terribly unlike God to take such an approach! But God is not controlled by these human limitations or defined by these cultural preferences. Though we do not even know the names of the vast majority of people who honored God in biblical times, particular people were elected to do specific things, sometimes extraordinary things, in God's plan throughout the ages. Our logic is inadequate, his goodness beyond our estimation. His justice will always be satisfied.

In his providence, God works in people's hearts and lives, and they, like the rich young man who turned away, must decide which gate to enter. And then, among those who trust him, and even some who do not, God's hand is, at times, heavy on some for a special task. Sometimes, for those God is calling to a particular assignment, there are special signs, a burning bush or a bright light on the Damascus road. But those called in such a way were not waiting or searching for the sign. God chose them, elected them, often after many years, decades, and, sometimes, centuries of suffering and silence, for a special task in his plan.

On the inside of the small gate, in our day, some are still chosen to do great things in his plan, but *all* of us are called to be humble, loyal, faithful servants trusting him in the events and routines of our daily lives. As such,

50. GOD CHOOSES SOME

we will fulfill his purposes and are in the center of his will for us. He intends to use us *in our situations* as salt and light in the world.

Scripture References: Gen 12:1-5, 45:4-8; Exod 3:1-10; 1 Sam 2:35, 13:13-14, 16:6-7; Pss 51:17, 115:3, 135:5-6; Isa 45:13, 57:14-15; Mic 6:8; Matt 4:18-22, 5:13-16, 7:13-14, 19:16-22; Luke 1:11-17; John 1:12, 3:16, 15:16, 21:20-26; Acts 9:1-16; Rom 12:1-2; 1 Thess 4:11-12.

51. "Biblical" Doctrine

Trust in the Lord.... Wait patiently for him.... For the Lord loves the just and will not forsake his faithful ones.

—Ps 37:3, 7, 28

It may sound like treason to say so, but we are not altogether objective when we come to the Bible. Some teachings of the Bible are quite clear and cannot be missed even if a person does not believe them to be true. But other times biblical doctrines become clouded as they are manipulated by our cultural preferences and personal needs. We might wonder how there can be any influence from our culture when we see this or that doctrine so "plainly" in the Bible. But the "plain meaning" may be plain *to us* because of our strong personal preferences, our need for it to mean one thing or another, or our expectations coming from our cultural frame of reference. Although not always adverse, our cultural values control us in unseen and powerful ways. Our social situation and personal experience also shape our perception, giving us a frame of reference for meaning. Our values and personal needs can enter our reasoning with a silent yet profound influence; our inclinations toward our social survival may cause us to see what we need, not necessarily what is actually there.

Our efforts may result in the legalism of adding rules and regulations where God has given us freedom; it is our human, religious, and cultural need for an objective do or don't-do list. Or we may need the assurance of God's love and affirmation through mystical signs and personal miracles because we find it hard to trust what he has told us. Some allow syncretism with cultural values, giving them an identity and feelings of worth among other Christians for their social survival through competitive self-assertion. Yet others seek a theology that satisfies their need for logic and fear of

51. "BIBLICAL" DOCTRINE

uncertainty, one that ties up all the loose ends into a neat system. When we insist on our way of seeing the Bible, we have yet to allow God to be God.

It's time to grow up in our faith. We must lean on the Holy Spirit, letting God speak for himself, trust what he says, and leave what he has not given us to know in his hands. We need not add to what he has given us, manipulate it to say what we want, or wring objective information out of it because of our fear of ambiguity. Our Western need for neat and organized data must be laid aside when God has not given us the information in that way. Though declarations of fundamental truth are often crystal clear in the Bible, they are frequently surrounded by the mystery of his providence and the paradox of his grace on the edges. Becoming mature in Christ is a matter of settled trust in God and thoughtful engagement with the freedom he gives us under grace within the boundaries of love for him and others. It is a way of love, faith, and wisdom, concepts the Western world finds difficult to understand and hard to accept.

Do not allow yourself to become a blind follower of someone else's personal preferences. Do not allow God's word to be twisted into an artificial system that invents what is not the intent of Scripture. He has told us all we need. "Be still before the LORD and wait patiently for him" (Ps 37:7). Read it intently and thank him for what he has given us, but *trust him* for all we do not know, what we do not understand, and for what is yet to come. All his ways are perfect; he controls the universe according to his purposes, and he loves you and me with steadfast, unchanging, unyielding love, and desires to bring about his purposes in our lives. Trust is the centerpiece of our relationship with him.

Scripture References: Deut 32:4; Pss 15:1–5, 23:4, 27:13–14, 37:3–7a, 51:17, 91:14–16, 115:3, 130:5–6, 135:5–6, 146:1–10; Prov 6:12–19, 16:25, 30:5–6; Isa 43:1; Lam 3:25–26; Dan 4:34–37; Mic 6:8; Matt 28:20; 2 Cor 3:15–18; Gal 1:6–9; Phil 2:12–13; Col 2:17–19; 1 Tim 1:3–7, 4:1–3, 6:3–5; 2 Tim 2:14–18, 23–26; 3:16; 4:1–4; Titus 1:5 with 9–16; 3:9–11; Jas 5:7–11.

52. God at Work in You

You intended to harm me, but God intended it for good.

—*Gen 50:20*

GOD INFLUENCES HIS PEOPLE by revealing his will and way in his word, convicting them of sin, intervening in their lives, and directing their way by bringing about opportunities and equipping them with abilities and resources. Such is the work of his Spirit and his good providence in our experience. He does not, however, make our moral choices for us or force us to have faith, loyalty, or love for him. These things cannot be legislated. People choose to follow or not to follow his way. They decide to trust him or not, to remain loyal to him or to themselves. Neither does he make everything easy for us in this broken world, but he promises to be with us in a powerful way through it all.

Though we must choose his way, God is at work in us. We are humbled, encouraged, and strengthened by his grace in our lives, forgiving us of sin and giving us the righteousness of Christ before him. He is at work in us in these ways that we might be loyal to his purposes and walk in his ways, giving us every reason, motive, and, by his good providence, every resource and opportunity to trust him in our lives and in the lives of others. We will be far from identical to other believers because God works in each of us for his purposes and has given us freedom in our living for him. But, in the essentials, we will be one with him and each other, having the same loyalty to God, purpose in life, and mission to accomplish.

We are told that "God works in *all things* for the good of those who love him" (Rom 8:28). That does not mean everything will be agreeable; it was not for Paul or Joseph or scores of others we read about in the Bible. But whatever God allows in our lives *will* be something he wants to use for

52. GOD AT WORK IN YOU

his purposes, and none of it can separate us from his love. Yes, even bad events in our lives, though they do not look like it at the time, will result in him using them through his good providence for his purposes if we trust him. They will strengthen our faith, encourage other believers, and make him known to those outside the faith. God is at work in us that we might desire and live in harmony with his good purposes. And he has given us everything we need to do so. Paul prayed that God would equip us "with everything good for doing his will" (Heb 13:20–21).

Scripture References: Gen 45:4–4 with 50:19–21; Josh 24:14–15; Pss 84:10–12, 118:6; Matt 6:25–34; John 14:21 and 27; 16:5–15; Rom, 8:28–39, 12:3–21; 2 Cor 5:21, 9:8; Gal 5:16–26; Eph 2:1–5, 5:15–18; Phil 1:3–11, 2:12–16, 4:4–9; Col 2:13–15, 3:15; Heb 13:20–21; 1 Pet 3:18, 5:7; 2 Pet 1:3.

53. I Believe It

Not everyone who says to me, "Lord, Lord," will enter the kingdom of heaven, but only he who does the will of my Father.

—*Matt 7:21*

THE WORD *BELIEVE* IN English does not encompass the breadth or depth of the Middle Eastern word in the Bible. Jesus showed surprise in Luke 6 when people called him "Lord," a statement of belief and loyalty to him, then did not follow his teachings. He later showed surprise, even astonishment, when the gentile centurion showed the genuineness of his faith by saying Jesus did not need to come to his house but just say the word, and he knew his servant would be healed. It was the authentic faith Jesus sought from those around him, and, here, he found it outside of Judaism. Religious as they were, the words and rituals of the Jewish people were empty. They did not know God and his intentions, only his laws and the ones they added to them. They were blind to the promised Messiah.

A peculiar idea in our Western culture is that a person can believe something without the behavior it demands—know something without living in response to that knowledge. This is partly because we are a literate, printed, informational culture. Instead of a message or truth being part of us, it is often on a page in a book, often on a shelf at home when we are at work or school, or on a website when we are driving down the road—just out of reach. The message remains on the page or website; in the podcast, words are forgotten. When Jesus said the word *believe*, he meant that the truth concerned should become part of us as if we ingested it. When we eat something, it, or its effect, goes with us wherever we go, is part of what we do, and becomes part of who and what we are physically. "You are what you eat," as the saying goes. It is not surprising that Jesus would say we should

53. I BELIEVE IT

ingest what he was, said, and did. He indeed was and is the bread of life and the living water.

In his day, among those of an oral culture, people were under the oral traditions the Pharisees gave them, and Jesus spent a good deal of his ministry trying to get them to root out what had control of them and drink the new wine he brought. They needed to be born again, to start over with the actual message from God that would become part of them. It is not without cause that he used eating the bread and drinking the wine of the Last Supper to be a reminder of his sacrifice that it might become the energy that motivates our lives.

Our Western word *believe* is dreadfully cognitive, carries no volitional overtones, and is very easy to use. However, belief is not biblical unless substantiated by natural, everyday behavior—reliably reflected in words and actions. As with wisdom, genuine faith is established in the Bible by the good works that demonstrate it. There is no alternative for us. Our behavior must bear witness to our faith if it is true. Just as saying you love someone but never showing it in actions is not true love, so it is with faith. Though many in the Gospels were changed profoundly when they had enough faith to come to Jesus and he attended to their needs, the mature expression of our faith in behavior is something most of us grow into like the disciples did while with Jesus. Zacchaeus (Luke 19:1–10) was one of the more striking examples of behavior reflecting his faith when he experienced Jesus' acceptance of him. He demonstrated his faith. The Pharisee in the temple of the previous chapter (18:9–14) is an example of the empty words and rituals of falsehearted "faith." Words are not enough; where there are many without action, deception is in the air.

Scripture References: Prov 3:27–28, 21:13, 22:9; Mic 3:9–12; Matt 5:14–16, 7:24–27, 8:5–10, 9:16–17, 15:8–9, 26:26–28; Luke 6:46–49, 18:9–14 with 19:1–10; John 1:10–11, 6:25–59, 14:6; 1 Cor 13:4–7; Eph 2:8–10; 2 Tim 3:16–17; Titus 1:16; Heb 11:1 with 6; 13:15–16; Jas 1:19–25, 2:14–26, 3:13; 1 John 3:16–18, 4:10–14.

54. Unreliable Feelings

God is our refuge and strength, an ever-present help in trouble. Therefore we will not fear, though the earth give way and the mountains fall into the heart of the sea.

—Ps 46:1–2

EMOTIONS CAN PLAY AN important part in motivating us in a good direction, but the important thing is not to depend on feelings for guidance, truth, or assurance. Feelings can be beautiful and enjoyable, but do not make bad things good for us. They can also be dark and negative without making good things wrong. Dysfunctional family life or legalistic churches in our background can breed negative emotions and false guilt. There must be discernment because these negative emotions can cause us to reject the very things we need in our lives because they were distorted in our past. They can destroy our ability to love and trust others, however trustworthy they may be. Some go through life crippled in every relationship, anxious and insecure about being around people who may hurt them again. Most importantly, these negative emotions can come between God and us, making it difficult to trust him.

Not only are negative emotions harmful, but some good feelings can be deceptive and addictive, leading us astray from truth and wisdom. Either can become a barrier in our relationships with God and other Christians or between us and family members. We simply cannot let emotions push us around. If our relationship with God is about feelings, we will crash at the first real setback in our circumstances. What should be an opportunity to trust God's providence and goodness in our lives causes us instead to look the other way for things to fix our feelings or wallow in self-pity. Satan likes nothing better. Like the snare of the fowler, he sets traps for us, catches us

54. UNRELIABLE FEELINGS

off guard to entangle us in negative emotions and weaken our confidence in God. But we are told to resist him by standing firm in our faith and loyalty to the one we belong to, and "He will save you from the fowler's snare" (Ps 91:3). This determined trusting in God must become our habitual pattern. It is the kind of sanctified stubbornness we see in Job as he resists the advice of his wife and "friends."

The disciples ran when the soldiers grabbed Jesus in the garden. Peter went further and denied three times that he had ever known him. After Jesus' burial, their emotions were pretty dark. They had all committed the failure of failures. They even refused to believe the first witnesses to his resurrection on that first day of the week. Their feelings, in this case, were justified. Things do not always go well for us, and sometimes it is *our* fault. But we must stop and realize things are not always what our feelings make of them. When Jesus appeared to them in the room that evening, he was not angry, not full of criticism but forgiveness. He said, "Peace be with you." In our darkest moments, the God of peace is there. We must believe his promise as he said to David, "I will not take my love from him, nor will I ever betray my faithfulness" (Ps 89:33). Asaph reminds us that even when we are at our worst, we are never out of his reach: "I am always with you; you hold me by my right hand" (73:21-23).

Emotions will come and go, but he remains stable. A growing relationship with God increasingly gives us feelings of contentment and assurance of his providential care and goodness, even in intensely adverse circumstances. Though our emotions may rage like the sea, and their swells pitch and toss our boat as the storm surrounds us, we can have peace, for "God is our refuge and strength, an ever-present help in trouble" (Ps 46:1). "Though ... the mountains fall into the ... sea" (46:2), our hearts can be undisturbed, trusting in God, who is present in mystery, power, paradox, and grace.

Scripture References: Exod 14:13-14; Josh 1:9; Job 2:9-10, 13:1-16, 16:18-21, 19:23-27, 42:1-2; Pss 9:9-10; 20:7; 33:16-22; 34:4-7; 46:1-3 and 10; 52:7-9; 56:3-4; 73:21-26; 84:1-12; 91:1-4 with 9 and 14-16; 107:29-30; 118:6; 119:10; 124:1-8; 140:4-5; 146:3-6; 147:10-11; Prov 3:5-7; Eccl 9:17-18; Isa 26:3-4, 12-13; 41:10; 43:1b-3a; Matt 6:25-34, 7:24-29, 8:23-27, 11:28-30; John 14:27 with 20:19-20, 16:33; Rom 5:1-2, 8:31; 1 Cor 3:11-15; Eph 2:19-22; Phil 4:6-9; Jas 4:7; 1 Pet 5:6-11.

55. Explaining God

How unsearchable are his judgments and his paths beyond tracing out!

—*Rom 11:33*

OUR THEOLOGY—OUR UNDERSTANDING OF God's word—is essential to our faith. But sometimes Bible teachers in our Western environment seek to be exhaustive in their explanation of God and his activities. Their commentaries can become complex, philosophical, logical arrangements of propositions, resulting in elaborate doctrines as they stretch their theory over the text. Some build rigid theological systems using this approach. As they read the Bible, what does not seem to go along with their organized system is explained away or twisted to fit. The system, then, becomes the framework for further understanding—the hermeneutic, or rule, for interpreting Scripture.

Though the essential, objective truths are clearly stated in the Bible, some Bible teachers interpret and arrange even these in a way that fits their preference. Some theologians then think their complicated, "watertight" scheme finally explains all of God's intentions. But it is bewildering to the "ordinary" Christian who wants to know and stand on the truth, taking God at his word, and wanting to be faithful to his intentions and purposes. This kind of theology is complex, uses specialized and exclusive vocabulary, ignores many verses that seem contrary, builds theological structures on vocabulary instead of its contextual meaning, and presumes a great deal not given to us in the Bible. The average reader can feel lost among the trees of this vast theological forest when they open the Bible. They may never see its help for the problems of getting through another day.

55. EXPLAINING GOD

Being a theologian is a risky business. It is possible for them to go about their task without thinking about God at work in their own lives. They may not consider how different he is from our cultural and logical preferences or our obsession with methodical systems of thought. They sometimes do not realize that knowing and trusting God is different from our trust in the printed page. For them, the thinking is finished. No mystery is left. The fear of ambiguity is assuaged, the paradox dismantled, and God explained. The boundaries are drawn, and the system may be arrogantly and divisively defended against all alternatives. When this arrangement of God's revelation is handed to students in the classroom or people in the church pews, they begin to filter all they see about God and his ways in the Bible through the sieve of these "sacred" propositions.

As a movement, the theological system can blind the masses. Such was the case with the counsel of Job's friends or the Oral Torah of the Pharisees in Jesus' day, and some of these confident theologians are still with us in our day. Just because some who have used the Bible to oppress others, or tell us God does not love the world, or insist that we need signs and wonders to affirm his acceptance of us, or have manipulated us out of our money call themselves "Christians" does not make it so.

As a result of theology gone wrong, we may not know God for ourselves but only as others "explain" him, a reflection of the real thing in a man-made mirror smudged with their personal and social preferences. Followers may begin to think that God cannot do anything outside the box created for him by the theological system. They may find belonging to their group gratifying and gain feelings of worth and identity as an insider. But the leaders of the movement may come from the wrong starting point and be headed toward the wrong destination. They start with what man says about God to interpret his revelation about himself. We must consider that trusting human information about God may not lead to knowing him. Satan and his angels have information about God.

The religious scholars had information about the coming Messiah before Herod when Jesus was born. The Pharisees, in Jesus' day, studied the scriptures diligently. But informed cleverness is not the same as godliness. Information alone, however neatly arranged, is not enough. We are not to come to the Bible with human, logical, and obsessive perfectionism or seeking a reputation of status. If we do, we may be worse off than not knowing anything about God. Not only is our own sin a problem but allegiance to our theological community comes between us and knowing him. We must come to the Bible with humility and eyes of faith to truly know its ultimate author, his grace, and his intentions for our lives.

God intends us to understand his message and see the implications of the truth in our lives and situations. Understanding the message and its application in our context is a process called theologizing, which is necessary and extremely helpful if written and read with the right attitude. It is not the final word, for there is much he has not given us to know and a good deal of mystery he has reserved for himself. The depth of God's wisdom is beyond our human grasp; the mystery of his providence and the paradox of his grace overwhelm our logic. God is not impressed with our intellectualism or the complexity of our explanations. He is not limited to our exclusive systematization. What he asks of us is our trust. Theology is valuable and extremely helpful as it tells us what the Bible means, but it must let God speak for himself and lead to trust and godliness in the life of the writer and eventual reader in "ordinary" life.

Ironically, in our modern world, where every word can be chased down electronically and scrutinized scientifically, ultimate commitment to the meaning of truth in the Bible continues to weaken. A return to the Bible itself and simple but ardent faith in its essential meanings and the purposes and providence of God are needed in our day. Not that we throw out every theology, but we look at each with the caution this faith should give us.

Scripture References: Pss 37:3–6, 91:14–16; Prov 3:5–7, 30:5–6; Isa 40:13–14, 55:8–9; Hos 6:6; Mic 6:8; Matt 2:1–6, 3:7–10, 7:15–23, 23:13–15; John 1:12, 3:16, 5:39–40, 15:5–8; Acts 16:31, 20:29–31; Rom 11:33–36; 2 Cor 11:4a with 13–15; Gal 1:6–9; 5:1, 6; 1 Tim 1:3–7; 2 Tim 4:1–4; Titus 1:1–3, 10–16; 2:11–12; Jas 1:2–18, 2:18–20, 3:13–18; 1 Pet 4:12–19; 1 John 4:7–10; Jude 3, 17–21.

56. Good People

Now there was a man in Jerusalem called Simeon, who was righteous and devout.

—*Luke 2:25*

Are we confusing righteousness with perfection? It is a common doctrine of man's depravity that grasps verses telling us no one is righteous and categorizes them with a sense of all-inclusive finality. Those holding the doctrine may go on to treat all the references to upright people and their righteous acts and good works with explanations not found in the text, or perhaps ignore them altogether. It is outside our system of logic and linear thinking to say there are none righteous and there is a remnant of the faithful and upright in the same book from God. We forget that such expressions of thought are not only permitted in other cultures, they are expected. We may need to remind ourselves, as well, that paradox is God's tool to reveal himself, and his ways are not ours. Not limited by our human logic or preferences, as with the mystery of his grace that brings dead people to life, both are true. God displays righteous and devout people who desire to honor him in biblical accounts as examples for our lives in an unbelieving society.

God does not call these examples perfect but upright, righteous, or blameless people. Six of them are mentioned in the birth narrative of Jesus alone. We know our perfection before God is based on our position in Christ. His perfect righteousness covers us, but it is also true that there were many good people in the Bible even before Christ's coming, and many were mentioned during his ministry. These people feared the Lord, trusted him, and wanted to honor him "in spirit and truth." They were not perfect but good, blameless, and upright *in their hearts*. And though they awaited God's work in Christ to cover them, they were, in God's words, and we can also be, dare I say it, are told to become, good and upright people. This is in no way legalistic; it has always been a matter of the heart not a matter of a perfect record. Jesus brings this intent of the Old Testament law to the attention of the Jewish people in the Sermon on the Mount. God wanted their hearts. He wants ours. He always has and always will.

People who know and trust God *can* do good things, and God calls them blameless. Can we permit that? Is righteousness different from what our cognitive domains, our mental compartments, can allow? We want it to be a black-and-white matter: since people are sinners, they can never do good. When we state this preference, we refer to a theory of their complete depravity. But many in the Old Testament and in the Gospels were called righteous. After the death and resurrection of Jesus, all who believe in him are given his righteousness and told to express it in good works done in humility and love. It has always been a matter of a person's desires aligning with God's, trusting him, and motives that intend to honor him. And he, in turn, will honor them.

Interestingly, none of the examples of obedience and exhortations to do good tells us God will do it through us. No, we really are expected to become good people, even if imperfect. The examples we are given are of people who were loyal to God and acted on it. The good things each Christian can do to honor God and serve those around them will look different given their personality, talents, situation, and experiences. But they are genuine signs of their faith.

Note the emphasis in the New Testament on good works and good relationships between Christians and with outsiders. It's everywhere. Is it possible that we cannot blame all our shortcomings on the fall, that some of the fault is ours, and that we could be better people and honor God more if we really wanted to? The solution is not that doing good is too hard for us or that we must let Christ do it through us. That is a teaching that has weakened the church. It negates all that Jesus, Paul, Peter, James, and John are telling us about putting off the old man, walking worthy of the gospel, living in the light, and bearing fruit. God asks *us* to do good works, nudging us toward them by his Spirit, giving us every resource and opportunity necessary, and promising to be with us always. God is looking in our hearts for humility, trust, and the desire to do good works, not a perfect record or a celebrity-style faith that works miracles to amaze others. Salvation through Christ is not found in our works. It is by grace through faith. However, it must indeed result in good works, the sign of that faith.

There is a difference between good works and good people, however. "Good" works can be performed with wrong motives, perhaps, for example, to be noticed by others. These are empty rituals before God. A lifestyle of

56. GOOD PEOPLE

these works, as with the Pharisees, proves the opposite, that one is not a good person. And if we think we can add any good works to help our salvation, Paul says we are alienating ourselves from Christ. It is a matter of the heart. Christians are forgiven because of their genuine faith and the grace of God in Christ. But they need to be in the process of becoming godly in their daily lives. This is the justice God wanted from the people of Israel in the Old Testament. It is the honesty, compassion, humility, love, and impartiality he sought in their hearts and seeks in ours today.

Scripture References: Exod 33:17; 1 Sam 2:35 with 8:1–5; 13:14; 1 Kgs 19:11–18; Pss 15:1–5, 91:14–16; Prov 16:2 with 20:27; 17:3; 21:2–3; 24:15–16; Isa 32:17, 58:6–12; Hos 6:6; Joel 2:12–13; Mic 6:8; Matt 1:19, 5:3–10; 6:1–8; 15:7–9; 23:23–24, 28; 25:40; Luke 1:5–6, 28–30; 2:25, 36–38; 18:9–14; 21:1–4; Acts 11:22–24, 13:22; Rom 12:1–3, 9–21; Gal 5:1–6; Eph 2:8–10; Phil 1:9–11; 3:12—4:1, 8–9; Col 3:1–14; 1 Tim 6:11, 18–19; 2 Tim 3:16–17; Titus 1:16; 2:11–14; 3:1, 8, 14; Heb 11:13, 13:15–16; Jas 2:17, 21–26; 3:13; 1 Pet 2:4–17.

57. The "Ordinary" Christian Life

And whatever you do, whether in word or deed, do it all in the name of the Lord Jesus, giving thanks to God the Father through him.
—*Col 3:17*

SOMETIMES WE OVERSPIRITUALIZE THE Christian life. *What?* Isn't the Christian life spiritual? Yes, but though it is sometimes a battle with the dark powers of this world, and we need God's Spirit to strengthen us in the valleys of grief or pain, it must more often be lived out in the ordinary events and encounters of this life, like the Samaritan walking down the road to Jericho. We live it, of course, for God, and do so by the work of Christ on our behalf and the help of his Spirit. And, yes, we are released from the kingdom of darkness, brought into the kingdom of light, and now live with an awareness of the spiritual universe. But the odd thing about now seeing life as a spiritual experience, only expressed by singing emotional choruses in church, attending Christian events, and reading our Bible, is that there are dirty dishes in the sink, dog hair in the corners, a laundry basket of dirty clothes in the hall, a lawn to be mowed, garbage to take out, and gutters and dryer vents to be cleaned. There are spouses and children to be helped and provided for, house payments to be made, difficult people at work to deal with, that family member to be visited, and cranky neighbors to encourage. Some might say, "Well, yes, but these things don't really matter like 'spiritual' activities." If it seems this way to us, we had better read a little further in the Bible. Some time in the book of Proverbs, where we see wisdom lived out in everyday life, would be helpful. Everything that is in the Bible is there for a reason. Our selecting some verses to emphasize and others to ignore does not change what God says is necessary for us to flourish in our Christian life.

57. THE "ORDINARY" CHRISTIAN LIFE

When we choose certain concepts in the Bible that we think are more spiritual and de-emphasize others, it confuses people about a life lived for God. You will, for example, hear much more emphasis on "Do not neglect meeting together [at church]" (Heb 10:25) and "*discover* your spiritual gift" (which is *not* in the Bible) and a good deal less on "Lead a quiet life and mind your own business . . . work with your hands" (1 Thess 4:11), "Live peaceful and quiet lives" (1 Tim 2:2), "When you pray, go into your room and close the door" (Matt 6:6), "*Whatever you do*, do it all for the glory of God" (1 Cor 10:31, emphasis added), and "Live in harmony" (Rom 12:16). Paul says the one who does not provide for his family is denying the faith and is *worse than an unbeliever*, and James says that pure service for God involves controlling your tongue and looking after orphans and widows. Jesus says what we do to help others, we do for him.

Paul wrote instructions for the churches to Timothy and Titus, emphasizing things like teaching the people to do good works to provide for daily necessities, not live unproductive lives, and have a good reputation in the community. But he does not mention unbending commands of God on church attendance, discovering spiritual gifts, or rigid spiritual disciplines. Hmmm . . . It is not that spiritual disciplines, worship, and Bible teaching are not important; *they are*, but that is not what God wanted him to say. The emphasis was on humility, honesty, and good works in everyday life.

Paul emphasizes living our lives in a day-to-day pattern of good works, caring for one another, encouraging one another, being responsible and loving in the home, and having a good reputation in the community. James emphasizes a good life displayed by deeds done in humility. Mowing the lawn or cleaning up the dishes does matter. Our attitudes and controlling our tongues do matter. The mention in Hebrews of not neglecting meeting together was to remind these believers to encourage one another during a time of severe persecution. But our regularity at church when our daily lives are a mess works against the gospel. It is not living in a manner worthy of the gospel. Humility, good works, and encouragement of others are the intentions of Heb 10:25, the signs Jesus said should reveal our identity to the world, the service to others that he says is done to him.

Scripture References: 2 Kgs 6:13–17; Ps 23:4; Matt 6:5–8, 25:37–40; John 1:4–5, 13:35 with 17:21–23; 1 Cor 10:31; Gal 6:9–10; Eph 4:1–7; Phil 1:27, 2:1–4; Col 1:13–14, 3:17; 1 Thess 4:11–12; 1 Tim 2:1–4, 5:8, 6:17–19; Titus 3:14; Heb 10:24–25, 13:15–16; Jas 1:26–27, 3:13–18 with Isa 30:15a and 32:17; 1 John 3:16–20.

58. The Ultimate Identity

Since we live by the Spirit, let us keep in step with the Spirit.
—Gal 5:25

SOME CHRISTIANS CLAIM TO have discovered their spiritual gift (as if God told us to search for one). Others constantly mention their years of service in ministry or some accomplishment (as if they had done this in their own strength). The ultimate establishment of "spiritual" identity may be a comment about finding God's will (as if it were lost!) or God's calling (though all are called to full-time faithfulness, to walk in the Spirit, and to make disciples). Though spiritual gifts and God's calling are found in God's word, they are often abused and used to claim a spiritual status. It is all too common and repels many outsiders from an interest in the church. At the same time, insiders may go from one church to another, seeking genuine faith and unity beyond the superficial clamor.

On the other hand, we may criticize these people while seldom noticing our own habits for social survival. These patterns have been in place our whole lives. Humility, honesty, and the Holy Spirit are our only guides to the truth. We must come to know ourselves as we come to know God. We will not hide anything from him. And as we get closer to him, we will feel less and less worthy of his grace in our lives. Everyone who knows God is also known by God as they are. He shows us our weaknesses and then assures us his grace is sufficient.

We must always be aware that we are very special to him. He knows our names and has written his on our souls; no one can wrench us out of his hand. Our part in his plan may never be known to others. Most faithful people go unnamed in the Bible and will continue to do so in our day. But that is of no matter. Our true identity and worth are in Christ. God has

58. THE ULTIMATE IDENTITY

made certain of that. Our calling is to remain in step with the Spirit, a matter of the heart.

Having this identity as children of God, each of us is unique in his care and plan. The Japanese use the word *oubaitori* to describe how trees blossom at different times. It refers to cherry, peach, plum, and apricot trees, each of which is different in color, blooms, scent, and, in its own time, fruit. For the Japanese, these trees are like us. People are different from each other. Each blossoms in their unique time and way and bears their own fruit. They cannot be compared to one another. This analogy resonates with the biblical truth that if you humble yourself, God will "lift you up" *in his own time* (1 Pet 5:6). If we trust and wait on him, he will make our unique identity in his plan known, the justice of our cause to "shine like the dawn" (Ps 37:1–11). Patience. As his children, we are different from each other, each with our gifts, abilities, and experiences, but each will bloom into *God's* purpose for us in his time as we seek to honor him.

Scripture References: Exod 33:17; Pss 15:1–2, 25:9, 37:1–11, 40:1, 69:32, 145:14; Prov 11:2, 15:33, 18:12–13, 20:27, 29:23; Eccl 5:1–3; Isa 43:1; Lam 3:24–26; Mic 6:8; Matt 5:9, 23:11–12; Luke 14:11; John 4:23–24; Rom 12:12; 2 Cor 4:7; Gal 5:16–25; Eph 4:2, 5:15–18; Phil 2:1–4; Col 3:12; Titus 2:14, 3:2; Jas 3:13, 4:10; 1 Pet 5:5–7.

59. Our Cultural Lens

New wine must be poured into new wineskins. And no one after drinking old wine wants the new, for he says, "The old is better."

—*Luke 5:38–39*

WE PERCEIVE GOD THROUGH the lens of our cultural frame of reference. It acts as a filter, only allowing particular views about God and his word to come through. While restricting some concepts, others are accentuated as they fit our cultural values and preferences. This influence of culture on our view of God is the old wineskin. And the truth God gives us about himself will not fit in it and cannot be defined by it. If we try to make God and his truth fit into our old frame of reference for meaning and combine it with our old set of values for application, we will miss the truth about him, and all our efforts will be lost (Matt 9:17). We have depended on our cultural system—the old wineskin—since childhood, using it daily to navigate our lives and understand our experience. It serves us well in many ways, but in other ways, it keeps us at a distance from God and people of other cultures. Our culture teaches us to value our independence and trust our achievements as we compete for survival in society. Some have done "well" in the eyes of society. Others are considered failures by these human standards. But this is not God's way.

Nonetheless, our cultural system is very important to us. We cannot just turn it off when we encounter God. We still need many things it provides, even though parts of it hinder knowing and trusting God. However, our dependence on cultural solutions for our personal, social, and mental survival must be set aside to acknowledge God, understand him on his terms, and learn to trust him.

59. OUR CULTURAL LENS

Our trust in logic, the objective, the measurable, and our preference for order and systems cause a dislike for mystery and avoidance of paradox. But there is much we do not know, a good deal God has not told us. And much of what God reveals to us is shaped by the paradox of his grace. Our individualist approach and materialism put the self at the center of our concerns rather than trusting God. Our preference for objective, direct information and answers to all our questions is not always helpful for understanding his ways. He will not fit in our black-and-white categories; our logic cannot explain his wisdom; our values are contrary to his goodness, grace, and love. We must let him be God, speak for himself, and use the cultural forms he chooses to reveal himself in his word. His ways are not ours; we must become more comfortable with that thought and can only do so if we trust him.

When we acknowledge God through the work of Christ, we are stepping into the spiritual universe through which he rules the physical one. The cultural ways of understanding ourselves, our experience, and the world around us—values we have counted on all our lives—do not serve us well in this spiritual universe. They unravel quickly and fall to pieces before God's wisdom, power, and ultimate authority. Our arrogance about our achievements and independence will melt in his presence. As Isaiah saw himself as undone, we will see ourselves as helpless. As Daniel saw the attributes of Jesus, we must acknowledge his authority and sovereign power and realize that his eternal kingdom is coming. Our cultural system is woefully inadequate. This is the spiritual universe, and the new wine of this understanding must go in a new wineskin of trusting *his* purposes and providence. We must acknowledge the God of the universe and allow his goodness and grace to have its way in our lives, though our culture may tell us otherwise. We must come home to our true Father.

Scripture References: 2 Kgs 6:15–17; Pss 20:7; 91:1 with 14–16; 127:1; 146:3–6; 147:11; Prov 3:5–7; 5:21 with 16:2 and 9; 18–19; 20:28; 21:30–31; 28:26; Isa 6:1–5, 40:28, 55:8–9; Dan 4:28–32, 7:13–14; Mic 6:8; Mark 2:21–22; Luke 5:36–39, 12:13–21, 15:11–24; Col 1:13–14.

60. Learning Is Not for the Faint of Heart

By wisdom a house is built, and through understanding it is established; through knowledge its rooms are filled with rare and beautiful treasures.

—*Prov 24:3*

WE HAVE DIFFICULTY LISTENING to someone telling us how to live our lives unless we want to become better people and value growing in wisdom for the encounters and experiences of the days ahead. It is part of individualism to think we already know what we need to make our own decisions. In our proud independence, we know what we want in life and have *our own ideas* for achieving it. But we are not as independent as we think. Many ideas we think are ours were actually pushed on us by the hippies of the 1960s or the woke movement of our day, and these with Darwin, Marx, and Freud in the background. We do not realize it, but our thinking is clouded by second-hand human theories coming from sick people. We are mesmerized when we should be insulted, and, in our arrogance, we have closed our minds to further thinking.

But what if we were man enough or woman enough to think again? What if we have missed something in the nature of the universe? Only a learner with common sense, someone who thinks about the direction of their life and is open to realities beyond this temporary one, can see what is truly significant for themselves and others. Usually the only new information we want is what helps us to live the life we have already chosen. But unless we are learners, we will miss many important things, even true life itself. This is the point of the book of Proverbs in the Bible. Those growing in wisdom take wise instruction seriously—instruction from those who respect the Creator-God of the universe. Not so the foolish. They take up

60. LEARNING IS NOT FOR THE FAINT OF HEART

the latest human theory if it is popular and try to look confident in the behaviors it leads them to. They have been duped.

Having been "rescued from the dominion of darkness" (Col 1:13-14) and realizing their freedom in Christ and God's forgiveness, Christians seeking to honor him learn from his word and other honest believers. They also learn from their experience in this relationship with God. Paul learned repeatedly from his difficult experiences that God's provision, grace, and providence were at work in his life. We, too, will learn over time that God's providence has been at work in our experiences and that trusting him always serves our well-being and his purposes in our lives. (Think of Abraham, Joseph, Moses, David, Daniel, and others.) We are not saying we should "trust" God to do what is in our power to do. Obedience has a very practical side. But we *are* to trust him for what we cannot do, for outcomes outside our control, for things we do not know, for the uncertainties and difficulties of life, and for the softening of others' hearts to receive his grace.

In choosing to know God and experience his grace, learners gain wisdom that begins to affect all of life and uncovers its very purpose. True faith is a worldview transformation that makes us a new person; what is true and possible for us changes forever. We are no longer blackmailed by culture's values and solutions for survival. We exchange these human theories for trust in the Creator-God's providence and promises for our lives. It will take humility to submit to God when we think we know how to do life, but it will make all the difference. Instead of responding to our circumstances with arrogance, anger, rage, or anxiety, we can trust his providence and wait for him to act on our behalf. Bathed in his grace and love, we can seek to honor him no matter what comes our way. He *will* care for us in *his* way and time. Trust and patience in waiting on God are rare and beautiful treasures of wisdom that fill a house built on the rock. Think how patient he has been with *us*. Can we not wait for his way in our lives?

Scripture References: Gen 45:4-7; Pss 37:1-11; 107:10-16; 119:71; 130:5-6; 138:8; 145:13-14, 18-19; Prov 1:1-7, 3:5-7, 9:7-10 with Eccl 7:8-9; Prov 12:15, 13:10, 15:31-33; Lam 3:24-26; Dan 3:16-18; Matt 7:24-27, 11:28-30; Rom 8:18 with 28-39; 1 Cor 1:26-31 with 2:14 and 5:15-17; 2 Cor 5:17, 11:13-15 with 1 Pet 5:8-9; 2 Cor 12:7-10; Eph 2:1-4, 5:15-18; Phil 4:10-13; Col 1:13-14, 2:13-15; Titus 3:14.

61. Truth

Taste and see that the LORD is good; blessed is the man who takes refuge in him.

—Ps 34:8

NOW AND AGAIN I mention our search for black-and-white information. I do not mean to say it is not there in God's word, but that we often seek it where God has intended to be qualitative instead of quantitative in his message and desires for us. On the other hand, many do not want objective information, specific values for life, or boundaries for behavior in our day. God's word for them is suggestive rather than definitive, descriptive but not prescriptive. Nothing is the ultimate truth but rather a personal opinion or preference. For them, morality and meaning are social constructs. In such thinking, they become their own gods, wise in their own eyes. However, society survives and flourishes only when we realize there are boundaries outside of which human beings cannot endure. God created us with a purpose, and there *is* truth and meaning outside ourselves, which to find and embrace means peace and contentment even though many outside Christ, and even among popular Christians, have never given it thought.

God's loving intention for us is founded on his grace and forgiveness in the sacrifice of Christ, a very objective fact in history explained in his word. From that quantitative fact comes the qualitative description of his goodness and kindness toward us who know that grace and his patience toward those who do not. Don't let religious legalism or cultural syncretism take that grace from you. Don't let the deception of evolutionary theory, postmodern theology, woke social values, or humanistic hedonism push it away; forbid your emotions to cloud it over. Do not take to heart the words of a fool. Do not assume God is not there, and build all your "proofs"

61. TRUTH

of it on that assumption. Seek the truth with an open heart where it may be found: in God's word, from genuine and honest believers—the pure in heart—and even in the created order itself. God promises to reveal himself to you in these ways. You will see that God cannot be erased. Though the world cancels all else, he remains. His purposes endure. His goodness and providence, his grace, and the freedom it brings, are there for you and me. It is his intervening love. "Taste and see that the LORD is good" (Ps 34:8).

Scripture References: Gen 1:1; Pss 14:1; 19:1-4; 20:7 with 33:16-22, 6-11; 34:4, 8, 15 and 17-19; 119:160; 146:3-6; Prov 1:28-29, 3:5-7, 19:3, 26:12, 28:26; Isa 55:10-11; John 1:1-5 with 3:19 and 8:12, 31-32; 3:16-21; 14:6; Acts 20:28-31; Rom 1:18-21, 3:22-24, 5:6-8; 1 Cor 1:18-25, 15:1-6; Eph 2:1-5 with Col 1:13-14; Phil 3:17-21; Titus 1:15-16; Heb 4:12, 1 Pet 3:18; 2 Pet 3:3 with Jude 17-19; 1 John 1:1-10.

62. Reaction

I tell you this so that no one may deceive you by fine-sounding arguments.

—*Col 2:4*

Reactionary behavior, instead of a well-reasoned and tempered response to an issue or statement, seldom accomplishes its goal. Its defensiveness reveals poor foundations, weak standards, selfish motives, insecurities, and lack of reason. We too often let people get under our skin; even if we do not react outwardly, we are angered inwardly. It is not only a waste of emotional energy, it eats up a good portion of our day or week and reminds us we are short on wisdom. People who set us off are often difficult, if not impossible, to avoid, as much as we try. It reminds me of the song of Ko-Ko in Gilbert and Sullivan's *Mikado*: "I've got a little list of people I could do without who never would be missed." But aggravating people keep showing up, so it is up to us to regulate our response, calm our hearts, and recalibrate our reaction to the patience and kindness of love God calls us to. Our world gives us plenty of opportunities to practice. It is a matter of wisdom; as Solomon tells us, "The end of a matter is better than its beginning, and patience is better than pride. Do not be quickly provoked in your spirit, for anger resides in the lap of fools" (Eccl 7:8–9).

But there is a more grave reaction to avoid. Many react against the truth about God. When they do, they may be defending their "right" to personal happiness based on social definitions and expectations around them. These inclinations to seek happiness using human values never find lasting fulfillment, and if they include reactionary and emotional defensiveness against God, they take people down the wrong path. It is a search for

62. REACTION

meaning, self-worth, identity, and happiness in the wrong places. We cannot find our way following blind guides.

Trusting human reason or passion against God's purposes will never result in the personal contentment we seek. Humility and truth lead us in a different direction. Happiness is found when we stop searching for it. It makes itself known in God's providential care for those of us under his grace—the paradox of his undeserved favor on those who were dead in their sin and enemies of his cause in the world. And, as I have said before, if you are going to fight God, you are going to lose. It will take humility, but unless we seek our well-being in him, we are reacting to the certainties of the nature of reality, to our Creator, the King of the universe, to the fact that Jesus is the only way, the truth, and the life. Arrogance has no stronger definition. Only the reactionary behavior of a fool tries to replace God in the world (Ps 14:1), substituting human explanations to deceive the hearts of others (Prov 28:26). Yes, it is through death that one finds life, but find it, we must. No other door opens to the contentment we long for.

Scripture References: Pss 10:4, 14:1, 18:25–28, 25:8–12, 27:13–14, 28:26, 33:16–22, 37:9, 55:19, 127:1, 130:5–6, 146:3–4 with 118:9; Prov 3:5–7; 8:13; 11:2; 14:12; 16:2, 5, 18–19; 17:3; 19:3; 20:7; 26:12; 28:26; Eccl 7:8–9; Isa 40:31; Matt 7:13–14, 11:28–30 with John 14:27; Matt 16:24–26; Luke 9:23–25; John 12:23–26; Rom 1:21–22, 5:1–11; 2 Cor 11:14–15; Eph 2:1–10, 5:1–7; Phil 4:4–7; Col 2:1–5; 1 Pet 5:5b–7.

63. Failings

If the Lord delights in a man's way, he makes his steps firm; though he stumble, he will not fall, for the Lord upholds him with his hand.

—Ps 37:23–24

CHRISTIANS OFTEN FAIL, AND "good ones" know it better than others. We are not perfect, but we know who is and find grace in him. He never stops helping his people. The Bible talks about walking (living) in the Spirit. This is not a mystical statement but refers to a sensitivity to our behavior that God gives us so that we notice when our inclinations and behavior are contrary to his word and, with his forgiveness and help, fix them. We make amends where necessary and set a better course for ourselves. Perfection is beyond us. But that is not an excuse to not be in the process of becoming the kind of people Jesus talked about in the Gospels and the writers of the New Testament urge us toward. We should continually grow into better people as we are surrounded by his grace, instructed by his word, made sensitive by his Spirit, and in fellowship with his people—all of God's plan for our growth to maturity.

We must never give up. As we keep our relationship with God our primary concern, we will become more sensitive to wrong thoughts and behavior and want to honor him. He looks for loyalty in our hearts; even though our thoughts and behavior might not always reflect our allegiance to him, he knows if it is there. Our concerns about falling short make us those Jesus referred to as "the pure in heart" (Matt 5:8). We confess our weakness to him, and his grace abounds in forgiveness.

If we desire to serve and honor him, with the help of his Spirit, we will get better at it as we go along. "If the Lord delights in a man's way, he makes

63. FAILINGS

his steps firm . . . the LORD upholds him with his hand" (Ps 37:23–24). He "will not forsake his faithful ones" (v. 28).

Scripture References: Pss 32:5; 37:1–11, 34a; 51:17; 130:3–6; Prov 24:16, 28:13; Matt 5:3–8; John 3:16–18, 5:24, 10:27–30; Rom 3:22–24, 7:14—8:1, 8:31–39; 2 Cor 9:8; Gal 5:16–26, 6:7–10; Eph 4:11–16; Phil 1:6, 2:12–16, 3:12–14; Col 1:9–14; 2 Thess 3:11–13; Heb 6:1–3, 9–12; 12:1–6, 13:20–21; 1 John 1:8–10.

64. The Mystery of God's Ways

For my thoughts are not your thoughts, neither are your ways my ways.

—Isa 55:8

THERE ARE A LOT of books in my library that try to explain God and his ways. Most authors realize that some of what they say only estimates God and his intentions when the text seems open ended and does not tell us all we want to know. But when the church thinks it has the final explanation, the complete account of God's ways in the world and in the hearts of humankind, that it has built the box that God fits into perfectly, it ceases to know God as he is. There is paradox in God's grace, mystery in his providence, and irony in his purposes that cause us wonder. We must sometimes set aside our logic and preference for the objective and measurable, our human and cultural expectations, and wait for what he might do, trusting his words, remaining faithful in the silence.

It may feel like we are risking everything, handing over control. And we are—brave and independent individualists, we are. We must turn our talents and abilities over to his purposes. Remember, he has never been obligated to satisfy our impatience or inclinations, driven frequently as they are by our cultural values, theological systems, or personal preferences. But he does obligate himself to his promises and assures us he will always be with us. We must welcome his omniscience, power, and authority, trusting his love, grace, good providence, and purposes in our lives, for we do not know everything; we do not know very much at all. Mystery and trust must come together for the pure in heart if they would see God. Sometimes the wait may seem long, but we are not risking anything worth keeping in exchange for knowing him.

64. THE MYSTERY OF GOD'S WAYS

A God without such mystery and paradox is made in human likeness according to our preferences for his being and activities, with the clear boundaries we give him. Each culture has its own image of him, which may make people feel more secure, but this is not the God of creation revealed to us in the Bible. He tells us there are things we do not know or understand, and we shall have to be content and grateful for what he *has* given us. We must rest in his goodness, power, and wisdom as he carries out his purposes. He *will* do so in his own time and in his own ways. The trust broken in Eden must be revived in our situation and circumstances. What he says is true and never without intent; his love for us is beyond measure, and his providence always achieves his purposes and our ultimate good.

Scripture References: Job 1:20–22 with 2:9–10; 38:1–3 with 42:1–6; Pss 62:5–8, 84:10–12, 100:5, 130:5–6, 138:8; Prov 16:9 with 19:21; Eccl 11:1–6; Isa 14:24, 46:10, 55:8–11; Lam 3:25–26; Dan 10:20—11:1; Matt 5:8, 24:36; Luke 9:23–25 with John 12:24–26 and Matt 6:33; John 3:8, 21:25; Rom 8:28 with 18 and 31–39; 11:33–36; Phil 2:12–13.

65. The Justice of Man and God

It would be better for him to be thrown into the sea with a millstone tied around his neck.

—*Luke 17:2*

IF THERE IS AN ultimate moral standard and people really matter, the punishment for crime and assaulting innocent people is necessary for the survival of society. The functional family should include loving correction for bad behavior to shape a child's ability to live responsibly in the community as an adult. This correction is out of love and respect for each child born in the image of God so they can honor their Creator and his creation with their life. If the family weakens in its responsibility or its efforts are neutralized by immoral educators, unethical political authorities, or godless social influencers, the natural results will be moral chaos, emotional confusion, and senseless crime. And these consequences will increase. We cannot blame guns or drugs. Deep in our political, educational, and social systems and revealed in our entertainment world is the wildly desperate attempt to remove God as the foundation for meaning in life, to teach the next generation that there is no wrong turn or destination in life. This rejection of the moral and ethical framework of God's word is the cause of social disintegration, no matter what else is blamed.

Our human situation is no surprise to God. Knowing the human heart, he ordained that justice be applied to the criminal. Though this human justice is often absent in our day, God's justice is never lacking. He will bring it to bear on all wrongdoing and oppression, on all who reject his truth. It will especially come to bear on those who confuse and lead the children and other innocent people in a society astray from his truth. As God-haters, these ruin lives and create a void in which selfish, immoral,

65. THE JUSTICE OF MAN AND GOD

and criminal behavior breeds. Only a turning to the grace of God in Christ can remove the condemnation his justice will bring on these. However, not all the damage to society can be undone, and we all live with the results of human sin.

When adequate punishment for evil is removed from adult society, it will have disturbing effects. The inconvenience of a few years of prison for intentionally taking the life of someone else or several others is an immoral disrespect for human life, not to mention the disregard for loved ones left without a parent, child, spouse, or friend. When criminals are soon freed to do their evil again, society suffers worse than before they were detained. But the religion of godlessness goes deep. Darwinian and Freudian beliefs naturally lead to the conclusion that we are only animals and morality is an arbitrary human construct of no ultimate significance. Human life is an accident without purpose and has no motives but natural and selfish impulses. It seems more "humane" in such a society to give everyone a break (if it serves our purposes). Animals will do what animals do.

The search for pleasure or survival, motivated by insecurity, hatred, or madness without consideration for others, comes naturally to creatures who have evolved from the mud. The pursuit of happiness takes on a very narrow and personal aspect. It becomes "the pursuit of my happiness at your expense." But where human systems fail, ultimate justice is yet to be revealed. As God's coming hand of justice was shown to his people by many Old Testament prophets, he will deal with all who turn from his ways or seek to turn others away from him in our day.

Our God sees all, but he also loves the world. He is a consuming fire but also a God of lavish grace. We must spread the news of that grace and live a life that shows the difference the light makes in a dark place while God waits in love and patience for all who will come to him. As he once brought light where darkness lingered over the deep waters of the earth, he brings the light of Jesus into the dark souls of mankind today, and the humble recipient will *never* be condemned.

Scripture References: Gen 1:1–5; Deut 4:23–24; Pss 15:1–5, 37:1–11, 89:11–18, 96:11–13, 97:1–6; Prov 29:4, 14; Isa 1:17, 42:1–4, 59:1–20; Jer 17:5–11; Mic 6:8; Mal 4:1–6; Matt 7:24–27, 23:13–15; Luke 17:1–2; John 1:1–5 with 10–13; 3:16 and 36; 8:12; Rom 13:1–7; 2 Thess 1:5–10; Heb 12:28–29; 2 Pet 3:3–11.

66. In the Ordinary Things

Make it your ambition to lead a quiet life, to mind your own business and to work with your hands, . . . so that your daily life may win the respect of outsiders.

—*1 Thess 4:11–12*

MANY THINGS IN LIFE are ordinary, yet nothing is ordinary; many activities become routine, but all activities matter; talking is normal and common, but words make a difference. It is in the everyday things of life that we often have the opportunity to express our loyalty to God and love for others. In fact, that is where it really counts. Living a life of respect and consideration for others does not go unnoticed. Jesus tells us he will remember the works of caring for the hungry, homeless, poor, sick, and wrongly imprisoned in Matt 25, and the author of Hebrews reminds us that God "will not forget" (Heb 6:10). It is in the more commonplace experiences where we rub shoulders with our neighbors (and perhaps "angels" [Heb 13:2]), and they see our genuine regard and concern for them; we will be known for honesty and good works by them (not perfection, however). We may never be experts at something those around us need, but all of us are there in everyday concerns and ordinary moments and can show kindness and help as an example of God's love for them. Paul tells us to prefer a quiet and responsible life that wins the respect of our neighbors.

God does not tell us that everyone will accept our efforts. However, kindness and respect should be our habits in everyday life, even though they may be cast aside by the recipients. If we are to lead others to God's kindness, love, and grace, they need to see it in us first. These actions cannot be compared with ritual behavior that we might carry out because we are obligated by social conventions, legalism, or peer pressure from a group.

66. IN THE ORDINARY THINGS

This should be natural, everyday behavior motivated by our desire to incarnate Christ in the world.

So there is no ordinary event in our lives that God cannot use to do the extraordinary in us or others. We are still human. We have all the human limitations of passing time, human reasoning and appetites, emotional states, physical weaknesses, and, eventually, death. And we still fall short of honoring him in every way. But God's grace has covered us, and he has his hand on us with purpose and intent in our human experiences. In his own words, "I am with you always" (Matt 28:20b) and "Never will I leave you; never will I forsake you" (Heb 13:5b). We may feel dull, pretty average, but he intends to "work in us," despite of our weakness, "what is pleasing to him" (20-21).

Scripture References: Lev 19:13-18; Ps 15:1-5; Prov 3:27-32, 14:21; Isa 58:6-7; Matt 5:16; 7:14-16, 22:37-40, 25:31-40, 28:18-20; Luke 10:30-37; John 13:35, 17:23; 1 Cor 13:4-7; Gal 6:9-10; Phil 1:6, 9-11, 27a; 2:12-13; 1 Thess 4:11-12; 2 Thess 3:6-12; 1 Tim 2:1-4; Titus 3:1-2, 14; Heb 6:10, 12; 13:1-3, 5b-6, 20-21; Jas 3:13; 1 Pet 2:12 with 15 and 3:15-17; 2:16-17.

67. Quiet People

Blessed are the meek, for they will inherit the earth.

—Matt 5:5

THOUGH THEY ARE BELIEVERS, we are not sure we like them. Quiet people must be hiding something or lacking in "healthy" social skills. Maybe they just don't have anything to say. Our Western culture admires the extrovert, the socially engaged—those who influence others with an outgoing personality. But, though God uses these outgoing believers to touch the lives of people for him, many in the body of Christ are not so gregarious. They are quieter, more sensitive, introverted. They see life from a different vantage point. They long for chords in a minor key, storm clouds in a warm summer sky, and the melancholy sound of the wind in the woods. In these effects, they recognize God's hand in the world and sense his power. They may creatively express this "quiet" faith in art, music, interpretive readings, and poetry. They may be writers instead of talkers.

These "quiet" ones sense contentment in God's ways and their part in his plan. They value time alone or with those who understand them and are less comfortable with the noise and commotion of a crowd. They know God's grace very personally and are particularly sensitive to their relationship with him. They may spend hours at a time thinking about it, reading about it in old books, and considering how to help others go deeper into it. They may not be suited to every public ministry, but they know service to others and empathize readily with their burdens and emotional pain. They may not talk as much but often have important things to say. We dare not neglect them just because our culture values other personalities.

Most faithful Jews in the Old Testament and honest Christians in the New Testament are unknown to us. Though some stand out in the Bible as

67. QUIET PEOPLE

people chosen to be the leading players in God's workings of the time, most go unnamed. They were people loyal to God who desired to honor him in the familiar routines of life. God mentions the seven thousand faithful when Elijah gets discouraged, but we do not know their names. The book of Acts begins with a mention of one hundred twenty believers. We may be able to name the twelve and a few others, but most were simply faithful followers. They may not have all been introverts, but they were content to follow God's leading through others. The majority of these people may be unknown to the world, but they had God's careful attention as unknown believers do today. Those who have gone before us are an example to us.

When accompanied by humility, extroverts and introverts alike can be pure in heart and honor God. And whether they are known for their public ministry or not, the quiet, the poor in spirit, and the meek are held as high as Peter or Paul in the Bible, though their names may not be mentioned. Though all the pure in heart will see God, these are given a special place in the Beatitudes of Jesus.

Scripture References: 1 Kgs 19:11–14 with 18; Pss 23:2, 131:1–3; Prov 17:1; Isa 30:15 with 32:17; 66:2b; Matt 5:3–10, 23:11–12; Luke 14:11; Acts 1:15; 1 Thess 4:11–12; 1 Tim 2:1–4; 1 Pet 5:6–7; Rev 7:9–17.

68. Why Go to Church?

Blessed are the pure in heart, for they shall see God.

—*Matt 5:8*

CHRISTIANITY MUST LEAD US beyond the ritual behavior of simple attendance at church, or we remain popular Christians riding on the superficial benefits of belonging without the substance of what it means to know God. The church must set us on the path to walk in the Spirit in a manner worthy of the gospel, in a relationship of grace and contentment with God. The structured ritual behavior of the church service is only the background that encourages godliness in the natural behavior of everyday life. As the old TV commercial said about their car tires, everyday life is "where the rubber meets the road." It is where theory becomes practical and prophecy, pragmatic. Love and kindness, encouraged in the church, put on their work clothes at home and in society. It is the incarnation of the biblical message. Anything less is missing the purpose of the church and God's intentions for our lives as salt and light in the world. We must each become good neighbors, exemplifying God's purpose for the Bible (2 Tim 3:17), for the church (Eph 4:12), and for salvation itself (2:10).

When the church does not encourage this purpose in life, it fails in its task and may become an enabler of popular or superficial Christianity. This is perhaps most evident when Christians become competitive and argue about nonessential or legalistic "theological" issues, dividing people and causing the world to see the worst instead of the work of God in our lives. We must get beyond these divisive, negative, damaging issues to the love and unity that are the marks of our faith. To do otherwise is to be responsible for the world turning away from God's grace. For it is by our example of "love, which comes from a pure heart and a good conscience

68. WHY GO TO CHURCH?

and a sincere faith" (1 Tim 1:5) that the world will know that God sent Jesus and that he loves us (John 13:34-35, 17:21-23). The absence of this example leaves the world without hope, a dark and broken place. The church must prepare us to be light in that world.

Scripture References: Matt 5:8, 9, 14-16; John 1:4-5 with 3:19 and 8:12; 4:23-24; 13:34-35; 17:15; Rom 12:9-13 with 16 and 15:5; 1 Cor 1:10-17 with 3:1-9 and 21-23; 13:1-13; Eph 2:8-10, 11-13; 4:3, 11-16; Phil 2:1-4; Col 1:13-14, 3:14; 1 Tim 1:3-7; 2 Tim 2:14-16, 22-26; 3:16-17; Titus 1:15-16; 3:1-2, 8, 14; Jas 2:17 with Gal 5:6; 1 John 1:9-11; 3:11, 16-19; 4:7-21; 5:1-5.

69. Reminders of Sin and Grace

If we claim to be without sin, we deceive ourselves, and the truth is not in us.

—1 John 1:8

Among other things the church is to do, it should remind us of our sins. That is not a popular theme among churchgoers. We go to church for other reasons and have a particular dislike for a meddling pastor. But the pastor must wear his armor and care for his duties, among which this is one, combining it with the message of hope because of God's grace, for we are all sinners in need. On the other hand, concerning this sin, some of us are too sensitive already—confessing sin we have already confessed and feeling guilty about what has already been forgiven. But it is gone. The pastor must help us understand God's mercy, grace, and justification for forgiveness. The very sensitivity and pain in our conscience prove that we desire God, are in his hand, and that his love and attention are fixed on us. But we have yet to understand the breadth of his grace and the depth of his love.

We must humbly accept God's forgiveness of our sins and, because of it, forgive ourselves and others. We will *never* be called to account for sin he has forgiven, for there is *no* condemnation for those in Christ. With God, forgiveness is the complete removal of sin and a reminder of the perfect righteousness he grants us in Christ. We make his grace of no account if we question his forgiveness or do not forgive ourselves. We make the sacrifice of Christ in vain on our behalf. Some Christians feel that falling into the same sin again somehow negates God's forgiveness, that he gets tired of us and, throwing up his hands, goes on to someone else who might better meet his standards. But that is not in the Bible. In fact, nothing could be further from the truth. God's love for us is not so fragile. His purpose for

69. REMINDERS OF SIN AND GRACE

us remains; our weakness cannot undo it. Our discouragement at failing him shows he has our heart, and it's the one thing he wants. He forgives even as he told Peter to forgive, "not seven times, but seventy-seven times" (Matt 18:21–22), a way of saying *always*. "He who began a good work in you will carry it on to completion" (Phil 1:6). He is "faithful," patient, and just to "forgive" (1 John 1:9)—to acquit us "once for all" of our crimes because Jesus took the sentence for our sin on himself, "the righteous for the unrighteous" (1 Pet 3:18).

Others are unaware of certain sins in their lives. Bringing this to their attention is a daunting task for the pastor. Pride, arrogance, a need to be recognized, false reverence and holy tones, and lack of consideration for others are sticky sins. It is very difficult to help people see these patterns in their lives. Their very nature causes resistance to the pastor or a friend mentioning them. Like strong glue demanding special solvent or bent and rusty nails needing the crowbar of God's word to pry them loose, these attitudes and habits are resistant. But even if these sins or others are ours, we are not without hope, not beyond the grace of God.

When people are authentic Christians, they have the Holy Spirit reminding and convicting them of their weaknesses. He will use God's word, the persistence of a pastor or friend, or maybe a Christian book, blog, or podcast to help them see the truth in humility and realize they are guilty of these deeply rooted tendencies that deny the truth and grace of God's word. At the cross of Christ, they will always find the grace so desperately needed by us all. It takes humility to accept that we are sinners needing God's grace daily, and must show that kindness to others. That grace covers all, every sin we confess, forever.

Scripture References: Ps 103:10–18; Prov 8:13; 16:5, 18; 18:12; 27:6; Isa 32:17, 66:1–2; Mic 6:8; Matt 5:3–10, 18:21–22; John 5:24; 13:6–10; 16:7 and 13; 17:23; Rom 2:1–4; 3:23–24; 5:1–11 with 15–19; 8:1 with 31–34; 10:4; 2 Cor 5:15–17, 21; Eph 2:4–7; Phil 1:6; 1 Tim 1:12–17; Heb 8:12; Jas 3:13–18 with 4:10; 1 Pet 3:18, 5:6–8; 1 John 1:5–10.

70. God Speaks with Purpose

But the Lord is in his holy temple; let all the earth be silent before him.

—*Hab 2:20*

When we open the Bible, God speaks whether we think so or not. We may see many verses as common and overused and be numbed against their impact. Yet, though they may seem simple, they are volcanic, earth-shaking statements meant to change our lives and affect those around us as they do. We must return to the realities of which these old and worn words speak. The question is whether we, insiders or outsiders, will allow God to speak at all, and, when we do, will we allow him to speak for himself, to say what we *need* to hear rather than what we want to hear. We must all come to the Bible with a sincere, thoughtful approach and an open mind if we would see what God is saying. If we only want to find what we have already determined must be there, we will find that instead. Honesty in our approach is the only way to hear him—it is the pure in heart who will see God. A sound hermeneutic, including cultural differences and trust, is essential.

In addition to the need for honesty, we must allow God to be God. He is above our limited logic, temporal orientation, linear thinking, and human preferences—a God of grace *and* truth but also of mystery in his providence and paradox in his grace, with some things known only to him. He wants us to approach him with persistent faith in his power, enduring trust in his goodness, and persevering loyalty to his purposes, even if we do not understand his way at the time.

God speaks with purpose. He informs us of his work in the world from its beginning and his plan to redeem those who trust him from the curse they brought upon themselves. That theme of redemption permeates

70. GOD SPEAKS WITH PURPOSE

the Scriptures from cover to cover. He holds out salvation to all mankind, not only to make them perfect in Christ but to begin his work in them, to bring them to completion in themselves as they learn to trust his goodness, grace, providence, and power in this world. When they accept his offer, he brings them into fellowship with him and gives them their part in his plan for the world.

Nothing is in the Bible by chance; all is there by the providence of God as he speaks to the needs of the original audience and to us today. We must listen to each verse as if hearing it for the first time, not turning it into a legalistic ritual but allowing it to shape our hearts. He speaks with the intent to turn us into a certain kind of people, not create a religion we must follow. We must meet him on his terms, become those who honor his name, grow into those loyal to his intentions, and live in the freedom he gives us to enjoy the good things of his creation. For God has spoken, and we are to let all his words become part of us.

Scripture References: Gen 1:31 with 2:15–16 and 3:6 combined with 3:15 and Matt 1:21, 5:8 and John 3:16–17, 14:23, 17:20–21 and Eph 2:1–10 with Rev 7:9–10; 1 Sam 16:7; Pss 37:3–7a, 91:14–16; Prov 3:5–10; Isa 43:10–13, 46:10, 50:10–11 with 55:8–11; Hab 2:20; Matt 5:3–10; Phil 1:6 with 2:12–13; 2 Tim 3:16–17, 4:1–4; Titus 1:15, 2:11; Heb 4:12–13 with Isa 55:11; Heb 11:1–39, especially 6.

71. Meaning and Purpose

What good is it for a man to gain the whole world, yet forfeit his soul?
—*Mark 8:36*

HUMAN NEEDS BECOME OVERWHELMING when those who think they are wise become fools and remove meaning and purpose from life. Reason and experience become difficult to balance. Both are framed and controlled by our cultural and personal values and interpreted by our worldview—our understanding of reality. Without meaning and purpose, our thinking has no basis, our experience no boundaries, and our assumptions about reality are hopelessly human and constantly manipulated by those who seek to avoid God. The result is not transparent like the laws of physics.

For many people, it is like a sort of hypnosis, a dull mixture of feelings and yearnings swirling around bits of misinformation, mostly out of control, and over time a creeping amnesia sets in. They slowly forget the God of order, meaning, and purpose as he is removed from their lives. Their deceivers say they are wise and know better than God how to do life, but, in the end, they release the powers of darkness on their prey. Others seem in control of their lives but have been charmed by wealth and status, mesmerized by the feeling of power. Under the spell of the dragon himself, they feel no need for God and find out only too late they have been deceived.

People, led by the popular influencers of society, become fixated on experiences that make them feel better about themselves in the world their ancestors have constructed, and their peers keep renovating and modernizing. The reality that can bring forgiveness and freedom, that can restore meaning and purpose in the confusion, God himself, is avoided at great cost. But they know nothing of the end of their road or the outcome of their doctrines. If there is one purpose among these people today, it is to

71. MEANING AND PURPOSE

erase any thought or memory of God from our society. They think lifting the ancient "barriers" in their pursuit of personal "happiness" and worshipping the gods of pleasure, power, and wealth will bring the fulfillment and self-importance they seek. But their gods will fail them, and they will know darkness instead of light, taking the masses with them.

But we have been rescued from the powers of this darkness, we who know the Creator and the power of his love and grace and the goodness of his providence. He shows us his will, and, though we may have a ways to go, we grow in the wisdom of his presence and purposes, wisdom from above, wisdom that gives life.

Scripture References: Pss 1:1–3; 10:4; 14:1; 37:1–20, 28, 34; 91:1 with 14–16; Prov 1:7; 3:5–7 with 13–18; 13:20; 14:12; 16:25; 17:24; 20:27; 21:2; Isa 5:20–21; 32:1–8 and 17; 50:10–11; Matt 15:12–14; Mark 8:34–38; John 3:19–21; 8:12, 31–32; 10:1–10; Rom 1:18–23, 11:33–36, 12:1–2; Eph 6:10–13 with Col 1:13–14; Phil 3:18; Jas 3:13–18; 1 John 1:5–7; Rev 20:10.

72. Worldview Gone Wrong

Although they claimed to be wise, they became fools.

—*Rom 1:22–23*

WORLDVIEW IS THE TERM used to describe a human construction of the nature of reality. It tells us what is real or actual in the world. As such, it is the frame of reference for interpreting our experience. It becomes the basis of our values, beliefs, and behavior. It is a collection of understandings we take as absolute—so fixed that we do not question them. Gravity and air are part of reality for everyone. (Except in Jainism, where bad karma clings to your body and holds you down to the earth.) However, private ownership and personal independence in the Western world, the goal of enlightenment among Zen Buddhists, or active ancestors, witchcraft, magic, and nature spirits in traditional Africa are examples of particular assumptions different peoples make about reality. The assumptions we make control our behavior all day, every day. Gravity causes us to buy a protective case for our cell phones, use the stairs, and put notes on our refrigerator with magnets. And we do not just take any car in the parking lot to go home from the grocery store; we take the one we came in. In the evening, a traditional Central African would take another route home instead of the shortest one if it meant avoiding water where nature spirits abound at night. The Zen Buddhist may spend a lifetime meditating and seeking an answer to the Zen master's question (koan). But how often do we think about gravity or wonder why our key only fits *our* car? And why do we think Central Africans and Zen Buddhists do strange things?

Our assumptions about life go on to many other things we take for granted. For example, our post-Christian culture assumes people are born good unless something they cannot control makes them act antisocially.

72. WORLDVIEW GONE WRONG

This assumption about the nature of man leads to thinking, behavior, and social organization that seems natural. So if the people of another country shout "Death to America," they don't really mean it. Punishments for violence and crime or killing others should not be too severe since the offenders cannot help it. Only in Western culture could the fix for rising crime become a movement to defund the police. A society follows its worldview without questioning its validity. Prisons may be bulging, drug use rampant, the streets full of homeless people, school shootings regular, and such a worldview might say it's no one's fault; it's the guns or the drugs, or it's in the genes.

Our worldview really does make a difference. In its attempt to exterminate God, the secular worldview has destroyed the only compass pointing north and devastated the soul of man. In the mayhem created, they have condemned themselves to the unthinkable without a second thought.

As we can see, the understandings of our worldview reach deep into our lives. When it comes to understanding creation or evolution as the core of life, what we decide makes a tremendous difference. Each is a way to describe the nature of reality. One is true, and one is false. Understanding that people are created in God's image or are animals appearing by the magic of chance affects relationships, social responsibility, justice, morality, and meaning in life. As the people of Israel turned from the living God to senseless idols in the Old Testament, many today turn from him to sick human theories, just as meaningless though made to sound sophisticated.

Like the story of "The Emperor's New Clothes" by Hans Christian Andersen, people are told they are stupid if they mention God. But when the worldview excludes his presence, people build their lives on what they want to be true, or hope might be true, without realizing their culture and human nature are blackmailing them with a false sense of worth, pleasure, power, or identity or the loss of all social rewards. Desperation to do away with God removes reason further from influence, leaving people with only experience and feelings—groping about in the dark while trying to act like they know where they are going.

Human worldviews never describe the complete nature of reality; they leave out the God of creation and the spiritual universe behind this physical one. God gives humankind the freedom to accept or reject the truth about him. Many popular Christians have chosen only part of that truth, their perception of it, or what they want it to be. In the end, fewer people genuinely trust God than we usually think. These popular Christians confuse cultural absolutes with biblical absolutes, personal preferences with God's desires, or their version of what they expect or want God to be like with what he actually says. This perception of God and his word becomes part of their worldview, and they allow it to interpret their experience, guide their behavior, and lead them away from his truth and grace as they really are. The results are more than obvious.

Life is too short to follow the human assumptions of those who do not know where their theory leads and have no idea of the outcome of their bold assertions. Jesus said *he* was the way, the truth, and the life. We have a decision to make that calls, at the very least, for honest consideration of his way. There is too much at stake to ignore God.

Scripture References: Gen 1:1, 20, 24, 27; 2 Kgs 6:15–17; Prov 13:20; Isa 44:9–20, 50:10–11; Ezek 14:6, 11; Matt 7:24–29; John 1:14–18 with 8:12, 31–32 and 36; 14:6; Rom 1:18–25; 1 Cor 4:4; 2 Cor 11:4–15; Eph 4:18; 2 Tim 3:5 with 7; 2 Pet 3:3.

73. Social Authority

The fool has said in his heart, "There is no God."
—Ps 14:1

WHEN THE INFLUENCERS OF a society ban the Bible as God's design for life, they can substitute another religion, give their worship and loyalty to the gods of their imagination, or surrender to human philosophy. When humans take over setting the standard, society is told to trust human leaders instead of God. Somehow they believe they know what is right or wrong for the rest of society, know more than God about how the community can survive and flourish, and think they know the future outcome of their ideas. But their promises are empty. All they really know is what *they* want from society, without knowing where their preferences lead and their path ends. In the name of freedom, they are intolerant of any alternative views. God has been canceled.

So, ultimately, secular society constructs its own boundaries for right and wrong, good and bad. But remember that they also say that humankind evolved accidentally from a lump of mud. This makes the social construction of their standard an arbitrary refusal of the God of creation for baseless human assumptions, leading to the dashing of all human inhibitions and enthroning self-assertion with its urges and ambitions. We are told to trust their "ultimate" understanding of reality for our survival, well-being, and destiny . . . because they say so.

This rearrangement is nothing new and has never succeeded, but human nature knows no other path. Only God's grace opens the way to know him, which is life—the true nature of reality. Jesus said he was the way, the truth, and the life. The decision between him and the social authorities of our day can be difficult. Each has a price tag. As with the previous theme of worldview gone wrong, either you trust a human who says he came from a pond to tell you the real purpose of life and where you are going, or you open yourself to the God who created you. The first demands surrender to a blind human leader taking you down a dark path, the destination of which he does not know, but "in the end it leads to death" (Prov 16:25). To refuse is to risk all the social rewards, however temporary, and face rejection. The second choice demands honest consideration and humble acceptance of the grace of God, a commitment to his lordship, and loyalty to his purposes. This path leads to life, wisdom, and eternity with God. Though it will cost the materialism and social rewards the world offers, it replaces them with God's expansive grace, his powerful providence, and our personal peace and freedom for deep-seated contentment.

It is a battle for the souls of men and women. Despite the great deception in the world, none are outside the reach of God's love and grace. God specializes in giving life to the dead who reject him and follow "the ways of this world" (Eph 2:1–2). The question is whether those outside will see grace and truth in us and come inside to meet the one they need.

Scripture References: Gen 1:1, 20, 24, 27; Pss 20:7, 33:11–22; Prov 3:5–7, 12:15, 13:20, 14:12, 16:2, 21:2, 28:26; Isa 44:9–20, 50:10–11; John 1:4–5, 14; 3:36; 8:12; 10:7–10; 11:25–26; 14:6; 17:3; Acts 28:24–28; Rom 1:21–25, 3:9–18 with John 3:16–21 and Col 1:13–14; 1 Cor 1:18–19 with 2:6–9; 4:4; 2 Cor 11:4–15; Eph 2:1–5, 4:18; Phil 4:6–7; 1 Tim 1:13–16.

74. Security

He who dwells in the shelter of the Most High will rest in the shadow of the Almighty.

—*Ps 91:1*

PEOPLE SEARCH FOR FEELINGS of happiness and security. But when they come from sources other than God gives us, they are superficial and temporary. We always need more of whatever makes us feel good about ourselves, and we need it more often. We frequently try to compensate for insecurities and fears from negative early childhood experiences. If we find something that masks our anxious feelings or makes us feel good about ourselves outside of God, we will have discovered a thin human counterfeit that Satan can use to blackmail us for a lifetime. We may be trying to prove we are someone of value, trying to fill the void left by critical peers or siblings or an aloof or stern father who never gave his approval. We may seek something to replace the affection we missed from a mother. But the accumulation of money, abuse of alcohol or sex, or control of others will not meet this need. It will actually lead to further unhappiness, destroy relationships, and end in despair.

Except for the grace and providence of God at work in our lives, failing to have a trust-filled relationship with parents when young brings a lifetime of insecurities and can result in unreasoned, even neurotic behavior, harmful attachments, and addictions. We will have difficulty trusting others and find it hard to trust God. We may become arrogant and see ourselves as better than others to offset the feelings of insecurity. In an individualist society, self-assertion and attempting to control others is often the sign of our struggle to gain an identity and place in our competitive society. We all have struggles. Only God's grace can intervene.

We must turn to God, accept his forgiveness, and allow ourselves to trust his providence, which has brought us to the reading of this page. We cannot forget, but God's grace can fill the void. Old habits for survival are not easy to overcome, but when we see his purposes for us now despite our experiences, good and bad, over the years, we can rest in our new security in him and grow in our freedom from the control our past has had on us. Of course, we must apply ourselves to encouraging endeavors and spend time with good and wise people. But our source for true security is ultimately God, who bathes us in his lavish grace and gives us the abilities, opportunities, friends, or spouses he can use to help us become the people he wants us to be, whole for him and those around us. We must renew our minds with his word and be grateful, always grateful, for our new life in Christ. When we set aside our anger, resentment, and selfish desperation, we will see his provision of these meaningful and encouraging people, things, and events among the not-so-encouraging effects of the broken world in which we live. Yes, Jesus said, "In this world you will have trouble" (John 16:33), but we will also have his gift of "peace" (John 14:27).

But, while God encourages us, we must be suspicious of the self that wants its way. It is always up to something, and, on our bad days, we are inclined to lean on the old survival system in our weak moments for the familiar, though temporary and superficial, feelings of security. We cannot trust those feelings. Even among Christians, we find those of weak faith who gain their feelings of security from ritual behavior, achievements, or popularity. You meet them on the street, and they are more concerned about church attendance than your well-being in the faith, your personal walk with God, or your spiritual and emotional reserves in Christ. They have yet to see that church attendance is not the issue but whether attending church shapes our lives around God.

Churches can be full of insecure Christians who depend on human social solutions for feelings of security. Our faith must go deeper than that. The church must help us to develop a heart that humbly trusts God. Some Christians have yet to learn that "true worshipers will worship the Father in spirit and in truth" (John 4:23). To do so is to admit that he is God, that his powerful providence controls the world and our lives for his purposes. It is to want those purposes fulfilled in us and to become part of *his* plan. The root of our security is not in our social identity, personal achievements, or a life of ease but in God himself—in dependence on his grace, purposes, and providence in our lives, and the peace beyond understanding it brings that guards our hearts and minds.

Scripture References: Josh 24:14–15; Pss 20:7; 33:16–22; 46:1–11; 51:6; 62:5–8; 91:1–16 with 32:10; 145:18–19; 146:3–6; Prov 3:5–8, 28:26; Mic 6:8;

74. SECURITY

John 4:21–24; 8:31–32 with 36; 14:27; 16:33; Rom 8:28–39, 14:5–10 with 22; 1 Cor 1:8–9; Phil 1:6 and 2:12–13 with Heb 13:20–21; 4:4–9 with John 14:27 and 16:33; Col 2:13–23, 3:12–17; 2 Thess 3:3.

75. Good Things Made Bad

To the pure, all things are pure.

—*Titus 1:15*

THE GOOD THINGS GOD created and the good he brings into our lives are never harmful in themselves, but they seldom remain unaffected by human interference in our world. Evil comes from good things God created being taken to an extreme, abused, or twisted into perversions of the original. Human nature allows resources and relationships to become mixed with greed and envy, employment with ambitions, time and authority with self-advancement, marital intimacy and commitment with adultery and divorce, a glass of wine with drunkenness, and plentiful food with gluttony. In the aggressive self-assertion of our individualism, God's gifts to us can be put to selfish uses, filled with selfish expectations, and used to manipulate or control others for self-fulfillment. The good in them becomes hard to recognize. It is contaminated with evil intent. But this does not mean we throw out the resources and relationships, give up on employment, champion celibacy, or stop eating. Every created thing is good as it comes to us, a gift from God for us to enjoy.

The abuses dishonor God. And because of the harm they cause, we are trained by parents, pastors, and Bible teachers to avoid the inappropriate uses of what God has given us and the human appetites that go with them. However, we can lose sight of the original good in the activities and their values when we constantly see them abused. We become negative, even hostile, toward the gift because of the potential harm of its abuse. But forfeiture of the good things, along with the rejection of their evil abuse, leads to legalism, undoing the freedom we have in Christ and canceling God's intentions.

75. GOOD THINGS MADE BAD

It is the human element in the use of God's gifts that can change them from blessing to curse. To say they are bad in themselves is like blaming rising crime and senseless shootings in our day on the guns we have always had among us. Something else has changed. We do not blame gluttony on spoons or make cell phones responsible for gossip. The evil lies elsewhere. Money, food, or intimacy are not tainted until they are abused by human beings. Our degenerating society, having turned people away from God and his moral purposes, has left people without a compass to find their way. You cannot delete God's creation of humankind in his image, destroy morality, and expect people to have a conscience, to do the right thing, to show valor and courage, or even to believe that people matter. Joy was turned to distress in the garden when Adam and Eve did not trust God, and that misery continues to have increasing effects on humanity in proportion to its increasing rejection of God.

All God has given us must be enjoyed with what the Bible calls purity of heart. This purity has to do with our motives. Many good things we might enjoy with the gratefulness God intended and do for the enjoyment of others can just as well be done for self-promotion and out of selfish ambition. That is why Paul can say, "To the pure, all things are pure, but to those who are corrupted and do not believe, nothing is pure," even if they claim to know God (Titus 1:15–16). This accounts for a great deal of abuse and for the extensive legalism we see in our day toward things God created for good and for our enjoyment.

The New Testament tells us that the boundaries for all behavior and the enjoyment of everything God created are love for him and our neighbor. So this freedom we have comes with responsibility. We must maintain the consideration and respect we should have for God's intentions and our neighbor's well-being. But it is not a sin to desire the enjoyment of something God gives us if we are grateful and aim to encourage those around us. He created much for our pleasure, and we honor him when we partake in it with these motives. From God comes laughter, enjoyment, pleasure, and freedom for us within the boundaries of love and discernment. This means monitoring our motives is of the highest order in living to glorify him.

Scripture References: Gen 1:31; Prov 16:2, 20:27; Eccl 3:11–14; Matt 5:8, 22:34–40; John 1:1–5 with 3:19; 2:7–11; 13:34–35; 17:23; Rom 12:3 with 9–10; 14:13–23; 1 Cor 6:12 with 19–20; 10:23–24 with 31; 2 Cor 9:8; Gal 2:4, 5:13; Phil 2:3–4; Col 2:16—3:4; 2 Thess 1:11–12; 1 Tim 4:4–5, 6:17–18; Titus 1:15–16; Jas 1:16–17 with 3:13; 1 Pet 2:16.

76. Cultures of the Bible

The seed that fell among the thorns is the man who hears the word, but the worries of this life . . . choke it, making it unfruitful.

—*Matt 13:22*

OUR CULTURE CAN GET in the way when we read God's word. Though sometimes inspired by the moral and ethical standards of a religion, or even the Bible, cultures are basically human. Therefore, we find and can experience flaws, inadequacies, and abuses to the extent of trauma and even terror in our social situation. Negative emotions, addictions, and insecurities caused by godless human approaches to satisfaction can abound. A functional culture, however, should tell its members what is important, valuable, necessary, normal, and trustworthy on the human level, giving people common sense about how to go about life and relationships. It should create a consensus for what adds to the common good, what is dangerous or helpful, and what is respectful or inconsiderate.

The context of a functional culture is made up of a social group that agrees, in general, with the rules and boundaries so that people can have expectations for the behavior of others and that behavior will have meaning for them. It also tells its members what behaviors should be discouraged or punished to preserve society. Finally, cultural values and beliefs help people interpret their experiences, both personal and collective. In these ways, culture functions as a powerful frame of reference. Agreement with it gives people a social identity and feelings of worth and belonging. But human cultural systems have just that weakness: they are human and easily go off the rails. They fall short of God's expectations and desires for his people, so reading the Bible should put our cultural values under his microscope. The

76. CULTURES OF THE BIBLE

more we know about our culture's influence, the better we understand God's intentions for us in our context.

A functional, cultural frame of reference is a guide for appropriateness and meaning in communication, whether verbal, nonverbal, or written. So if we don't understand the cultural frame of reference that shapes a message, we may not understand the message as intended. This is sometimes the case when we read the Bible. It is a cross-cultural experience, and the need for a cultural frame of reference combined with our unfamiliarity with the biblical one may cause us to unconsciously read our own cultural values back into the text as we study it. If we don't understand the influence of our culture on our understanding, we will not know when it is leading us away from the truth in God's word. It is the only framework for meaning we have, so we fall back on it instinctively and unconsciously. It is what we call the law of ethnocentrism. We bring our modern Western logic, common sense, and conscience to the text. We would all do well to gain more personal and cultural self-awareness so we can be more attentive to what God is saying to us on his terms instead of ours. Our own values, concerns, and needs may choke the message, distorting its original meaning.

Unfortunately, it is generally a social taboo to bring up this subject of the influence of culture in the hearing of independent individualists in Western cultures—even among Christians—even though these Western values represent the largest culture gap and cause the most dissonance in understanding cultures of the biblical Middle East. We can never assume that people in other cultures, such as those in the biblical text, hold the same values and beliefs or see the world the same way we do. They do not. But a word of caution. These differences in Middle Eastern cultures must not be used as an excuse for things we do not want to be true for us in the Bible.

The people of the Bible see their world through the social controls of honor and shame, patrilineal kinship, patron and client relations, collective community, low contact and high context communication, and all that in a nonindustrial, nonscientific, nontechnological world. It is the opposite of our world. They found meaning and identity in shared, qualitative social values and tradition, while we find ours through quantitative individual achievements, personal advancement, and social change.

Despite the magnitude of these differences, in God's providence, the Holy Spirit helps us understand what he is saying to us. He enlightens our eyes and teaches us, giving anyone willing to read the Bible with an open mind an understanding of the fundamental truths. But he does not remove our cultural frame of reference. As God reveals himself and the spiritual universe through the cultural context of the ancient Middle East, we must ensure that our culture and worldview do not get in the way. The new wine

AN INTERVENING LOVE

of his message calls for a fresh, uncontaminated wineskin. That is the point of being "born again" (John 3:3, 7) and "renewing" our minds (Rom 12:2).

Scripture References: Deut 29:2–6; 2 Kgs 6:13–17; Prov 18:13; Isa 40:13–14, 55:8–9; Matt 9:16–17; 11:15; 13:1–9, 22–23; Mark 4:9, 23; John 3:3–8, 14:15–27 with 16:33; Rom 12:1–2; Col 3:1–4; 2 Tim 2:14–15 and 23–26; 3:16–17; Jas 3:1; 1 John 2:15–17, 4:1–6; Rev 2:17.

77. Walking Worthy of the Gospel

For it is God's will that by doing good you should silence the ignorant talk of foolish men.

—*1 Pet 2:15*

WHAT ARE WE REVEALING about God to the people in our community? What do they see and hear about God in our routine lifestyles and ministries? What do they understand from the marquees in front of our churches? Is it just the natural offense of the gospel that turns the world away from Christianity, or is our expression of that faith part of the problem? As Christians lose their credibility in the West, secularism dominates society, bringing its darkness with it. Are our "successful" institutions helping or standing in the way of a relevant Christian witness? Are legalistic tendencies alienating the people around us and moving public opinion away from God? Can our faith easily be identified as authentic and life-changing? Or do they see little difference between Christians and non-Christians? Do we go through the motions of Christianity without thinking seriously of the one we worship, as the people of Israel did so many times? Have we been inaccurate about the meaning of the gospel? Is it possible the world has not seen the real thing and therefore criticizes or denies its existence?

People without Christ often become adversaries of the gospel and God himself, about whom they know nothing. In light of this critical need of our society to know the God they refuse, we must incarnate the message of the gospel—embody that grace and freedom in our broken world. We will not be perfect, but we will become evidence of his purposes and providence in the lives of his people and the difference it makes. God uses our faithfulness to intervene in the lives of others.

Scripture References: Matt 5:13–16, 7:13–21, 9:16–17, 15:7–9; John 1:4–5, 10; 3:19; 8:12; 12:23–26; 13:34–35; 14:6; 17:3 with 20–23; Acts 1:8; 2 Cor 5:15; Phil 2:12–16a; 1 Thess 4:11–12; 1 Tim 2:1–4; Titus 1:15–16, 2:11–14; 1 Pet 2:11–17, 3:13–17, 4:1–2.

78. Our Part in Making Disciples

Unless the LORD builds the house, its builders labor in vain.

—*Ps 127:1*

IN INFLUENCING THE WORLD with our faith, we must be mindful that even the best methods of man are useless apart from the activity of God. Those who share and demonstrate the life-giving message of Jesus Christ must acknowledge their utter dependence on God. After all, even the breath we have to speak, the health and energy to act, are from his hand. But more than that, his Spirit is at work through our efforts, convincing, convicting, and drawing people to himself, an intervention accompanying our part in making him known. It is not our message alone that may be heeded or rejected; it is the Spirit of God.

Nevertheless, God does put the task before godly men and women to represent him in their lives and have a part in making disciples. In fact, the same apostle who acknowledged God as the ultimate source of salvation also said, "I have become all things to all people so that by all possible means I might save some" (1 Cor 9:22). There is dependence but also responsibility.

We are to reveal Jesus as Savior and Lord in word and deed in a relevant way in our broken world. But, though each person is unique and their path to God may look different on the surface, the path must lead to Christ. Peter, Nicodemus, the Samaritan woman, and Zacchaeus all came to Christ differently, and lived for him, each in their own way. So will each person who encounters him. We are only to introduce them to Jesus as the way to God through our lives and words, and pray for God to help them to accept his grace. After they choose Christ, with discipleship and teaching, they will continue on a path toward maturity in their faith, and walk it with him, who is also the truth and the life, as God works in them. Their journey on that path may not look like ours, but their essential commitment and loyalty will be to the same person of God through Christ. Though his providence may be difficult to discern, we must all be patient. He is at work in each person for his purposes.

Scripture References: Ps 127:1–2; Matt 28:18–20; Luke 5:8–11, 19:8–10; John 3:9, 4:28–30, 14:6, 16:5–8, 21:17–22; Acts 4:12; Rom 11:33–36; 1 Cor 3:5–9, 9:22; Phil 2:12–13; 1 Pet 3:18.

79. Information About God

. . . the knowledge of the truth that leads to godliness.
—Titus 1:1

WHEN KNOWLEDGE ABOUT GOD results in realizing what that information means, especially what it means for us, we have moved beyond knowing to understanding. It remains for us to act on that understanding if we believe it is true. This realization of God's intentions in our lives is spoken of in the Old Testament as the fear of the LORD and is the beginning of wisdom. It is rooted in humility and grows into a relationship with God built on trusting his omnipotent providence, unconditional grace, and meaningful love. Being built on trust, this relationship does not have to, and realizes it cannot, know everything about God. It results in freedom: freedom from fear, legalism, selfish ambition, the need to control or manipulate others, etc. We are free to let God be God and enjoy all he has given us in creation. We do not have to make him fit our expectations and definitions. We can let him speak for himself. When our intention to honor God is clear, we have contentment. We place our destiny in his hands; we do not need to try to save ourselves but to live responsibly with what he brings into our lives.

Biblical information always leads to something. It should result in a relationship of trust, expression of worship, freedom from fear, and intentional behavior that honors God. However, much of this information is objective, and it can be accumulated and organized into a system, answer questions, and give its owner a feeling of accomplishment. This may satisfy our need for order and logic, but we must not fall in love with it instead of the God of whom it speaks. By itself, it remains ink on paper destined to perish with time or disaster. Only the results of God's word go on forever in our hearts and lives. As Paul said, the goal of his teaching was "the knowledge of the truth that leads to godliness" (Titus 1:1). He then describes godliness as love coming "from a pure heart and a good conscience and a sincere faith" (1 Tim 1:5). The intended outcome of what God gives us in his word is that we each become a certain kind of person.

However, biblical information can be twisted, refusing the actual truth about God or his ways. The Pharisees wanted their own way of doing what they said was of God. But it was not of God; it was of themselves. Paul said of others, "They claim to know God, but by their actions they deny him" (Titus 1:16). They were corrupted. He said this in contrast to the pure in heart: "To the pure, all things are pure" (1:15). There are two kinds of wisdom, but that "from heaven is first of all pure" (Jas 3:13–18).

Scripture References: Pss 33:18, 91:1–2, 111:10, 147:3 with 6a and 11; Prov 9:10, 22:4; Isa 33:6, 41:10, 58:6–12, 66:2b; Hos 6:6; Mic 6:8; Matt 5:8, 7:15–27; John 14:23–24, 15:9, 17:3; Rom 12:1–2; Eph 5:15–17; Col 3:1–3 with 12–17; 1 Tim 1:3–7, 6:17b; Titus 1:1–3, 15–16; Jas 1:22–25, 3:13–18; 1 John 2:15–17, 3:16–20, 4:15–18.

80. Fatal Mixture

> Everyone who hears these words of mine and does not put them into practice is like a foolish man who built his house on sand.
>
> —Matt 7:26

WE CAN READILY SEE contradictions between biblical faith and some of the cultural values that run our lives. Some of these values indeed lead us away from God. Yet most Christians are not interested in looking at these aspects of culture that compete with God's desires and purposes for us. If we examine it, we will find that truth from God is often contrary to culture's definitions of reality, its idea of morality, or its superficial values of self-assertion or the achievement of self-worth.

The fact is that culture is either influencing the truth or the truth is influencing our culture. When culture affects the truth of God in our lives, the mixture is called syncretism. The truth becomes integrated with the cultural norms into a new understanding for survival. The distinctions of the truth are eventually blurred by cultural understandings, values, and personal preferences. We hardly know it's happening as the truth becomes contaminated, its potential and intentions diluted, its sharp edges blunted. It can no longer speak in a relevant way to our needs. God's work in and through us is impeded if not ended.

Eventually, instead of worshiping in spirit and truth, attendance and membership in denominational churches become the issues of importance, the buildings the central feature, the charisma of the pastor the engine, and divisiveness the reputation instead of harmony. If the situation continues, the mixture hardens, and the longer it goes unattended, the harder it gets. As in the parable of the soils, the true message gets choked out by the weeds of cultural values until it bears no fruit. In our numbness to God's way for us, the mixture feels natural; we see no inconsistency. It becomes something to be desired and maintained, but culture has poisoned the truth, and the salt has lost its savor.

The Jews had turned the temple into a marketplace. It seemed natural and was quite profitable. Today, many churches have changed. They have normalized many contrary cultural values in their midst in the name of relevancy and go on as if nothing has happened. Leaders become celebrities, worship services become performances, and members who give are promised prosperity and health. Perhaps they feel it makes them more acceptable or attractive to the world around them. We have a great deal of freedom in Christ, but it is bounded by devotion and loyalty to God, as well as consideration and love for one another. If we are building on sand instead of rock, we will not be able to withstand the gathering storm. The enemy is on the loose, and we must be prepared to resist him or be devoured as he takes advantage of our apathy.

Scripture References: Prov 16:25; Matt 5:13–16, 6:19–21, 7:24–29, 13:7, 19:30, 21:12–13, 22:34–40; John 2:12–16, 8:31–32, 16:33, 17:20–23; Gal 5:1 with 13–15; Col 3:17 with 1 Tim 4:4–5 with 6:17b and Titus 1:15–16; 1 Pet 5:8–9; 1 John 2:15–17; Rev 2–3.

81. Perfect Christians

Blessed are the pure in heart, for they will see God.

—*Matt 5:8*

THERE ARE BIBLICAL "HEROES of the faith" that sometimes generate idealistic thoughts and descriptions of "perfect" Christians that we hold up as the model for all of us, but these were not the norm then, nor should we require it of ourselves now. Though they are excellent biblical examples of trusting God that can greatly encourage us in our own situation, not many of us will be known for our faith like Joseph, Daniel, Esther, or David. Like most of God's people in the Bible, we will be called on to be faithful in common situations and trust God in the more ordinary things of day-to-day life. Some of us may become outstanding examples in very difficult circumstances. But, though our challenges and problems seem as threatening as Goliath was to Israel or the lions were to Daniel, most of us will face trials more common to Christians in this broken world: challenges in family relationships, at work, with finances, and in the community. Some struggle with loneliness, anxiety, anger, or physical illness. Facing these difficulties with grace and trusting in God's providence, though our highest calling, may go unknown to any but our closest friends. But God is aware and never forgets our trust in him. Not many of us will be known as heroes of the faith, but God will always know each of us by name as his own child, even when we fall short and fail him. He is with all who love him and acknowledge his name. He doesn't sleep, doesn't change; he remains, and he cares.

People always need God's forgiveness and work in their lives. Perfection is yet to come. There are many mentions of righteous and upright people in the Bible. Though none are perfect, it is a way of saying that some are faithful and pure in heart. There were times in Israel's history when

AN INTERVENING LOVE

the people were so unfaithful that God described the situation as none being righteous, that is, none doing the right things with the right heart and the right spirit. Talking about the righteous and unrighteous people was a common speech convention of the language and culture of the times, and people understood its meaning. They did not confuse this "righteousness" with "perfection" where people were concerned. People always need God's grace. Only God acts with perfect righteousness, but we are made righteous before God "through faith in Jesus Christ" (Rom 3:22–24). It is not ours but his, and he has covered us with it in our weakness. No one can change our position in Christ.

Life will be filled with temptations to do that which dishonors God. Temptations are not sinful. Our human leanings toward satisfying selfish desires are fueled, and the opportunity for fulfilling them is presented by the enemy. Stepping into his trap by acting on our sinful desires is sin. It is familiar to sensitive Christians. Though our position in Christ bathes us once and for all in *his* ultimate and perfect righteousness before God, we must often get our feet washed by God's grace in our daily lives.

Righteousness in our daily walk is up to us. We must choose intentionally to honor God. That choice is called walking in the Spirit and walking worthy of the gospel. Yes, we will occasionally fail, but no sin is beyond his forgiveness for those in Christ. There is no condemnation for those whose sins have been forgiven, but they may expect some directive discipline to help them see their faults. He loves his own too much to let them go their own way without his intervention of love. There are many good Christians; there just are not any perfect ones. Faithful Christians know that very well.

Scripture References: Gen 37:21–28 with 41:41; 1 Sam 13:14 with 16:1 and 6–13; 2 Sam 12:7, 9, and 13; Pss 34:17–22, 91:14–16, 102:25–28, 121:1–4; Prov 3:5–7, 15:8–10; Isa 43:1, 53:4–6; Matt 1:19, 5:8; Luke 1:5–6, 2:25; John 5:24, 10:28–30, 13:6–11; Acts 13:22; Rom 3:9–24; 7:14—8:1, 31–35; 1 Cor 10:11–13; Eph 4:1–6, 5:17–18; Phil 1:27, 2:12–13; Col 1:22; Titus 1:15; Heb 6:10; Jas 1:1–18; 1 Pet 4:12–19, 5:6–11; 1 John 1:7–10.

82. Never Good Enough

It is not the healthy who need a doctor, but the sick.

—*Matt 9:12*

People do not have to be good for God to welcome them. God's purpose is to take those who realize they are not good and need him and give them the goodness of Christ. Yes, Jesus did not come to condemn but to save bad people. When they come to know God through Christ, people learn even more about how imperfect they are and realize more and more how much they continually need God's grace. Sinners who know it are the only kind of people God saves. Their gratefulness becomes a deep-seated attribute of their lives.

The proud cannot be saved without the humility it takes to trust God. It is impossible. The self-satisfied go on as if they were good and did not need God. But self-assertion, which seems their friend, is instead their enemy. It has taken them to where they are now and keeps them from where they need to go. They cannot see the end of their path. It seems to them that self-satisfaction is the goal of life, and they pursue it at all costs. But the final bill is yet to arrive in the mail. "There is a way that seems right to a man, but in the end, it leads to death" (Prov 14:12). If you think you are good enough or are, at least, better than most, you are dead wrong. Your thought tells the tale. Your pride has numbed your heart to your precarious situation. Your need for God's grace is urgent, and your time is running out.

Scripture References: 2 Chr 7:14; Ps 51:16–17; Prov 11:28, 14:12, 16:18–19, 19:3, 26:12, 28:26; Jer 9:23–24; Dan 9:18b; Matt 9:9–13, 19:16–22; Luke 5:31–32, 12:15–21, 18:9–14; John 3:17–18, 14:6 with Acts 4:12; Eph 2:1–10; 1 Tim 1:15–17; Heb 7:23–25, 11:6.

83. Maybe God Doesn't Mind

If we claim to be without sin, we deceive ourselves and the truth is not in us.

—*1 John 1:8*

SOME THINK THE FIRST sin was some massive moral collapse that separated man and woman from God. But it was actually something simple; it looked innocent and was quickly and easily done. A desire, a doubt, a simple twist of the wrist, a bite of the sweet fruit, finished. Eating the fruit of the trees was not a bad thing, and this act was the same as eating from other trees . . . except for God's clear statement that this one was off limits. It was against his will for them, and a matter of *trusting* him. That is how easy it was to break trust with the God of the universe.

    The couple learned that one can do what one wants, and the immediate reward can be quite agreeable. Such a small thing, they thought. And it seemed the serpent was right; nothing happened. God doesn't mind after all (or what he says doesn't really matter). Perhaps everything *was* theirs; there was *no* limit, and it would go on forever. What an exhilarating feeling to be in control. Then they heard God's voice in the garden. Their hearts were struck with fear. In an anxious panic, they tried to hide, but it was useless, and, when found, they deflected the blame. We are not told of their repentance. God covered their shame, explained the suffering and death they had welcomed into their lives, and sent them out of the garden. Things were never to be the same, yet the sin was, in a similar way, to be repeated over and over by humankind to this day. Satan would like us to think it's a small matter. But trusting God is the most crucial matter in the world, and disregarding him brings deep and enduring consequences.

83. MAYBE GOD DOESN'T MIND

Man and woman never knew perfection again on earth until Jesus came. But they were again defensive. In their pride and anger, they rejected and killed him. Even in the best of times, maybe especially in the best of times, we choose self-contrived and self-centered gratification over trusting God as if we could achieve our own happiness without him. As Christians, we can slip back into these old patterns. Israel did it time and again throughout their history and continues in it today. They are an example for us. It is time we gave it up and put our complete trust in him, who can save us from ourselves and give us the peace we seek. God does mind when we stray from his guidance in his word. He cares out of his love for us. His patience and grace are ready to intervene and forgive us yet again. His forgiveness will restore our relationship with him *every* time we humble ourselves and return to him. He is faithful, just, and full of mercy. You and I are the variables.

Scripture References: Gen 3:1–13; Deut 32:4; Pss 25:9, 145:14; Prov 5:21 with 16:2 and 20:27; Isa 5:20–21, 26:12–13; Luke 18:9–14, 19:41–44; John 3:16–18, 16:33 with 14:27; Acts 7:51–53; Rom 1:21–22, 3:21–24, 10:16—11:36; 1 Cor 10:1–13; 2 Cor 4:4, 11:14; Eph 3:20–21; 1 Tim 1:15; Heb 12:1; 1 Pet 3:18; 2 Pet 3:8–10; 1 John 1:8–10.

84. A Lifetime

Teach us to number our days aright, that we may gain a heart of wisdom.

—Ps 90:12

SEVENTY OR EIGHTY YEARS seems like a long time, especially to the young. But it goes by quickly like a mist that disappears or wild grass that soon withers. This bit of time we have is usually full of efforts to meet social expectations, achieve feelings of worth, and gain personal satisfaction. These years can only go so far in the hands of a human being. Solomon would call all our straining for self-assertion, achievement, recognition, and ease a chasing after the wind. It is a useless spending of the rapidly vanishing moments of our lives.

We must stop and think. We must notice the good God has given us, see the blessings, savor the moments. Every day is the first day of the rest of our lives; every day is new and full of possibilities; and every day may be the last one we have to live for God and those around us. What we do not do or say today may never get done or said. What goodness to be enjoyed will be missed, tears of sharing someone's pain will be left unshed, or promises left unfulfilled? How much contentment forfeited? What good deed will be left undone when the curtain is pulled on the act of our lives? We only have today to do it. We cannot finish it all today, but we can make progress.

What if these years were in the hands of God, given to him—to the best of our ability—to honor his name and trust his purposes, which endure forever? It is not as common a pattern as we might want for our lives, but, when it is, though the person who seeks God in this way may never be known by society, they are known and treasured by God. They will be people who do that one good deed, say that one helpful, loving word, enjoy

84. A LIFETIME

that one small gift from God each day he gives them. They will live their short time on earth in the shadow of his power, faithfulness, and protection and abide in his presence for eternity, lifted above all earthly rewards.

Each year of our lives can be an investment in the future, familiar with the contentment of knowing God, even in difficult times, ground sown with good works and compassion. Then, when the curtain falls, we will join loved ones lost on earth and know joy with them forever, with no needs, no sorrow, and all suffering ended. Seventy or eighty years is not long, and it will soon pass. It is a small investment to entrust them to God's providence, the dividends of which are so enormous they cannot be weighed and of which there will be no end.

Scripture References: Pss 16:11; 25:4–5; 33:11; 84:10–12; 90:10–12 with 17; 91:1–4, 14–16; 103:10–18; 139:15–18; 145:18–19; Prov 20:27; Eccl 4:4; Isa 64:4–5a; Matt 5:1–10, 6:19–33; John 4:23–24, 14:6, 16:33 with 14:27; 1 Cor 2:9; Jas 4:13–17; 1 Pet 1:24–25; 2 Pet 3:8; Rev 21:1–4.

85. The Nature of Worship

True worshipers will worship the Father in spirit and truth.
—John 4:23

WORSHIP IS THE HUMBLE and grateful recognition of God's greatness, grace, and providence on our behalf. It is a specific experience, and it must include the loyalty and allegiance to him that should be present in our lives—a loyalty and allegiance that people in our Western culture give to the self. What we worship, we serve. Until our conversion, we worship the individual achievement of our identity, independence, and social and material wellbeing. After we meet God, the object of our worship must change from self to him and his ways. This change is difficult enough, but our preference for informality, need for distraction, desire to avoid uncertainty, passion for the new, aversion to the old, and fear of silence make true worship of God even more difficult for us. What should call for more trust in our God tends to breed anxiety and self-centered behavior. Once again, our cultural conditioning is getting in the way.

So not everything called worship is authentic. When we mix our cultural values and personal preferences with what we call worship, we are in the center and God is on the outside. We have yet to humble ourselves. Worshiping God will take a new wineskin, which will require discarding the old one. Jesus talked about the process as a necessary death to bring about life. His choice of terms, along with being "born again," are striking but not inappropriate. They are well-suited to a process leading to a "new self."

We must remember that God does not *need* our worship; it is for us. He is worthy of unending worship, but we also have an essential and desperate need to worship him, to extol his greatness and grace for our sakes, to humbly express unceasing gratitude for his intervening love.

85. THE NATURE OF WORSHIP

Not all we do is worship, but what we worship will affect all we do. All our activities must honor the one whom we worship. We glorify God with all our endeavors—make his greatness, grace, power, and providence known—or we do not. We must incarnate his love in our relationships, demonstrate his justice in our vocation, and express his grace and generosity in our actions. This is the developing outcome of a life that revolves around the true worship of God. When we do otherwise, we step outside that loyalty and allegiance, that love and devotion for God. We, as humans, are not perfect at this kind of loyalty. Therefore, we must constantly remind ourselves of our need for his grace. True worship does that. Deep down, we know that the worship of self must go. One cannot serve two masters.

Scripture References: Pss 15:1–5, 29:1–2, 37:3–6, 46:10, 96:11–13, 100:1–5, 145:17–21; Prov 3:5–6, 16:2, 20:27, 21:2; Isa 29:13, 46:9, 66:2b; Ezek 33:30–33; Mic 6:8; Matt 6:19–24 with 6:33; 9:16–17; 19:16–24; 22:34–40; Luke 4:8, 6:43–49; John 4:21–24, 12:24–26, 17:3; Rom 11:33–36, 12:1–3; Eph 4:20–24 with Col 3:10.

86. Commanded to Worship?

They worship me in vain.

—Matt 15:9

GOD DOES NOT DESIRE us to worship because it is commanded. He wants our willing hearts. He knows our salvation and happiness come from a relationship with him that involves the willing choice to accept his grace, love him for it, recognize his power, accept his providence, and make him the center of our lives. Worship should be a result of who he is and what he does. Brought about by obedience to a command, worship becomes legalism not true worship, and God seeks people whose worship is authentic. Though sovereign in every respect, he does not force his way into our lives to make that worship happen. It is a natural result of realizing he is worthy of our undistracted devotion, admiration, and awe. It is a voluntary, though often overwhelming, response to God's person, attributes, works, power, and grace coming from the pure in heart.

God is worthy of our worship, but it is *not* the purpose of our creation. It is, instead, the *result* of being created by such a God. His creation, including that of humankind, reflects his glory, the manifestation of his power, majesty, and sovereignty. His interaction with the people of his creation reveals his love, grace, patience, providence, and justice. Worship is the result of knowing something of God as he really is, something about his extraordinary works in the universe and his intention for and attention to humankind, something of the mystery of his providence and the paradox of his grace. All this we extol in our worship. If we let God be God, we will find that love, loyalty, worship, and obedience come from a willing heart. We will give him our allegiance, and, though we often fail, it will be our heart's intent to honor him in all we do.

86. COMMANDED TO WORSHIP?

In putting God first, we share loyalty with no other god, even, or perhaps especially, the god of self. Just as God told Adam and Eve not to eat from the tree in the middle of the garden, he tells us not to neglect him as the center of our lives (as we are overly inclined to do), and to trust him for our present and eternal good. For Satan is still after our hearts as he was with Adam and Eve and later with Jesus in his temptation. And the result of his victory is the worst kind of death. God insists on our need for him, but the choice to trust and worship him is *ours*. When we humble ourselves, desire turns from self to worshiping him as we recognize his utterly undeserved, intervening love and grace for us. Blessed are the pure in heart, for they will see God.

Scripture References: Exod 20:1–6; Deut 6:4 and 13; 2 Chr 7:14; Ps 51:16–17; Prov 3:5–7, 21:3; Isa 1:11–20; Hos 6:6; Mic 6:8; Matt 4:8–10, 5:8, 15:8–9, 22:37–40; Luke 4:5–8, 9:23–25; John 15:1–8; Rom 1:18–32, 12:2 with Matt 7:21 and Eph 5:15–17; 2 Cor 5:15, 11:13–15; 1 Pet 5:6–11.

87. Glorify God

Live such good lives among the pagans that . . . they may see your good deeds and glorify God on the day he visits us.

—*1 Pet 2:12*

To GLORIFY GOD IS different than to worship him. Though it happens in worship, glorifying him is an ongoing honoring of him in all we do. To glorify him is to display his significance, goodness, grace, power, and love in our words and works—in the way we live our lives. All things should be done with a grateful attitude and an attempt to honor God, but worship is that specific response to his being, attributes, and works. He is worthy of the undistracted attention of the worshiper; everything else must stop and fall silent in his presence. To glorify God is different from "Be still, and know that I am God" (Ps 46:10); it is to be active and interactive in displaying his goodness, grace, and providence in society.

While worship begins deep in the heart, where communion with God in spirit and truth is ignited, it can remain there, secret, silent, and powerful, or come out in grateful praise. But the commotion of the world stops for it. We glorify God, however, in the noise and bustle of daily work in that world, in conversation with others, and in our attitude while everything is going on around us. Amid the confusion, distractions, and frustrations around us, we are to make his goodness, grace, and love known by our lives out in the world. One of the purposes of the church is for gatherings of his people to, with one heart and mind, give praise and recognition to the God of the universe. How we live our lives outside the church takes this recognition to the world around us; it glorifies God.

87. GLORIFY GOD

Scripture References: Pss 29:1–11, 96:6–9, 100:1–5, 105:1b, 145:1–21, 150:1–6; Matt 5:13–16; Acts 3:11–16; 1 Cor 10:31; 2 Cor 5:15; Eph 2:1–5; Phil 2:1–11; Col 3:17; 1 Pet 2:11–12, 4:1–2.

88. To Do or Not to Do

So, if you think you are standing firm, be careful that you don't fall.
—*1 Cor 10:12*

BECAUSE OUR WESTERN CULTURE is not friendly to the ideas of submission, duty, or humility, we seek ways, even in our Christianity, to work around the difficulties they bring to personal survival in our social context. One of the problematic lines of faulty thinking is the phrase "Let go and let God." Some people say, "We cannot live the Christian life we are called to in the Bible; we must let God do it through us. The Holy Spirit must take over." However, that is not what the objective reader with an open mind will find in the New Testament. We will see there instead that we really are told to do things: to practice self-control, to love and serve others, to seek his kingdom, to renew our minds, and to think on things above. We do not see "Let go and let God do these things through you." We see that we are to be careful to devote ourselves to "doing what is good" (Titus 3:8).

If it were the teaching of God's word to let go this way, it would be part of every exhortation or reference to putting off sinful behavior. In fact, there would be something unethical about making it sound so very much like God is asking something of *us*. The word *obedience* would have to be removed from the text. Waiting on God to do good things through us, as much as blaming Satan when we are proud and selfish, is a movement away from responsible behavior that creates spiritual arrogance. It does not reflect the humble trust God looks for in the hearts of those who seek to honor him. Along with a lack of emphasis on freedom in Christ, this ideology has weakened the church.

Through his Spirit, God is very much part of the transforming journey of renewing our minds, setting them on things above, and working out our

88. TO DO OR NOT TO DO

salvation to fulfill his purposes for us in the world. He encourages us in his word with every reason to move ahead. God provides resources, wisdom, opportunities, and people to support and inspire us. But he waits for our loyalty and the trust needed to walk worthy of the gospel. He wants that willingly from us. The only real loyalty and trust are those displayed in behavior, faltering though it sometimes is. He will add his grace to every effort to honor him.

We are not alone when tempted to stray from this desire to "please him" (Col 1:10–11). The question is whether we turn to the one who is there with us. In him, we find every reason and encouragement to "keep in step with the Spirit" (Gal 5:25). He gives us a way to weather the storm of temptation if we are willing to take it. Do we fail at times? Of course we do. God knows it, and his grace is present in those moments. When we turn to him in our failings, he bends to wash our feet because he knows our hearts.

Scripture References: Pss 25:9, 51:17, 91:14–16, 103:10–14; John 13:5–10; Rom 12:1–2; 1 Cor 10:12–13; 2 Cor 9:8; Gal 5:16–25 with 6:9; Eph 4:1; 5:1, 22, 25, 33; Phil 1:9–11, 27a; 4:4–9; Col 1:9–14, 3:1–17; 1 Thess 2:10–12, 4:11; Titus 2:11–12, 14; 3:1, 8, 14; Heb 12:1–4, 13:15–16; Jas 1:13–25; 1 Pet 1:13–16, 2:12, 3:13–17, 5:6–7; 2 Pet 1:3–11; 1 John 1:5–9, 3:18.

89. Heaven or Hell?

Man is destined to die once and after that to face judgment.
—Heb 9:27

God created heaven for his children and hell for Satan and his demons. Then why are we told that some human beings may end up in hell? How can God do that? Well, he does not. But in his wisdom, it is one thing he has chosen to not prevent if we choose it. He sends no one to hell. But he will not tread on the freedom he has given us to choose our loyalties and loves, and thereby, our destiny. That freedom is shockingly authentic. He made heaven available to all. What would be unjust is if, after giving us that freedom, he were to force people to go to heaven who do not want to take that road, those who do not want God to exist or meddle in their lives, those who pledge no loyalty to the King. Yes, he sends his Spirit to convict people of their waywardness, gives them opportunities to choose him, and tells them openly in the Bible of the consequences of rejecting him. God longs for everyone to come to him and trust him, but though he encourages and convicts through his word and his Spirit, he leaves that choice ultimately up to us. He has given us the sacred gift of free will as he did with the first man and woman. We must choose who we will trust, or the word will have no meaning.

Our original question about how God allows some people to go to hell comes from not wanting the responsibility for the freedom he has given us. Though Western people desire independence, they often want the rewards of loyalties they have not chosen, i.e., heaven without the cost of humility and the submission of faith. The rich young man in the Gospel of Matthew wanted heaven, but not at the expense of his earthly treasures. While not choosing God's way, people ignore the current and future consequences

89. HEAVEN OR HELL?

of what they *have* chosen. They have strange ideas of freedom and justice. They think God is not just unless he gives them, without the requirements, what they have categorically refused, his grace. This is very foolish thinking until we realize that Christians, too, sometimes want God's blessings without the humility faith demands. Even those headed for heaven do well to take inventory of their values and choices.

Our minds might go to those who have not heard, are not mentally capable of understanding, or are too young to grasp the importance of the gospel. They have not chosen God. What will he do for them? But we forget. He is a God of perfect love and perfect justice. He can be trusted without question to express that love and justice in perfect ways. These have not chosen him, but they have not rejected him either. But for those who have heard of the work of Christ and God's grace, not trusting him is a rejection with consequences.

We are called to allow his truth and grace to restructure our thinking. God is a God of love who never forces people to love him. It would not be love if extracted from the unwilling. But he is also a God of justice. He never forgets those who are his, but neither will he forget those who reject him, who seek to erase the memory of him from society, and especially those who seek to destroy his children. Though it is not his desire that any should perish, he will allow each the the consequences of their chosen destiny.

Scripture References: Exod 17:8–16 with 1 Sam 15:32–33 (four hundred years later); Deut 32:4; Josh 24:14–15; Isa 42:1–4; Ezek 33:11 with 2 Pet 3:9 and 15a; Matt 7:13–14; 11:20–24, 25:41; Luke 17:1–2; John 3:16–21, 36, 8:42–47; Rom 3:21–26, 12:1–2; Titus 2:11; Heb 2:1–4; 2 Pet 2:17.

90. Encouraging Popular Christianity

For it is God's will that by doing good you should silence the ignorant talk of foolish men.

—*1 Pet 2:15*

OF COURSE, THE FULL promises of heaven are not a reality in the here and now, but some may look at Christians and see no sign of them at all. There are places where we have failed in our responsibility as Christians on this side of heaven. Though we are to be evidence of his love and grace, too many of us are in love with Christianity instead of God; we are fooling around with it for what it can give us rather than living in the reality of its intended purpose. In our numbness to truth and grace in our daily lives, we may be responsible for others rejecting God. There is a fine line between this kind of thoughtless detachment and actually helping the enemy by intentionally leading others away from God. Jesus' words for that person are strong: "Better for him to be thrown into the sea with a millstone tied around his neck" (Luke 17:1–2).

We must examine our faith and be alert and careful. While the weakest efforts to live for him will be rewarded, some will answer for foolish "faith" that has pointed others in the wrong direction. They have led people away from God instead of toward him. This is a serious affair. Jesus told Jewish people to love others using Roman soldiers and Samaritans as examples. But he did not tell them to love the Pharisees. Those who lead others away from God, no matter how religious, are enemies of God himself. Paul was once among them and called himself the worst of sinners, for so he was. He saw himself as an example of the magnitude of God's grace.

Some of this comes from "pastoral preparation" that does not train students in the deeper motivations for the faithful Christian life. Sometimes

90. ENCOURAGING POPULAR CHRISTIANITY

preparation rests on information and sometimes on emotions, but it must instead rest on the meaning of the truth, which, if truly believed, actively changes our lives. Information about God should lead students to a deep sense of loyalty to his purposes, humility in place of their individualism and recognition of achievement, and a deep trust in his providence, wisdom, goodness, grace, and love. The knowledge of the truth must lead to godliness. If we are more intent on handing out information and preparing students to pass it on in attractive, even emotional, ways that will grow large churches, we are missing the mark. If we keep the goal of leadership before them, they may become enamored with its social status. The idea is attractive as it agrees with the influence of their culture to achieve and be at the top of their profession. Some may become indifferent to their own spiritual well-being, unaltered by the information at the foundation of their training. As pastors, they may go on to encourage a popular, culturally influenced, materialistic Christianity. This energized, human-shaped ministry does not lead others to godliness but to human "success."

Popular Christianity does not see the connection between truth and godliness in daily life. Those who claim God's grace must become practical examples to their spouse and children in the home and to friends in the community, show honesty and kindness at work or school, practice loving intimacy in marriage, and desire to honor God in everyday life. Again, as Paul told the young pastor Titus, the knowledge of the truth must lead to godliness. Yet pastors of megachurches are dropping out of the ministry at an alarming rate. Popular Christianity offers no more hope than "springs without water" (2 Pet 2:17). It will not do.

We can't tell which popular Christians are in Christ but need forgiveness, which ones are collaborating with the enemy, loyal to self instead of to God, or which are caught in ritual behavior bred of secret legalism. Let us find ourselves on the right side of the battle for the souls of men and not enabling popular Christianity. While on this side of heaven, we should not judge the weak in faith but encourage them to bear fruit and not give room to the foolish deceptions of society and selfish ambition. We must encourage worship in spirit and truth and lead people away from a self-centered perspective, however informed, to a God-centered life. We are all imperfect here and need a growing relationship with the God of grace. It is a process rather than an event. But it is a process that must be in motion.

Scripture References: Matt 7:13–23, 23:13–15; Luke 17:1–6, 22:31–34; John 4:23–24, 15:1–8; Rom 14:1–4, 15:1–2; 1 Cor 9:19–23, 15:2 with 2 Cor 13:5; 2 Cor 2:10–11, 11:14; Gal 5:19–26, 6:9–10; Eph 6:11; 2 Tim 2:22–26; Titus 1:1–3; Heb 10:19–25, 12:28–29; Jas 3:3–6, 13–18; 1 Pet 2:12 and 15; 2 Pet 2:17; Rev 20:11–13.

91. Life as a Christian

Whatever you do, whether in word or deed, do it all in the name of the Lord Jesus, giving thanks to God the Father through him.
—*Col 3:17*

GOD WAS CLOSE TO Adam and Eve and gave them dominion over the creation, the tending of the garden, and intimacy in their relationship so that they might be fruitful. Though they would soon fall from these perfect relationships as sin entered the world, life would continue to have many of God's blessings for engaging the world around them. Many generations later, Jesus returned to his creation to redeem it, and entered its society, attending weddings, funerals, feasts, and dinner parties. He made wine to complete a joyous wedding occasion and brought Lazarus back from death, relieving the sorrow of Mary and Martha. Jesus had concern for a wayward Samaritan woman, a wealthy Pharisee, and a crooked tax collector. He returned many people to health and physical well-being. He had compassion for the masses as lost without God, and was angered at the abuse of the temple and at the Jewish leaders who led the people away from their Creator and Savior.

Later, Paul and Peter were concerned that Christians lead quiet family lives and engage in vocations with a good work ethic so they would have good reputations in the community and not be dependent on outsiders. They taught that marriages must be loving, and one's spouse never neglected, older people should be respected by the younger ones, and children should be loved and introduced to a God-centered worldview. Paul took for granted that Christians would visit nonbelievers in their homes, enjoy their hospitality, and enrich their lives with the gospel.

91. LIFE AS A CHRISTIAN

Everyday life goes on after a person becomes a Christian. It is not to be legalistic but entered into with freedom, enjoyment, and purpose. Much of it is the same as before we were Christians, but we go about it with different attitudes and approach it with different values. We must empathize with others, helping them in need and sharing their joys and sorrows. Life is not one long Bible study or spending all day in prayer. It is engagement with the world and living out the message of God's grace. We have been sent into that world to announce forgiveness in Christ, bring joy, carry one another's burdens, be faithful in friendship, and be dependable on a work team. We are to be harmonious in our gatherings of believers, answer questions about our faith, and love our families and neighbors. Not every day will be without suffering, but it is our calling to embrace the gift of life before us in an inclusive way, good things and bad, under the powerful wing of God's providence, in the cool shade of his grace, with the relief and rest of freedom in Christ supported by an undying loyalty to his honor.

Scripture References: Gen 1:26 with 28 and 2:15; Matt 21:12-17; Luke 5:27-31, 14:8-12, 19:1-10; John 2:1-11, 3:16-17, 4:17-26, 9:1-41, 11:17-44, 13:34-35, 17:23; 1 Cor 2:1-8; 1 Pet 3:1-7, 13-17; 5:5.

92. Sustaining Faith

God is Spirit, and his worshipers must worship in spirit and in truth.
—John 4:24

UNDER THE SURFACE OF the noise and activities of organized Christianity, some long for a more functional faith and calm contentment amid the demand for achievement, performance, and competition for affirmation or control that surrounds them. They desire to see the rapidly disappearing moments of our human experience from God's perspective, gain assurance from trusting him, rest in the certainty of knowing they are in God's will, and experience the quietness of wisdom. They find this peace in their relationship with God, bound by his grace and cared for by his providence, whether in church, with their family and friends, or alone in his creation.

But for others, how to move beyond the demands of life in the world escapes them. They continue to seek their well-being, feelings of worth, and identity in the recognition of their performance by others. They have not found trusting God the solution to their restlessness. The need for more affirmation and control persists, and the church becomes an ideal context for expressing these culture-shaped human inclinations. They do not realize that such selfish attainment is temporary and superficial, costing them and everyone around them the peace they long for.

If one is looking for a religion of rules to obey that will earn God's approval, I can hardly recommend Christianity. It is not a religion, and it soundly rejects legalism. And it is no kinder to those seeking signs affirming God's love and promises. The Bible teaches a faith that is much different from what most expect. Our search for God's will in our lives is not to be an endless and frantic pursuit for his approval. Unless we let go of the need for human achievement and culture's rewards, we will not arrive at the ongoing

92. SUSTAINING FAITH

rest and freedom of sustaining faith and trust in his providence. The way to our goal is not a checklist of commands we have compiled. Nor is it a secret formula that only a few can figure out. It is on every page of the Bible. It is a matter of trusting God more than ourselves and our achievements, valuing our relationship with him more than our own recognition, seeking to honor him instead of to be honored, and allowing for his providence in our lives. A sustaining faith allows God to be God, combines truth with grace, respects his mystery, and worships him in spirit, truth, humility, and gratefulness. Peace is a gift from God wrapped in the paradox of his grace.

Scripture References: Pss 37:3–4; 42:8; 51:6, 17; 62:1–2; 63:1–8; 84 10–12; 91:1–16; Eccl 9:17–18; Isa 32:17, 66:2; Mic 6:8; Matt 6:25–34, 8:23–27, 11:28–30, 14:28–33; Mark 8:21; Luke 10:38–42; John 4:23–24, 14:27, 17:3; Rom 1:17; 1 Cor 1:20–25; Eph 2:8–10; Heb 11:1 with 6.

93. Biblical Christians in Ordinary Life

Make it your ambition to lead a quiet life.

—*1 Thess 4:11*

THERE ARE NO PERFECT Christians. There never have been. But many have an honest and humble faith in God's grace and a steadfast allegiance to his purposes. Therein lies authentic Christianity. It is a realistic category of Christians loyal to Christ as God. They trust his work on their behalf and his providence in the circumstances of life. They know they are forgiven daily by his grace and loved by him. They desire God's will more than their own. They are resting, trusting, missional people who do not seek their own recognition but make God known—glorify him—in the ordinary routines of life. They find their identity, meaning, well-being, and peace in Christ rather than their achievements. Since they won't be talking about themselves, it may take you some time to figure out who they are and why they are content without mentioning their accomplishments or social position. But a well-placed question or two will reveal their lives are centered on someone other than themselves. In contrast to popular Christianity, which is superficial, biblical Christians are settled in their faith, secure in their identity in Christ, and confident in God's providence. They are becoming more devoted to God's purposes in their lives each day.

Instead of being shining stars of spiritual excellence, they are godly in the routine and commonplace things of life. The everyday honesty and reliability of biblical Christians win the respect of outsiders. A few are called to public life and ministry or to the Christian leadership of others, but all are called to a life of faithfulness to the God of their salvation. To trust him is of the highest order in our lives. It is the heart of any ministry to others.

93. BIBLICAL CHRISTIANS IN ORDINARY LIFE

Becoming a biblical Christian is a process rather than an event; some go through that process under more difficult circumstances than others. God's providence will look different in each person's life. The process is longer for some people, but the goal is the same. In our broken world, it is learning to trust him in difficulty or plenty, trials or blessings, sickness or health, even in our final walk through the valley of death. That, not perfection, is being in the center of God's will. Biblical Christians have not "arrived" but are *on their way* to maturity in Christ. They know that in all the ups and downs of life, he is at work in them "to will and to act according to his good purpose" (Phil 2:13), to "work in us what is pleasing to him" (Heb 13:20-21). They know his intervening and enduring love is behind the mystery of his providence and the paradox of his grace.

This providential work in us, this journey toward maturity in Christ, is made up of many events and experiences in our lives, sometimes shocking and tumultuous, sometimes peaceful and gentle, sometimes lonely and sometimes with friends, and sometimes just commonplace. These come together to serve his purpose if we can see it. It is like words with only dictionary meanings on their own brought together in an arrangement to build a larger meaning in a paragraph. The individual words are given context and purpose as they are carefully assembled and connected, leading to the author's construction of an idea or a conclusion.

God uses life events and experiences like words to write our story. We did not understand them at the time; they did not look like things God could use. But when put together, when we consider them in the light of the truth and grace revealed in the Bible and see the experiences of those in its stories (Joseph, Esther, Daniel, and so many others), we see his providence and purpose at work. He can use them in our lives, pulling them together into meaningful paragraphs, shaping us to trust him for today and tomorrow. Each story is unique and can serve his purpose; each character can be shaped into a biblical Christian if they trust him.

Scripture References: Gen 37:12-28 with 41:41-45 and 45:4-8; Esth 3:10-14 with 4:11-17 with 7:1—8:13; Pss 62:1-2 with 5-7; 63:1-5; 84:10-12; Prov 3:5-7 with 28:26; Isa 26:3; Dan 1:1-6 with 6:1-28; Matt 6:33, 11:29; John 14:27; Rom 5:1-2, 8:28-39; 2 Cor 5:15; Phil 2:12-13, 3:12-17, 4:4-9; 1 Thess 4:11; 1 Tim 2:1-4; Titus 1:1, 2:11-12; Heb 13:20-21; 1 Pet 4:2, 5:5-7; 1 John 1:5-10.

94. For the Love of God

They claim to know God, but by their actions they deny him.
—*Titus 1:16*

SOME PEOPLE IN LOVE with evangelical Christianity are missing the essence of the gospel. They may find it wholesome to be part of a church and find encouragement in the social interaction to keep them going. They may see it as a way to gain status, meet social expectations, or hide other distractions in their lives from those in their group. They may find people at church who will listen or who they imagine are listening to them as they go on and on about themselves. They may be pursuing their own agenda for personal achievement and affirmation. They may find that attending church helps assuage guilt, or they may not know what else to do on Sunday. However, the teachings of God's word do not make measurable changes in their approach to life and fundamental loyalties. They are what I call popular Christians.

We cannot tell if they are people of true faith or not. Christianity cannot save. Only God, in the work of Christ, has given us the way, and it is a way of faith demonstrated by humility, trustworthiness, and good works that honor God whether one is a member of a church or not. Of course, there is also the issue of what kind of teaching the church offers. Sometimes it leads people to believe that the church should be at the center of their loyalties. However, even good biblical teaching does not always move people to a functional and vibrant faith, an engagement with God that motivates their behavior. There is no substitute for the humility and trust required for them to rely on God's providence and welcome his work in their lives.

Popular Christians must move from loving Christianity or church to loving God, from syncretism with culture to trusting God's way, and from ritual to natural behavior representing Christ in daily life. This is biblical

94. FOR THE LOVE OF GOD

Christianity, and it will take a genuine conversion from the old life with Christianity tacked on to a new life of faith and trust in God alone. The love of God will be its motivating influence. Faithful churches teaching God's word will be its instruction and encouragement, and like-minded fellowship will be its reinforcement. Good works in love and consideration of others will be its sign to the world.

Scripture References: Matt 5:14–16, 9:16–17; John 4:23–24, 13:34–35, 15:12–13; Rom 12:1–2, 9–13; 14:5–11; 1 Cor 13:1–13; Gal 5:1–6; Eph 4:1–16; Phil 2:1–8; Col 2:6–8, 3:12–17; Heb 3:12–13 with 10:24–25; 11:6; 13:15–16; 1 Pet 2:12, 3:8–12; 1 John 3:16–18, 4:16.

95. Freedom from Cultural Conscience

Then you will know the truth, and the truth will set you free.
—John 8:32

SINCE HUMAN CULTURES EVOLVE as systems of solutions for the survival of a group of people, they become highly influential in people's lives. They are so essential and valuable that they are assumed to give us the only way to live. Cultures become so natural that, like fish in water, people are unaware of how much they depend on their value system and worldview or how powerfully these cultural elements control their behavior. But no cultural system is entirely functional for our survival. All are human and, therefore, flawed in their lack of biblical values and virtues at the core. When values and virtues wane, people, however irrational it is, come to chafe under the old restraints and boundaries of the system. They forget the problems the traditional values solved and disregard the principles that maintained the society. Then the old problems come back and exact their toll. This is the beginning of cultural decline and eventual disintegration.

However, the intended role of culture, though never entirely successful, is to ensure the well-being, security, and survival of individual members. It is not surprising, then, that Christians sometimes grant spiritual value to a human cultural theme, and it becomes a matter of conscience. These might be values of individualism, self-assertion, personal achievement, or an internal locus of control for North Americans and Western Europeans. An example would be when a Christian feels embarrassed and even guilty for not standing up for themselves or not taking advantage of an unfortunate event at someone else's expense. Western values say we should "take care of number one" and "nice guys finish last." If these Western values become attached to our definition of a good Christian, we are

95. FREEDOM FROM CULTURAL CONSCIENCE

confusing cultural absolutes with biblical absolutes. This causes a great deal of confusion. Who's in charge? And where do ultimate security, worth, and identity come from? What is real freedom like—freedom from guilt, social demands, fear of failure, dread, anxiety, and an uncertain future? Biblical solutions become confused with cultural solutions—a mixture that hardens the longer it sets.

The Jerusalem Council in Acts 15 dealt with this problem in early Christianity when converted Jews felt the law of Moses should still be binding on believers in Jesus, but the difficulty continues to plague us. Though the expression of biblical faith must be relevant in its cultural setting, if culture has the upper hand in shaping the truth to be expressed, at the very least, it creates uncertainty. It, more often, leads to legalism and false guilt, or syncretism and loss of biblical purpose, or a mysticism that seeks signs and wonders to confirm God's presence and approval. Freedom in Christ goes beyond culture to find its realization in God's word, though it must find its expression in cultural forms (words, activities, routines, products, etc.). We are free to use these forms with caution and discernment to serve God and further the gospel.

The boundary of this freedom of conscience is love for God and others. We are freed from anxiety by trusting God, giving us assurance and security as we rest in his good providence. The world's ways, our culture, cannot begin to provide this abundant life. And when society weighs down our conscience with its rules and regulations, it must be limited in its influence by God's word, our loyalty to him, and his grace in our lives.

Scripture References: Matt 5:8; John 8:31-36; Acts 15:1-29; Rom 14:5-8, 16-18, 22; 15:1-6; 1 Cor 9:19-23, 10:23-33; 2 Cor 4:4-6; Gal 5:1 with 6; Col 3:17; 1 Tim 1:18-19, 4:4-5, 6:17b; Titus 1:15-16; Jas 4:4; 1 Pet 2:16, 3:14-18; 1 John 2:15-17; 3:18-20, 4:1-6.

96. Early Impressions

Train a child in the way he should go.
—*Prov 22:6*

CHILDREN GAIN AN IMPRESSION of God and his ways from adults and the teachings and examples at church. Adults may not realize how much they are part of that impression. Though there is much they cannot understand at a young age, what children see in the lives of grown-ups, especially their parents, leaves an impression. As parents, we don't always give the best example of trusting God's providence. Or we let our strong preferences get in the way, such as an overbearing father from whom the child can never sense approval. This makes it difficult for the child to relate to God as their father and nearly impossible to understand and welcome his love and grace or that of others. But we can do better. One of the best examples we can give is the love, trust, acceptance, understanding, and grace parents have for each other.

We don't always feel very spiritual and are distracted by the many cares of earning and managing a living, social engagements, and being a parent. But in small ways, and by example, we are planting seeds in another life and must make the best effort to show them God's hand in creation, his true grace and love, and our freedom in Christ. You may never remember something you did that God used in a young heart. Later, when the world's distractions compete with the seeds of loyalty to God planted early on, the child, now adult, may falter, but God will use your example in their memory. Society intends to remove thoughts about God from young hearts, but impressions about God and his love and examples of trusting him from those they love and respect go deep and are not forgotten. Unfortunately,

96. EARLY IMPRESSIONS

impressions of legalism or mysticism will not be forgotten either and may keep them away from Christianity later in life.

Many are the soils of the hearts of men and women, but a child trained in the ways of God will not forget it when they are old. They may or may not trust God later, but if they do not, it will not be because they do not know about his grace. Many factors in the world will be competing for their hearts and minds, and many deceptions of the enemy will surround them. But we will have done what we could so that our children have the best chance of owning God's truths for themselves as we pray for God's work in their hearts.

Scripture References: Gen 3:1–7; Deut 6:4–9; Prov 4:1–27, 22:6; Eccl 7:8–9; Matt 13:1–9 with 18–23; Luke 1:37, 10:41–42 with Matt 13:22; John 1:12, 16:33; 2 Cor 11:13–15; Eph 6:4; Col 3:18–21; 1 Tim 4:4–5, 12; Titus 2:6–7; 1 Pet 5:8–9.

97. In the Stillness

... in the shadow of the Almighty.
—*Ps 91:1*

OUR MODERN CULTURE IS crowding into our understanding of how to approach God. Some acts are worshipful, such as Michelangelo painting the Sistine Chapel or chiseling the statue of David, the artisans building the tabernacle, or Handel composing the "Hallelujah" chorus. But not all is worship. And some of what we call worship may distract others from seeking this personal engagement with God. We see in the Bible that everything else stopped when Moses was in God's presence. Jesus sought solitude to talk to the Father. Isaiah was not distracted when he found himself before God's throne. Fear and awe, submission and humility, overwhelming gratefulness, and singular attention are aspects of worship, leading to and preparing us for a desire to honor and glorify God in our day-to-day lives and express our allegiance in obedience.

In church, we should consider God's holiness and mystery, the depth of his grace, the expanse of his power, glory, and majesty, and his particular love for us in this world. We do this in a community of those doing the same and respond in praise and prayer. Being together in worship can be a great encouragement. But we each need times of stillness in our busy lives to contemplate our relationship with him alone in humble submission and worship. Amid the clutter of our lives on earth, we must step back, look into the mirror of his word, and see ourselves as we are, him as he is—acknowledging our unworthiness but never forgetting his grace, power, love, and providence. The cool water of his grace extinguishes the hot coals—the burning memories of our despair, rejection, abuse, or guilt. We are his, and,

97. IN THE STILLNESS

in the stillness of his presence, we continue to rest in the peaceful but powerful shadow of the Almighty.

Scripture References: Exod 33:7–11; Pss 33:18; 34:15 and 18; 46:10; 62:5; 91:1–2, 14–16; 91:1; 95:6–7; 100:1–5; 121:1–8; Isa 6:1–8; Hos 6:6; Mic 6:8; Matt 6:1–8, 14:23; John 4:23–24; Eph 2:1–10; 2 Tim 3:17; Titus 2:11–14 with Isa 43:1; Jas 1:22–25; 1 John 1:8–10.

98. Miracles

The heavens declare the glory of God.
—Ps 19:1

WE DON'T KNOW HOW aware of it they were at creation, but miracles surrounded Adam and Eve on every side. Every tree, every animal, and every bug were miraculous examples of God's power and wisdom. Perhaps more remarkable than all was the miracle of each other before them. It, of course, was not the kind of place we, in the modern West, would expect it to be. No electricity, plumbing, transportation, internet, AI, or smartphones existed. But, then, most of what God does is not what we would expect, yet everything in his works is a miracle. We have come to accept the miracles around us as the ordinary order of things, and we spend a great deal of time, effort, and resources adapting them to suit us. Having normalized the truly miraculous, we wish for miracles outside that norm. But we are wrong. We need to appreciate the miracles already there to know something about the nature of their Creator and his powerful providence that is still at work today.

Not only is the creation a universe of miracles, but the God of that creation pouring out his grace on us, who, like Adam and Eve, have made many wrong and selfish choices in life, is the greatest miracle of all. In his patience, he waits for us to choose that grace, and then, in his providence, he cares for us, seeking to develop in us a patient faith in him and loyalty to his purposes for humankind and the universe as a whole. Truly, God is good, his lovingkindness is forever, his purposes are just, his grace is overwhelming, and miracles belong to him.

98. MIRACLES

Scripture References: Gen 1:31—2:1; Pss 19:1-14, 34:4, 33:1-11, 100:5, 139:13-18; Prov 3:5-7; Matt 6:25-34; John 1:1-3; Rom 3:21-24; Eph 2:1-10; Phil 1:6, 2:12-13; Col 1:15-16; 2 Pet 3:9; Rev 4:11.

99. Improvements to Worship

True worshipers will worship the Father in spirit and truth.
—John 4:23

HUMAN SKILLS ATTEMPT TO bring improvement to worship. It seems to have been relatively simple in the early church, but today social expectations around us have their influence. Professional worship leaders design high-tech worship experiences. More and more resources are being given to the equipment for worship experiences to meet our need for involvement in worship, get emotions going in the "right" direction, and get people out of the boredom or apathy their everyday lives seem to instill. But how much of our culture's influence is good for our worship of God? No one seems to know, and no one is asking.

However, not everyone is excited about this energetic trend in churches. Some people present are not apathetic. They come in the door ready, with a passion to learn more about and contemplate the God they worship in spirit and in truth, in reverence and in awe. These often need fewer distractions, not more. They may be more reserved in their worship; the flurry of excitement is not their primary objective. The simplicity of bowing before the Creator of the universe in the silence of humility, deep chords of gratefulness, and subdued tones of adoration may be more what they anticipate and need. They may feel that the intense tones of a minor key help them in worship more than lights and rhythm. Words are sometimes wholly inadequate. There must be room for silence before the mysteries and wonders of our great God, who has put his name on his own. It is often then that the Spirit stirs the souls of these more quiet worshipers to see themselves next to their Creator, causing repentance, worship, and wonder from the depths of their being to emerge.

99. IMPROVEMENTS TO WORSHIP

The music and prayers of human voices in the community before God are important to this expression of worship, but the reserved soul may find some of today's trends distracting. That does not make him or her more spiritual, just different. And, lest our emphasis on the reserved here make worship seem overly somber, we must be reminded that humility, trust, and gratitude are a matter of the heart for everyone, and cause music and prayer to fulfill their purpose for anyone, the reserved or the expressive. Worship leaders today have the challenge of helping both introverts and extroverts express their inner worship. But our culture tells us extroverts succeed in life. That brings us to the question of what a "successful" church looks like, sounds like, and acts like.

The more culture influences our means and methods of worship, the more danger there is that the results will emulate those of the culture—professional achievement, celebrity status, entertainment, etc. We must take care that our purposes are the same as God's for the church, worship, and service to him in the world. And we must encourage the sincerity of the heart in worship as in all other aspects of living for God. Before making the next "improvement" to worship, we need to ask why. After we look at the cultural reasons and the biblical teachings and examples concerning the change, we may be able to make an honest and reasoned decision about the meaning, values, and motives involved. It is sure that not everyone will agree with a change or the lack of one. Personality, age, and experience differences exist among us, and popular Christianity does not mix well with biblical Christianity. If we can just remember that it is always a matter of the heart. Outward activities are secondary.

Scripture References: Pss 51:6; 95:1–7, especially 6–7; 100:1–5; 145:18–19; Prov 17:3, 21:2–3, 22:4; Hos 6:6; Matt 6:1–8 with John 5:44; Matt 15:8–9; Luke 6:12; John 4:21–24; Acts 2:42–47; Heb 12:28–29; Jude 24–25.

100. Glorify (?) God in Our Lives

Whatever you do, do it all for the glory of God.

—*1 Cor 10:31*

WHEN WE USE THE word *glorify* in daily conversations, we may mean a makeover of something plain, a renovation, or the addition of some attribute to an ordinary object to make it look better than it is. But God is not asking us to add glory to him in these ways. We cannot add anything to God. As strange as the expression is in Western culture, Christian use and interest in the word pertaining to God is prolific these days. We usually mean to worship or praise him; to that end, it is often translated as "praise." But it has a more specific meaning.

Glory in the Old Testament spoke of the significance and weightiness of God, the magnitude of his worth, power, and lovingkindness. To glorify God meant to elevate or to *make known* the extent of his goodness, attributes, grace, and providence in the world and our lives. Though glorifying God is part of worship, it goes beyond that to how we live our lives before a watching world. How we interact with our families and neighbors, care for the unfortunate, carry out our vocation, encourage justice, or love one another glorifies God, or it does not. It makes his attributes known or hides them from the world. These good works point to him, and their absence denies his existence. We must bear fruit that glorifies God—makes him known—in all we do.

Scripture References: Isa 24:14–16, 28:5–6, 44:23; Matt 5:14–16; Luke 5:22–26; John 8:54, 12:20–29, 13:31–35, 14:11–13, 15:7–8, 16:14, 17:20–23; Acts 11:18; Rom 15:5–6; 1 Cor 10:31; Gal 5:22–23; Eph 2:10 with 2 Tim 3:17 and Titus 1:15–16, 2:14 and 3:1, 8, and 14; Phil 2:9–11; Col 3:17; 2 Thess 1:9–12; Heb 13:15–16; 1 Pet 2:12.

101. What Is Your Name?

Yet to all who received him, to those who believed in his name, he gave the right to become the children of God.

—*John 1:12*

IN THE PATRILINEAL, STATUS-ORIENTED, honor-and-shame society, names in the Bible were far more meaningful than they are for us in our day. Names carried the authority, honor, and values of one's father and maintained the family lineage. They spoke of God's hand in the people's history, beliefs, and traditions. Shame, the strongest social sanction, and honor, the highest social standing of a parent, would be attached to the family name and, therefore, to descendants, bringing social blessing or punishment for three or four generations for the sin or honorable actions of an ancestor.

In this social context, names for God were important as the outward recognition of his power, glory, singleness, authority, and grace. People acknowledged something about God using the significance and implications of names given to him. When they heard the name El Shaddai (Almighty One), they were reminded of his power to do anything he purposed to do. When they called him El Elyon (Most High God), they acknowledged he was the supreme God above all gods. *Yahweh-Jireh* means the LORD will provide. Depending on how you count them, there are some twenty names of God in the Bible. Making these attributes about him known through his names and their faithfulness to him was to glorify him among the nations. God rescues, protects, answers, accompanies, delivers, honors, and satisfies those who acknowledge his name (Ps 91:14–16).

Believers in the New Testament were first called Christians at Antioch. It was a weighty matter in that day. They were not only followers, but their lives echoed the values Jesus expressed in his life. As God's children, we, too, have taken on the name of Christ, and, today, our lives are to become indicators of his significance in the world, and pass that on to the next generation. To acknowledge him for who he is in everything we do is to glorify him in our lives. It is all about letting God be God and making the significance and consequences of that known. To acknowledge his name is to recognize all he is and all he does and has done. He is the Savior of all those who know his name and trust his grace.

God sent Jesus, whose name describes him. The name Jesus (*Yeshua* in transliterated Hebrew), the equivalent of Joshua in the Old Testament, means "God saves" or "The LORD is salvation." We remember the angel's reason for his name: "for he shall save his people from their sins" (Matt 1:21). Those who carry his name are to go along in life ("As you are going" in Matt 28:19a) in a way that signifies they belong to God's lineage as his children, being loyal to his purposes and making his grace known in their day-to-day lives. This is the essential component in influencing others to listen to the gospel and become his disciples. And because we who acknowledge him love and trust him, he is our ultimate security and protection, and he will honor us. Think of it. God will honor faithful people not because they are perfect but because they acknowledge his name and, as part of the family (lineage group), are covered by the righteousness of Christ.

Scripture References: Exod 20:4-6 with 34:6-7; 33:17; Pss 9:10; 20:1 with 6-8; 29:2; 37:3-6 with 23-24; 89:8, 14-18; 91:14-16; 139:7-12; 148:13; Prov 3:5-7; Isa 43:10-13; Mic 4:5; Matt 1:20-23, 28:18-20; John 1:12, 12:26, 14:15-21; Acts 4:12, 11:19-26; Eph 1:15-23, 2:8-10, 5:17-20; Phil 2:9-11.

102. The Fear of God

The fear of the LORD is the beginning of wisdom, and knowledge of the Holy One is understanding.

—*Prov 9:10*

THE FEAR OF GOD is a heightened sense and careful regard for his sovereign power, ultimate justice, sufficient grace, and omniscient providence that he brings to the lives and situations of those who acknowledge him. It can bring joy to the salvation of those who honor his ways or devastation to those who disregard him—the unmerited favor of salvation or the furious fire of judgment. Acknowledging the consequences and magnitude of these extremes in his person and making them known is to glorify God. Mystery and awe are on one side of this fear. But respect for his sovereignty, humility in his presence, utter dependence on his providence, hope in his unfailing love, and gratefulness for his grace are also responses of his people, giving them overwhelming confidence. Their security is sure. The terror and dread of this fear await only those who refuse to acknowledge him. Those who "rest in the shadow of the Almighty" are delivered (Ps 91:1–7).

Isaiah's vision of meeting God in his heavenly temple was exceptional, but his response was not so extraordinary. He responded in the *only way possible* for one who already knew of God's glory and now saw it. The contrast with his people was only too obvious, and his reaction was an attitude of total resignation, an overwhelming humility lost in our day. In the Bible, you will never find someone talking about being in God's presence or experiencing God's glory with casual informality or flippant clichés. The God who saves us from every enemy is not cozy; his justice is administered as an intolerable purifying fire, and it always prevails. Were we not covered by his grace for even a moment, we would be consumed, but because we are in his care, the sheep of his pasture, his children, we rejoice. The fear of the Lord and humbly receiving his grace are our salvation.

The Bible also tells us that the fear of the Lord leads to wisdom for life, the rewards of which, though they vary for different people, are listed as life, riches (not necessarily material), honor, protection, peace, and blessings. It is worth any cost and is the supreme purpose of life in the book of Proverbs. It seems strange that we should overlook this outcome of the fear of the Lord, but it is natural for those of a culture of doing rather than being, of achievement rather than prudence, and of self-assertion rather than patient faith. However, those who fear God are not limited by their cultural situation. They are indeed free of its limitations.

Scripture References: Exod 3:1–6; Job 28:28; Pss 16:5–11; 19:9; 32:10; 33:11, 18; 73:23–28; 89:8 with 14–16; 91:14–16; 96:6–9; 100:3; 147:1, 6a, 11; Prov 1:7; 3:5–7, 13–17 with 4:1–13; 9:10; 10:27; 14:27; 15:16, 33; 17:3, 24; 22:4; Isa 6:1–8, 11:1–3a; Lam 3:22; Hab 2:14 with 20; John 1:12, 8:31 and 36; Gal 6:7–8; 1 Thess 1:9–10, 5:1–11; Heb 10:26–27, 12:28–29; Jas 3:13–18; 1 Pet 1:17; 2 Pet 3:1–7.

103. Religion or Righteousness

For Christ died for sins ... the righteous for the unrighteous, to bring you to God.

—1 Pet 3:18

WHEN WE ACCEPT GOD'S grace in the gospel, God covers us with the righteousness of Jesus Christ. Our relationship with him is assured on that basis, not a life lived perfectly on our part. Then he sets his moral will and desires before us, and we see even more how his grace in our forgiveness is always needed and present. He shows us how he is the alternative to what our culture offers as thin solutions for emotional and social survival and that religion is not capable of the ultimate solution for our salvation. We learn that the temporal survival of the self is not the point of life. There is an existence outside this world, the meaning of which is well beyond this one. Mankind lives in the shadow of a spiritual universe known only to those who open their eyes to Christ.

Human culture has no dimension for the real thing, this spiritual universe. It is the old wineskin, dry and stiff. Religion may be used to attempt to fill this cracked wineskin of culture, sometimes becoming the central theme. However, ritual behavior is human activity that never reaches the reality of a grace relationship with God that he initiates with us in offering Christ's righteousness. The parched skin of our culture cannot expand to include this reality of God in the world. It takes a new wineskin. We must start over, beginning with God, and putting culture in its place. To know him this way is an intentional choice of the heart and results in experiencing meaning and purpose in this life and our ultimate survival, an eternal presence with God. It is not about our performance or our circumstances. It is about being renewed, born again, redeemed from the old, and walking into the new. It is, and always has been, a matter of the heart, and results in the rewards of trusting him, some now, some much later in life, and some after this life.

Scripture References: 2 Kgs 6:15–17; Job 19:25–27; Pss 33:11, 53:1, 73:25–26; Prov 16:2, 17:3, 21:3; Isa 29:13; Ezek 33:30–33; Hos 6:6; Matt 5:3–10, 7:13–14; John 3:3, 5–7, 36; 4:21–26; 10:7–10; 14:1–6; Acts 4:12; Rom 5:6–11, 11:33–36, 12:1–2; 1 Cor 2:6–10; 2 Cor 5:15–18a, 21; 1 Tim 2:5; 1 Pet 3:18.

104. Beauty with Tremors

> I pray also . . . that you may know . . . his incomparably great power for us who believe.
>
> —Eph 1:17-19

THE SAME WIND CAN be a gentle breeze or a roaring, devastating tornado. We climb a majestic mountain with wonder and exhilaration while it is also a sleeping volcano of enormous energy capable of frightful destruction. We are struck with the beauty but also feel the tremors. Our God of grace and lovingkindness is also a consuming fire, and those two perspectives come together for the attentive person reading the Scriptures. Gratefulness for his grace is combined with respect for his power, just as the joyful warmth of the sun comes from a raging cauldron of unbearable heat and penetrating light. Beauty, love, mystery, and power meet in him. His ultimate justice and quiet grace come together in our salvation. We may feel breathless and overwhelmed, yet the immense energy of his good providence moves in our small lives, making way for his purposes in us. We converse in prayer with the Creator-God, the power of the universe, but also our loving and patient Father. He who rules all knows us; we are his, and no other power can change it.

As we humble ourselves and trust him, this powerful God will lift us up "in due time" (1 Pet 5:6) to honor him in the way he gives us. We cannot add to God's glory or diminish it, but we can "glorify him" when, in our lives and message, we make him known as he really is in the world around us. And we must. For mankind must know him, who can make flowers of beauty come up from the ashes of our lives. But the door may not be open for much longer. His patience will not endure forever.

Scripture References: Pss 25:9, 96:9; Nah 1:7–8; John 3:12–21, 8:12; Rom 11:33–36; Eph 1:15–23; Phil 1:6 with 2:12–13; 1 Thess 5:1–11; 2 Thess 1:5–10, 2:16–17; Heb 10:26–31, 12:25–29; 1 Pet 5:6–7; 2 Pet 3:3–15a; Rev 22:7, 12, 20.

105. God's Work

Though he stumble, he will not fall, for the LORD upholds him with his hand.

—Ps 37:24

GOD IS AT WORK in us so that we might desire to act according to his purposes—in accord with the true nature of reality instead of human assumptions about reality. Human understanding places an evolved mankind at the center of his world; achieving personal success and individual well-being are his sole purposes in life. But the true nature of reality is centered on the Creator-God, the cause of all that is good and infinite. This God of grace and power sits on the throne of the universe as the ultimate reality. As a result, we who know him obtain the lasting well-being and lavish rewards he bestows. He is at work in us, making himself known and his promises clear through his word. God's purpose is carried out in us as we learn to trust his power, providence, and purposes in our lives. This power of God raised Jesus from the grave and is displayed in our salvation.

So does God expect us to live the Christian life just as we are? No, there is a "letting go" demanded of us, but it is not of our efforts to honor his will and walk worthy of the gospel. Instead, we must let go of culture's solutions for our pain and survival and the self-centered motives they give us. It is letting go of social rewards and putting our reputation, relationships, well-being, and happiness in his hands. We can only do this if we *trust* him for it all. There should be no looking back except to remember that from which he has saved us.

We are not always so good at letting go. The last paragraph may make it sound easy and even natural for the Christian to "trust him for it all." But it is not easy or natural. That is why we are reminded over and over to trust him in the Bible. Trusting him for the damaging experiences of our past and the emotional baggage they have left with us will take determination and endurance. We are bruised reeds near breaking, smoldering wicks about to go out, but he will care for our injuries and compensate for our weaknesses as we grow in our loyalty to him.

Many of us have been trapped in harsh situations by a clever adversary. But it is not God's intention for us. There is a way out. He will honor our desire to trust him and bring it to fruition in our lives as we keep that desire and hope before us. We are never perfect in our walk with God, but he looks at our hearts and fills their longings with his purposes for us. In Ps 37:1–6, replace "evil men" in verse 1 with the enemies of your life: evil thoughts, negative self-talk, flat emotions, anxiety, feelings of guilt and doubt, or of never achieving enough to sense God's approval. Then follow the advice of verses 3–5. You will arrive at the results in verse 6, and a reminder to wait on God in verse 7. He is at work in your life.

Scripture References: Pss 37:1–7; 73:23, 28; 91:14–16; 130:5–6 with Isa 40:31; Ps 145:13–19; Prov 3:5–7; Lam 3:25–26; Matt 6:33, 12:20; Luke 9:62; John 15:7; Rom 1:16, 8:38–39, 12:1–2; 1 Cor 6:19–20; Eph 1:15–23; Phil 1:6, 2:12–13, 3:12–16, 4:4–9; Heb 6:1, 13:20–21; 1 Pet 1:17–21, 3:18, 5:6.

106. Bargaining with God

Trust in the LORD with all your heart and lean not on your own understanding; in all your ways acknowledge him, and he will make your paths straight.

—*Prov 3:5–6*

WHEN WE SAY TO ourselves that God may give us this if we do that, we are bargaining with the God of the universe. We are attempting to obligate him to meet our needs. A few years ago, someone told me they hoped God would forgive them for missing church one Sunday. This tally sheet mentality holds many back from experiencing a relationship of grace and freedom with God in Christ. It keeps them trapped in a popular Christianity that remains superficial. We cannot bargain with God and do not earn karma chips for doing what we think he demands of us. He is not a vending machine where you get the item you want if you put in the right amount of money. God does not want your money or your works; he wants your heart, your loyalty, your will. He wants you.

When God has our hearts, what we do can honor him, so it is less about doing and more about being. What you do that honors him will result from knowing him, from loyalty and trust, not from a guilty conscience. It will not be done with a begrudging spirit but with a grateful heart. If we put what we do for God into a favor bank, thinking now that he is in our debt he will have to come through for us, we will one day find that our works did not tip the scales in our favor. It is not about working for God to get what you want but about trusting him for who he is and having confidence in *his* providence for our lives.

So, all along, God has been measuring the genuineness of our faith—a matter of the heart. We cannot bluff our way through or push the right buttons to get him to do things for us. Above all, he is not measuring our feelings but our loyalty, which is a matter of the will. That is where he wants us to be "perfect," that is, complete (Matt 19:21). Feelings typically come along the way as a result. We will often feel grateful, confident, and secure as we trust him, and our works for him, and the love and unity that come with them, will become the signs or marks of that loyalty to outsiders. But, even so, emotions are not a reliable indication of this commitment. We cannot make ourselves feel "spiritual" all the time. Efforts to do so will take us away from his purposes, not toward them. We will have to trust him more than ourselves for our hearts to be filled with the gratefulness and peace he intends. He will lead us to this end, but we will have to follow.

Scripture References: Deut 8:2–3; Pss 37:1–7, 40:6–8, 51:16–17; Prov 3:5–7, 16:2, 17:3; Isa 26:3–4, 12–13; 66:2b; Hos 6:6; Joel 2:12–13; Mic 6:8; Matt 5:9, 12:1–8, 15:7–9, 16:24–26; John 8:32 with 36; 14:27 with 16:33; Gal 5:1; Phil 4:4–9; 1 Tim 4:4–5; Heb 11:6.

107. God's Sovereignty

This is good, and pleases God our Savior, who wants all men to be saved and come to a knowledge of the truth.

—*1 Tim 2:3-4*

WE KNOW GOD TO be entirely free in his movements and decisions. He alone acts as he will; no one can undo what he does; no one can stop him. But his purpose for creation is not without its mysteries, especially the paradox of his lavish grace. In his wisdom and providence, he has maintained one intention that requires an external cause. He intends that the essence of human life be a relationship with him. Any relationship must depend on intentional choice, trust, and loyalty. In his sovereignty, he has given this freedom of choice to humankind. Once we understand what he asks, we will or will not choose to be his. God elected from eternity past that all who, when they hear and believe the word of truth, embrace Jesus as Christ and accept his grace through the cross would be included for eternal life. It is his fixed decree that it should be thus, and no one can change his will. We can play with words and arrange Bible verses to say something different, but we cannot force God's hand. His decree stands.

It was a decision of costly love for God. As pearls among the swine, it is often a tragic love trampled in the mud. He risked a great deal in giving this free will to humankind. His love and devotion for his creation were behind that risk, for true faith, loyalty, and love are voluntary. It is a choice to love and trust him. In the Old Testament, God longs for his chosen people to enter the land he promised them, but the generation he brought out of Egypt refused to trust him and died in the wilderness. Today, he longs for people to have peace and contentment in this broken world and all that is reserved for his bride in the next, which blessings come only through choosing him. Those who reject that love will live forever without it.

We should not be surprised that the gospel is not transforming the world. It is intended to transform people in that world. Jesus said they would be few. The broad road is enticing, and the enemy treacherous in his lies about God. Those who choose God's way will be like flowers here and there coming up out of the ashes people have made of our societies. Beautiful is their faith to God, who have chosen his way. They are his through the righteousness of Christ who made it possible, a righteousness they chose to receive as a gift held out to them by the sovereign God and Creator of the universe. And out of gratitude for unmerited favor they cannot repay, they give him their hearts. Yes, God wants something he has decided not to take for himself. He wants our true loyalty and trust; he wants you and me.

Scripture References: Pss 33:11; 73:23, 28; Isa 43:10–13, 46:10; Matt 7:13–29; John 3:16–21, 36 with Eph 1:11–14 and Titus 1:1–2; Rom 5:1, 8:1 with 28–39; Eph 2:1–6; Phil 3:18–21; Col 1:21–23, 2:13–15; 2 Thess 1:5–10; Titus 2:11, 3:3–8; 2 Pet 3:9; 1 John 4:7–8.

108. Good Is Evil, Evil Is Good?

But the chief priests and the elders persuaded the crowd to ask for Barabbas and to have Jesus executed.

—Matt 27:20

WHAT HAPPENS TO A society if the people decide that the old ideas of good and bad are antiquated or that things and behaviors thought good and respectable by older generations were actually abuses, that what they called evil is actually good and what they called good is evil? This would mean, of course, that those original people were not very good. In fact, they were very bad people, and they taught their children to be bad people. But the more unthinkable crimes are happening today after the influence of older generations on society has been marginalized. Mass shootings of innocent people, road rage, and car bombs are relatively recent social problems threatening our survival that come from the disintegration of society. They are no more the fault of guns and cars than dinner plates are of obesity. The responsibility lies with a society that has removed certain meanings and values of life for a lie.

Though people have never been perfect, much of what those past generations of Western society called good has its roots in the Bible, so today's "progressive" people say it, too, is evil. By their acidic determination to cancel God, they remove the only moral standard for humankind, the only authentic freedom in Christ, and open the door to any and all abuse of God's creation. They install the gods of human power, pleasure, and wealth, the god of self. They teach children that there are no wrong roads, that any destination they choose is right for them. But calling good evil and evil good is thinking that ends somewhere. Forcing this unreasoned blindness on the masses results in something. Many outspoken "experts" in our

Western society today would like to think they know what that is. But they do not. These leave devastation in their wake while they make the world a "better place" for themselves. But while thinking they are clever, they are headed for the darkest night.

The ignorance not only prevails, it grows deeper. And it is nothing new. Previous civilizations have done the same and shown us the result. They are gone forever. As it was in the days of Noah and later in the days of the prophets when the Jews turned away from God and were taken from their land by the enemy, it is among us today. It is not unforeseen except by those who accept human philosophies over God's revealed truth. This social corrosion set in motion by those who deny God and their effort to gag and cuff any who would try to stop it leads to an end for them that is fatal and final.

The leaders of the Jews were just as blind in the days of Jesus. Having missed the birth of the Messiah altogether, they were busy substituting their own ideas about God's laws that denied his true intentions, something Jesus contradicts in his early sermon on the mountainside. Lost in their theology and drunk with the prestige and power their control of the masses gave them, they led the people away from God and his intentions for them. The entire chapter of Matt 23 gives us Jesus' evaluation of the hypocritical blindness of these foolish leaders. The scathing criticism rings in our ears: "Better a millstone tied to their necks and they be thrown into the sea" (Luke 17:2). Harsh words for the God of love? Yes, our God is good, but is also a consuming fire. His dreadful vengeance toward those who led people away from him and strong vindication of the innocent and forgiven cannot be missed.

We no longer have to guess where the modern-day movement to erase God from the minds of the people may end for its perpetrators. Unless they turn to him, God will, in the end, erase them from the earth as he prophesied to do to the Amalikites and later to Babylon. It may be a dark world in which we must be light, but there is tremendous hope for those who belong to God, for no matter what happens, "The LORD Almighty is with us" (Ps 46:7). He is our refuge and strength, the Savior of all who will come to him, and he *will* be exalted in the earth.

Scripture References: Exod 17:8 and 13–14 with 1 Sam 15:2–3; Pss 37:1–6, 7–11; 46:1–11; 73:27–28; 91:1–16; Prov 17:13, 21:3; Isa 1:1–4; 5:7, 12, 20–21; 13:1 with 9–13 and 19–20; 59:14–15; Jer 9:23–24; Hos 6:6, 14:9; Amos 5:7, 14–15; Mic 3:1–2a, 6:8; Nah 1:3; Hab 1:1–4; Matt 5:1—7:28, 23:1–39, 24:36–51, 27:15–23; Luke 6:43–45, 17:1–2; Rom 2:5–11, 12:17–21; Heb 12:28–29; 1 John 1:5–10; 3 John 11.

109. Look at Me

But many who are first will be last, and many who are last will be first.
—Matt 19:30

THE CULTURAL URGENCY FOR people in the West is to establish an identity and achieve recognition and affirmation as someone special. It might be through wealth, performance, looks, outrageous behavior, or the self-assertion we are taught is necessary for survival in Western society. People seek a reputation. We believe admiration and respect will lead to feelings of meaning, belonging, and self-worth. Individualist cultures like that in North America and Western Europe do not offer other options for feelings of security. But this thin and fragile feeling of social acknowledgment is short lived. People attached to it have to constantly remind others of their attainments, or succeed in other achievements that meet individualist expectations, so they can move back into the light of social distinction and feel at ease with themselves again. It becomes a lifetime of seeking approval and maintaining status.

Such is the individualist's situation in their culture, and it becomes an addiction. The need for personal and social survival is no less desperate in collective cultures, though the goal looks very different, and the avenues to it are not the same. What if these values and their attitudes enter the door of the church? What if those claiming Christ are still trapped in this worldly passion for identity and recognition? What if their actions toward God are done to seek his approval or recognition from others? What if they are in search of becoming "Christian" celebrities? Jesus had words on that for the Pharisees. Through their actions and attitudes, they always said, "Look at me." Nothing could be less biblical, no behavior less typical of Jesus' example. And yet many Western "Christian" lives are compromised by these values of individualism. The word for mixing cultural absolutes with biblical truth is *syncretism*. It is a mixture of elements that resembles neither of the original ingredients. And the longer it sets, the harder it gets. We have yet to learn that the first will be last. Our identity must rest on our relationship with God through Christ. If we do not trust God for our reputation, we are not letting him be God. We belittle the sacrifice of Christ and ignore his providence in our lives.

Scripture References: Prov 3:5–7; 15:33; 16:5, 18; 26:12; 28:26; Isa 66:2b; Matt 5:3–10; 6:1–8; 16:24–26; 19:16–22 with 29–30; 20:16, 25–28; Luke 9:25, 12:15–21, 18:9–14; John 5:44, 8:44; Gal 6:3; Jas 3:13–18, 4:1–10; 1 John 2:15–17, 4:1–6.

110. Hard Times

If we are thrown into the blazing furnace, the God we serve is able to save us. But even if he does not . . . we will not serve your gods.

—Dan 3:17–18

COMING TO KNOW GOD through Christ gives us a new understanding of reality. His word tells us what is really true and possible in our lives and the world around us. We own new values about what is good or bad, what is honoring to him, or what is a breach of our new loyalty. We are asked to live in light of these new realities in our decisions and behavior. We are no longer prisoners of our culture's ways of survival, no longer victims of its blackmail. It is not that we never sin but that our culture's selfish ways and interests are no longer in charge of our hearts and minds, nor do we want to serve them.

If we trust his love for us, his wisdom, and his powerful providence in our lives, we can rest in him. The worry, fear, anger, frustrations, and anxiety that used to motivate our behavior are examples of not trusting God in difficulties. He has given us his way to know well-being and security. We will grow increasingly in our habit of trusting and resting in him. It is not a secret that we need to discover nor a miracle for which we must wait. Will there be hard times, disappointments, illnesses, accidents, and sorrows along the way in this broken world? Of course. Since Eden, there always have been. In the worst of times, the earth splitting and mountains quaking, the sea roaring and pounding, raging wars and falling kingdoms, whether literal or figurative of our lives, God asks us to "be still" and know that he is God (Ps 46:10); he reminds us that he "is with us" (46:7) and is our "refuge and strength" and "help in trouble" (46:1).

AN INTERVENING LOVE

We must grow in allowing his care, good providence, and love to relieve our anxieties. For there is nothing this broken world can do to us that cancels his love for his own. There is no surging storm that he cannot still if we wait on him, for "God is our refuge and strength, an ever-present help in trouble" (46:1). When life is severe, we never need despair. Though we may not feel like it, he is with us and accomplishing his purposes in and for us to the end of the age.

Look at the examples of good people that are given to us in the Bible. They knew hard experiences and difficult circumstances. That is the world we live in, disfigured by human choice. But we are never alone, and the suffering is temporary in light of his plan for us and for the world. His providence is at work, bringing about his purposes in all of this. It is for us to trust him. We will know difficulties, but we will know who bears them with us and find contentment in him. We will also know times of joy and deep satisfaction because of his gifts to us. These also will comfort us in demanding and troublesome times as we keep our hearts set on things above.

Scripture References: Josh 1:9; Pss 9:9–10; 23:4; 37:1–11; 46:1–11; 62:5–8; 73:28; 84:10–12; 91:14–16; 118:1–9; 119:71 with 92–93; 130:5–6 with Isa 40:31; Ps 138:6–8; Lam 3:24–26, 33; Matt 28:20b; John 16:33 and 17:15 with 14:27; Rom 5:1–4, 8:18, 12:1–2; 2 Cor 4:16–18, 11:21b–29; Phil 2:12–13 with Matt 28:20b; Phil 3:7–11; Col 3:1–4; 1 Thess 3:1–5; 2 Tim 10:10–17; Heb 13:5b; Jas 1:1–18, 5:7–11; 1 Pet 1:3–7, 4:12–16, 5:10–11.

111. I Have Been Wronged

Make every effort to live in peace with all men.... See to it... that no bitter root grows up to cause trouble and defile many.

—Heb 12:14–15

PAUL BECAME FRUSTRATED WITH the Christians at Corinth. Among other things, they were taking each other to court to resolve their grievances. After some advice on handling these things among themselves, he tells them that if they cannot come to an agreement, "Why not rather be wronged?" (1 Cor 6:7). It would be better to be cheated than to disgrace the name of Christ. These are hard words for the Western Christian.

Our culture comes in the door of the church with us, bringing our sense of personal ownership, "my rights," and the self-assertion it trains us to use with it. We do not realize the danger this presents. Even among Christians, sometimes kindness and consideration do not come to mind readily when we are wronged. When someone takes advantage of us, takes what is *ours*, beats us out of what we have coming to us, surpasses us where we ought to be recognized, our culture trains us to assert our rights or retaliate with litigation. This cultural conditioning might allow strong emotions to push patience and wisdom aside, even in the church. But those reactions are part of the old wineskin, and it must be replaced.

When we are wronged by other Christians, we learn how strong our trust in God really is. When we should be walking in the confidence of having seen his hand on our lives in the past and in our present salvation, we are inclined instead toward defensiveness. As individualists, in our old life, we have had to call on our self-assertion for personal survival—to hold up our pride, preserve our image, protect our interests, and claim the respect of others. When the old ways come out among believers, the harmony and love we are to emulate, that which should set us apart in the eyes of the world, is lost. The new wine has been put in the old wineskin, resulting in disaster. We must not allow it among us. The constant reminders for unity and harmony among believers in Jesus' ministry and the letters of the apostles to the early churches tell us how badly we need to maintain it and how often we forget it.

His grace is sufficient in every way. We no longer need the old understandings that kept us in a prison of what is only humanly true or possible—the old, culturally bound solutions for personal identity, feelings of security, and self-worth. Our emotional, mental, and spiritual survival is now secure no matter what the world dishes out or what other "believers" may do. He fulfills all our needs. Now we must trust him. Now we know the truth, and it sets us free from the demands and requirements of the old life. Now there is room for humility, kindness, patience, consideration, and wisdom ... that the world might know that God's love has intervened.

Scripture References: Pss 37:3–11, 90:10–12, 138:8; Prov 16:18–19; Eccl 7:8–12; Matt 5:9; John 8:31–32 with 35; 13:34–35; 17:20–23; Rom 12:17–18, 15:1–6; 1 Cor 6:1–8, 13:4–7; 2 Cor 5:15–18; 9:8; 12:7–10, 20–21; Gal 5:13–15; Phil 2:1–8, 4:4–9; Col 2:13–15; 1 Thess 4:11; Heb 12:14–15; Jas 3:13–18, 4:1–10, 5:7–11; 1 Pet 2:16–17, 23–25; 3:13–17; 2 Pet 1:3–11.

112. The Power of Darkness Undone

Whoever follows me will never walk in darkness, but will have the light of life.

—*John 8:12*

THE DARK POWERS OF Satan are all around us in this world. But we have been called "out of darkness into his wonderful light" (1 Pet 2:9), rescued by our conquering God "from the dominion of darkness, and brought into the kingdom of the Son he loves" (Col 1:13–14). That light shines in the darkness as it did on the first day of creation, and the darkness cannot extinguish it. This is God's power, the same that raised Jesus from the dead, working on our behalf so that we might be free of Satan's power, the world's deception, and, ultimately, death itself. His overwhelming and irreversible justice through Jesus' death and resurrection is stamped deep on the souls of all who believe—sons and daughters of light.

In the past, you may not have experienced trust, or even had your trust in someone else betrayed. Some have not known it, even with parents, siblings, or friends. These harsh conditions may make it difficult, but God knows your situation and wants you to know that you can trust him in strong contrast to the world around you. It is the good news that changes our lives in every respect. He is worthy of our trust and faithful to us in every way. It may seem a paradox to the self-made individualist, but trusting him deeply generates patience and endurance, strengthening us to "live a life worthy of the Lord, and please him in every way: bearing fruit in every good work" (Col 1:10).

We realize that Satan is powerful, but though we are careful of his treachery, we no longer fear his domination. Neither can we be blackmailed by our past failures. They are forgiven and covered by Christ himself. We are finally free, though we continue to live in that broken world. Satan knows it and will try to discourage us. We will know difficulty, suffering, and sorrow while here, but not as those without Christ. Though we may experience the emptiness and fear of grief, and all the promises sound hollow, we are *not* alone; God grieves with us. He never wanted it this way, and for those who trust him, it will not always be this way. Even now, in our dark hour, God sees (El Roi), God knows (El Deah). You matter to him, and he brings the light of a living hope into the night of your day: "He who believes in me will live even though he dies" (John 11:25-26).

Yes. "The people walking in darkness have seen a great light; on those living in the land of the shadow of death, a light has dawned" (Isa 9:2). Though many reject it, and though we once walked in darkness with them, we now walk in the light of life and can be that light for others. The spiritually dead can come to life, and the spiritually blind see if they come to the life and light Jesus offers.

Scripture References: Gen 1:1–3, 16:13; 1 Sam 2:3; Pss 9:9–10, 107:14; Prov 3:5–7; Isa 9:2, 50:10; Lam 3:22–26 with 33; Matt 12:20; John 1:4–5, 10–12; 3:19–21; 8:12, 31, 36; 11:25–26; 12:35–36; 14:1–4, 6, 27 with 16:33 and 17:15; Rom 7:24–25; 8:1–4, 31–39; 2 Cor 4:6, 11:13–15; Eph 1:15–23, 4:1–6, 5:8–17, 6:10–18; Phil 1:27, 2:12–13 with 1 Thess 5:24; Col 1:9–14, 21–22; 2:13–15; 1 Thess 2:11; Heb 5:14–16; Jas 4:7; 1 Pet 2:9, 5:8–11; 1 John 1:9, 3:7–10; Rev 12:10.

113. Culture and Conversion

Don't be deceived.... Every good and perfect gift is from above.
—Jas 1:16–17

CHRISTIANS NEED HELP UNDERSTANDING the cultural conditioning they struggle with in their new life. Traditionally, our culture has promised a respectable social identity, personal fulfillment, protection of individual rights, and material success to the self-made, hardworking man or woman. These values are commendable within the boundaries of personal virtue and respect for others. But the values of the self-made man and material success have become a snare over the years as virtues waned and greed, fraud, and arrogant self-assertion took over in the fertile soil of free and democratic capitalism. Nevertheless, even though this "American dream" is temporal and tainted, it is hard to express strongly enough how resilient those desires and values are in our lives or how they can limit our perspective of a new life in Christ.

The powerful result of our socialization blinds us to the alternative of life in God's care, under the cover of his grace, within the boundaries of his providence. Since we can remember, we have been in charge of our own lives, seeking to survive socially and mentally, if not physically, as independent people in a world of individualists. Our egalitarianism, internal locus of control, and legal and equal right to pursue personal happiness put many on a reckless track of self-assertion and personal ambition for success. These illusive goals of our culture are not handed to us freely, and we can become desperate to achieve them, for our society offers us nothing else. Not all have fared well in the endeavor, and if we meet God later in life, the inclinations for them are strong, the habits ingrained, and the will hardened. But we *do* have a choice.

Letting go of this old system of survival to trust God—to trust his providence, love, and grace—is not easy. It is truly being born again to start over, putting life together in a new way on a new foundation, renewing our minds to know God's will, and setting our hearts on things above. It is new wine that demands a new wineskin. We step onto the path of becoming all we were meant to be in Christ. But the old system of survival is still there, and we have a natural inclination for its familiar patterns and values. Satan will use it to deceive us if he can. He will bring back feelings of desperation to which we are no longer slaves. We must not let him blackmail us. We must be on our guard to give our trust and loyalty to our new King. Good and perfect gifts and the deep and enduring peace they bring come to us only from him.

Realizing the enormity of his grace to forgive and accept us as we are is the primary building block of our new life. He did this for us at a great cost to himself, and he will do everything else we need of him in life. We will still work hard and face difficulties in this world. But though we sometimes fail, our desire to trust him for our survival, meaning, and purpose in life will grow. We are now part of his plan, walking by faith instead of by sight, our loyalty to him showing in what we do, our desire to honor him evident in our decisions. His providence is our confidence, and those he has entrusted to us, our treasures to love, encourage, or shape for him. All is now in his hands, and we must leave it there.

Scripture References: Pss 8:1–9 with 13:5–6; 37:3–11; 84:10–12; 91:1–16; Matt 9:16–17; John 3:3, 16; Rom 8:28–32, 12:1–2; 1 Cor 10:31; 2 Cor 5:15–18; Eph 2:1–5, 4:11–16; Col 2:13–15; 3:1–4, 12–17; Jas 1:16–18; 1 Pet 4:1–3a; 2 Pet 1:3.

114. God's Goodness and Our Freedom

To the pure, all things are pure.

—*Titus 1:15*

GOD KNOWS WHAT IS truly good for us beyond our imaginations and expectations. He created all things good and good itself. There was nothing evil in God's creation. Even Satan was created as a beautiful and powerful angel. But in the goodness of God's creation, he also gave the human and angelic beings he created the gift of free will. Satan used that freedom to rebel. He chose his own way and has been trying to take us all with him ever since. Humankind fell early into his trap, doubting God and twisting the good of creation toward the self, making evil use of God's gifts. Our potential and human inclination for this reordering of God's purposes for us is alarming. Satan planted doubts about God's goodness in Eden, and they continue to flourish among us. After deceiving us, he then accuses us before God. All things were created good and plentiful, but Satan tapped into our human desire for something more. This opened the door to a greedy and selfish appetite for control, wealth, pleasure, and prestige.

When we become Christians, God purifies us through the sacrifice of Christ, and we are released from Satan's grip. As we put the old self behind us, God intends that we enjoy the things he created, good and pure, though now they are often contaminated in our broken world. That is why the apostle can say, "To the pure, all things are pure." Christians can welcome God's good things into their lives. It is part of our new freedom in Christ within the boundaries of love and gratefulness. The malicious use of good must be corrected by God's grace and truth, and legalism must be shattered.

Legalism is one reaction of human perspective showing our doubts about God's goodness and misunderstanding his grace. Another human and misguided perspective is to need, even require, God to continually prove his goodness and express his approval by meeting our expectations for signs and wonders. I often refer to this as mysticism in the ranks of Christianity. But these approaches are not for us. He has revealed his goodness and love for us in his word, in the great sacrifice of his Son, and in his careful and beautiful creation. By that same good purpose, he has been and is now at work in our lives through his good providence, and has brought us through a great deal to this day, to the reading of this page. We now live lives of trusting him and walking in the freedom he gives.

Yes, there are things we do not know. God's ways and thoughts are much higher than ours, and he has only revealed what we need. There is mystery about his being and ways that we may never understand in this life. This limited understanding of his unlimited being demands our trust—trust he is waiting for, looking for in our hearts. If we do not trust him to be good, we do not trust him at all. When we trust his goodness and grace, we grow into freedom from fear, anger, anxiety, and guilt, even in a world eroded and worn by sin. He is there, and he intends us to trust his goodness.

Scripture References: Gen 1:31; Pss 18:25–28, 23:4, 33:6–9, 100:5, 103:10–14 with Isa 55:8–11; Zech 3:1–2; Matt 5:8, 12:15–21; John 8:31–32 with 36; Rom 1:18–22; 8:1, 28–39; 14:16–18; 15:1–2; 1 Cor 6:12, 10:23–24 with 31; Eph 2:1–5, 6:10–18; Phil 1:6 and 2:12–13; 4:4–9; Col 1:13–14, 2:20–23; 1 Tim 4:4–5, 6:17b; Titus 1:15; Heb 13:5b; Jas 1:25; 1 Pet 3:18, 5:6; Rev 12:7–12.

115. God's Help

> He who began a good work in you will carry it on to completion until the day of Christ Jesus.
>
> —*Phil 1:6*

WE OFTEN HEAR THAT God gives us power over sin in our lives. Then we wonder when we are going to get it. But God does not barge into our lives, forcing his way on us, making us do the right things. The sacred gift of free will is too precious and central to his purposes for us. He wants our voluntary love and loyalty; he wants our hearts. His word and the Holy Spirit are before us and in us and central to his transforming work in our minds and hearts, giving us every reason we can imagine to want to honor him, and creating in us a deep motivation of gratefulness for his love, forgiveness, and providence. "He has given us his great and precious promises" (2 Pet 1:4). He makes us aware of our sins, reminds us of his grace, and shows us how to walk worthy of the gospel. He answers our prayer for wisdom and shows us the many opportunities we have to do what will honor him. Any doing of his will is not an achievement but a humble response to his goodness and grace in our lives. It will not be a response of obedience to legalistic laws but our progress in love and submission, our trusting of his providence in our lives.

This is the power of God in us. We will not be perfect at living for him, being products of human culture in a broken world, having a weakness for the old solutions for survival. But his grace is sufficient, and we will improve as we pursue maturity in his purpose for our salvation while he works in us. Through our willingness, humble trust, and pursuit, our hearts and minds will be transformed through his word and the Holy Spirit. We are learning to trust him and his way as we might learn to ride a bike or play the piano. It takes a while to learn to swim.

The disciples were with Jesus for three years, seeing him, knowing him, and yet found trusting him to have a steep learning curve, even after seeing many miracles. Some of them struggled to the very last before he ascended. Paul struggled with his sinful nature and trials all his life. We can expect there to be effort needed on our part as well. We are headed toward maturity in Christ, toward wisdom, but it is a journey. Journeys, by definition, mean making progress toward a destination. They may include mountains to get over and rivers to cross, and there may be detours, but a journey has an end, and, in this case, it is worth all the effort and cost. God's work in us as we put one foot in front of the other will continue until the day of Christ's complete victory over all.

This humble realization of the measure of God's grace and providence in our lives is highly motivating and will give us the desire to live for him, strengthening us. We are free from the condemning law of sin, free to choose his way. All he has done for us moves us to trust him, have a new perspective, and be loyal to his purposes. There is no credit for ourselves in this; it is his work in us as we take each step by faith. No magic, secret words, or special rituals are necessary. It is the reality of the powerful presence of God's Spirit in his word and in his love, grace, and providence in our lives every day. And it is there whether we feel like it or not.

Scripture References: Gen 3:6; Josh 24:14–15; Pss 25:9, 91:14–16, 138:8, 145:14; Prov 9:10, 11:2; Mic 6:8; Mark 4:35–41, 8:11–21; John 4:23–24, 16:33; Rom 5:6–8, 6:1–14, 7:14–25, 8:1–2; 1 Cor 10:12–13; 2 Cor 4:7, 5:15–18, 12:7–10 with 9:8; Gal 5:16–26; Eph 4:11–16; Phil 1:6, 2:12–13; Col 3:1–17; Jas 1:14–15, 22–25; 3:13–18; 1 Pet 5:5–9; 2 Pet 1:3–4; 1 John 1:8–10.

116. Human Religion

Shall I bow down to a block of wood?
—Isa 44:19

THERE IS SO MUCH emphasis on religion, but it is a trap for humans, the snare of the fowler, of Satan himself. Religions are human attempts to stay right with the gods for protection, release from suffering, personal peace, general well-being now, and attainment of a better state after death. But *none* grant the rewards they promise; they are deceptions that lead the blind away from the real God of the universe who intervenes with an everlasting love for us. Like the idols laid bare by Isaiah, the religions are exposed by the weakness of their human invention, their political and materialistic ends, and the false hope and suffering they bring. In reaction, and to avoid the true God, many Western people have turned to the final religion of Darwinian atheism. Evolution outstrips the other religions in its political and human trappings. It is less credible than any, defying human reason and demanding blind faith in the god of chance without purpose or meaning. The clay pot has rebelled against the potter, saying it became a pot by itself.

And then there is Christianity. If I am exposing human religion here, why would I bring up Christianity? Well, I'm not; not biblical Christianity anyway. It is popular Christianity that is in question. Much organized Christianity has been compromised by institutional needs and purposes, materialism, and the desire for human recognition and reputation. These contaminations make it look and function like a religion. Christianity does not save people in any form; only God saves people as they come to him through Christ, which biblical Christianity insists on and which separates it from the religions. It is not a religion of works that saves us but a grace relationship with God himself. Popular Christianity leads people away from that relationship to the gods of human values and social rewards. To truly know God and his grace is to know the peace so many seek in a world of many gods, full of trouble, confusion, and desperation. How can we worship a block of wood instead of this God of the universe?

Many churches still seek to honor God and his word, encouraging a relationship of trust with him. These are authentic expressions of God's intention for the church. Though imperfect, you can find those of honest faith and humble hearts who seek to walk in the truth and live out their freedom in Christ in an authentic church. Other churches only act out the rituals of religion or cater to cultural and social expectations. Trusting in *anything* or anyone other than the Creator-God who has revealed himself and sent his Son leads away from salvation, not toward it.

Scripture References: Exod 20:2-3; Pss 20:7-8, 146:3-6; Prov 14:12 with 28:26; 16:2; Isa 44:1-20 with 50:10-11; Matt 7:13-29; John 1:10-18; 3:16 with 36; 3:19-21; 5:24; 6:40; 8:12; 14:6, 27; 16:33; 17:3; Acts 4:12, 5:1-2 with 6; Rom 5:1-2; 2 Cor 4:4; Phil 2:12-13, 4:6-7; Col 3:15; 1 Tim 2:5; 1 John 5:11.

117. Doing Good

Jesus . . . gave himself for us . . . to purify for himself a people that are his very own, eager to do what is good.

—*Titus 2:13–14*

PAUL TELLS TITUS TO continually remind the people in the church at Crete to do good works. He mentions the theme five times in a letter to Titus that takes only one and a half pages in my Bible. Paul does not say God will do the good works for them; they are to be instead a result of God's grace and providence in the lives of his people, proof of the power of God in their salvation, showing them to be people who trust him and witnesses to the watching world. He tells them that Jesus redeemed them and set them apart as his very own, as those who would be "eager to do what is good" (Titus 2:14). Paul tells the Ephesians that good works are the purpose of God's grace in our lives, and Timothy that they are the purpose of the inspired word of God for us. James does not cut us any slack on the subject. Our faith must result in good works if it is authentic. The wisdom he tells us to ask of God in chapter 1 is shown by a "good life, by deeds done in the humility that comes from wisdom" (3:13).

So there really is this matter of submission and loyalty to the King based on his love and grace toward us that results in good works. Kindness, compassion, helping, loving, and using our talents for his purposes are all evidence of the gospel's truth. None of these passages in the Bible tell us that, saved by God and indwelled by the Holy Spirit, we are still unable to glorify God in this way, that, in our weakness, he needs to do these things for us (some would say through us). Jesus tells us to do good works to let our light shine in a dark world and show the way of God in our lives. Giving us every

AN INTERVENING LOVE

reason, every encouragement, every motive, and every opportunity in his providence to do good, God allows us to honor him in the world in this way.

These acts of kindness and consideration, this sharing of love and hope, should characterize our lives. To say we cannot do these things, that God must do them through us, confuses people. It overspiritualizes the very practical results of his intervening love in our lives. On the other hand, legalism, a list of things to do or to avoid to maintain God's approval, is not the goal. He accepts us through the sacrifice of Christ and measures our commitment by the attitudes of our hearts. After our salvation by God's grace, we must not allow ourselves to become prisoners of doctrinal systems that remove God's desire for us. We serve him now in freedom.

Our position in Christ frees us from self and society, blackmailing us at every turn, telling us that we will never know happiness or satisfaction if we do not do things their way. The threat of that deprivation has lost its leverage and power; the attraction has lost its magnetism. We are free to walk away, live differently, and have the treasures we seek securely from the hand of God. He has given us and gives us all we need to honor him. We are not perfect. We are more like recovering alcoholics coming out of the habits, patterns, and addictions that have shaped our lives. Paul calls us "jars of clay" (2 Cor 4:7), brittle and fragile with cracks, so it is clear that the message of Christ we bring to the world and its power to save is from God alone. But, though fragile and prone to cracks, his forgiveness is there for us each day, and, having Christ's righteousness, we can begin to walk worthy of the gospel of Jesus. But it takes "correction and training" from God's word (2 Tim 3:16–17) and practice—more structured at first and more natural as we go along—to glorify God (reveal his attributes) in our lives.

God has a huge part in this process of transformation to walking in the Spirit. But he looks for hearts and minds set on things above, those who approach him in spirit, truth, and humility, those who are eager to do good works, and those who pray for his will to be done in their lives and the wisdom they need for their part in it. These, whose hearts are his, are his very own.

Scripture References: Ps 37:3; Prov 3:27; Isa 43:1 with Titus 2:14; Matt 5:16, 28:18–20; John 13:34–35 with 14:15 and 15:10; Rom 12:1–2; 2 Cor 4:5–7, 5:21, 9:8; Gal 6:9–10; Eph 2:8–10, 4:1; Phil 2:1–4; Col 1:9–10, 3:1–4; 1 Thess 2:12; 2 Tim 3:16–17, 6:18–19; Titus 2:11–15; 3:1–2, 8, 14; Heb 6:10, 13:15–16; Jas 1:2–8, 2:14–17, 3:13; 1 Pet 2:11–17, 3:13–17; 2 Pet 1:3–4.

118. Faith

Faith is being sure of what we hope for and certain of what we do not see.

—*Heb 11:1*

GOD NEVER TIRES OF us, though we sometimes act in ways that do not honor him. His grace is not like ours, given or withheld based on our feelings and, perhaps, the weather or even our digestion. He asks us to trust him, but often we choose to assert ourselves, live with anxiety, or feel we can't go on another day. Yet he is there for us, waiting for us to turn our heads in his direction and see his providence again, full of goodness, power, grace, and love that no human theory can cancel or remove. We must trust him for what we do not know and cannot see or feel, and move ahead with confidence.

Of course, trusting God is not a natural human response to the ups and downs of life. We have expectations for him that do not fit the reality of who he is, of what his helping us should look like. Part of this comes from the values of our culture, such as logic, efficiency, prosperity, and predictability. Part of these expectations come from our personal preferences for certainty and clarity or our desperation in times of need. But he is above and his ways greater than these expectations, his responses to us more perfect than our imagination, his understanding of our needs deeper even though his ultimate plan may be unknown to us.

Faith is trusting God. We might want it otherwise, but he insists. That is the lesson of Abraham, who was called to a place God would show him but had to leave his home without knowing where or how he and his family would survive. Later, he trusts God by being willing to go beyond reason to obey him in the sacrifice of Isaac. God considered him righteous because of his faith, *not* because of a perfect life. Ultimately, God called him his friend and blessed the world with Jesus through him. Then there are Joseph, Moses, Joshua, Daniel, David, Rahab, Ruth, Esther, the prophets, and all the others who trusted God, named and unnamed. Is our situation harder or more severe than theirs? Is God's providence weaker in our case; is he less able to sustain us? Let his grace overwhelm you, wisdom from his word guide you, his providence control your situation, and his peace comfort you. Trust him.

Then let the kindness God has shown you flow out to the world around you. It is the culmination and sign of our faith, the result of knowing and trusting God. We must set our minds and hearts on things above to guide our living here on earth.

Scripture References: Gen 37:12–36 with 50:19–21; Josh 2:1–24 with 6:24–25 and Heb 11:31; Ruth 1:1—4:22; 1 Sam 13:14 with Acts 13:22; Esth 4:1–17; Pss 9:10, 91:14–16; Prov 14:26–27; Dan 3:15–18; John 16:33 with 14:27; Gal 5:6; Phil 1:18b–27 with 29; 4:4–7; 1 Thess 1:8; Heb 5:14–16, 11:1–40; Jas 1:2–8, 2:14–26; 1 Pet 5:6–7.

119. Quiet Loyalty in Times of Trouble

I have told you these things so that in me you may have peace. In this world you will have trouble. But take heart! I have overcome the world.

—John 16:33

LIFE DEALS ITS BLOWS. People can be unkind and selfish, damaging our personal world, stealing our peace, and ruining our attitude. How is it that we allow inconsiderate people to control us in this way? Are we not already given to the one above all others? Is he not with us even in the valley of death? To him, we must show a steadfast and unending allegiance, confident trust, and loyalty, quiet but fierce enough to deflect the world's worst acts against us. It is then that we stand tall, not in our own strength but resting in his.

With understanding and caution, we can return kindness to those who abuse us. We are to be wise as serpents and harmless as doves. This is part of a good life lived in humility and wisdom, wisdom from above. Anyone can react with defensiveness and selfish ambition, but we are to be peacemakers, in so far as it depends on us, while not enabling evil.

Yes, we may stumble, but he is with us. We must turn our eyes again to him in devotion and faith. His ways are not our ways, but his strong love and lavish grace are abundantly clear and unquestionable. He will bear the weight of our troubles and discouragement and is there for us in our loneliness. Our purpose is fulfilled in him, and his becomes ours. We can stand above our circumstances, knowing his hand controls all. Quiet loyalty to him, who moves granite mountains and calms raging seas, can still our anxious hearts. Blessed is the man or woman who trusts in the LORD, the Creator-God of the universe.

Scripture References: Pss 9:9–10; 23:1–6; 27:1–6; 37:3–9, 23–28; 42:5; 46:1–3, 10; 61:5–7; 62:1–2; 84:12; 91:1–16; 118:6; 121:1–8; 130:5–6; 145:18–19; 147:3, 6a, 11; Prov 3:21–26, 15:16, 16:8; Eccl 7:8–9; Isa 30:15; Matt 5:9, 10:16, 12:20; John 16:33 with 17:15; 18:36 with 14:1–4, 27; 17:3; Rom 5:1–5, 8:31–39, 12:14–21; Phil 4:4–7; 1 Thess 4:11–12; 1 Tim 2:1–6; Jas 3:13–18; 1 Pet 5:6–7.

120. The Builder at Work

He who began a good work in you will carry it on to completion until the day of Christ Jesus.

—*Phil 1:6*

IF WE LOOK BACK and see God's hand of providence in the events of our lives, we may come to Solomon's conclusion that "Unless the LORD builds the house, its builders labor in vain. Unless the LORD watches over the city, the watchmen stand guard in vain" (Ps 127:1). It does not mean that the builders or watchmen do nothing. It means that doing their best if God's hand is not in it will not have the outcome they need. Jesus' words are parallel when he says we must build the house of our lives on the foundation of his teaching, the rock that will anchor it and hold it together in the hurricanes of life. All the efforts of those who build on some other foundation will, eventually, be in vain. The house they put so much effort and hope into will be swept away.

If God should literally build a house, what sort of house would it turn out to be? We have seen his work in creation. Before human choice marred it, it was perfect, incredibly beautiful, intricate, and precise. What, then, do we expect that God has in mind for his work in our lives? Will he be satisfied with a mediocre result? Will he sign his name to a rough idea of what he wants? I think we should expect the same creative God in our lives who made the world and the universe it inhabits.

First, his part in it is so essential he will use whatever is necessary to get our attention. He will insist on starting with the firm foundation of our faith in him rather than ourselves. Then, in his providence and wisdom, he will put all the necessary parts in place. He has an end in mind that we may not expect and means to that end we may not understand or desire. It will take work, perhaps a painful process, to bring it about. But we must not be anxious. You and I are the projects of an infinite, loving, and persistent craftsman. And he will finish his work in us as we allow him his way. He is preparing us to be his lights in a dark and broken world and to know an eternity with him.

It is not yet the seventh day of his work in us, so we must not be wearied by the inconvenience of the improvements he seeks to put in place. It takes time to make us fit for a life that honors him and helps those around us. And though the life he prepares us for is on earth, the finishing touches are yet to come. They will be realized in a place where they cannot be contaminated by human desires and expectations. Be patient; he works, and the good he has in mind for us is beyond our imagination, beyond anything we may have hoped for in this life.

Scripture References: Pss 27:13–14, 37:3–7a, 40:1–3, 46:10, 84:10–12, 127:1, 138:8, 139:13–18, 143:8; Prov 3:5–7; Lam 3:25–26; Matt 7:24–29; Rom 8:28; 2 Cor 12:7–10; Eph 1:11–12; Phil 1:6, 2:12–16, 3:7–9, 4:4–7; Heb 12:9–13; Jas 1:2–8; 1 Pet 1:3–7.

121. Independence Has Its Dangers

Blessed are the poor in spirit, for theirs in the kingdom of heaven.
—*Matt 5:3*

IN A WESTERN INDIVIDUALIST culture, independence and self-sufficiency are deeply and passionately valued ideals. Decisions about how we live are highly regarded as our personal prerogative. Freedom can be a blessing for us, but feelings of independence bolstered by self-reliance, self-sufficiency, and self-assertion make it very difficult to think about the need for God in our lives, and most do not. Many resist him, and others say he cannot exist. "If there is a God, then we are not in control," which is unthinkable for the hardened individualist. "It shall not be so." It is why few of the wealthy and powerful turn to God. Their trust is in something else. The kingdom of heaven is available only to the poor in spirit—those who know they have no worthiness before God, no achievement that can earn his favor, meet the requirement for salvation, or substitute for him in their lives. They rely on his mercy and grace alone. He is with them now, and they will be with him in the future.

Individualists have an internal locus of control in this culture that values and rewards self-assertion and personal achievement. They believe they can change their circumstances in their favor one way or another, that it's up to them, that life is what you make it. Most of them are confident that they manage life quite well without God. They value their achievement, which adds to their feelings of personal worth and social recognition. Even though some see their lives falling apart now, others only know they have taken the wrong road at the end of the journey. They have been deceived by their own pride and by the many counterfeits that are called "Christianity." Satan can indeed appear as an angel of light and his servants as servants of "righteousness." But God continues to wait for the proud and self-sufficient to look in his direction. He pursues them not because he needs them but because he wants them. He may go to great lengths, using even the difficulties in life to get their attention. He longs for them to know him in spirit and truth and bless them with his grace.

Scripture References: 2 Chr 7:14; Pss 10:4, 14:1, 51:16–17; Prov 11:28, 14:12, 21:2, 28:26; Isa 29:16, 57:15, 66:2 with Matt 6:24 and 7:13–14; Jer 9:23–24; Dan 4:28–34; Matt 19:16–26; Luke 12:15–21 with Prov 3:5–10; Luke 15:11–24; John 17:3; 1 Cor 1:26–31; 2 Cor 11:13–15; Heb 12:11; Jas 4:6; 1 Pet 5:5–6; 2 Pet 3:8–9.

122. Confusion in the Church

The Spirit clearly says that in later times some will abandon the faith and follow deceiving spirits.

—1 Tim 4:1

WE MUST NEVER CONFUSE God with Christianity, nor the local church with true believers. Sometimes the church is not so good at teaching about the true nature of God or about people who worship him in humility and honesty. Many today are leaning toward political correctness to seem more welcoming of the world around them and more user-friendly. But the gospel is quite direct in its message, and these efforts can give a false impression of its exclusiveness. Sometimes this is because of the church budget. Any time there is money to be gained or investments to maintain, there may be a leaning in the direction that seems to benefit the cash flow. Other times it is because of what the leaders consider "success" for the church. Sometimes their way of getting that reputation is to condone and enable lifestyles contrary to God's word, or even use the church to further political agendas.

Leaning toward a politically correct church goes against God's purposes. But so does the church used for the personal agendas of its leaders or members. Though these people may seem numb or favor church growth with the wrong motives, their primary use of the church is for the social recognition they cannot find elsewhere. A reputation for being spiritual is easily put in place by playing a few trump cards no one there can argue with. No one knows their heart motives, and they make it seem unspiritual to question them.

Other churches react to these approaches with legalism. Their efforts to avoid ambiguity and deal with insecurity under the guise of "literal, biblical" obedience are attractive to some in our objective society. By creating their own lists of expectations for Christians and using their position of authority to enforce them, they ignore the grace that should accompany the truth, and destroy the intended freedom in Christ for believers. They also believe the gospel is against the world, and we must separate ourselves from people outside the church. It appears by their behavior that God does not love lost people, a rather strange idea after seeing the behavior of Jesus in the Gospels and the kind of world he died for.

We do not talk about these issues in the vocabulary I use here. We are pretty good at making what we do sound spiritual, telling people that somehow it is all about God. But these approaches do not represent the truth of the Bible about the church or true believers. They reveal a gap between God and Christianity of our own making. He loves the world and wants us to be salt and light, offering hope, showing the results of God in our everyday lives, and giving credibility to the gospel among the lost. He is waiting for them to come to him. We must be relevant and genuine in our God-and-neighbor-centered lifestyle. At the same time, there are limits to our acceptance of the world's ways and our efforts with those who are violent in refusing him and fixated on destroying his work. His grace has appeared to all, free and powerful, but salvation can only be realized by those of humble faith who come to God in spirit and truth.

Scripture References: 1 Sam 16:6–7; Pss 20:7, 51:16–17; Prov 21:3, 28:26; Isa 58:6–12; Hos 6:6 with 14:9; Mic 6:8; Matt 5:3–10; 7:6, 13–23; 10:5–16; 18:20; Luke 12:15, 18:9–14; John 3:16–17, 4:23–24; Acts 20:28–31; Rom 16:17–19; Phil 3:2; 1 Tim 4:4–5; 2 Tim 4:1–5, 14–15; Titus 2:11; 1 Pet 5:5b–6; 2 Pet 3:9; 1 John 2:15–17.

123. What We Don't Know

Does the clay say to the potter, "What are you making?"

—Isa 45:9

IT IS DANGEROUS TO think we know everything about God and his ways. He has told us that we do not, and has given us only what we need. Realizing there is much we don't know is cause for caution in our thinking about his ways and the reason to trust him. Some theologies among us purport to settle all the questions about what God does and how and why he does it. As with the theologies of Job's friends or that of the Jewish religious leaders in the Gospels, God is not allowed to do things these theologies have not outlined for him. But in this, *we* are formulating the definitions, strapping God with our logic, making the rules, and not allowing God to be God.

There is mystery and a good deal of paradox in God's ways, and some of us informational people are afraid of it. What we individualist problem solvers cannot quantify and control causes us to feel insecure. We want a predictable God. But we must recognize that, along with what we know, there is much we do not know about God. We must trust him without doubting his good providence, lavish grace, and deep love for us, even when we cannot see very far down the road. We cannot trust our expectations of his actions. We do not know precisely what he will do in answer to our prayer or how he must work in the lives of others. It is God's intention that we trust him instead, and he gives us every reason to do so. He is always right, his way is always best, his grace always enough, his power always sufficient, and his justice always complete.

Scripture References: Deut 32:3–4; Job 34:11, 36:11, 40:1—41:34, 42:7–9; Pss 37:3–7, 111:7–10; Prov 3:5–7 with 28:26; Isa 29:16; 40:13–14,

28–31 with 41:10; 46:10; 55:8–9; Matt 2:3–6; John 21:17–22; Rom 11:33–36; 2 Cor 12:7–10.

124. The Pride of the Self

Come to me, all you who are weary and burdened, and I will give you rest. . . . Rest for your souls.

—*Matt 11:28–29*

PRIDE IS AN AWKWARD enemy. It comes in all shapes and sizes and is seldom recognized by its owner. It can be subtle in its expressions or loud and boisterous. We are none of us completely free of this battle with the self. It seems Christians are as vulnerable as anyone else. Every caution is required. For many, this desire for recognition, achievement, competition for affirmation, and quiet dislike for those who have achieved more has become the theme of their lives. It is one of the indications of emotional insecurity and must give way to God and his ways out of a heart of trust.

For generations now, many have grown up denying God in the Western world. The self becomes all-important, and survival, success, and feeling good about themselves become the essential values. When they think they are better than someone else, they feel better about themselves, and their insecurities are veiled. Typically, the strong individualist must be first; no one else matters except if they recognize and add to that individual's self-esteem. Society can support only so much of this defensive, self-centered pride before it comes apart, for societies are communities of people working together for survival. Without consideration for one another, they cannot flourish. Without God, the foundation is removed, the insecurities laid bare, and dark places become their haunts. Doubts and uncertainties breed anxiety for some and self-assertion for others. This kind of society will disintegrate and collapse. It is a house of cards, and the events of our times keep shaking the table. It is just a matter of time. Rest from it all is found only in Christ, and only if we trust him.

AN INTERVENING LOVE

The Old Testament prophets give us insight into God's feelings about the self-centered pride of his people and the sin it bred among them. Isaiah is one of those chosen to expose their proud hearts. Destruction and deportation were called on to bring them to their senses, but the heart of man hardened toward God deceives even itself. They continued their sacrifices and fasting, but their hearts were far from God. Humility, justice, and compassion were not found among them. Instead, they called good evil and evil good. Rest and peace were in a different direction altogether, but they would have none of the blessings promised them. If only they had acknowledged God for who he was.

However, God's love did not give up, and he held out hope and compassion for the people of Israel in the future, a hope that would include us with them. It would come in the person of his Son and the greatest sacrifice of all, the promises of which are strewn throughout the Old Testament. They would have every blessing of a future kingdom if they followed the coming Messiah. But, again, when the day came, they would not, so though he has come and died for us, except for a few, their pride still rules their hearts. We who know God through him know that trusting him instead of ourselves brings that rest and peace so desperately needed.

Scripture References: Pss 10:4, 62:5–8; Prov 3:5–7; 8:12–13; 16:2, 18; 21:24; 26:12; 28:26; 91:14–16; Isa 1:1—2:22 with 5:20–23 and 30:15 but 26:3 and 32:17 with 40:28–31 and 41:10; 42:3; 9:6–7 with 52:13–15 and 53:1–12 with Mic 5:2; Isa 57:15 with 66:2b; 58:6–12; Jer 9:23–24, 17:5–10, 31:3–6; Hos 6:6; Obad 1:2–4; Mic 6:8; Matt 1:20–23; 7:13–14; 11:28–30; 15:8–9; 23:5–7, 11–12; John 14:6, 27 and 16:33; Gal 6:3–5 with 14; Phil 4:6–7; Jas 4:6; 1 Pet 5:6–7; 1 John 2:15–17.

125. Knowing or Not Knowing

Blessed is the man who does not . . . sit in the seat of mockers.
—Ps 1:1

KNOWING A LOT ABOUT God is not the same as knowing God. Those who have information about God without knowing its meaning may seem clever with it, but it is not the God of the Bible about whom they talk; it is an exhibition of what they take as intelligence. To get closer to knowing about God without faith is to be further away than true believers who know only elementary things about him. Others deny God outrightly. But those who keep saying, "It is not true, it is not true," are often afraid it *is* true. There is hope for even these if they take a moment for honesty in their hearts, humble themselves, and turn to God for his cure for us in Christ.

The honest person who seeks to know God cannot help but find him. The grave danger is that it can be more profitable in the temporary rewards of this world to use information about God to advance oneself. Others find that even a slight allusion that God might not exist can impress others and reward the braggart with a feeling of importance and inclusion. It gives some people feelings of security, though quite thin, to say with the crowd that the world and its human beings are an accident. Though their theory is highly insulting to the honest intellect, they allow their pride and insecurity to bolt the door to the truth. However, the social rewards for these people are superficial and short lived; their path leads to self-destruction.

While it can be good and helpful, becoming a theologian is second to trusting God, and information about him must be handled with honesty and humility. And while becoming an atheist may include a person among those with popular names, the blind lead the blind toward a gaping pit that swallows up the unbeliever. Neither the superficial theologian nor the arrogant atheist will know God. That is reserved for the poor in spirit and the pure in heart who trust God's grace.

Scripture References: 2 Chr 7:14; Pss 1:1–3; 10:4; 14:1; 91:1 with 9 and 14–16; 145:13b–14; Prov 14:12, 16:26, 26:12, 28:26; Jer 29:13–14; Matt 5:3–10; 7:15–23; 11:20–24; 15:7–9; 23:1–4, 13; Luke 6:39–40, 18:9–14; John 1:10–13, 4:24, 17:3; 1 Tim 1:3–7; Jas 3:1.

126. I Don't Feel Like It

My God is my rock, in whom I take refuge.

—Ps 18:2

THE DECEPTIVENESS OF FEELINGS is a battle for everyone, even Christians. One day, we feel like we are on top of life, looking down, and the next, we are at the bottom, looking up. The fact is that feeling spiritual is not proof of it, and feeling unspiritual does not change our relationship with God. Just because you do not feel like walking down the hall and taking the stairs down to get to your car doesn't make jumping out the second-story window a good idea. Gravity is not based on feelings. Just because I don't feel like getting a haircut doesn't mean I don't need one. A look in the mirror tells me that, and a look in God's word assures me of the reality of his unchanging and unconditional relationship with us who know him.

We may feel pretty flat about our relationship with God, and perhaps we have ignored his presence in our lives. Maybe things have become so confusing and difficult that some feel there might not be a God. But these feelings don't change the fact that we have his attention, that his providential care is active in our lives, and that his love for us, not based on feelings, is stronger than any we can imagine. That does not mean that your difficult times do not matter. They matter a great deal to God, and he is asking you to trust him.

A quick overview of the Old Testament leaders, kings, judges, and prophets shows us that God uses people, events, circumstances, and experiences that are very different from what we might imagine, expect, or desire to accomplish his work in the lives of his people. We are each on a journey toward maturity in Christ, and ours is not like that of other Christians. We may feel ours is harder than someone else's, but there are always those facing more difficult challenges than ours. Jesus told Peter that John's journey was none of his business. He was to be faithful to what God gave *him* to do. God told Paul that his grace was sufficient in his sufferings. Joseph, Daniel, and many others faced suffering. Jeremiah, Ezekiel, and many other prophets must have thought their misery would never end. Harder still, it was intended to help the Jews turn back to God, which they never truly did. There were times of discouragement and depression, but what is conspicuously absent in the stories of these prophets is doubt that God was at work in their situation. Even Job, though at times discouraged and confused, came back to his trust in God's sovereign and powerful providence.

Feelings will always be a part of life; there will be good and bad days. The question is whether we let them control us or allow the truth to offset them and be the reason for our actions. If we build our lives on the rock-solid foundation of the truth of God's word, our house will weather life's inevitable storms and floods. Though an emotional volcano erupts, threatening our personal world, it will not overcome us, for "God is our refuge and strength. . . . The LORD Almighty is with us" (Ps 46:1, 11), and he will accomplish his purposes.

Scripture References: Deut 31:6, 8; Josh 1:9; Job 42:1–6; Pss 23:4, 34:1–22, 42:1–11, 46:1–11, 56:3–4, 103:11; Prov 19:21; Isa 40:28–31, 41:10, 42:1–4, 43:1, 55:10–11; Lam 3:19–24; Hab 3:16; Matt 7:24–29, 14:22–33, 26:36–46, 28:20b; John 14:27 with 16:33; Rom 7:24–25; Phil 2:12–13, 4:6–7; 1 Pet 5:6–7.

127. Taking Others Seriously

I am the light of the world. He who follows me will never walk in darkness, but will have the light of life.

—*John 8:12*

OUR CONSIDERATION OF OTHERS is fundamental to living in our communities of all kinds of people. Taking others seriously does not mean they are all good people, but our responsibility is to be kind, though perhaps cautious, despite their lifestyles. Some are kind and considerate, but we must be patient with other neighbors as God was and is patient with us. They are created in God's image, and he longs for them to be under his grace, love, and protection. He loves them. Each is eternal; family members, friends, neighbors, and strangers are all, potentially, part of God's family. The choice is theirs. We may detest their lifestyle; they may be corrupt, abusive, inconsiderate, angry, and immoral, having pushed God aside. Their character and behavior may rest on deep insecurities and emotional pain. Though they have settled for society's temporary and futile rewards, God desires them to know him and the forgiveness, peace, and rest he holds for them. Regardless of what they have done with his gift of life to them, he waits for them to turn to him.

The pride of some neighbors prevents us from having any helpful relationship with them. They may be beyond our help but not beyond God's. Others we are advised to avoid. But toward all we must be humble and leave evidence of love and concern in the wake of our lives as we pass by them. Our purpose must be that they might see something of Jesus. He is the light of the world, and, like the moon reflects the sun, we are to reflect the light Jesus brought in the darkness around us. It is a critical part of others becoming disciples of Jesus. It may be the only part we play with many.

That light will not be welcome for many who have found some faint feeling of security in the dark corners of their lives that they do not want disturbed, shadowy values they do not want exposed by the penetrating light of God. When that light came into the world, "men loved darkness" (John 3:19), and they were unwilling to receive it, so they continue today, "but with God all things are possible" (Matt 19:26).

Scripture References: Ps 1:1-3; Prov 22:24-25, 23:6-9; Matt 7:6, 15-23; 9:9-13; 19:23-26; Luke 20:46-47; John 3:16-21; 8:12 with Matt 5:13-16, 28:18-20; John 17:3; Acts 20:28-31; Rom 5:1-2, 16:17-18; Eph 2:1-10; Phil 4:5-6; Titus 2:11; 1 Tim 1:15-16, 2:1-5; 2 Pet 2:11-12, 3:9; 1 John 1:5-9.

128. Roadblocks to Knowing the Truth

Then you will know the truth, and the truth will set you free.
—John 8:31–32

POWERFUL CULTURAL PREFERENCES, NEGATIVE personal experiences, pride, false ideologies, and the arrogance of thinking we already know everything about God are conditions and influences that block our understanding of his ways and intentions for us and for the creation. Sometimes it is better to begin with what we do not know. *What?* Yes, knowing there is a great deal about God that we do not know is an excellent starting place for our theology about what we can know. Realizing what we do not know and considering what we do know can shape us to worship him in spirit and truth with wonder at his greatness and respect for his mystery. Yes, we can know God better than we do, and churches should help us, but not every church leads us in the best way toward this goal; not every church respects the mystery surrounding his goodness and teaches us to trust him without reservation, without conditions.

Much that is called Christianity gives us false ideas about God through legalism, syncretism, and mysticism. Some churches are so institutionalized by liberal, "politically correct" approaches they can no longer answer our questions. The standard has been removed; the fire of the Spirit extinguished; the sword dulled; the mystery "explained" away. Only cold ashes remain, bringing no comfort to the troubled heart. But God wants you to know his true grace, freedom, and providence. Our loyalty must be to him. Don't fall in love with Christianity but with God himself. Then find in Christianity what helps you to grow in him in your understanding, faith, and loyalty.

All this means we must be careful where we get our thoughts about the true nature of God and what it is to worship him in spirit and truth. His word is our primary source, but we must not allow twisted doctrinal systems to interpret it for us. Sound Bible teaching is becoming harder to find in our day; we must seek out good churches and teachers. Above all, do not give up on learning about the nature of God and his plan for you. Read his word with humility and openness, and pray for God's help and leading, for his Spirit to be at work in you, shaping you, transforming and renewing your mind. Read books written or recommended by Christians you respect, and talk with friends who are further along than you in their walk with Christ.

At the same time, remember that no teacher or church is perfect, and not everything others apply for themselves necessarily applies to you. Christianity itself is not unflawed; it is made up of people who are all at different places in their maturity in Christ. But do not allow spiritual arrogance to creep in. Be patient and kind. Those who attend but do not belong in the church will be sorted out by God himself in the coming days. In the meantime, while each may see his freedom in Christ differently, we will know true men and women of God by their commitment to the essential truths of God's word, the humility of their hearts, and the good works of their hands, "deeds done in humility that comes from wisdom . . . that comes from heaven" (Jas 3:13, 17).

Scripture References: Prov 21:2; Isa 55:8–9; Matt 2:3–6, 5:13–16, 13:24–30; John 13:34–35; 15:3–5 with 8; 16:33 with 17:3, 15–18; 21:17–22; Rom 11:33–36, 12:1–2, 14:5 with 13 and 22 and 15:5–6; Col 3:1–4 with Phil 3:18–19, 4:4–9; 1 Thess 5:19; Heb 12:28–29; Jas 3:13–18; 2 Pet 1:3–11, 2:1.

129. To Be Free of Anxiety

And the peace of God, which transcends all understanding, will guard your hearts and your minds in Christ Jesus.

—*Phil 4:7*

MOST OF US LIVE our lives with shades of anxiety nagging at the edges. Our human socialization, being just that, human, was not perfect; it never is. It did not meet all the needs of our developing emotions. It left us with certain insecurities, especially in our individualist society, where we are expected to achieve an identity by ourselves and find our worth in it. In our early years, with immature and superficial thinking, we sought to cope with the absence of affection or approval, a missing parent, spiteful siblings, social bias, tragedy, or abuse and fill the gap of growing insecurities with substitutes or distractions that never quite met the need.

For some, arrogance and self-assertion set in to deny these feelings and attribute them only to others. These "confident ones" set about to control life to meet their needs and find, however superficial, feelings of self-esteem in conquering those around them and proving their worth to the world. Some decide to out-achieve everyone, at any cost, to prove their worth. For others, irrational behavior sets in as an effort to fight back, replace the emptiness, and put feeling back into life, even if it is painful. This can lead to obsessive behavior patterns that are difficult to deal with later in life. Yet others go on in life emotionally unstable, needy, vulnerable, and anxious. But, of course, none of these reactions are God's intentions for us. They come from dark shadows of negative experiences that blind our minds to him, clouding his image in us and his purposes for us.

These reactive emotions and behaviors can twist the good things God created for us to enjoy into obsessive abuses. As such, they become self-focused values and solutions for happiness and survival. We can resist God's help and become our own gods, or we can, in humility, see ourselves as the bruised reeds or smoldering wicks for whom Jesus would come with empathy and deliverance. These are the brokenhearted and crushed in spirit the psalmist speaks of; many are among us. We must stop replacing God's will for us with human attempts to control the insecurities of life, leading to further insecurities and feelings of inadequacy.

For many, the busyness of life and the effort put into their achievements distract them from these unfulfilled needs most of the time, but the needs are there and creep back in at the most inconvenient times. Then there are times, short experiences of seeming release from it all, brief moments of freedom when a person can feel as light as air. We all have them. We want those moments to return, but they are not at our command. So those who do not know God return to their distractions.

God's word gives us the solution to our problems. He tells all who listen to trust him, give their anxieties to him, and let him care for the things we have no control over. But, even as believers, we have been so conditioned by our broken world that, try as we may, we often find it difficult. We were brought up to depend on our efforts and are afraid to let go. We do not have much experience trusting other people; they have often failed us. So, in a natural way, we are not good at trusting God. We are not sure he will come through for us and that we will find happiness and security in this broken world.

Unless we trust God, waves of anxiety creep in like dark clouds over which we have no control; we may have no awareness of their causes. But in those stomach-churning moments of uneasiness, we must recall God's generous grace, powerful providence, and everlasting love. As believers, we belong to him. We must trust God, who cannot fail us, though his ways may be beyond our understanding. When we first believed, he made us his children; he wrote his name on our souls. If he gave us his Son, he will freely give us all we need—he will be our rock and fortress in hard times. And, one day, he will roll back the clouds, coming in victory over every deception of Satan. All evil will be exposed for what it is, and all anxiety destroyed forever.

Our God does not sleep; he is not unaware of our struggles, and wants us to leave them all to him. It is not his desire for us to suffer, but he does not plan to take us out of this troubled world just yet. He intends, instead, to protect us from the evil one, and reminds us that his grace is sufficient if we will trust him. The psalmist often cried out to God because the wicked sought to destroy him. The "wicked" for us may be our pride, fear, or anxiety. But he is our help in trouble, our refuge and strength against

129. TO BE FREE OF ANXIETY

these enemies. Read the Psalms with that in mind. We may not like it, but these very insecurities, different for each person, as much as we hate them, are opportunities to depend on God and practice our trust in him. We are in his hands as his projects, which is a good place to be. When we trust his deep love, good providence, and eternal purposes, we find rest for our souls.

Scripture references: Pss 9:9–10; 34:1–22; 37:3–7a; 46:1–3 with 7 and 10; 56:3–4; 73:23–28; 91:1–16; 95:6–7; 100:5; 103:10–18; 119:71, 92–93; 121:1–8; 138:8; 147:3; Prov 3:5–7, 28:26; Isa 40:28–31 with 41:10; 43:1; 50:10; Matt 11:28–30, 12:20–21; John 1:12; 14:25–27 with 16:33; 17:15; Rom 5:1–4, 7:24–25, 8:18–32; 1 Cor 1:26–31, 15:9–10; 2 Cor 12:7–10; Phil 1:6 with 12–13; 4:6–7; Titus 2:11–14; Heb 4:14–16; Jas 1:2–12; 1 Pet 1 3–7, 5:6–7; 2 Pet 1:5–8.

130. The Value of Weakness

My grace is sufficient for you, for my power is made perfect in weakness.

—2 Cor 12:9

PAUL TALKED ABOUT HIS weaknesses and even delighted in them because being weak in various ways showed that the results of his life and ministry were from God's strength, not his own. He was amazed at this display of God's grace in his life. We never have cause for personal pride. The farther we go in our Christian lives, the more we realize how unworthy of his grace we are. Paul said that we have this "light of the knowledge of the glory of God in the face of Christ . . . in jars of clay" (2 Cor 4:6–7). In that day, those jars were simple, brittle, and commonplace.

We must be humbled by our weaknesses. Knowing them, we realize how dependent we are on God and how the social rewards we might gain from *our* achievements are thin, superficial, and short lived. We recognize how grateful we should be for his grace and power, for any good influence our actions and words may have, and for any damage from poor behavior that is avoided when we mess up.

We recognize our strength in life is from him, and the results of our work and ministry depend on his providence. Our weaknesses do not prohibit the good things we can do to honor the one who saved us. They show us to be people of truth who trust God. But we realize that it is by his grace and love that he uses us in his plan in this way, and blesses us with the love of others, knowing all about us. It is not that we cannot do good things; it is often knowing we can but don't. God's blessings come to us, not because we deserve them but because of his goodness and grace; all we *do* accomplish that is good is because he is good. We are weak but have no other purpose

130. THE VALUE OF WEAKNESS

and meaning in life than to honor him just the same. That purpose is owned by sinners saved by grace. There are no others in his kingdom. Look up and thank him for his grace in weakness.

Scripture References: Pss 9:9–10, 46:1, 85:9–13, 91:14–16, 119:71, 130:1–8, 138:8, 145:14; Luke 18:1–14; John 7:18; Rom 7:24–25, 12:7–10; 1 Cor 1:27; 2 Cor 4:7, 12:7–10; Eph 2:10, 4:12; Phil 1:6 with 2:12–13; 2 Tim 3:17; Titus 2:14 with 3:8 and 14; Jas 1:16–18; 1 Pet 1:3–9; 1 John 4:12–16.

131. Personal Peace

Peace I leave with you; my peace I give to you.

—*John 14:27*

JESUS OFFERS PEACE BUT says he does not give it to us as the world gives. We should not expect that happiness from him is the same as our culture defines it. We may think we want our culture's substitutes, but, though they look good on the surface, they are shallow, easily disturbed, and short lived. They are dependent on human understandings and feelings that come and go. Trusting them is building a house on the sand instead of on the rock. It will not withstand the storms of life. His peace is steady, deeper, and stronger. It depends not on our emotions but on his constant goodness and grace. We need not be anxious or afraid. In his time and providence, he will care for us.

This peace has a door, and we enter that door by trusting God even when, mostly when, things are really falling apart and we are close to feelings of anxiety, fear, dread, or despair. That trust means leaving it to him even when we have prayed about the situation and he has not responded as we wanted or expected. To trust him is to want *his* way more than our own ideas and preferences. "*Your* will be done on earth as it is in heaven" (Matt 6:10, emphasis added). Daniel's three friends knew God could save them from the fire but said that, *even if he didn't*, they would not bow down to Nebuchadnezzar's idol.

God's timing seldom meets our expectations. Some twenty-four years passed before the promised Isaac was born to Abraham and Sarah. God sent Samuel to anoint David to be the next king of Israel, but it was twenty years before he sat on the throne. Seven hundred years after Isaiah spoke of the coming Messiah, Jesus was born. Simeon had waited long years to see him.

131. PERSONAL PEACE

God is at work, but he is not limited by our personal or cultural expectations, by our time constraints, or by whatever logic we apply to define a good result. Patience and trust are required.

Trust is not about working up an emotional state of "faith" or using some gimmick to increase the chances of God's attention to our prayers. We can never make him more inclined to listen; he *always* listens to those who acknowledge him. Neither is the trust required for the peace Jesus gives measured by how strongly we believe he will grant something we ask for. It is the faith of accepting and living in the reality of his good providence, a quiet confidence in his grace, love, and justice, regardless of whether *our* expectations are met.

"My peace I give to you" (John 14:27). But you'll have to step into *his* way if you want it. As C. S. Lewis would say, you'll have to stand by the fire if you want to get warm. Following love and humility, peace is a true sign of faith, for it comes from trusting God, and will guard our hearts and minds. There is no lasting peace outside of knowing and trusting God.

Scripture References: 1 Sam 16:6–13 with 2 Sam 5:4; Pss 37:3–6, 55:22, 56:3–4, 91:14–16, 118:6, 127:1–2, 138:8; Isa 9:6–7; 26:3–4, 12–13; Lam 3:26; Dan 3:12, 15b, 16–18; Matt 6:5–13, 25–34; 7:13–14, 24–29; 11:28–30; Luke 2:25–32, 12:6–7; John 6:16–21; 14:25–27; 16:33 with 14:27; 17:3; Rom 5:1–2, 14:16–17, 15:13; Phil 2:12–13, 4:4–7; 2 Thess 3:16; 2 John 3.

132. A Broken World

The light shines in the darkness, but the darkness has not understood it.
—*John 1:5*

Men loved darkness instead of light.
—*John 3:19*

THERE ARE MANY THINGS in life about which we have no choice. We can fight the idea, but we live in a damaged and fragmented world. Humans chose not to trust God in the garden, and today they still prefer that destiny, loving darkness rather than light. We will all feel the increasing pain and sorrow of that choice. The resulting suffering is everywhere, and people try to fix it with nonsense, continuing to reject God's ways. We can complain that it is unfair that others make a choice and we pay the price, but if those without sin living in a perfect environment chose against God's desires for them, could we be far behind them in a damaged and degenerate world where Satan's lies fill every corner? We would have made the same choice and do so often enough.

But our perspective is human. As bad as it is, it is only in such a situation that love and compassion can exist. It is where we learn loyalty in our relationship with God, trust in his startling providence, and genuine concern and kindness for others. We would not give God a moment if we did not, in the humility of our desperation, realize our need for him. And his response is love and grace toward us in this situation of suffering, in high contrast to the hatred and vulgarity of our times. Our choice of God's kindness and our trust in his good providence cannot flourish without the free will of mankind that creates its need, however we may dislike it. We who know God may suffer, too, but it is in his purpose for us and those around us

132. A BROKEN WORLD

to keep us in this world a little longer, where we serve others, helping them in their desperation and suffering, and in doing so, serve Jesus. It is in this dark world that we offer light and hope, salvation itself. Even when the way seems unclear, we can "trust in the name of the Lord our God" (Ps 20:7). None of the answers people make for themselves to replace God will lead to life. Though free to choose their own path, they are not free to choose its consequences. We bring them the bread of life, the living water. Those who eat at Christ's table and drink at his well know freedom and grace now and the final outcome of their choice.

Scripture References: Pss 20:1–9 with 19:14–16; Isa 50:10–11; Lam 3:33; Matt 5:14–16, 25:31–40; John 1:4–5 with 3:19; 15:18–21; 16:33; 17:15; Rom 3:22–24, 8:35–39; Eph 2:1 with 4–5 and 8–10; Phil 1:18b–27; 1 Pet 1:3–9, 3:8–18, 4:12–19, 5:8–11; 1 John 1:8–10; 2:15–17; 4:4–6; 5:4–5, 19–20; Rev 21:1–4.

133. The Power of Culture

> For everything in the world—the cravings of sinful man, the lust of his eyes and the boasting of what he has and does—comes not from the Father but from the world.
>
> —1 John 2:16

WE DO NOT TAKE the culture around us seriously. We have no idea how powerfully it shapes our expectations, needs, preferences, and decisions. Because of this, we do not see its influence on our understanding of Scripture, our emphasis in ministry, our conscience, or the expression of our faith. Culture is a socially controlled frame of reference for the meaning of the events in our lives. It is the product of our understanding of reality and our experience on which we base what we believe is true or possible. Rooted in these beliefs are our values about what is important, good, necessary, reasonable, beautiful, helpful, etc. These values lie behind behavior. They tell us *why* we do what we do.

That's why culture is so important. Through this filter, we unconsciously screen, sift, and sort everything in our experience for its meaning, authenticity, worth, and usefulness. Knowing something about culture, especially our own—*why* we see things the way we do, *why* we do what we do—will help us keep it from contaminating our understanding of the Bible and the expression of our faith with its old values and solutions for survival. Otherwise, we will fail to distinguish between cultural absolutes and biblical absolutes. We will tend to mix them up unintentionally in favor of our cultural preferences. Though our friend in many ways, culture can also be an enemy of the Christian. The Bible calls it "the world" (1 John 2:15–17) when referring to its harmful influences on Christians. It makes the terminology of being "born again" (John 3:3) make sense.

133. THE POWER OF CULTURE

Culture's influence on the expression of our faith is enormous. A few years ago, I wrote a book about its turbulent but hidden effects on us as Christians in the Western world (*The Gap Between God and Christianity: The Turbulence of Western Culture*). We like feeling independent and in charge of our lives, making our own decisions and plans. But we do not realize we are highly influenced by social preferences around us. I often asked my college students in a course on cultural anthropology why they dressed the way they did that day. They thought it was because they liked this or that style or color or felt more comfortable if they had a few holes in their jeans. When I asked them to look around the room, they realized everyone was dressed similarly. Though it is possible to wear pajamas to class, no one did. We also discovered that though it was possible to eat cornflakes for dinner, no one did, possible to sit on the floor, possible to wear your shirt inside out, possible to wear lipstick on your forehead, . . . no one did. And why did the students in a class picture of my college days look so odd today? Hmmm. Who is in charge here? Who is making the rules? This becomes a serious consideration when culture normalizes values and activities outside God's desire for us, and we embrace them without question and haul them into the church.

It's true. Our culture is making the rules. We adhere to those unwritten rules within a certain margin of variance between us, but it is less of a margin than we think. A little too much variance in a person makes them odd, illogical, inefficient, dull, or even . . . stupid, because of our cultural preferences. The dangerous thing is that these preferences are invisible to us. They just feel like the natural way to see the world. Can you imagine the issues in moving to live or work in a different culture? How hard is it to own one culture, one frame of reference for meaning and values, while trying to live in another? It is more difficult than most imagine.

The question is how much we let our culture influence our Christian views of the faith, of the Bible, of ministry, or of God himself. How much adaptation is okay and needed for a relevant ministry in our society, and how much is based on the relativity of underlying, nonbiblical values in our society? It matters who makes the rules. Are values of the world compromising our interpretation of the Bible and the purpose of the church?

What do these values look like? Among other things, they are values on individualism that encourage self-assertion, personal achievement, competition, the desire to control situations, the preference for a secular worldview that leaves out the spiritual universe, or an inclination toward legalism instead of freedom in Christ. Our value on an internal locus of control (we can control our situation) does not let God have *his* way.

It will not do. If what is true or possible has changed because God is now at the center of our frame of reference, our values should reflect that. The new wine must go into a new wineskin. We must show love and loyalty to God. We must emulate the values of justice, mercy, understanding, and empathy with neighbors—in ways they understand. We must "do nothing out of selfish ambition or vain conceit, but in humility consider others better than [our]selves" (Phil 2:3). With believers, there must be unity around the essentials of our salvation. Yes, our faith must be relevant *in* the world but not shaped by the values *of* the world.

Scripture References: Deut 6:5; 2 Kgs 6:15–17; Prov 16:25; Mic 6:8; Matt 7:13–14; Luke 5:37, 6:46–49; John 1:10–11, 3:16–21, 8:12, 9:4–5, 12:23–26, 14:6, 17:15, 20–23; 1 Cor 6:12; 10:23–24, 31; Eph 2:1–5; Phil 2:1–11; Col 3:12–17; 1 Tim 4:4–5; Heb 12:1; 1 John 2:15–17 with Jas 1:17; 1 John 3:18, 4:1–6.

134. Problems Reading the Bible

For the word of God is living and active.

—*Heb 4:12*

SOME PEOPLE LOOK TO the Bible for what they "expect" should be or "needs" to be there. Their cultural values, personal needs, or social expectations operate in the background. These self-centered influences can interfere and not allow God to speak for himself, accomplish his intended purposes, and meet our true spiritual needs. The danger is that these human inducements habitually go unnoticed, deflecting the truth we need in our lives. We must be careful that our desires for personal recognition and acceptance, or our love for this world, do not lead us away from God's true intentions for us.

We need to see, understand, and avoid these filters through which we may see God's word so we can come to the Bible with an open mind and heart. We need a humble attitude that allows him to speak for himself. We must carefully seek out good Bible teaching to help us to this end, teaching that does not give us legalistic rules, syncretistic expressions, mystical signs, or promises of prosperity. Though mystery surrounds God and his ways that calls for our faith, there are no secrets that you must discover. All God wants you to know is in his word with his intention that it leads to a renewing of the mind, a vibrant faith, and a flourishing life of good works and missional purpose.

Scripture References: Ps 25:9; Prov 11:2, 29:23; Matt 19:23–24; John 8:31–32, 17:16–18; 2 Cor 4:1–7; Eph 2:8–10, 4:1–6; Col 3:12–17; 2 Tim 3:16–17, 4:1–4; Heb 13:15–16; 1 Pet 5:5–11; 2 Pet 1:3, 1:20—2:3; 1 John 2:15–17, 20–25.

135. The Barrier of Culture

As the heavens are higher than the earth, so are my ways higher than your ways and my thoughts than your thoughts.

—*Isa 55:9*

IN STUDYING THE BIBLE, our cultural bent is to collect information, organize it, and put the data into theological categories. Our cultural preferences are behind this process, for our style of thought and communication is as infused by the reasoning, logic, and values of our culture as was the heart and mind of the Middle Eastern person by theirs—the context God used to reveal himself and his will for humankind. The Western mind is influenced along the lines of an anxious need for logic, order, and information, made worse by an aversion to uncertainty, fear of ambiguity, and aggravating feelings of insecurity. While information is essential and good, we may be forcing the Middle Eastern document into a Western mold when reading the Bible. We must use caution when systematizing it and wringing logical information from verbs and lexical probabilities from nouns. The structure and vocabulary of the language are linked to a system of reasoning and values very different from our own.

Our theologies, excellent and helpful they may be, are only maps, as C. S. Lewis would say. They are not God but limited descriptions of his ways and will, leading us to his purposes for our lives. They are not without error or the influence of personal preferences and cultural expectations. In some cases, they are wrong, as were the theologies of Job's friends, or the Pharisees in Jesus' day, or the many heresies down through the centuries. In other cases, they are incomplete, leaving out vital understandings essential to living our lives for God. The map is not the destination; we must not mistake it for God himself.

135. THE BARRIER OF CULTURE

So we must not think we know all there is to know about God, that our theology is the final explanation or systemization of all the Bible says. God is not bound by the systems we create or the demands of our culture. We must let his love, faithfulness, and kind but sometimes severe providence have their way; trusting him must overcome our uncertainties and insecurities. Respect for his greatness and mystery and caution concerning the influences of our culture and personal needs on our understanding are fundamental to knowing God and his will for us.

Scripture References: Job 11:13-16, 18:19-21 with 13:1-15 and 19:25-27; Pss 57:2, 91:1-16; Prov 3:5-7; Isa 46:10, 55:8-11; Jer 23:29; Matt 23:13 with 23-24; John 1:1-14, 17:3; Rom 11:33-36, 12:1-2; Phil 2:3; 2 Tim 3:16-17; Heb 4:12; 2 Pet 1:19-21.

136. Satan Makes No Friends

"You will not surely die," the serpent said to the woman. "For God knows when you eat of it your eyes will be opened, and you will be like God, knowing good and evil."

—Gen 3:4–5

THE BIBLE IS AN irritation to those who want to be independent of its boundaries, those who want it to not be true, those who do not "know" God (John 17:3). They may experience an initial feeling of great relief when they finally say, "There is no God" (Ps 14:1). They convince themselves they are, at last, free from the penetrating "moral demands" and the perceived misery of submission—the withdrawal of all our culture tells us brings satisfaction and happiness. But they have been blackmailed by the great deceiver and willingly substitute thin worldly pleasures and the temporary social rewards offered to those foolish enough to leave God behind. They jump into a new identity as one who finally understands "true human freedom" in life. But they are not really free. The lack of meaning and purpose persists. Many must constantly distract themselves from a lingering fear that it might be true. And even if they seem to have defeated this fear, they will know the reality of the one they reject soon enough.

The truth they are trying to escape remains an irritation. Moments of doubt must be conquered. To maintain their new faith and feel good about their choice, they join others and follow celebrities who have made the same move away from God. But the day passes quickly, for Satan makes no friends. They do not realize that their movement away from God, which felt so good, will end in devastating misery, and their "friends" will be no help. All of them will find the same bleak desolation, and each will face it alone.

136. SATAN MAKES NO FRIENDS

They do not know that it is Satan's way. In his bait-and-switch strategy, he deceives with honey, but in his dungeon they will find only vinegar.

As God deniers grow stronger in their new "freedom," finding new ways to disguise their insecurities and rejecting all that is good to fulfill their selfish appetites, there comes a day when it is too late to do anything about their fateful decision. We don't know where the boundary is for them, but in their blindness they let the opportunity given to them freely by God in Christ pass them by. Authentic freedom in Christ has been forfeited. The disease has destroyed the organism, and it can no longer respond to God's grace. The battle is over; the great chasm closes over them; the enemy is satisfied.

Scripture References: Gen 3:1–7; Pss 10:2–6, 53:1; Prov 16:25, 26:12; Isa 45:5–6; Matt 4:1–11, 7:13–14; John 8:12, 14:6; Acts 4:12; Rom 1:24 and 28; 1 Cor 1:18–20; 2 Cor 4:4–7, 11:13–15; Phil 3:18–19; 1 Pet 5:8–11; 2 Pet 2:17–19; 1 John 2:15–17; Rev 20:15.

137. The Journey

Come to me . . . and you will find rest for your souls.
—Matt 11:28–29

GOD PURSUES PEOPLE IN different ways to get their attention, and their journey may go through several stages. In his providence, God may cause or allow certain circumstances to help a person recognize their need. These sometimes lead to guilt, fear, shame, anxiety, or insecurity. People may seek various solutions to this lostness—these dark clouds surrounding their souls. They may seek to escape the insecurity in their lives through achievement and the recognition of success, wealth, power, and social affirmation. Some seek relief in religion, and others, though fewer, find it in God himself. Those seeking answers in organized Christianity rather than in God himself will form commitments to it in terms of ritual behavior, trying to let God be a part of their lives. This is a level of what I call popular Christianity. These may eventually come to know God himself. But many stay at this level, and others ultimately give it up, not having an authentic relationship with God.

For their commitment to result in actual spiritual survival, popular Christians must understand and, in humility, accept God's unlimited grace on their behalf. Then they must change from the syncretism of wanting God to bless their plans to a welcoming of his plan, from commitment to Christianity to loyalty to God himself, from ritual behavior to natural behavior that expresses genuine faith in everyday life, from legalism or mysticism to God's true intentions in his word. The goal is to rest in God's providence in all things, the contentment of trust, the certainty of knowing God's will, and the quietness of wisdom. Biblical Christians are progressing toward this, and, of course, no two journeys look quite the same, but what is sure and

137. THE JOURNEY

the same for all of them is that they are deeply grateful for God's grace and know that rest for the soul is only found in Christ.

Scripture References: Ps 62:5–8; Prov 3:5–6, 11:28, 28:26; Isa 32:17 with Eccl 9:17–18; Matt 5:8, 9:16–17, 11:28; John 17:3; Rom 3:21–24; 2 Cor 5:17; Phil 3:12—4:1, 4:19; Col 2:8–10; 1 Tim 1:3–7; Titus 1:15–16 with 2:11–15; Heb 4:1–2 with 14–16; 2 Pet 2:20–22.

138. The Importance of Names

Salvation is found in no one else, for there is no other name under heaven given to men by which we must be saved.

—*Acts 4:12*

NAMES ARE PART OF a person's identity; they become connected to our personality, character, and lifestyle by which we are known in our individualist society. In the patrilineal society of the Bible, they spoke of one's heritage, and each person carried the honor or shame of their parentage. In either case, names are very personal. In the Old Testament, God put his name on his people. What could be more meaningful in his acts toward his people? He also gave new names to several key people in his plan to connect them to his destiny for them. In the initial stages of God's plan for the old covenant, Abram is called Abraham, Sarai, Sarah, and Jacob, Israel. Simon is called Peter in the early stages of the new covenant. After the death and resurrection of Jesus, Saul meets Jesus on the Damascus road and is later called Paul. Then believers began to be called Christians. Once again, God has put his name on his people.

Such was God's personal attention to central figures in his plan. It was a sign of the change from the old way of life to God's new purposes for these people—his way of marking them as his special representatives. But we may not often think about being God's people or what it means to have his name. We may be in love with our own names and, even as Christians, desire an identity that brings affirmation—to be known in our social circles as someone of importance, worth, and celebrity. But though our names, through human achievement, may allow us to advance ourselves, names are not bad in themselves.

138. THE IMPORTANCE OF NAMES

God gave Adam and Eve their names and told Adam to name each kind of animal. He writes our names down in heaven, and considers names so necessary and significant that we will each be given a new and unique name in heaven known only to him and us. Nothing could be more descriptive of his personal attention to each of us, his desire to have us near him, and our intimate relationship with him. But while we look forward to a new name and address in heaven, we must live up to his name, not ours, during our time on earth. We are Christ-followers, those who have "believed in his name"; we have "become children of God" (John 1:12) and should be known for love, harmony, humility among ourselves, and compassion for the lost in a dark world. With a reputation for good works, we can bring the news of God's grace, a message of light and hope, to a broken world.

Scripture References: Gen 17:5-8, 15-16; 32:27-28; Exod 3:13-14; Num 6:27; 2 Chr 7:14; Pss 9:10, 91:14-16; Isa 43:1; Matt 5:13-16, 16:13-19; Luke 10:20; John 1:12 with Acts 4:12; John 3:16-17; 13:34-35 with 17:13-23; 8:12 with 14:6; Acts 11:25-26, 13:9; Eph 2:1-10; Phil 2:1-4 with 12-13; 1 Thess 4:11; Titus 2:11-14; 1 Pet 2:12; Rev 2:17, 3:11-13.

139. Different from Each Other

So in Christ we who are many form one body, and each member belongs to all the others. We have different gifts, according to the grace given us.

—Rom 12:5-6

THE BIBLE TELLS US the body of Christ comprises many members, and each person has their place and function. His providence in our lives is different for each of us. We cannot compare ourselves to others except in the essentials of our faith. Each person has their own personality, life circumstances, and challenges. Each has different experiences that demand and shape our trust in God. Each has talents and abilities for serving others in ministry. This results in each person's unique expression of their faith and good works of service. We all must be grateful and humbled by his grace, which should be evident, but it does not erase our particular place and function in the body.

We are all responsible for the unique abilities and talents God has given us to serve him and honor his purposes. But we are not responsible for someone else using their abilities and skills for him. They do not have to be like us or do it our way. We must seek to be faithful to the part he has given *us*. That part in God's plan may be with the crowd or in personal encounters. The extrovert and the introvert both have a role. Some teach, some give counsel, some lead, some follow, some defend the faith, and some bring encouragement and show mercy. The strong in their faith must be considerate of the weak, and the wealthy must be generous to the poor. In this regard, we are not all equal. Each of us is special in God's plan. This should create humility among us and appreciation for each other.

139. DIFFERENT FROM EACH OTHER

It becomes quite clear that the proud heart has no place in the church, and legalism is a deadly denial of our freedom to be who God has made us in Christ by his grace. Faith, humility, love, freedom, and grace are signs of all who are in Christ, though each will express these virtues in service to one another in different ways. To use the talents God has given us to serve ourselves—to gain the reputation of being more spiritual, more gifted, or more essential than others—is among the worst sins. Unity and harmony, requiring humility, in the body of Christ are of the highest emphasis in Jesus' teachings and prove or disprove his sonship and the value of his sacrifice on our behalf in the eyes of the world.

Scripture References: Ps 51:16-17; Prov 11:2, 15:33, 16:18, 18:12; Luke 18:9-14; John 13:14, 34-35; 17:20-23; Rom 12:3-8, 10-16; 14:1, 13, 16-18, 22; 15:1-2; 1 Cor 12:12-26; Gal 5:13, 6:2-5; Eph 4:1-7, 11-16, 32; Phil 2:1-4; 1 Thess 4:11, 5:11; Titus 2:14, 3:14; 1 John 3:18-19.

140. Truth and Experience

Do not be foolish, but understand what the Lord's will is.

—Eph 5:17

TRUTH AND EXPERIENCE ARE necessary parts of our Christian lives; without the other, either can be deadly to an authentic and biblical expression of our faith. The experience of God's *grace* and knowledge of the *truth* came to us in Jesus Christ, but neither alone is a complete expression of his purposes. Mutually, they give us understanding and gratefulness, coming together in wisdom. Too much emphasis on one or the other can derange a Christian life or make a church dysfunctional. Truth is information that can be abstract and intellectual outside the experience of it in our lives. Experience, on the other hand, is personal and emotional and can be given inappropriate influence if not connected to the truth.

While truth can remain objective, predictable information in a system and give us feelings of security, it can also lead to legalism if we do not experience a grace relationship with God and the freedom and good works that are its outcomes. But experience can be unpredictable, subjective, and risky. On its own, it can lead to mysticism, syncretism, or sentimentalism. But when together, truth and experience give us the full picture of God's grace based on the truth of Jesus' sacrifice at work in our lives. There is, however, a need for caution. While truth should inform experience, there are dangers in what we *want* to call truth and what we *want* to accept as the experience of that truth. We cannot pick and choose what we want to be true in God's word, prescribe the experience we want from it, and explain the rest away as irrelevant. We need to let God speak for himself and bring the whole of what he says to bear on our experience. This is the working out of our salvation with transformed minds and the illuminating help of the Holy Spirit.

140. TRUTH AND EXPERIENCE

Scripture References: Prov 21:2–3; Isa 58:6–12; John 1:14–18; 8:31–32 with 36; 10:10; 14:6; 14:26 with 16:13; 17:3, 17–19; Rom 12:1–2; 2 Cor 5:15; Eph 1:17–20, 2:10, 3:14–21, 4:11–13, 5:15–18; Phil 2:12–13 with Rom 12:1–2; Phil 4:6–7; Col 3:15–17; 1 Tim 1:3–7; 2 Tim 3:16–17; Heb 4:12; 3 John 1:4.

141. Approaching God

The knowledge of the truth that leads to godliness—a faith and knowledge resting on the hope of eternal life.

—*Titus 1:1–2*

THEOLOGY IS THE STUDY of God's word and ways leading to knowledge about God, but it must also lead the writer and reader to encounter God himself. It will take a passion for God in our study of the Scriptures to fully understand his intended message—a humble awareness of God's *grace* to have the proper perspective of the *truth* in the Bible. This spiritual submission to the ultimate author and dependence on his Spirit must precede our study and result in wisdom rather than just information. In addition to these attitudes, we must empathize with the human author God used. We must be sensitive to his situation, his cultural frame of reference, and the values and needs of his original audience. We must hear the words as they were heard by them. This means the theologian will need a proper hermeneutic—a historical, grammatical, and *cultural* exegesis for their work.

In the end we must live what we have learned, or we have not learned it. Many theologies have damaged the faith in their communities. The friends of Job in the Old Testament or the Judaizers Paul fought against in the New Testament worked against God's purposes. The sin of the Pharisees in the Gospels and Acts is an example of theological study gone wrong. It was not just hypocrisy; the seed and the result of their sin was legalism, which gave birth to pride. They added to God's word what they interpreted was to be required, and then, claiming their information was from God, they blackmailed the people of Israel into submission to their Oral Torah. There may be no sin greater than misleading God's people.

141. APPROACHING GOD

It is no different today, except that there are many more wrongheaded and wrongly motivated theologies among us than ever before, denying huge swaths of God's revelation to emphasize what they desire to be true. Though they claim to reveal God's true intentions, they put their words in his mouth or twist his to their advantage. Honesty and humility must describe our approach to knowing God. They must precede our study; submission to what we learn and trust for what he does not tell us must follow it. If we let God speak for himself, we will find grace blended with truth. It is there for all who will accept it, for God is "not wanting any to perish" but for all "to come to a knowledge of the truth" "that leads to godliness" (2 Pet 3:9, 1 Tim 2:4, Titus 1:1).

Scripture References: Ps 25:9; Prov 15:33, 21:2-3; Isa 58:6-12; Dan 10:12; Hos 6:6; Mic 6:8; Mark 7:6-8; John 1:17; 7:18 with 8:32; 17:3; Rom 12:11; Gal 1:6-9; Eph 3:11-13; 1 Tim 2:1-6, 4:1-8; 2 Tim 2:15, 3:16-17; Titus 1:1, 5-16; 2:11; Heb 4:16, 11:6; Jas 1:22-25, 3:13; 2 Pet 3:9, 17-18; 5:6; Rev 22:18-19.

142. Beginnings of a Life with God

Therefore, if anyone is in Christ, he is a new creation; the old has gone, the new has come.

—2 Cor 5:17

THE CHRISTIAN JOURNEY BEGINS for many in the storms of life, in the hours following a tragedy, or in a narrow escape from disaster with a rather sudden realization that they have forgotten God and desperately need his help. For others that realization comes more slowly in the ordinary routines of life. Some only realize after years of church attendance that, in their superficiality, they have not allowed God to have his way in their lives. But all must recognize what God has done for them in Christ, his far-reaching forgiveness of their self-centered values, and his lavish grace regarding their pride. The amazement should never weaken, the gratefulness never fade. Undeserving and humbled, we come to regret and detest our past sins. As C. S. Lewis would say, God's declaration of grace is an "intolerable compliment" we must humbly accept as true.

We must, then, begin growing in the knowledge of God and his ways. We learn to go along in life with an awareness of his presence and an acknowledgment of him in the events and circumstances of life, growing in confidence and trust in his providence. We will want to honor his name in everything, even though we do so imperfectly. Because we have let him in, we will grow in virtues such as compassion, kindness, love, humility, loyalty, etc. They will increasingly motivate our everyday behavior on our journey to God's destination. This growing relationship with him lasts a lifetime. When we get old, we look back and see that even on our worst days, he was faithful to us and his purposes for us. And if we pay attention, we see his continued work in us today. He promises to be faithful to it until the day of

142. BEGINNINGS OF A LIFE WITH GOD

Christ. We are his projects. Each is a work of art different from the next but with unmistakable evidence of the hand of the Creator.

Scripture References: 2 Chr 7:14; Pss 91:14–16, 145:14; Prov 3:5–7; 1 Cor 13:1–13; 2 Cor 5:15–17; Gal 5:22–26; Eph 1:3–13, 2:1–10, 3:14–21; Phil 1:6, 2:12–13, 4:4–9; Col 1:9–14; 1 Tim 1:12–17; 2 Tim 3:17; Titus 2:11–14; 2 Pet 1:3–11.

143. What Is It to Be Spiritual?

Abraham believed God, and it was credited to him as righteousness, and he was called God's friend.

—Jas 2:23

SOME PEOPLE GET STARTED in their life with God and then get sidetracked, if not totally derailed, by an emphasis on discovering their spiritual gift, searching for God's will, wondering about a call from God for their life, or waiting for a sign. These are complexities people have added to the life God has asked of us. These people are taking one side or another of a Bible verse and are leaning on their personal and social needs instead of God's intentions. In their search for the key to knowing God, discovering what he wants us to know, and finding the secret to a "successful" Christian life, these may fall into syncretism, mysticism, or legalism. This is not the way; Jesus is.

Throughout the Bible, God tells us he is looking for those who are faithful, those who trust him. He does not tell us to "understand what the Lord's will is" (Eph 5:17) and then hide it from us so that we spend a lifetime searching for it, trying to discover the secret key to pleasing him. What he wants from us is and always has been before us in his word. But that sounds too simple, and many struggle to feel "spiritual." They wait anxiously or search frantically: surely, God will open the door to the mysteries of being spiritual or the behavior necessary to maintain his approval. But all the while God is looking at our hearts. Will he find we trust him or lean on our efforts to pursue secret discoveries?

It's not a game of hide-and-seek. It is a matter of being. Being grateful for God's grace, trusting in his providence, and desiring to honor him in the renewing of our minds puts us on a path of knowing and doing his "perfect

143. WHAT IS IT TO BE SPIRITUAL?

will" (Rom 12:2). Seeking to live in this relationship with him results in contentment, peace, and the right motives for behavior that honors him. We are becoming "the pure in heart" (Matt 5:8). We don't have to stew about what we should do; we realize he is more interested in what we are and that we are allowing ourselves to be "transformed" (Rom 12:2). We are not perfect in this life for him. But we are overwhelmed with who he is and what we are in Christ—children of the all-powerful, sovereign God of grace and love, who hears and answers our prayers while moving his universe toward the consummation of his plan.

Scripture References: Pss 15:1–5, 51:16–17, 91:14–16; Prov 21:2–3; Isa 58:6–12; Hos 8:6; Mic 6:8; Matt 5:3–10, 6:33–34; Luke 7:9; 18:1–8, 9–14; John 1:12; 4:24; 7:18; 14:6, 27; 17:3; Acts 20:25–31; Rom 5:1–2, 12:1–2; Eph 5:15–21; Phil 1:9–11, 3:17—4:1 with Col 3:1–4; Phil 4:6–7; 1 Thess 4:11–12; Titus 1:14; 2 Pet 3:3; 1 John 1:9.

144. The Simplicity or Complexity of Faith

For in the gospel a righteousness from God is revealed, a righteousness that is by faith from first to last.

—*Rom 1:17*

BEING A FOLLOWER OF Christ in the Gospels was a "simple loyalty"—that is, it was costly but not complicated. No one was worried about what their spiritual gift was. No one was anxious about getting a special call from God. No one was worried about whether they should be missionaries in a foreign land. Those who *were* called to some extraordinary part in his plan were not expecting or seeking it and, when it came, could not have missed it. It was not long, however, before this simplicity developed into complexity as influential people added requirements to the faith of the early believers. Some required obedience to the law of the Old Testament (Judaizers), and others, miraculous signs, wonders, and spiritual gifts to prove one's spirituality (Corinthians).

Paul dealt with this complexity and confusion in the early churches in the book of Acts and his many Epistles. Later, John gives us God's response to seven churches in Asia that were missing the mark. It seems, however, that we have not yet learned our lesson in the institutional Christianity of our day. We have taken it upon ourselves to add definitions, rituals, competition, and materialism, or seek special attention from God beyond this faith to get what we want from him or stand out among other believers. Our individualism in Western culture, pushing self-assertion and the desire to be special, is part of the driving force behind this insistence. We are already *very* special to God, but we are so because we trust him, a matter of the heart. So there is something in human nature that wants more than God says we need. Adam and Eve allowed this desire to capture their hearts.

144. THE SIMPLICITY OR COMPLEXITY OF FAITH

In our organized churches, figuring out if you are doing the right things for God is difficult. In some cases it seems you are endlessly trying to meet the approval of other members, trying to attain some standard that has been subtly, or not so subtly, put in place. Some wonder if they can ever achieve the levels of spirituality others have erected. Everyone is supposed to talk like they enjoy whatever trend is shaping the worship service. Theological systems are put in place, and the average person can't figure out the definitions, why some Bible verses are more important than others, and some do not matter at all. Many people feel like they can never give enough, serve enough, or attend enough meetings to meet the demands.

What have we done to the faith? One gets the feeling that some questions are not supposed to be asked because they "rock the boat" or are too "unspiritual" to ask. There are politically correct Christian ways to talk about certain issues that are a mystery for the average person in attendance, and only certain groups are "in the know."

Christians in the early churches also had disagreements and struggled to act like the body of Christ. New Testament writers constantly sought to bring them back to the essentials of the faith. It is time for us, too, to return to the simplicity of humble acceptance of God's grace, loyalty to Christ, trusting God's providence, pursuing his honor, serving him in whatever we do, and having respect and love for our brothers and sisters. If human demonstrations of "spiritual success" are required, if it is about achieving a certain status above others, or if money is proof of God's favor, people are left to struggle with the resulting complexity we have added to God's word; we are talking about "a different gospel" (2 Cor 11:4 with Gal 1:6–9). Faith is still costly, but it has never been complicated nor has it demanded the discovery of secret or hidden things.

Scripture References: Ps 51:6a and 16–17 with John 4:23–24; Ps 62:10b; Isa 66:2b; Mic 6:8; Matt 5:3–10, 6:21, 7:13–14, 8:5–10; John 3:16, 7:18, 8:12, 12:24–26, 14:6, 17:20–23; Acts 16:31; Rom 14:1 with 5, 8, 10, 13 and 22; 1 Cor 14:12; 2 Cor 9:8, 11:1–6 with Gal 1:6–9 with 5:1–6; Phil 1:21 with 3:13–16; 2:1–8; 4:8–9; Col 2:8–9; 2 Pet 1:3–8; Jude 3; Rev 2:1—3:22.

145. Spiritual Disciplines

True worshipers will worship the Father in spirit and truth, for they are the kind of worshipers the Father seeks.

—John 4:23

THE SPIRITUAL DISCIPLINES THAT draw us near to God are mostly unseen. Personal prayer is to be done with the door closed, and true worship is in spirit and truth. Though we may often worship with the community of believers, personal worship in our hearts strengthens us for each turn on the journey of our lives. Growth in this relationship with God and trust in his goodness and providence means sticking close to his word and living in communication with the one who created and oversees the universe. Opportunities to serve him will present themselves as we pursue a natural, everyday expression of his grace in our lives.

But there is a danger of using "spiritual" disciplines as personal achievements, to make an impression, to assert legalistic control over others, or to compensate for feelings of guilt. Some even find satisfaction in controlling themselves with rigorous disciplines and look down on a more spontaneous Christian life, even though it is the natural expression of faith that Jesus taught us. Others turn these disciplines into secret ways to earn God's approval or blessing, but there is no magic in prayer, Bible study, or worship, public or private. Putting a spiritual discipline on the schedule can do as much harm as good. It is a matter of the heart. Perhaps the worst motive for spiritual disciplines is self-centeredness—seeking personal status among other Christians. The results of using Christianity for selfish reasons may not be readily seen by others in this life . . . but God knows our motives.

As good and helpful as scheduling, order, and planning might be, God is not impressed with our personal discipline records, and he will not be put

145. SPIRITUAL DISCIPLINES

on an agenda. No gimmicks or rituals make him more inclined to listen or help. He looks at the heart, always the heart. Once again, it is more about being than doing. He seeks our loyalty. He knows those who honestly and humbly seek him. They are not perfect, but his grace in their lives is.

He is at work in us, shaping and molding us as we meet him in his word and prayer, and practice our faith in the blessings and challenges of our circumstances. He wants to "work in us what is pleasing to him" (Heb 13:21). The truth, humility, and depth of faith are usually expressed outside the structure we try to give to life. Unfortunately, these unplanned occasions are often seen as interruptions or inconveniences when they are God's opportunities to grow in faith and loyalty, opportunities for us to serve him by encouraging and helping others. We frequently do not notice these occasions, passing over them even though we may have said our prayers on time and made it to another meeting at the church. Faithfulness is about living our lives for him not checking things off our schedule. Honesty, humility, and wisdom must accompany discipline that prepares us for service.

Scripture References: 1 Chr 29:17a and 18b; 2 Chr 7:14; Pss 15:1–5; 33:18; 51:6, 16–17; 91:14–16; 145:17–19; Prov 15:26; 16:2, 25; 17:3; 20:27; 21:3; Jer 29:12; Hos 6:6; Mic 6:8; Matt 6:1–8, 25:34–40; Luke 16:14–15; John 4:23–24; Rom 8:26–27; Eph 2:8–10 with 4:12 and 2 Tim 3:16–17; 1 Pet 3:15.

146. Missionaries?

> We continually remember before our God and Father your work produced by faith, your labor prompted by love, and your endurance inspired by hope in our Lord Jesus Christ.
>
> —*1 Thess 1:3*

SOME PEOPLE HAVE THE particular task of being cross-cultural missionaries, but every Christian needs to be a missional person. The biblical priority is on what we are rather than what we do. So being missional depends on our motives and purposes. It means seeking to be part of God's plan rather than letting him be part of our plan for life. Instead of bringing recognition, for most people, it will be the faithful Christian life, loving others, and trusting God in the home and on the job. It is simply being faithful to God and his message, doing all we can to incarnate his will and way, and making his intervening love, the mystery of his providence, and the paradox of his grace known in the everyday events of life.

But what about a "call"? God called certain people in the Bible to do particular things in his plan. However, there is danger in thinking that we must each be called in the same way. It makes people feel special if they believe they have received a specific, individual call from God for a special task, and, as individualists, we may fall into the trap of desiring to be special in that way. But we have *already been called* to be disciple makers anywhere and everywhere. Geography is not the main thing in this calling. Any cultural context is a "mission field." Yes, God called some in the Bible to participate in particular and far-reaching endeavors for him, but they were not waiting on or seeking that call. God stepped into their lives, and, most of the time, it was not an agreeable experience. It did not often bring recognition and applause from those around them. If God wants you to do something

146. MISSIONARIES?

special in his plan, you can be sure, like Saul on the road to Damascus or Joseph being sold into slavery by his brothers, you will not miss it. However, the vast majority of God's people do not have such an experience.

We are "called" to a life of loyalty to his purposes and trust in his providence in day-to-day faithfulness at home, at work, and at school. This loyalty and trust become a lifestyle that gives an authentic witness to his goodness and credibility to the message of his grace in a lost world. In all this, we have a part in making disciples. It is the high calling of God in our lives. His providence may indeed open the door to cross-cultural missionary work or pastoral ministry for some of us. These particular endeavors require special training and preparation to serve God well, which is also part of that calling. But unless or until his providence and Spirit lead in such a direction, we are called to loyalty and trust in the part he has already given us in making disciples.

If God is leading you in the direction of ministry outside your own culture, pray for his continued guidance and be sure to lean on wisdom more than emotions. Not everyone is called, sent, or even intended to go to a foreign culture to make disciples. The participle we translate as "go" in Matt 28:19 might better be translated as "going" or "as you are going" (as you are going through life). Instead of giving us a command, an imperative to go somewhere to make disciples, he is calling us to a lifestyle that can contribute in many ways to help make disciples anywhere.

As a Christian, you are a personal agent of God in his mission in the world, your community, the next town you visit, or on longer journeys and in other lands. It is a full-time calling for everyone committed to God and loyal to his purposes, not just missionaries and pastors, as important as their ministries are. He saved us by his grace "to do good works" (Eph 2:8-10) and gave us his word so that we might be "thoroughly equipped for every good work" (2 Tim 3:16-17). So keep yourself in shape for good works. Stay focused. Stay faithful. Trust God. Set your mind on things above. Allow God to work out his providential plan for you. Don't count on your feelings. Recognize that God is good even when the way is rough. Never doubt that he is in sovereign control of his plan, even if we do not know how he has decided to accomplish it and how he will use us in it. These attitudes and values make a person missional.

Scripture References: Dan 3:16-18; Matt 5:14-16, 28:18-20; Acts 1:8; Rom 12:1-2, especially 2b; 2 Cor 9:8, 12:7-10; Eph 2:8-10; Phil 2:12-16a; Col 3:1-4; 1 Thess 4:11-12; 2 Tim 2:15, 20-21; 3:16-17; Titus 2:13-14; 3:8 and 14; Heb 13:20-21; 1 Pet 2:12; 2 Pet 3:10-12a.

147. Motives and Ritual Behavior

For I desire mercy, not sacrifice, and acknowledgment of God rather than burnt offerings.

—Hos 6:6

STRUCTURED BEHAVIOR CAN SERVE a purpose for Christians, especially in our early days, to help us grow in our understanding of God and trust in his providence. But we must grow in our faith beyond the necessity of ritual and regimented behavior, the elemental things of the faith, to walk with him in our natural behavior of everyday life. As Paul would say, we must get beyond the milk of early days to the solid food of a mature faith. Wisdom from God's word, not legalism, must guide our faith, directing our choices, thinking, and behavior. Recognizing we are in a process, on a journey, we must be considerate of those at earlier stages of their walk with Christ.

Ritual behavior is repeated activity that can, unfortunately, be performed by anyone and with various motives. Natural behavior is how we go about our daily activities. Ritual practice is a means but not an end in itself. We often assume its role in our Christian lives is always good, but it can also become a legalistic way of life and may be thought to earn God's approval. But God is looking at us through the righteousness of Christ and at our hearts and motives for what honors him. Ritual behavior is only good in so far as it takes us there.

It is not that we do not need to hear biblical teaching or have fellowship with other believers, but as soon as missing a Sunday at church produces feelings of guilt, we have given ritual a way to control us. If having devotions trumps loving your neighbor, something is wrong. If showing up at a Bible study is meant to show others your dedication, attendance is for the wrong purpose. There are things prescribed for Christians in the Bible, and

147. MOTIVES AND RITUAL BEHAVIOR

spiritual disciplines have their place—in secret. Rituals can strangle faith and become a matter of personal pride if not kept in their place. External practice should be driven by the internal desire to flourish in our relationship with God, honor his name, fulfill his plan, encourage others, and be salt and light in the world. This godliness often does not meet the social expectations institutional Christianity has generated nor fit into a planned schedule. Making disciples and teaching them can take many forms, but the genuineness of the disciple maker will matter more than the structure we give to a program. Their approach must be "from a pure heart and a good conscience and a sincere faith" (1 Tim 1:5).

Scripture References: Ps 91:14–16; Prov 3:5–7, 21:3; Hos 6:6; Mic 6:8; Matt 5:8, 6:1–15, 28:18–20 with John 17:15–23; Rom 14:1–8; 1 Cor 3:1–2, 10:23–31; Gal 5:13–14; Phil 1:9–11; Col 1:10–12; 1 Tim 1:5–7; 2 Tim 3:5, 7; Heb 5:11–14; 1 Pet 2:16–17, 3:15.

148. The Human Jesus

He was despised and rejected by men, a man of sorrows, and familiar with suffering.

—Isa 53:3

IT IS CRUCIAL THAT we understand that Jesus was both God and man. God contextualized himself in our situation so we could see and feel him, so our human minds could know him. In becoming a man, he reveals God's attitude toward the human body he created, that it is good and not evil. But Jesus also accepts all the limitations and weaknesses of a body and the social expectations living in a collective community can generate. It is essential to see Jesus as a real human being. But we often see him more in terms of his divinity during his days on earth, which removes him from being our example for this life.

In his humanness, Jesus knew what it was to be exhausted, frustrated, and misunderstood; he knew sorrow and longing. Somehow, we hardly think his temptations could have been anything like ours or that he had to learn obedience and submission as we have to. But it is true. Jesus was tempted the same way we are. He also had to submit to God when, in his humanness, he preferred something else. Yet he overcame human weakness to serve and honor his Father in each instance, to the very end. Jesus tells us, "Take heart! I have overcome the world" (John 16:33). We will not do so perfectly, but his example is before us so that we can shape our inclinations and calibrate our intentions toward the goal.

He can and does empathize with us on our worst days. He is there, understands, and has written his name on our souls and ours in his book; we belong to him, and he will help his own, though it may not look like we expect it to. His love and grace—his steadfast love in the Old Testament

148. THE HUMAN JESUS

(*hesed*) and far-reaching grace in the New Testament (*charis*)—still overflows. Though not always in ways we readily perceive, even on our bad days, he is at work in us, shaping us and moving us toward his purposes. He brings meaning and purpose into life when we allow him his way and trust his providence in our situation. It is true that when we are weak, as we often are, he is strong. His attention is on us, the last of any we would expect him to notice, but the first shall be last, and the last, first.

Scripture References: Pss 31:5, 15–16, 21–24; 34:18; 77:1–12; 103:13; 142:1–7; Isa 43:1, 53:1–6; Matt 5:3–10, 12:20, 20:13–16, 26:36–46; John 10:28–30; 16:33 with 17:15 and 1 John 1:1–4, 2:15–17; 2 Cor 4:6–7, 9:8, 12:7–10, 13:4; Eph 3:12; Phil 1:6, 2:12–13; 1 Thess 5:24; Titus 2:14 with Isa 43:1 and Rev 20:11–15; Heb 2:5–18, 4:14–16, 5:7–10, 10:19–23; 1 John 1:1–4.

149. Behavior and Freedom in Christ

If you hold to my teaching, you are really my disciples. Then you will know the truth, and the truth will set you free.

—*John 8:31–32*

OUTWARD BEHAVIOR IS ROOTED in our values and motives, which make up the expression of our personalities, good or bad. God looks at these intentions of the heart. Our freedom in Christ for behavior is based on new inclinations from renewing our minds in Christ, which conditions and transforms our intentions, values, and motives. As this happens, we can express ourselves and live our lives with the freedom of knowing that all God created, when used as he intends, is good; it is pure. We enjoy this freedom within the boundaries of love for God and neighbor. Why we do something is often more important than what we do. We must seek to glorify God, that is, to make his character, attributes, and works known. If we reject this freedom in Christ for a legalistic pattern given to us by grace-starved "Christians," their social expectations and unrelenting demands, and the grim self-determination behind them, become cold and unrelenting laws in our lives, dividing grace from truth that came together with Jesus.

Under the cloud of legalism, "spiritual disciplines" intended to shape our hearts to live for God in freedom become a prison of efforts to earn God's approval or favor, prove our repentance, and even gain forgiveness so we will feel better about ourselves. But grace does not demand works for forgiveness, spiritual achievements for acceptance, or rituals fulfilled for approval. Spiritual disciplines have a different purpose altogether. They are not intended to be benchmarks to measure spirituality. The New Testament gives us a different measuring stick. We are to know people by their fruit—their natural behavior in everyday life—not their ritual behavior. When our

149. BEHAVIOR AND FREEDOM IN CHRIST

motive is to love and honor God, there is a great deal of freedom in our lives, for "to the pure, all things are pure" (Titus 1:15), and "everything God created is good" (1 Tim 4:4-5).

The traditional beliefs about these Christian disciplines are not always biblical, but they are not always human and dated either; we have to measure the traditional against the biblical standard. In the Bible, spiritual disciplines are meant to change us for *his* purposes, not ours. They are not intended to make us feel better about ourselves or look better to others but to shape us into people he can use in his kingdom. Instead of people who think they have to earn God's approval, we need to be people who know that, undeserving as we are, we are already bathed in his grace. As such, we become people who know and trust God in life's ordinary and extraordinary events and circumstances, making him known (glorifying him) through behavior shaped by freedom in Christ and bounded by love for God and neighbor. Spiritual disciplines and life in the church should help us grow in these values, motives, and the resulting wisdom.

Scriptures References: 1 Chr 29:17a and 18b; Prov 15:26 with 16:2 and 17:3; 20:27; Isa 58:6-12; Hos 6:6 with Mic 6:8 and Prov 21:3 and Ps 51:16-17; Matt 5:8; John 1:12, 14, 17; 3:16; Rom 5:6-8, 8:31-32, 11:6, 14:16-18; 1 Cor 10:23-24 with 10:31 and Rom 14:22; 2 Cor 3:17; Eph 1:6-8, 2:8-10; Col 2:16-23, 3:17; 1 Tim 1:12-17, 6:17b; Heb 4:16; 1 Pet 3:18 with 2 Pet 3:18.

150. God's Ways Are Not Our Ways

God chose the foolish things of the world to shame the wise; God chose the weak things of the world to shame the strong.

—*1 Cor 1:27*

DO NOT EXPECT GOD to answer you on your terms as if you understood every detail of his plan in the world. In his providence, he uses what we consider nothing, the weak and foolish things of the world, the things that appear adverse to us, to bring about his plan. In his paradoxical manner, the last will be first and the first, last. It is a question of whether we want his purposes more than ours. There is mystery, and we do not know everything about his strategy, but we can trust his goodness, that his plan has its purposes, and that those purposes are perfect. Why and how God has decided we can participate in his workings in the world is beyond our understanding. But he has, nevertheless, chosen to hear the prayers of his people in his Son's name, and act in ways of response that change the course of events and, perhaps, suspend natural laws.

Let God be God. Beware of people who design doctrines that, because they need a neat theological package that emphasizes their preferences, decide what the Bible says about God and what he says to us so it fits their system. Their theology may identify them as part of a popular group, but they do not allow God to act except on their terms. Theology should not use the filter of our human preferences when it is distilled from God's word. It should help us understand *God's* mission in the world and *his* intentions and desires for his children. It is extremely valuable when and as long as it does this faithfully. But they are all human systems, and when they limit God to their "complete" understanding of his ways or require him to meet their human expectations or preferences, we need to give them a critical

150. GOD'S WAYS ARE NOT OUR WAYS

eye. Such was the theology of the Pharisees in the Gospels and the Judaizers in the Epistles. Such is some theology today.

His thoughts are not like our thoughts; they do not fit our limited human logic and its frantic requirements to avoid ambiguity and uncertainty, or its obsessive need for systematic order. He is not limited by the restraints of our perception of time. Whether we like it or not, he is God. He will do what is good and necessary in his own way. We bend the knee to the God of unlimited power, flawless justice, lavish grace, and endless wisdom.

Scripture References: Deut 32:4; Pss 33:11 with 20–22; 89:8, 14; 103:6–18; Isa 40:13–14, 28; 46:10; 55:8–11; Hab 2:20; Matt 7:7–12, 13–23; 21:21–22; Luke 4:24–30; John 15:5–8; Acts 20:25–31; Rom 11:33–36; 1 Cor 1:18–31; Gal 1:6–9; Eph 1:7–8; Jas 2:5, 4:13–17.

151. The Good and Evil of Humankind

Woe to those who call evil good and good evil, who put darkness for light and light for darkness, who put bitter for sweet and sweet for bitter.

—Isa 5:20

WHAT IS TRADITIONALLY RIGHT or wrong in people's minds is more than merely a social construct. These boundaries developed over time and are hard won through generations of painful trial and error for the survival of society. They are then passed on to each new generation. No matter how "primitive," every society has some version of social rules, a human moral code, a community conscience with values and virtues at the core, and even if they are not perfectly expressed, they are called up when things go wrong. Though other moral codes are expressed quite differently than ours, these values stand behind what is considered good or bad behavior for each group. It is some version of respect for others contrasted with concern only for oneself, showing up in inconsideration or disregard for the well-being of others. However, people can rise against this traditional, cultural, moral code, and their self-interest brings about antisociety—oppressive regimes that seek to blackmail the world through terrorism. Judicial enforcement in each community is an effort to maintain moral and ethical standards, justice, and peace for the safety of the people. It can prolong social survival until it becomes corrupt itself or the people try to extinguish its authority, which brings about the demise of that survival.

In light of these existing human moral codes and traditions, we must use caution when encouraging social change. Since they were put in place over time to provide for the security and survival of society, their removal risks that survival, allowing the problems once solved to return in a socially

151. THE GOOD AND EVIL OF HUMANKIND

destructive way. Robert Frost said that we should not take fences down until we know why they are there. If this is true of human social systems that eventually fail, how much more critical are the boundaries God has given humankind for their survival.

The necessity for morality, justice, consideration, respect, and good works in society is greater than each individual imagines. It is a constant need in human cultural systems—a minimum law for survival. Without it, all perish. But where does this cultural conscience in every society come from? It is not generated afresh within each society, but rather its themes, however expressed, are common to all people from a beginning point outside the human race—the seeds of this conscience come from God himself. However, they are taken over by human understandings, preferences, and religions as he is forgotten. The knowledge of good and evil is a fundamental law in the universe since the garden of Eden and cannot be erased On the human level, this law operates on the free will God gave to each person to choose the good he gives us or the evil that separates us from him. On the spiritual level, every person is accountable to God for this choice of trusting or rejecting God.

Unable to fix the guilt and shame of our sin against God by ourselves, God intervened in our situation with his grace through the sacrifice of his Son on behalf of all humankind. For all who accept it, this sacrifice purchases the only ultimate justice and forgiveness for the wrong between humans and God himself, and becomes the basis for forgiveness between people. So the two roads exist for the choosing. By God's grace, loving him and others leads to the flourishing of life—a law that cannot be canceled. Rejecting God's grace and living in hatred is endless death—separation from God, another law that cannot be erased. Depending on the road they choose, people are either closer to one end of that continuum or the other. Some are better than others on the good end, and some worse than others on the evil end, but all at either end are headed for the outcome of their decision for or against God. Those unable to make such a decision are in the hands of God, whose goodness, justice, grace, and wisdom are perfect. He will do what is good and right for them.

Scripture References: Eccl 3:11, 7:16–18 with 9:17–18; Isa 5:20–23; Matt 7:12–14, 24–27; 13:3–9 with 18–23; 25:31–46; John 1:10–12 with 3:16–17 and 36; 8:12; 14:6; 15:1–5; 17:15; Rom 3:21–26; Eph 2:1–10; Titus 2:11; Heb 13:15–16; Jas 3:13; 1 Pet 2:12 and 15; 3:18; 1 John 1:9; 3:16–19, 36; 4:7–21.

152. Personal and Social Choices

Light has come into the world, but men loved darkness instead of light.

—*John 3:19*

THE SURVIVAL OF A society has its source in God alone. Each person must respond to God's grace to be included among those who have the peace of trusting his goodness and providence. The Creator of human beings knows what will make a society flourish and what will be its ruin. But mankind follows the natural inclination to be loyal to self and human social rewards instead of to God. A few choose God, and, though each has their weaknesses, their lives can affect the lives of others as God uses them. But in their natural condition, people are influenced by their experiences, preferences, and desires, as well as by the choices of others in their group, and the group is influenced overall by the cultural values of their larger community. These influences are not toward God but away from his grace and toward the disintegration of society.

People have to decide to honor God with their lives or feel included in society among those who do not. As those choosing to serve themselves become more powerful, they lead society away from God. This leads to its disintegration and, unless corrective measures are taken, to its ultimate and inevitable end. But all is not lost. God waits for people to turn to him, to his grace, and to give him their loyalty. When individuals find his peace, they can be preserving salt and hope-filled light to the rest of society as they influence others around them through their faith and good works in everyday circumstances, and some in a more public and direct manner. Some people will see the goodness of their lives, listen to their message, and find God's

152. PERSONAL AND SOCIAL CHOICES

grace. But most will not, and God will not wait forever. He who is rich in grace and shows mercy is also a consuming fire.

Scripture References: Prov 16:18; Isa 26:3–4; Matt 5:13–16, 7:13–14 with John 3:16–21 and 1:5; John 3:36, 5:24; 8:12; 11:25; 14:6 with 27; 16:33; 17:15–19; Acts 1:8; Rom 5:1–2; Eph 2:1–10; Phil 3:18–21, 4:4–9; 1 Thess 5:1–11; Heb 12:25–29; Jas 4:1–7a; 2 Pet 2:1–3; 3:8–11, 15a; 1 John 2:15–17.

153. Human "Justice" Judged

Evil men do not understand justice, but those who seek the LORD understand it fully.

—*Prov 28:5*

IN OUR HUMAN COMMUNITIES, we thrive on the hope of justice. Knowing wrongs can be set right, evil aggression stopped, and the downtrodden vindicated gives people hope. Though some will exploit the disadvantaged for political reasons and will attempt to force them to accept ridiculous and violent courses of action, some people put their shoulders to the wheel and work to help build up society. They know that if justice prevails among them, it will protect them and all people can have the same fair treatment, whether encouragement of their good deeds or punishment for their wrongdoing. This hope gives people strength. But justice is never perfect in human society. And when the hope for it is diminished, when justice is twisted to favor the strong or the rich or the immoral, when it turns a blind eye to illegal and criminal behavior, the community cannot survive; the society will perish.

As God's children, we may suffer injustice in this life. We may be accused, mistreated, and abused regardless of the good we try to do for the community. We live for God as lights in a broken world that loves darkness instead. All human justice eventually erodes. No society continues forever. We must wait for him, whose justice endures, to set things right. Even when everything is falling apart, the psalmist says, "Be still before the LORD and wait patiently for him" (Ps 37:7–8). Jeremiah reminds us, "It is good to wait quietly for the salvation of the LORD" (Lam 3:26). God tells us, "Be still and know that I am God" (Ps 46:10). He means we should *stop* our natural reaction and start trusting him. Our anxiety, fretting, defensiveness, and anger must be pushed aside, for "The LORD Almighty is with us" (46:7). "He

153. HUMAN "JUSTICE" JUDGED

will judge the world in righteousness" (9:8). He will come with light that will reveal every wrong disguised and every injustice thrust on his people. As imperfect as we may be, God knows our hearts, and we belong to him at a very great cost to himself. We are indeed his very own to whom he has shown perfect justice in Christ.

Scripture References Deut 32:4; Job 8:11–19; Pss 9:7–10; 37:3–9; 46:1–11; 49:16–20; 96:11–13 with 98:7–9; 130:5–6; Prov 16:8, 28:5–6; Isa 43:1; Lam 3:25–26; Mic 6:8; Hab 1:4 with 2:9–10; Rom 13:3–4; Col 1:21–23; Titus 2:14; Heb 10:23–24; 1 Pet 1:13–21, 2:13–17, 3:13–17, 5:10–11; 2 Pet 2:17–19, 3:8–11.

154. The Human Heart

Above all else, guard your heart, for it is the wellspring of life.
—*Prov 4:23*

WE SELDOM REALIZE HOW strong our self-interest is. But if we stop and think, we recognize how concerned or worried we are about . . . *me*. Our insecurities in the background, we want to keep *us* safe and avoid the things that might upset our personal well-being. We should not be surprised. The Bible tells us how self-concerned and wayward the human heart can be. Even great men of God like David and Solomon were not exempt from very human hearts that went their own way. We can never be off our guard; never forget how human we are. We must accept that we are slow to do good and swift to do that which will benefit our own satisfaction. With this spiritual alertness, we must continually direct our hearts toward the good before us, resisting selfish inclinations, and living for our God and those around us. Of course, we cannot be perfect. But we know who is, and we can ask him for forgiveness and help whenever we fail or feel overwhelmed. He knows us better than we know ourselves, freely forgives, and still loves us as his children.

Good works for others must become habitual for us, for God uses our faithfulness to strengthen people around us, and we must try not to fail them. It takes discernment, for we have been told to avoid some people, and we want to be careful not to enable bad behavior that creates problems for others. But when we can, we must help who we can, even in small ways. It is not that they deserve it, for neither do we, but because God asks it of us, and it is him we serve. We must show compassion that might bring them closer to God or encourage them to consider his grace. We are, after all, servants of a loving God who loved us who were least worthy of it. We will

154. THE HUMAN HEART

not be perfect at it, but his ways must come to characterize our lives more and more.

Scripture References: 2 Sam 12:13; 1 Kgs 11:1–6; Ps 1:1–3; Prov 3:27–28, 4:23–27, 13:20, 20:19, 22:24–25; Jer 17:7–10; Matt 5:16, 25:31–46; Luke 10:25–37; Rom 16:17–18; Eph 2:10, 3:7–13; Phil 2:1–4; 2 Tim 3:17; Titus 2:11–14; 3:1–2, 8, 14; Heb 6:7–12; 1 Pet 2:11–15, 3:18, 5:6–9; Jas 4:7; 1 John 3:16–18.

155. Theologians and Everybody Else

Now this is eternal life: that they may know you, the only true God, and Jesus Christ whom you have sent.

—*John 17:3*

KNOWING GOD IS VERY different than knowing things about him. There is no difference between the average plumber, delivery truck driver, school teacher, or housewife and the theologian before God if they all have honest faith and know the depth of God's grace for themselves. The simplest person may be miles ahead of the theologian in knowing God, though we often think quite the opposite. Of course, the reverse can be true as well. But the theologian draws a map of the details of God's being and works for the rest of us to follow so that we might know him better. Unfortunately, a person can draw a map without the smallest interest in the landscape. It can just be a job—a job he knows more about than someone who is not a theologian, but, as any cartographer, the job may not cause him to fall in love with the main feature of the terrain. And it is just as true that the piano tuner knows more about pianos than the cartographer, but he may or may not love music. So they are equal regarding knowledge of their particular vocations, and perhaps in their indifference about the intended outcome of their work. But the issue is not a matter of what they know. It is a matter of who or what they trust for meaning, purpose, and salvation in life, who or what they depend on to get through another day and to manage tomorrow. They must come to terms with the issue of the Creator-God who gave his Son to make us right, and with his purpose for our lives.

I don't mention feeling spiritual here. It doesn't matter if the theologian or piano tuner *feels* spiritual. Though imperfect, an honest heart and a life of practical faith and loyalty is what God looks for and, in Christ, is

155. THEOLOGIANS AND EVERYBODY ELSE

worthy before him. Honesty and humility are the essentials, not feelings of spirituality.

Scripture References: Ps 91:1 and 14–16; Luke 12:13–21 with Prov 3:5–10 and Mic 6:8; Luke 18:9–14; Rom 12:2; 1 Cor 1:18–31; Gal 5:5–6; Eph 2:1–10, 4:1; Phil 1:27; Col 1:10, 3:11–17; Titus 2:11–14; Heb 11:1 with 6, 8–19.

156. The Kingdom of Heaven First

But seek first his kingdom and his righteousness, and all these things will be given to you as well.

—Matt 6:33

SEEKING GOD'S KINGDOM FIRST is not a mystery we must solve, not a hidden path only a few can discover. It is made quite clear to us in the Bible. We are not looking for something but pursuing ways to honor God's purposes, ways to become good subjects by living, as much as possible, according to his ways in that kingdom. This is not a set of rules to obey but a cultivation of our hearts so that, as people who have a great deal of freedom in Christ, we desire to honor him with our choices and activities. We seek to become people of pure motives, commitment, loyalty, and grace. Though we are very different from one another, opportunities to honor God and serve his purposes are before us all the time and everywhere—in our homes, our neighborhoods, at work, and at school, in all our relationships.

We are not always at our best in serving God. Helping and encouraging others by incarnating God's love is his way and always a need. But it does not come at the most convenient times for us, and our lives are terribly busy with our schedules and needs as we multitask our way through the day to accomplish all our society says we must. So we are already putting a kingdom first, ours. But the time, energy, and talent we may use for our own purposes are not ours—the resources are God's; he gave them to us. He also gives us those opportunities in our busy lives to serve others while not neglecting ourselves. It is a matter of seeking the values of his kingdom first, not forgetting everything else but putting first things first. The story of Mary and Martha puts the concept in work clothes.

156. THE KINGDOM OF HEAVEN FIRST

Introverts and extroverts do this differently. God knows the challenges introverts face around other people. But he has grace for that, and they can effectively encourage others indirectly and reach out to other introverts around them. God gives them opportunities not available to extroverts who may struggle to be sensitive and empathetic, having their own challenges and risks in serving God. We are all different and must serve his kingdom in the way he gives us and allow others to do the same.

Living for God's kingdom is not all public ministry. For most it will be a wholesome family, our responses to frustrations, setbacks, and disappointments, helping our neighbors, or honesty and reliability on the job. It is, most importantly, carried out in our everyday tasks. No more for a pastor than the layperson, our personal lives and families must have the respect of those around us, win their trust, and show wholesome values. We must be responsible members of the community. This is a lifestyle of pursuing the values of his kingdom.

Scripture References: Ps 138:8; Matt 5:13-16, 20 with 6:33-34, 7:1 and 12; Luke 10:38-42; John 21:17-22; 1 Cor 10:23-24 with Phil 2:1-4; 2 Cor 9:8; Eph 4:1-7; Phil 1:6, 2:13; Col 1:9-12; 1 Thess 4:11-12; 2 Thess 3:6-13; 1 Tim 3:7; Titus 1:15; Heb 6:10.

157. Bad Maps to Knowing God

Show me your ways, O LORD, teach me your paths; guide me in your truth and teach me, for you are God my Savior, and my hope is in you all day long.

—Ps 25:4-5

ONE NEED NOT BE a theologian to know God. But godly and learned Bible teachers can help us understand more about God's intentions in the world and the blessings of our salvation. As we read the Bible with this help, we see his grace more clearly and understand more about the boundaries of our freedom in Christ. Theological studies can give us a richer and deeper view of who God is and how he would have us live as the whole of his revelation in the Bible is considered carefully.

On the other hand, helpful as some may be, other theological systems can limit our understanding instead of broadening it. Like a map in the wilderness that leads us to water or a compass on the high seas leading us to a safe haven, theology should lead us to God and a better understanding of his ways—but we must be careful of choosing just any map. Getting the wrong package from the delivery truck driver because of a faulty address can be sorted out. However, an inaccurate theological map can dilute or change the message of the Bible and keep us from God's goal of maturity in Christ. Syncretism (mixing cultural values with biblical values), mysticism (seeking confirmation of God's promises through signs and wonders), or legalism (adding rules and laws to what God has given us) twist God's message. Liberalism destroys the message, the prosperity gospel deceives the listener, and romantic sentimentalism is superficial, producing a popular Christianity without answers. These give us wrong ideas about God's ways and intentions for humankind. Worse, they can take us to a catastrophic

157. BAD MAPS TO KNOWING GOD

destination with irreversible consequences of loss and suffering—separation from God himself.

Yes, there are bad theologies. And sometimes theologians spend a great deal of time answering questions no one is asking about nonessential issues, adding detail to a complicated system that confuses and intimidates believers wanting to know God better. Others throw out half the Bible and accentuate the other half to make their system go in the direction they want and need. We must know God personally through Christ and have the help and wisdom he gives us in his word through his Spirit before we attach ourselves to one theology or another. We must hold any such system loosely since there is much we do not know, and divisions over what we think we know that he has not given to us are detrimental to our spiritual well-being and our witness to the world. Each map must be held up to the light of the Bible to see its veracity and limitations.

Scripture References: Lam 3:24–26; John 3:16–17; 1 Cor 10:23–24 with 31–33; Gal 5:13; Eph 1:3–23, 2:1–10; Phil 2:1–4, 3:18–19; 2 Thess 1:11–12; 1 Tim 1:3–7; Titus 1:5–16; Jas 1:5–8, 3:1; 1 Pet 2:16–17; 1 John 3:7, 4:1–6.

158. Love

Love is patient, love is kind.

—*1 Cor 13:4*

THERE ARE SO MANY uses of the word *love*. Here, we want only to think about that highest sort of love that intends the best for its object. Though we may desperately want love in the sense of kindness or making us feel special, the highest sort of love goes beyond this to expressions we may not like as well. Being selfish, we want happiness and may expect someone else's love to give it to us. And it may, but more may come of it. If it is the devotion of one who truly loves us, they will want our happiness but not necessarily seek to arrive at it in ways we would choose, and it may not look like what we imagined. A parent's love for a child will mean shaping them out of their selfishness into those who can be considerate of others and one day love their spouse, children, and neighbors unselfishly.

This type of love shows empathy and engages with those in need. Initially, it means taking the time and effort and setting our needs aside long enough to listen to them, taking a genuine interest in what they have to say. When people who love you listen to you, they do not get distracted in the middle of your sentence; they seem to have a lot of time for you and go out of their way to show consideration for you in your situation. These qualities are rare in our Western culture, and even among Christians where they should be characteristic in some measure, even though sometimes we must listen with the caution of wisdom. Creating continual dependency of others on us is not the object of love. It should make others more complete in themselves so they, in turn, can love those around them.

This kind of love finds its source in God, and has a certain seriousness and particular intentions for the best outcomes for its object. It carries tones

158. LOVE

of consistent loyalty, steadfast commitment, and deliberate purpose, bathed in honest, though sometimes severe, kindness to obtain the best ends for its object. So is God's love for us. It is not a static pronouncement but a working love of great cost to himself. Neither is it a sentimental sweetness but a sturdy and strong, purposeful relationship. He carries it out through his generous grace and good providence in our lives for his good purposes. If we accept his love, he will shape our lives as a potter, the clay. Not all that he does will be to our liking at the time, and early molding may not look like the finished vessel, but he has a purpose in mind, and he intends to achieve it. We may want to be a mug, but he is making a beautiful vase. He will constantly work to help us be better people, to better serve him, and to love others with the abilities he has given us. Each of us is "handmade," with noticeable variations between us to fit his purpose for each. Understanding that God has this goal and trusting his providence to accomplish it gives us peace and contentment, even in hardship and adversity, and will end in eternal happiness. As he said to Israel, he says to us, "I have loved you with an everlasting love" (Jer 31:3).

Scripture References: Deut 32:3–4; Prov 13:20, 14:7; Isa 64:8 not 29:16; Jer 31:3–6; Hos 11:1–4; John 3:16; 13:12–13, 34–35; 14:15 with 16:33; Rom 5:1–8, 8:28–39; 1 Cor 13:1–13; Eph 2:4–5; Phil 1:6 with 2:12–13; Jas 1:2–5; 1 Pet 1:3–7; 1 John 4:7–21.

159. Common Sense

O Lord Almighty, blessed is the man who trusts in you.
—Ps 84:12

A GOOD DEAL OF common sense about living for God is overlooked in our culturally shaped Western churches. We often look for something spiritual, like a special power not to sin, a distinct individual calling, a spiritual gift, or a miraculous change in our circumstances. But trusting him is the one thing he has asked of his people since the garden of Eden. Living our everyday lives in faithful loyalty to God and personal integrity is difficult when we are looking for something else, and we often need his grace and forgiveness. But keeping the goal before us is what is called for and is what he looks for in our hearts. The Old Testament based this faithfulness on an ongoing fear of the Lord and connected it directly to wisdom.

Modern individualists who love change and the latest trends are often bored with simple faithfulness. We try to add spiritual excitement to what seems like just another day in our lives. The movie industry, values on achievement and doing, or cultural ideas of success, self-worth, and importance influence us more than we realize. God would have us stop (be still) and realize the magnitude of his power, the unlimited rule of his sovereignty, and the extent of his lavish grace and good providence in our lives. It is *never* just another day.

It is not just you and me. Everyone has a personal battle, often known only to them, for which they need God's help and grace. They may think that help will come through spiritual acrobatics and miracles. But God is looking for simple, humble, and honest faithfulness in each heart—the desire to trust him in the negative associations, conflicts, and adversities of life. It will affect what we say and do. With the grace of God's continual

159. COMMON SENSE

forgiveness, this faithfulness becomes the core of our being and makes us worthy of the gospel. With it, he will accomplish his purposes in us and in the world. God does not use perfect people; he uses people like you and me who trust him.

Scripture References: 1 Sam 16:7; Pss 25:9; 33:11; 37:3-9; 46:1-3 with 7 and 10; 84:10-12; 111:10; 147:11; Prov 1:7, 3:5-7, 9:10, 12:11, 15:21, 16:2, 22:4; Isa 33:6; Hab 2:20; Rom 8:28; 1 Cor 1:26-31, 12:7-10; Eph 4:1-7; Phil 1:6, 27a; 3:13-14; 1 Thess 2:12; 2 Thess 1:11-12 with 1 Tim 2:1-4 and Titus 3:14; Heb 11:1 with 6; 1 Pet 1:13 with Col 3:1-4.

160. Confusion in Difficult Times

God is our refuge and strength, an ever-present help in trouble.
—Ps 46:1

DURING THE PANDEMIC OF 2020–2022, fear, frustration, and inconvenience touched every area of life. Worse than that, it was a time of sorrow for many at the loss of those they loved. It was a time of confusion and desperation. An earlier generation went through World War II and the great depression on the heels of World War I. It's never easy. But, even as Christians, we seemed less able to bear it in our generation. We were less prepared and unused to trusting God. We couldn't see it or feel it for our pain, but God was not absent. Our weakness did not limit his concern for us or his grace in our lives during the hard and often tragic times. During such adversity, commitment is tested, and some of us may still feel the pain. It may blur our ability to trust him, but he patiently waits for us to call on him and trust his response. He knows we live in a broken world of fragile peace and well-being. He has compassion for us. He didn't want it that way either. He gave mankind a perfect world but also the gift of free will, and our situation is the outcome of the choice not to trust him. But, though life is demanding, and many of us who know him may not recognize it, he is at work in us to give us *his* peace, and will accomplish *his* purposes in us now and on into the eternity with him that awaits us.

We never face desperate times alone. He may be giving us a measure of grace to live for him in our need, using the circumstances to build our faith or our example to encourage another, but he is patient. He knows it is difficult for us. Calmness in our confusion, comfort in our sorrow, and rest in our frustrated and worried hearts are his to give us if we trust him and

160. CONFUSION IN DIFFICULT TIMES

accept his peace, who has all grace in abundance. We must "be still before the Lord, and wait patiently for him" (Ps 37:7).

Scripture References: Deut 31:8; Josh 1:9; Pss 9:9–10, 23:4, 37:3–7a, 46:1–11, 62:5–8, 84:11–12, 91:14–16, 103:13–18, 139:1–12; Prov 3:5–7; Isa 26:3–4, 41:10, 42:3; Lam 3:24–26; Matt 6:25–34, 11:28, 12:20, 28:20b; John 14:27 with 16:33; 20:19–20; Rom 5:1–5, 8:18 with 31–32; 2 Cor 12:7–10; Phil 1:6, 2:12–13 with 4:6–7 and Eph 2:10; Heb 13:5b, 20–21; Jas 1:2–5; 1 Pet 1:3–7, 5:6–7.

161. Never Alone

So do not fear, for I am with you; do not be dismayed, for I am your God. I will strengthen you and help you; I will uphold you with my righteous right hand.

—*Isa 41:10*

IN OUR DARKEST HOUR, we do not face misfortune or tragedy alone. Some find it difficult, they may say impossible, to consider God as always being with them. They have faced trials beyond what they thought they could bear, and he seemed absent, far away, unconcerned. But we are trusting our emotions instead of reality. Though he does not force anyone to embrace his peace or know his comfort and safety, the fact is they are there as sure as the fact of gravity, though we may seldom give it a thought. Stressful circumstances are crossroads or moments of truth in people's lives that allow them to realize their inadequacies and need for God. But he seldom barges in. He waits for their invitation, their move in his direction, in a word, their trust.

Our cry for help may be conditioned by a reluctance to give him too much freedom in our lives, a fear that he will take us where we do not want to go, a dread that we are being asked to be like other Christians we have seen. But it is our imagination. If anything, it is a call not to be like other Christians we have seen but to know not religion, not legalistic demands, but a life-changing relationship with God and freedom in Christ you cannot now imagine and cannot otherwise know. The safety and security of his love cut us loose from the demands of culture and the social expectations of the crowd. His forgiveness is not conditioned on ritual behavior. It is free, so we might not be trapped in rituals, clichés, endless arguments and demands, hypocritical smiles, and pious frowns. He wants us for real, knowing all about us, to be his own, in humble gratefulness for his grace, and he

161. NEVER ALONE

reminds us every day that we are not alone. Our emotions and imagination may not lead us to this awareness, but trust in him does.

Scripture References: Deut 31:8; Josh 1:9; Pss 9:9–10, 16:11, 23:4, 33:16–22, 34:4–8, 37:3–7a, 56:3–4, 62:1–2, 73:23–26, 91:15, 94:17–19, 121:1–8, 130:1–4, 139:5–12; Prov 3:5–7; Isa 40:28–31; 41:10; 43:1, 5a; Matt 28:20b; John 14:21–27, 16:33, 17:3; 2 Cor 3:17; Eph 3:10–12; Phil 4:4–9; Titus 2:11–14; Heb 13:5.

162. Doubt

Did God really say, "You must not eat from any tree in the garden"?
—*Gen 3:1*

WE ARE GIVEN GOD'S words in the Bible. Yes, it has been abused by those who "say" they believe it to the point that we are repulsed by what is called "Christian" in some circles. Others try to cancel it, saying it is outdated, unreliable, and the source of unsubstantiated guilt from an ancient moral code that no longer serves our needs. They do not know its true value as they remove all its "undesirable" teachings. But those words are still his. Satan has and continues to plant doubt in people's minds so they will not pay attention to the grace and freedom God is offering to us. He pollutes the message with the lies of the world, false teachers, and poor examples of believers. His purpose is to keep God's word from bringing life to people. But his way leads to death—separation from God and the grace, peace, and security of his providential care for us. These are conditions we cannot know without opening our hearts and minds to God. He waits to make us his children and write his name on our souls, but many have long been looking the other way. Still, as he loved his chosen people, Israel, he loves us with an everlasting love.

We may not always understand what God is doing in us or in the world, but we need not be anxious. We can thoroughly trust the Creator-God of the universe and lover of our souls. What he wants us to know is clear if we let him speak for himself. We must read his words with fresh eyes and open hearts, not those twisted by Satan or tainted by our culture and social situation, not those of personal preference. Our culture may laugh at us, for they need us on their side in their insecure and uneasy boldness of rejecting God. But we must, nevertheless, let God speak, show us his truth, and wait patiently for him to act. He will never forget his own.

Scripture References: Gen 3:1-7; Pss 27:13-14, 37:3-7, 46:1-11, 56:3-4, 130:5-6; Prov 3:5-7, 12:15, 14:12; Isa 30:15 with 18; Jer 31:3-4; Lam 3:25-26; Hab 2:20; John 5:24 with 8:12, 42-47; Acts 20:28-31a; 1 Tim 1:3-7; 2 Tim 3:1-5, 16-17; 4:1-4; Titus 1:10-11; 2 Pet 3:8-9.

163. Remember

I remember the days of long ago . . . and consider what your hands have done. . . . I have put my trust in you.

—Ps 143:5, 8

GOD HAS BROUGHT US through many adversities in life. Through one thing and another, here you are, reading this page. Whatever troubled you yesterday and will come today and tomorrow are events not outside his awareness. And if he should allow us to suffer some injustice, physical pain, or emotional hurt, we must look back to his care for us in the past and trust him for today. As the Jews were to remember his deliverance of them from the power and slavery of Egypt, we too must look back to his power and providence, as well as to the cross of his sacrifice and grace in our lives, delivering us from the powers of darkness. Leaning on his word and trusting him in this broken world is our comfort and peace that nothing can take from us, and it must occupy our restless minds and hearts when everything seems to be going wrong. We should "not fear, though the earth give way and the mountains fall into the heart of the sea" (Ps 46:2). We live in the shadow of his great works and are embraced by his love, covered by the grace he has lavished on us.

Though he gives us much to enjoy in his creation—friends, pleasures, family, and nature—our lives are not primarily about our happiness here, but allow us to be part of the happiness of others. We can be part of their peace of mind through our help, our example of trusting God, and our reminder that he is able. Remember how he has cared for us in the past. His providence regarding our well-being is still at work. Though good or trouble is part of his plan today, his love takes us to where their definitions

163. REMEMBER

fade. Good will be beyond our expectations, and trouble will not exist to compare.

Scripture References: Judg 6:7–10 with 1 Sam 10:17–19a; Job 2:9–10; Pss 23:4; 28:7; 42:1–5; 46:1–11; 77:1–20; 78:40–43; 90:1–2, 14, 17; 91:1–2, 14–16; 145:13–14 and 18–19; Isa 26:3–4; Matt 6:31–34; John 14:27 with 16:33; Eph 6:12; Phil 2:1–4, 12–13; 4:4–9; Col 1:13–14; Jas 1:13–18; 2 Pet 3:8–17, 5:6–11; Rev 21:4.

164. Get Busy

Let us not love with words ... but with actions and in truth.
—1 John 3:18

SOME CHRISTIANS TEACH THAT people cannot do good since the fall of mankind in Eden. For there is none who is righteous, and all have sinned. These teach that all people are totally depraved. But people can do good and often do, though none are without sin. Many are called righteous throughout the Old Testament and were honored by God because they had faith with honesty and humility. They were not without sin, but in faith they did good things that honored God. Many Christians think they cannot do good works on their own, that somehow we have to let God do them through us. However, though we must give God all the credit for enabling us, spiritualizing the needed activity is not helpful. Doing good is exactly what we are told and reminded to do throughout the New Testament. Do we sin? Yes. Can we do good? Yes. We must not be laden with guilt for past sins God has forgiven. We must forgive ourselves and get off our knees. There is much good to be done, and the grace of God that forgives our sins gives us every reason, encouragement, resource, and opportunity to do it.

We are not to just listen to what God tells us, not to love with only words, but to do what he puts before us. To have concern that results in action, caring for the truly unfortunate and discouraged, living godly lives, building healthy families, and doing whatever is possible to show God's goodness as lights in a dark world is God's will for us. Jesus intended that people in the world around us would see "our good deeds" (Matt 5:16) and become those who praise God. God's work of grace in our lives is to result in the "good works" he has planned for us (Eph 2:10), and his word is to prepare us for "every good work" (2 Tim 3:17). As one of Jesus' "very own," we are to be "eager to do what is good" (Titus 2:14).

It is because of this that the qualifications for the selection of elders and deacons in the church can be so high. We can and should expect them to be people transformed by Christ into upright people who do good. They will not be perfect, but they must pursue godliness in their personal and public lives. Even non-Christians do good, some of them putting believers to shame, though it is not to honor God, and they lack saving faith. But we have every reason and admonition to walk worthy of the gospel and live lives of good works for God and for our neighbors.

Scripture References: Isa 64:5, 66:2b; Mic 6:8; Matt 1:19, 5:16, 25:40; Luke 1:6, 28; Rom 3:9–11, 22–23; 12:17–21; Gal 6:9–10; Eph 2:8–10, 4:1–6; Phil 3:13–14; 1 Tim 3:1–13, 6:18–19; 2 Tim 2:20–21, 3:16–17; Titus 2:14; 3:1, 8, 14; Heb 6:9–10, 13:15–16; Jas 1:22–27, 3:13; 1 Pet 2:11–12 with 15; 1 John 1:9, 3:17–18.

165. Simple Faith

Now faith is being sure of what we hope for and certain of what we do not see.

—*Heb 11:1*

WE HAVE MENTIONED THE theme of simple faith several times, and here we are again. Why is it so important to realize that God is looking for simple faith (humble trust) in the hearts of his followers? Part of the answer is our propensity to make spiritual things complicated, and part of it is our difficulty sorting out cultural values that influence us. We can get pretty foggy-headed about our faith if we do not realize it is a straight-up honest trust in God's relationship with us in Christ, and that it comes before everything else. Jesus talks about the simple faith of a child: "Anyone who will not receive the kingdom of God like a little child will never enter it" (Mark 10:15). He spoke of faith the size of a mustard seed—a tiny seed with tremendous potential. By "simple faith," I do not mean trusting God is naive or easy. I just mean it is not complicated or superspiritual. It is quite practical, actually, touching the ordinary things of life. But simple as it is, trusting God's grace and providence can be very hard, and most of us have far too little experience with it.

Though faith is simple, it is an absolute that cannot be overlooked without consequences. Without an acknowledgment of God, people become prey to every empty-headed philosophy from even a very small minority telling the masses, "It doesn't matter what you do." With this comes confusion about good and evil, making the prey even more vulnerable. The finishing touch is the blackmail of withholding social rewards, and even making it illegal not to follow their nonsense. All this for lack of rock-solid,

165. SIMPLE FAITH

clear-minded, commonsense, simple faith. There is a way that seems right to a man, but its end is not so good. Only a fool says there is no God.

Jesus counseled Martha, who had legitimate things to do with her time but was worried and bothered by the many tasks in the seeming urgency of the moment. He told her that one thing was worth more than all of that, looking to him. Did those things still need to be done? Of course. But peace is not to be found in getting everything done; it is found in him. Worth and value are not found in accomplishment but in the simple faith that honors him. We must seek his kingdom first. He looks at the heart for this trust and loyalty. Just as with worship—an expression of that faith—our trust in him is assurance bounded by humility and truth because we know him.

The complexity of doctrines does not make them more profound or grant the owner spiritual maturity, and a list of ministry accomplishments or display of emotional fervor does not necessarily reveal a depth of spiritual commitment. It is not about being a celebrity among Christians. True faith is an unassuming attitude of the heart, which may be found in the least expected people. The last will be first, and the least of these, the greatest.

We have many examples in the Bible of those who have gone before us with deep-seated faith. Hebrews, chapter 11, gives us a list of them. Though they did great things for God, their remarkable quality was their faith. We are inspired by those who trusted God, but this kind of faith is not just for exceptional people; there were many others among them whose names are not mentioned. Your name may never appear in a history book, but God is not looking for that. Though a few of us may be called on to demonstrate our faith in an outstanding way, God calls all of us to trust and faithfulness in the ordinary things of life. That is what Paul calls walking worthy of the gospel, worthy of the calling we have received. It is the trust in God we are all capable of, though we often fall short of it.

After the stunning intervention of God at the confrontation with the prophets of Baal on Mount Carmel, Elijah becomes discouraged, thinking he is the only one left who is faithful to God. But God tells him there are seven thousand who are still faithful to him. Interestingly, Elijah didn't know this, and, just as interesting, we are not given their names. Social recognition seldom comes with trusting God, but if we wait on him, personal peace does.

Scripture References: 1 Kgs 19:9–18; 1 Chr 29:17–18; Pss 14:1, 15:1–5; Prov 14:12; 15:26; 16:2, 25; 17:3; 20:27; 27:19; Isa 66:2b; Mic 6:8; Matt 5:3–10; 6:1–8, 33; 11:25 with 13:11; 17:20–21; 18:1–4; Mark 10:13–16; Luke 10:38–42, 17:6; John 14:27 with 16:33; Rom 3:18; 1 Cor 1:26–31; Eph 4:1; Phil 1:27, 4:4–9; 2 Thess 1:11–12; Titus 1:15; Heb 11:1 with 6; Jas 2:5.

166. Knowing God and His Purposes

Then you will be able to test and approve what God's will is—his good, pleasing, and perfect will.

—*Rom 12:2*

KNOWING AND DOING GOD'S will is possible for us all. Paul tells us it comes from a renewing of the mind—a transformation of the worldview and values we have allowed to control us in the past. In discussing God's will, the word *doing* might not be the best way to start the conversation since it is more about *being* a certain kind of person who knows and honors God in a relationship. It is a relationship in which we trust God, realize the richness of his love and grace, and seek to be faithful to his desires and loyal to his purposes. This new kind of person seeks to do what honors God. Though it begins with being something, knowing and doing God's will is not about being perfect.

For much of life, we will ask for his wisdom and then, using reason within the boundaries he has given us in his word, choose what we will do, say, and think. Occasionally we will be part of a movement of his providence in our lives for which we do not see his purpose or know the outcome. We will have to trust him. Gratefulness will follow, but it often takes time to appreciate what God does, to realize its importance for his purposes, and to see his grace at work. Sometimes we will suffer just because we are part of this world damaged by sin, but he is there for us and can turn these experiences into what honors him in our lives. Sometimes, we will never know his purpose for some event in this life, but our trust must be in the one who is always just and whose purposes never fail. God *will* accomplish his will, and it must become our desire for it to come about "on earth as it is in heaven" (Matt 6:10).

166. KNOWING GOD AND HIS PURPOSES

The Bible prepares us for maturity in Christ and the good works he desires. As we said earlier, knowing God's will does not make us perfect people, and our attempt at doing it sometimes proves the fact. But God does not put perfect people in the center of his will. There aren't any; if there were, it would deny that we need his grace, making it of no account. But as we come to him each day, he forgives us and uses us for his purposes as we seek to honor him. That is being in his will.

Though mystery surrounds God in many ways, the path to knowing him and his will is to rest in his grace, welcome our freedom in Christ, and allow his Spirit to change our thinking through his word. He looks at our hearts for trust in him and is satisfied to call those who believe, his children and heirs of his kingdom.

Scripture References: Deut 31:8, 32:4; Josh 1:9; 1 Sam 16:1–13 with 13:14; Jer 9:23–24; Pss 23:4, 25:8–10; Prov 16:2–4, 9; 20:24; Matt 5:3–10; John 1:12, 17:3; Rom 12:1–2; 1 Cor 10:31; Eph 1:15–23, 2:8–10, 4:11–16, 5:15–18; Phil 1:9–11, 2:12–13; 2 Tim 3:16–17; Titus 2:14; Heb 11:6; Jas 1:5–8 with 3:13–18; 1 John 1:8–10.

167. The Fall of Humankind

You must not eat from the tree of the knowledge of good and evil, for when you eat of it, you will surely die.

—*Gen 2:17*

MANY DOCTRINES, TOO MANY to count, have become parts of overly complex theological systems seeking to explain God or his works on our behalf. The doctrine of the fall of humankind is one of these. But this is where humility must find expression. Our knowledge is quite limited, and much has not been made known to us by God. We know we inherited death from Adam but are unsure how we could have sinned "in Adam" and Eve. Some think what they did was a unique action that put us all in a position of helpless sinners who can do nothing else. Yes, all men and women, believers or not, know suffering and death now that the original couple unlocked that door, and we are all indeed sinners, but it does not mean Adam and Eve are to blame for our sins today. They have the regrettable reputation of being the first humans to act on selfish ambition; they spoiled the perfect conditions God gave them, the ruins of which come down to us today, but we are sinners just as they were. They made their choice in a perfect situation. We make ours in a broken and spoiled world of suffering they passed on to us.

Though sin entered the world by one man and woman, and all suffer the results of that selfish choice, all have sinned and are sinners of their own accord. One of God's gifts to mankind, all of which were good, was the freedom to choose our allegiance and actions. Adam and Eve abused this freedom and decided to serve themselves above God, just as we do today. The results of their choice are known in the highest contrast to the perfection surrounding them. We may think we would not have done the same, but we are wrong. Their failure did not make it impossible for us to

167. THE FALL OF HUMANKIND

decide not to sin. We have fondled that belief for far too long. We are also responsible for the sacred gift of free will, and we choose to trust God or not to trust him daily.

If we could not choose good, the decision to not choose it would not exist. We could never do any of the good things the New Testament writers constantly tell us and remind us to do. We could not love, trust, or have compassion, or, for that matter, obey anything God is asking of us. The New Testament does not say, "Let God do it through you." It actually tells us to do things that honor God, to walk worthy of the gospel we have received, to do good works, and to make disciples. It is our own selfishness that makes us prisoners to sin as we allow it. God will give us wisdom and strength as we come to him for it, but we must choose to do what he has set before us as his children. We will not do this perfectly. That is the reason for his grace. But he looks for the humble acceptance of that grace and the desire to serve and trust him in our hearts.

Adam and Eve revealed the damage to our relationship with God that results from abusing our freedom. Every day humankind adds to the evil and suffering the original two people brought into the world. As those who know God's grace, we must confess our selfish choices and recalibrate our relationship with the Father. Our potential to abuse our freedom is always there, and Satan takes advantage of it. We need God's help to identify Satan's ways and then must resist his deception. God's love and sacrifice for us is a great motivation; his Spirit will strengthen our desires to serve only him and change our thinking about him and ourselves as we read his word, but God does not barge in. He gives us the privilege and responsibility to act. Though he prepares the way ahead of us, he waits for us to take a step in the right direction. It is hard to say what happens in the spiritual universe when we resist Satan to follow God's way, but he provides "a way out" (1 Cor 10:13) for us if we are willing to take it, and we know we have him to thank for helping us.

As the proverb says, we must guard our hearts. Though we are never alone, we have been instructed to walk worthy of the gospel with our own two feet. The world has many muddied places since Adam and Eve, so our feet will need to be washed from time to time, more often, no doubt, than we might expect, by God's grace and forgiveness.

Scripture References: 1 Sam 16:1–13; Pss 34:17–19, 37:23–24; Prov 3:5–7, 4:23, 21:2 with Ps 25:9; Prov 21:3; Jer 17:9; Lam 3:33; Hos 6:6; Mic 6:8; John 5:24 with 8:31–32; 13:6–10; Rom 3:21–26; 5:12, 18–19; 1 Cor 10:13; 2 Cor 3:17–18; Eph 2:1–10, 4:1; Phil 1:27; Col 1:10; 2 Tim 3:16–17; Titus 2:14; 3:1–2, 8, 14; Jas 1:2–8, 13–15, 22–25, 4:7; 1 Pet 5:8–9; 2 Pet 1:3–4, 3:8–9; 1 John 1:5–10.

168. Creatures of Habit

And let us consider how we may spur one another on toward love and good deeds.

—*Heb 10:24*

WE ALL HAVE ROUTINES and habits that we lean on to get through the day. Many of these are set in motion by the options our culture gives us for survival, though our particular way of accomplishing them expresses our personal preferences. We get up at a specific time and go through the habitual motions of getting ready for the day. We pat the dog and head out the door for the day to face a competitive, individualistic, often aggressive world. There, we practice habitual adaptive behavior at work or school, shopping, or running errands. Our behavior in these ways is mostly on autopilot to get the usual things done and meet the social expectations for the best outcomes.

These regular patterns are normal for us and facilitate our well-being. But because they are habits, they do not require much thought or intentionality. This means they are not often evaluated regarding their usefulness or appropriateness in our Christian lives. This makes some habitual behavior dangerous to our spiritual well-being. Some patterns can become self-survival techniques that disregard family members or neighbors. We can get into habits of self-assertion to control our surroundings and the people in them to our advantage, keeping things the way we want them for our personal preferences or to contain our insecurities.

Though we may be more careful in our public engagements, sometimes our routine actions are not so helpful in our personal world. They may be patterns of behavior that hurt us or those around us. We would do well to assess these patterns of our lives for their value. A primary concern

168. CREATURES OF HABIT

should be where God fits into our ordinary routines of life. Do we normally look to him each day? Do we trust him? The Bible calls us to intentional activities of love and good works that honor him and show concern for others around us in our families and communities. How are we doing?

I emphasize the family. It seems to be where we let down most from our strenuous efforts at survival in the world around us and, in our stressed-out, tired state, fall into selfish habits and patterns that take others for granted, insist on our own preferences, and harm the people God has given us. Those we hurt often become defensive, triggering confrontation, resistance, and rivalry; disagreements become arguments; what should be love can become resentment. It may become a lifetime of wounds for the children in such a situation. We must be intentional in the family. It is the primary place where we must emphasize our love—our sensitivity, consideration, and willingness to serve. God planned it to be the incubator of loving people, the nest of care, love, and security for children. He intended parents to be an example for their children through their love for each other and an example to the world of his love for his people. Love needs to become the motive of habitual behavior regarding God and family if we are to take it with us out into the world.

Scripture References: Prov 11:29; 12:14–16, 18; 14:12; 17:1; 22:6; Matt 5:13–16, 18:1–6; Luke 10:25–37; John 13:34–35, 15:12; Eph 5:8–10, 5:22—6:16; Phil 1:27; 1 Tim 3:4–5, 5:8; Titus 2:1–8; Heb 13:15–16; 1 Pet 2:12, 3:1–7.

169. The Ways of God

How unsearchable his judgments, and his paths beyond tracing out!
—*Rom 11:33b*

WE ARE FAMILIAR WITH God's words that his ways are not our ways, but we seldom realize just how different they are. Of course, there is much we do not know, but there is also much he has shown us to which we do not give careful attention. Sometimes his ways seem backward from ours in that he puts the last first and the first last. Our culture has strongly influenced us to put "successful" people first and those who are weak or "failures" last. But we judge success or failure on purely human grounds based on what our cultural values tell us.

God deals with his people in paradoxical ways. We see it in stark reality at the birth of Jesus in Bethlehem, where God becomes man without ceasing to be God. This is God's Son, the King of kings, Creator of the universe, born to a simple peasant girl in an animal's stall and sleeping in the feeding trough? And *no one* is there for the occasion? While the religious leaders are confounded by their own theology, and the people preoccupied with their Oral Torah for their social survival, the only ones who notice God's hand moving on earth are coarse and ragged shepherds and, a couple years later, strange pagan priests he calls on for the occasion, the outcasts of Jewish society and gentile "dogs" of the earth. The irony of God does not stop there; it begins to shape the life and work of Jesus, who would go the dishonest tax collectors and sinners of the night, the sick and the poor, avoiding the rich and powerful unless they came to him. Eventually the body of Christ would come together of the weak and lowly, the despised and unknown of the world. Those who are nothing believe and become the children of God. He has shown the worldly wise to be fools, and those who are "fools" in their

169. THE WAYS OF GOD

eyes, as those who have found the wisdom of true life. We cannot lean on human understanding.

It is not a new approach. God had used it before that day. Moses, who cannot speak well, is sent to put the king of Egypt in his place; the prostitute Rahab saves the spies at Jericho; and an orphan and captive Esther saves her people. A Moabite widow, Ruth, becomes the wife of Boaz, the great-grandmother of King David, and a link in the lineage of Jesus. Sometimes the low are raised up to serve him. An outcast woman of dubious reputation and a history of five husbands becomes the link between the Jewish Son of God and the Samaritan people. Sometimes the high are brought low to serve him. Paul, a high-ranking Pharisee and persecutor of Christians, is called to become the messenger of Christ to the gentiles. We could go on. God's ways are very different from ours.

God uses very few celebrities in society to make up his church; he uses people like you and me—those whose names will never be on the top one hundred list of famous people. Only the humble who answer his call are in his kingdom. God will use the foolish and the weak to shame the wise and the strong in the world's estimation. He will lift up those who are nothing in the eyes of the world to accomplish his purposes for the universe. You and I are very special to him, his very own, set aside to do the good he has planned for us.

Scripture References: Exod 3, 4:1–17; Josh 2:1–16; Ruth 1; 1 Sam 2:3 and 7; 17:1–58; 2 Chr 7:14; Esth 1:1—10:3; Ps 25:9; Prov 3:5–7; Isa 40:28, 53:3, 55:8–9; Matt 15:21–28; Mark 9:33–37 with 10:29–31; Luke 1:46–55, 2:1–7, 10:25–37; John 1:12, 4:4–28 with 39–42; Rom 11:33–36; 1 Cor 1:20–31, 15:9–10; Eph 2:8–10 with 2 Tim 3:16–17 and Titus 2:14; Jas 2:5 with 25.

170. The Grace of God in Christ

Blessed are they whose transgressions are forgiven, whose sins are covered ... whose sin the Lord will never count against him.

—*Rom 4:7–8*

GOD MEETS PEOPLE WITH his intervening love at the most unexpected times and places, perhaps walking down the road to Damascus or Emmaus, at the well near Sychar, or in the grocery store parking lot. He gives us the opportunity to know him and experience his grace. If we welcome that encounter, if we embrace that love and recognize him as its source and Jesus' sacrifice as its door, he covers us as he did Adam and Eve in the garden. We no longer stand before him naked; we are clothed.

We are said to be "in Christ" when, because of our faith in his sacrifice for us, God's grace forgives us. God puts us in the position of being covered with the righteousness of Christ himself. We come to him; he changes our status in the universe. Though we remember how bad it was, how rebellious or self-centered we were, our shame is erased. So great is his grace that our past is wholly forgiven, never to be mentioned again; there will be *no* condemnation. God's justice has been served. Yes, he forgives and continues to forgive. It should make us humble and grateful beyond words to express it.

But, grateful as we are, Satan may still try to bring back the old attitudes to rule us or feelings of guilt to control us. We must remember we are forgiven and free of them. Though we sometimes fail God, he welcomes us to come to him in our weaknesses and failures, accept his continued forgiveness, and improve in our walk with him. As undeserving as we are, the granite mountain of separation has been removed, the curtain ripped in two for us to enter his presence as his sons and daughters. We do so without

170. THE GRACE OF GOD IN CHRIST

the guilt of our sin in the righteousness of Jesus Christ. It is beyond belief but absolutely true. We are in Christ.

Scripture References: Gen 3:21; Pss 32:1–2, 103:10–13; Matt 27:50–54; Luke 24:13–32; John 1:12, 5:24, 15:1–8; Acts 9:1–6; Rom 4:7–8, 8:1; 1 Cor 1:27; 2 Cor 5:15–17, 21; Eph 1:3; 2:1–10, 13; Col 1:9–14; Heb 5:14–16; 1 Pet 2:24–25 with 3:18 and 4:1–2; 1 John 1:9, 2:2.

171. Confidence in Being Right

> He will make your righteousness shine like the dawn, the justice of your cause like the noonday sun.
>
> —Ps 37:6

PROVERBS 3:5–7 TELLS US to trust in the LORD with all our heart and not lean on our own understanding but in all our ways to acknowledge him. It is then that he will make our path straight for us—known to us—as echoed in Rom 12:1–2. Following that, it tells us not to be wise in our own eyes but to fear the LORD and turn away from evil, as does Rom 12:3. It is a walk of confidence in *his* wisdom and way. God takes responsibility for the outcomes if we desire to honor him with humility, gratitude, and trust. It allows us to go in the direction given us in Ps 37, where, after telling us again to trust in the LORD and do good, it tells us to delight ourselves in him. Then he will give us the desires of our hearts. We are to commit our way to him in unbending trust of his providence, and he will care for our needs. We may not understand all he is doing or how and when he will act, but we will trust God and his way for all the conundrums of life and mysteries surrounding his ways.

One day, God will make it clear to the world around us that we are right to trust him, acknowledge him in everything, delight ourselves in him, and commit our way to him. But we must be patient and wait for him. The criticisms of our culture against us and against him will one day be exposed for their foolishness, and we will inherit safety and well-being, happiness and peace, beyond all expectations for days without end with those who have walked with us or have gone before us in the faith. In the meantime, our choices in life must bear witness to his love and grace.

Scripture References: Pss 1:1–6; 28:6–9; 37:1–11; 84:10–12; 91:1 with 4 and 14–16; 130:5–6; Prov 3:5–7, 21–26; 26:12; 28:26; Isa 30:15 with 18,

171. CONFIDENCE IN BEING RIGHT

50:7–9; Lam 3:25–26; Rom 12:1–3; Eph 3:10–13; Heb 4:14–16; 1 John 5:11–15; Rev 21:1–4.

172. The Weakness of Wealth

Better a little with the fear of the LORD than great wealth with turmoil.

—*Prov 15:16*

IN OLD TESTAMENT TIMES, many leaders trusted in the military might of their horses and chariots. They are told by God to trust instead in his power and providence to protect them. Others trusted other people. God tells them not to do so, for men are temporary, and their words die with them. Others trusted in themselves, but God calls them fools. Perhaps above all, prosperity has been the god people in modern societies worship for their security, and many are God's warnings of its deception. Hard times are frequent, and the loss of wealth is always just around the corner. Those who are able to keep it in this life tend to trust it and thereby forfeit their happiness and, perhaps, their souls. Only knowing God and acknowledging him in all we do is life and the beginning of wisdom, even for the poorest among us. God help us not to be distracted from it by temporary wealth.

Money is not evil in itself, and we should be careful to manage what God gives us so we can care for our needs and those of our family and not be dependent on others. But when we trust it for our emotional security, as the solution to all our problems, money becomes our enemy, creating distance between us and God, if not displacing him altogether. He says not to love the world or the things in the world, "for the world and its desires pass away, but the man who does the will of God lives forever" (1 John 2:15–17).

There is so much more in trusting God than in amassing riches for our well-being. Accumulating things on earth and preserving them creates worry and anxiety. Our security is found elsewhere, and meaning and purpose are embedded in helping others with what God has given us. We are

172. THE WEAKNESS OF WEALTH

to be prudent, of course, but generous and encouraging. Our resources can enable us to be salt and light in a dark world, introducing people headed for ruin to the God of salvation. However, we must be careful with what God has put in our hands. Many would take advantage of us if we gave no thought to our resources coming from God. If we have wealth, it is a temporary blessing he intended for his purposes. We must seek first his kingdom and set our hearts on our true treasures in him.

Scripture References: Pss 20:7, 33:16-19, 52:5-7, 62:10b, 84:4-7, 118:8-9, 146:3-6, 147:10-11; Prov 3:13-18, 27-28; 11:28; 22:4; 23:4-5; 26:12; 28:26; Eccl 5:8-15; Matt 6:19-34, 19:16-24; Luke 9:23-25, 12:13-21 with Prov 3:9-10; 1 Thess 4:11-12; 1 Tim 6:6-10 with 17-19; 2 Tim 4:9-10a; Titus 3:14; Heb 13:5; 1 John 2:15-17.

173. Feeling Saved

For the Son of Man came to seek and to save what was lost.
—Luke 19:10

Though some may feel exuberant, others may feel less saved than ever when they first come to Christ. As we come to know him, we know more than ever how bad we are—how far we are from his desire for us. We do not yet fully understand his grace. But as we read his word and seek his ways, we grow more grateful for it each day. Other more mature Christians can help and encourage us in our growing faith. Sound teaching of the Scriptures can increase our trust in God's providence.

However, some who say they are Christians do not know this way of grace. Some people cloud knowing God with human speculation about his ways, pressure us with professional salesmanship, or confuse us with requirements for sensational events to prove his acceptance of us. Others push a theology that burdens us to earn God's approval by our own efforts rather than accept it in Christ and live for him in the freedom of pure intentions. If we enter any of these other doors, we may feel saved when we do what they say God requires and do not do what he forbids. We may think we have accomplished what it means to be saved. But the feeling will be temporary, and guilt will overcome our confidence. If we are honest, we will realize we can never keep up with such requirements.

When we walk with God by faith instead of seeking his approval through works or sensations, our feelings will not always assure us, but, then, it is not about feelings. It is about facts. We were lost and now are found, blind, but now we see. We were dead in our sins and are now alive in Christ, standing before God in *his* achievement of our salvation. We are called now to good works, but they are not the cause of his acceptance; they

173. FEELING SAVED

are, instead, the results of his grace in our lives. We experience grace, truth, and freedom in Christ, and our gratitude motivates our good works. It is a very apt description to say that we have been born again.

Scripture References: Jer 9:23–24; Luke 15:1–7, 19:10; John 1:10–13, 3:3, 9:1–41; Rom 3:21–26; 2 Cor 5:15–18, 21; Gal 6:9–10; Eph 2:1–10; 1 Tim 4:4–5, 6:18–19; 2 Tim 3:16–17; Titus 1:15, 2:14; Heb 11:1 with 6; 1 Pet 2:12, 3:18.

174. Theological Maps

I am the way and the truth and the life. No one comes to the Father except through me.

—John 14:6

THE COMPARISON OF THEOLOGIANS to cartographers we mentioned earlier is a common one. The significance is that the one following their maps depends on them to reach their destination. They are putting their safety and welfare in the hands of the cartographer or theologian. But if either produces a map with inaccuracies or leaves out important information, the journey does not end well. If you navigate your ship using a map with errors, you may crash on the rocks of an unmarked shoreline or strike a hidden reef. If the theologian goes off on syncretism with culture, legalistic standards, the mysticism of sensationalism with its secret codes and messages, or denies truths God has given us, we will run aground spiritually. If the theological map gives us information without leading us to know God as he is and experience his grace, it has served some purpose other than God's intention. The outcome is farther from the destination than the starting point.

It is a vocation of weighty responsibility to lead others in God's ways. Theologians, pastors, and teachers of God's word must first establish that there are no other ways, no shortcuts to knowing God other than faith in the one who created the seas we travel in life. Then they must guide us by correctly interpreting the perfect map of his word, leading us on the journey to *his* destination, and helping us be lights for others lost at sea. We can have confidence in God's map even when the fog of life's worries is thick and we cannot see very far ahead. You do not have to be a theologian to be saved, but you do need to know and experience God's grace through Christ

174. THEOLOGICAL MAPS

in humility and trust. It is where the journey begins, and will be our true north all along the way.

Scripture References: Ps 107:23–31; Prov 30:5–6; Matt 5:14–16, 7:13–14, 8:23–27, 15:14; Luke 6:39, 46–49; 8:22–25; 17:1–2; John 1:12, 14:6; Acts 4:12; Eph 4:11–16; 1 Tim 1:3–7, 2:5, 3:1–7, 5:17–22; 2 Tim 3:7; Titus 1:5–11, 16; Jas 3:1.

175. Human Culture in the Church?

Do not think of yourself more highly than you ought.
—*Rom 12:3*

IN AN INDIVIDUALIST CULTURE, our feelings of self-worth are calculated by social standards and comparing ourselves to others. By these, we gauge our progress in achieving whatever our culture calls success. Then we go to self-improvement seminars and learn to calibrate our approach and how we present and express ourselves to achieve more. We think that performance at a higher level than others and a display of success is how people will recognize our worth. These are ruinous attitudes in the church but extremely difficult to root out since, in our society, they are the core of self-esteem. Without warning, with the most natural feelings, they can motivate our behavior, whether we are the leaders or those attending a service. Church leaders sometimes gauge their ministry by how good they are at getting our emotional attention, how novel they can be in their approach, or whether the service looks and sounds professional or has the right touch of informality. Did participants express appropriate praise for the events and the people leading them? Did they use the right words? Those in attendance often concentrate on their feelings of self-worth, while the pastor speaks about honesty, humility, and loving one another. Their personal values get in the way, and they often rationalize the message to advance their aims.

All this is disturbing to worship in spirit and in truth. It must all be laid aside for us to focus on the God of our salvation, for a sense of humility before him, for gratefulness that his grace is at work in us. We should always do our best, but our performance does not enhance our worth. The attribution of Christ's righteousness does that. The fact should humble our hearts and purify our love. It must change our attitudes in church. If we

175. HUMAN CULTURE IN THE CHURCH?

are not careful, our cultural emphasis on professional leadership, emotional sermons, impressive worship arts, and celebrity testimonies may lead us away from instead of toward the simplicity of his welcoming grace and the humility of trusting him it must produce. Yes, the church is made up of people at all levels of maturity in Christ, but it is charged with helping them move toward it, not away from it. Don't let competitive cultural values lead the way. What we need is not found among them but in God himself and in his grace on our behalf.

Scripture References: Pss 33:18; 37:3–7a, 34; 46:10; 51:6; 96:9; 138:8; 145:13b–14, 17–19; Eccl 5:1–3; Luke 18:9–14; John 4:23–24; Rom 12:2–21; Eph 4:1–3, 11–16; 5:1–2 with 8–10 and 17; Phil 1:6 with 2:1–4 and 12–13; Heb 12:28–29, 13:21; 1 Pet 5:1–7.

176. Our Part in God's Plan

All these people were still living by faith when they died.... The world was not worthy of them.

—*Heb 11:13, 38*

TRADITIONAL JAPANESE UNDERSTAND THAT each person's life in the present connects the past and the future positively or negatively, giving that connection strength or weakness. It is a good concept for us as Christians. As I have mentioned elsewhere, the Japanese use the word *yo* to speak about this. It is the word for the growth span between the joints of a bamboo cane. It connects what has gone before with what follows. If it is weak, it diminishes the healthy effect of past lives on the present and our present life on the future. If it is strong, it connects the exemplary lives of the past (think of chapter 11 of the book of Hebrews) with the possibility of a flourishing future for others. That connection is our faithfulness to God's purposes today. Each person's life has connections to the past, present responsibilities, and future consequences in the chain of human existence, either for good or for ill. Another Japanese term, *naka'ima*, adds that each day is the "middle present," the meeting point of the past and future, and we occupy that center of time. How we live today affects the outcome of history; it sets the foundation for people who will follow us. The thing about a *yo* is that it has a beginning and an ending. We only have so much time to be a meaningful link in the chain of lives around us.

When we know God and choose to honor him, our lives have a positive effect, though we often have little idea of the consequences of our trust in God on others. Doing our part affects many other lives and sets many things in motion in God's plan. Our sometimes labored, sometimes habitual faithfulness to some duty or task, kindness shown, and words of advice

176. OUR PART IN GOD'S PLAN

or encouragement add to what faithful people have done in the past and will affect others for generations until Christ returns. It may not seem like much at the time, but we each have a part to play in the body of Christ, and God wants to use that part to accomplish his plan on earth. Endurance and patience are required, for we may not see the outcome in our lifetime. In haiku poetry, Yosa Buson uses a candle to penetrate us with this meaning: "The light of a candle / Is transferred to another candle— / Spring twilight."[1]

We must be faithful to do what is before us today—homework, housework, care for our spouses or children, bathing the dog, the needs of a neighbor, a day at the office, at school, or in the shop—for his honor and glory, so that others in the present, our children, friends, students, customers, coworkers, and brothers and sisters in Christ, can benefit in some way today. Others after us may have a stronger faith and a more resilient loyalty to God when they remember the consideration and kindness shown to them. We may not have a role in God's plan like Mary's, but we can all become part of her song, telling of God's grace "from generation to generation" (Luke 1:46–50). If you are among the "children of God" (John 1:12), you matter to him as much as Mary, and though your part in his work in the world may not be as earthshaking, it is just as important as you become a link in the gospel message touching those who follow you.

Scripture References: Ruth 4:13–17; Esth 9:26–28; Pss 22:30–31, 78:3–6; Matt 17:20, 25:21; Luke 1:46–55; 1 Cor 4:2; 2 Cor 5:7, 15; Eph 4:11–16; Phil 2:3–4; 1 Thess 4:11–12; 1 Tim 1:12–17; Titus 3:8; Heb 11:1–40 with 12:1–2; 13:15–16.

---

1. Yosa Buson, "Lighting One Candle," trans. Robert Haas, My Poetic Side, https://mypoeticside.com/show-classic-poem-4825.

177. God Uses the Most Unlikely People

They spread the word... and all who heard it were amazed at what the shepherds said to them.

—*Luke 2:17–18*

WE TALKED ABOUT THE ways of God earlier and saw that one of the most extraordinary things about God's ways is how he uses the opposite of what we expect to accomplish his purposes. It is the paradox of his ways. The King comes through the back door when no one expects it, no one is watching or listening, and uses the least expected people to accomplish his unstoppable purposes—his will on earth. It cannot be mistaken as the achievement of solely that person. Those seen by the world as the "weak," the "foolish," the "nobodies,"—the most unlikely—are used by God to shame those of the world who appear strong, clever, wealthy, prominent, intelligent, or attractive so that his will is accomplished, his promises fulfilled, and his name is honored. It seems God continues to create things out of nothing.

In addition to the examples of Moses, Rahab, Esther, and Ruth mentioned before, we also notice the youngest brother, Joseph, who is so unceremoniously sent to Egypt to save his people. We see God using Gideon, small on faith and from Manasseh's smallest clan, to overcome the Midianites, Amalekites, and other Middle Eastern combined armies with an extremely small contingent of soldiers. David, youngest of the sons of Jesse, a forgotten, disheveled boy in the fields watching the sheep, is chosen by God, even to Samuel's surprise, over all his brothers, to be the king of Israel, slayer of the giant, and centerpiece of God's plan for Israel. Though unknown as a boy and not a perfect adult, he was a man after God's own heart.

Jonah, of all people, brings God's message to the Assyrians, causing a vast pagan city to turn to God. Peter preaches on Pentecost after denying

177. GOD USES THE MOST UNLIKELY PEOPLE

Christ, and God uses Paul, who had been passionate in his persecution of Christians, to reach the gentiles with the gospel despite his weakness from a "thorn in my flesh" (2 Cor 12:7) and his battle with "the evil I do not want to do" (Rom 7:19). We see it in the lineage of Jesus: God uses the most unlikely people, those our culture considers weak or offensive, to do some of the most important things in the world for him.

We see with human eyes and judge according to the human values our culture gives us, but with God the last shall be first, and from what looks like the end, he makes the beginning. Nothing can keep God from using us if we seek his grace, trust his providence, and desire to honor him. For most of us, it will be serving him in the "ordinary" events of each day. For a few, our part will be of a more public nature. But we are all part of his work in the world, called to honor him with the life he has given us. Always allow room for the mystery of God's providence and the paradox of his grace that show up in the most unlikely places at the most unexpected times. In the harshest circumstances, the waves are calmed, and the hardest of people melt as God's grace pressures through the fissures in the granite of their hearts. You and I may be the channels for that grace to flow.

Scripture References: Gen 37:19–28 with 41:41–46; Exod 3:10–14; 4:1, 10, 13; 5:1; Josh 2:1–14; Judg 6:14–16 with 7:1–8, 12; 1 Sam 13:14, 16:1–13, 17:1–58; Pss 33:11; 89:3–4; 145:13–14, 18–19; Prov 21:2; Jonah 3:1–10; Matt 1:1–16; Luke 1:46–53, 2:8–20 with Matt 2:1–12; Luke 2:8–20, 13:29–30; Acts 2:14–41, 13:22–23; Rom 7:14–25; 1 Cor 1:20–31; 2 Cor 4:7, 12:7–10; Titus 2:14; Heb 11:6.

178. God's Providence at Work

As it turned out, she found herself working in a field belonging to Boaz.... Just then Boaz arrived from Bethlehem.

—Ruth 2:3–4

WHO ARE WE THAT God should choose to use us in his plan for the world? In these years we have known him, we have to admit that we often followed him in weakness and that our faith has not been what his faithfulness to us deserves. There is no room for arrogance. Even if some of us are talented, intelligent, or accomplished, these are *his* gifts to us, and we live and act only by the breath he gives. By his grace, strength, and wisdom, he uses such as us in his plan, often the most unlikely and insignificant people, in improbable, unpredictable, perhaps impossible situations. "It just so happened" that Ruth found herself working in the field of Boaz, and, afterward, she was never the same.

In the book of Daniel, King Nebuchadnezzar is an example of one who arrogantly thought he had accomplished everything in his great kingdom on his own. But God brought him low so he might recognize his hand in everything. King David was different; he was aware of his sin. But he thanked God for his grace and the strength he had given him to rule the kingdom of Israel. God was at work in both cases to bring about his will. In some cases, his providence may not seem like it could be God at work, but we may be too close to the details. When we step back from the biblical accounts, we see with what large letters it is written from cover to cover that his providence is at work in and through us.

Most of us are nobodies in the eyes of the world, or at least our strengths are not respected because we are Christians. But if we want to honor him, God will use us and accomplish his purposes. He will do it in such a way

178. GOD'S PROVIDENCE AT WORK

that the credit belongs to him, for he strengthened us for it and protected us from many evils to bring us to this day, to this book, to this paragraph. He was not obligated to do so; it is by his grace. We must not ignore this hand of God on us. By giving us light in our own souls, he gives us the possibility to be light to others, and, by his providence, has shaped us to do that in ways others cannot. We cannot claim recognition for his work through us; we can only express humble gratefulness. We are the sheep of his pasture today, as Israel was in the past. It is often when we are weakest that he shows himself strong. When the mountains around us are trembling (Ps 46:1–3, 10), he leads us "beside still waters," guides us "in paths of righteousness" (23:1–3).

Scripture References: Ruth 4:13–17; 2 Sam 22:1–4; 1 Chr 29:14–16; Pss 23:1–6, 28:6–9, 46:1–11, 73:23–28, 95:1–7, 100:1–5; Prov 16:4, 27:2; Isa 41:10–13; Ezek 34:30–31; Dan 4:28–35; Matt 5:14–16; Luke 1:37; John 8:12; 1 Cor 1:20–31, 4:7; 2 Cor 12:7–10; 1 Thess 4:11–12.

179. The Real Me

The wisdom of the prudent is to give thought to their ways.
—*Prov 14:8*

How we view or think about ourselves is significant—how well we know ourselves and the accuracy of our estimations are crucial to wisdom. Life is often referred to as a play on a stage. Before we encounter the grace of God through Christ, we act with those in our lives and surroundings in various ways according to the script our society provides—the social norms of our people—and try to arrange the props to serve our needs. We play the part through a character our experience has shaped and our efforts have constructed within our social context over the years. We do not often think about the real person in us while on stage. Most of us never meet our authentic selves until we meet Christ. Then, like the rich young man who asked Jesus what he needed to do to gain eternal life, we finally get a glimpse of the self behind the one acting on the stage. At that point, we face an important decision.

In their proud hearts, the Pharisees rejected the image Jesus showed them of themselves. Because of his love of money, the rich young ruler turned away. The rich fool built new barns without thinking about the final outcome of his course in life. Demas fell in love with the world and left Paul while he was in prison. But Peter realized his sinful self when he met Jesus, much like Saul (Paul) on the Damascus road. Some of us, in love with the person we have constructed, may find it difficult to end the affair. But to turn away from Jesus is a fatal decision. He holds out life while we are courting death. We must leave the old self behind and put the new wine Jesus gives us into a new wineskin.

179. THE REAL ME

It may seem like a terrible risk to trust him. But when we do, we will find ourselves in the entryway of the house of wisdom. Giving ourselves to him, then, we must not underestimate the extent to which he wants to work in our lives and use us in the lives of others by his enablement. We must not confuse "my idea of me" with God's thoughts about us. He sees what we cannot, has purposes for us we are not yet aware of, and values us beyond our comprehension. We are now his very own, and he wants our lives, weak and untalented as we may think them, to bear the fruit of good works he has prepared for us.

Scripture References: Prov 14:12, 16:18 with 29:23; Isa 43:1; Matt 5:1–8, 33; 7:13–14; 9:16–17; 19:16–24; 23:1–39; Luke 5:1–11, 6:20–26, 12:13–21, 18:9–14; John 1:4–5 with 5:24 and 8:12 and 14:6; 12:24–26; Rom 12:3; Eph 2:10; 1 Tim 1:12–16; 2 Tim 3:17, 4:10; Titus 2:11–14; Heb 13:15–16; 1 Pet 5:6; 1 John 2:15–17.

180. Born Again—A New Beginning

I was blind, but now I see!
—John 9:25

WHEN WE ACCEPT CHRIST and are born again, the old self must be dealt with. All things become new, and we begin a process of change to fit our new identity in Christ. As it took time to construct the self we were before knowing God, we begin a journey now, with his help, of transforming that self into what he wants us to be. We have a new script now, and neither our society, our selfish desires, nor our need for control are to direct the play anymore. Though our new understanding of his will motivates us to act accordingly, we do not forget the old self very soon; some never do. It may be for the best since that is the sharpest perspective from which to view and appreciate God's overwhelming grace in our lives. The danger is that it keeps popping up, wanting to direct the play here and there. But we must resist our enemy at every turn.

This is why the Bible tells us to put off the old man, to die to self, and to transform our minds. It is the intent of the words *born again*. That old self is no longer the real you but the old one that wants to re-exert its influence over you. The real you is reborn. Opposition to the old selfish preferences taking over is the real you now in action, and it is possible in Christ. However, though it is possible to oppose the enemy, avoiding the encounter is not possible. Everyone has a battle to fight, for our lives were occupied territory, now being retaken through Christ. Your battle will be different from that of other Christians, and it will not be easy. There is still resistance in the land as it is returned to its rightful owner. Satan and self have had their way and do not give up without a fight. It is in the new script. It is part of the play, and the director is well aware of it. He reminds us daily to fight the

180. BORN AGAIN—A NEW BEGINNING

good fight and gives us the encouragement and strength we need. We were blind, but now we see and must grow in that realization.

Scripture References: Ps 103:6–18; Isa 41:10; Matt 6:33, 16:24–28; John 3:1–21, 9:1–41; Rom 12:1–2; 2 Cor 5:15–21; Eph 4:17—5:1; Col 3:8–10; 1 Tim 4:7–8, 6:11–12; 2 Tim 2:22; Heb 12:1–4; Jas 3:13–18; 1 Pet 1:13, 5:6–11; 2 Pet 1:3–11.

181. The Mirror Doesn't Lie

Be very careful, then, how you live—not as unwise but as wise. . . . Do not be foolish, but understand what the Lord's will is.

—*Eph 5:15, 17*

THERE IS THE PERSON I am and the person I think I am, inside and outside. In their Shinto beliefs, as we said earlier, the Japanese use the word *makoto* to talk about a mirror's reflection of the truth. They see it as an analogy of how the *kami* (gods) "see the truth in all things." A physical mirror only tells us what is there on the outside. We might wish it were different, but the mirror does not lie. We can dress it up, try to cover the blemishes, and choose clothes that help it not show so much. But we know. The Japanese beliefs are a human explanation of where truth lies. But God has given this ultimate truth in his word, in his revelation of himself and his Son.

Christians have the true mirror of the Bible. The Creator-God of the universe uses it to look deep into the soul and show us things hidden even to us. Through his word, he reveals *only* the truth. If we see the truth about ourselves as God's word reveals it, we must take it seriously. We are wise to make every effort to, as Paul would say, leave the old self behind and put on the new self in Christ—forgiven, free, loving, and grateful, a new person in our encounters with family, friends, and community. But this is a process rather than an event. As James would say, we must not walk away forgetting what we look like but *continue* looking into the mirror of God's word and doing what is given to us there to clean smudges from his reflection through us.

We are told to walk in the freedom Christ gives us bounded by love and gratefulness, to be slow in judging others, and to become humble in spirit, helpful, and encouraging. We know what we have seen in the mirror

181. THE MIRROR DOESN'T LIE

and must respond to it biblically and personally, just as all Christians must. We must all seek to walk in this wisdom from above. If we do not, we deceive ourselves; we are not walking in the Spirit but in our desires and preferences. We must build on the foundation of the truth God gives us in his word.

Scripture References: Job 28:12–13 with 20–23 and 28; Ps 119:45; Matt 6:4; 7:1–5, 24–27; John 8:31, 36; Rom 12:9–12; Eph 5:15–18; Phil 2:1–4, 3:13–14; Col 2:1–3 with 9 and 13; 3:1–17; Heb 4:12–13, 12:1; Jas 1:5–8, 22–25 with 4:10 and 17; 3:13–18; 1 Pet 2:16–17; 1 John 1:7–9.

182. The Demands of Culture

Do nothing out of selfish ambition or vain conceit.
—*Phil 2:3*

SOCIAL VALUES MAKE DEMANDS on people in every culture. Ours demands we be self-confident, self-assertive, and in control of our lives and, as much as possible, our surroundings. In a way, it blackmails us, telling us we will not be happy unless we meet the demands. Some learn to act out these values pretty well, but we may not be good examples of them ourselves, even though we feel pressured to act like we are. This creates insecurities for us, doubts, and even false guilt.

Then there is the church culture, which is usually a hybrid situation—a mixture of human and biblical values demanding certain attitudes that people might muster up for a Sunday morning that are not really part of their lives otherwise. It is a mix of biblical and Confucian values in many parts of Asia, creating competing loyalties. In the West, a blend of biblical and individualist values creates the confusion. The more uncomfortable and distracting the situation is, the less value people get from the worship and teaching. Of course, being polite and kind is always called for, whether we feel like it or not, but other cues are often used to determine if people are "spiritual." In an Asian church, people may ask if others are respectful enough and submissive to church authority. In our Western situation, people may ask if they are informal enough. Are they extroverts? Again, these values seem natural at church for some, but others may not be good examples of them, while feeling pressured to act like they are comfortable with them.

It is difficult to be entirely honest with God when we have social and church values to juggle, but we must. He cares about us personally, not our

182. THE DEMANDS OF CULTURE

ability to compete with the world or how well we perform at church. He has a master plan for the universe, but he also cares about each of us as his very own so that we might be more like Christ in humility, truth, freedom, and grace. These are not natural values in our society and are often not compatible with the human aspects of church culture. We will have to be honest with ourselves and with God to know him, trust him, and have his peace. It is the wisdom that comes to us through Christ.

Scripture References: 1 Sam 16:7; Ps 51:6 with 16–17; Prov 21:3; Hos 6:6; Mic 6:8; John 14:27; Rom 5:1–2; 1 Cor 1:18–31; Eph 4:11–13; Phil 2:1–13, 4:4–9; Col 3:1–4; Titus 2:11–14; Jas 2:1–4, 3:13–18; 1 John 2:15–17.

183. Weakness and Walking Worthy

> My grace is sufficient for you, for my power is made perfect in weakness.
>
> —*2 Cor 12:9*

I AM GRATEFUL THAT the apostle Paul was willing to be vulnerable with us. He talks of his struggle to do good, but the habits of the "old man" in him, his sinful nature, were pushing him to do what he hated. The Old Testament law showed him just how bad his sin was. He called it evil, or sin, living in him, while he desired to live for God in his heart and mind. He is describing the human situation, and we all share that condition. The answer is Christ, who saves our souls now and one day will redeem our bodies and all of creation. Many of us go through our Christian lives thinking we are very poor at living for Christ but that others are nearly perfect at it. But it is not true. We all are examples of those struggling to trust God at some level in our spiritual battle.

If you think you are without weaknesses or sin, then you are deceiving yourself and have yet to know God's truth. Some of us are better at covering it up, acting like we are free of the humanness that the Bible tells us is ours, but we delude ourselves. We are but jars of clay, intended to carry God's grace to the world around us, but easily broken when we do not trust him. On the other hand, constantly whining about our vulnerabilities so others will feel better about theirs is not what the Bible teaches. It is simply a fact that none of us is free of the need for God's grace every day, in abundance, and lavished on us if we are to live for him. It is why we are entreated to walk in the Spirit, worthy of the gospel, and God gives us every incentive and provision to do so. The Holy Spirit gives us spiritual self-awareness, sensitivity to what we read in God's word, and guidance in the way of God for us.

183. WEAKNESS AND WALKING WORTHY

We have no fear in this grace relationship with God. It is an amazing paradox; he knows us better than we know ourselves, yet forgives all we bring to him and wants us near him. He intends to fulfill his purposes for us in his plan. Such is his grace when we come to him through Christ.

Scripture References: Pss 23:3; 25:4–5, 8–9; John 5:24, 14:25–27 with 16:12–13; Rom 3:21–26, 7:14–25, 8:1; 1 Cor 15:42–58; 2 Cor 4:6–7, 5:15–18, 9:8, 12:7–10; Gal 5:13–16; Eph 1:6–8; 4:1–3, 17–24; 5:15–21; Phil 1:6, 27; 2:12–13; Col 3:8–10; 1 Thess 4:13–18 with 1 John 1:5–10; Jas 1:22–25; 2 Pet 1:3–9.

184. The Essentials of God's Word

For the word of God is living and active.
—*Heb 4:12*

CULTURAL VALUES, CONTEXT, GRAMMAR, vocal inflection, nonverbal cues, intentions, and associations with personal experience formulate the meaning of words between people in communication. The same words would mean something different if any of these elements changed. Reading God's word is no exception. God carefully chose to use particular people in specific contexts, using their vocabulary and grammar, with their individual and collective experiences to reveal himself and "breathe" his message to us through them. Those he used, who spoke to him and for him, were real people with minds, hearts, and souls shaped by their cultural values, intentions, and experiences. These and other elements add a dimension to their words and actions that may be foreign to us while intended by God. But we must not forget. The Bible is not like other ancient texts; it is alive. It is a sword that cuts deep, as the Holy Spirit shows us our rejection of the Creator and also the light that gives hope, for it tells us of his works and wonders, of his grace and providence. Through it, he continually reminds us of his way for us and in us.

God used human beings to inscribe his desires for us in this life, his intentions for our peace in this broken world through trusting him, and his providence shaping us for his purpose of making him known. The human authorship has an enduring and unbreakable divine connection. We must pay attention, for the truths given to us in foreign languages and contexts are to be lived out in ways relevant to our situation today. They cross all cultures and times to come to us with infinite value and importance. We cannot survive without them. What we are to do to love one another will be

184. THE ESSENTIALS OF GOD'S WORD

different from what they might have done, but the essential truth endures for all time.

When the ancient words are God's revelation of himself and his instructions as to what people are to be or do for him, we in our modern, Western context must consider these cultural, linguistic, and situational variables. But we must also approach the Bible with the understanding that it was not only true for the people of those times and for us in our situation today but for anyone, anytime, anywhere.

Seeing it in English gives us a feeling that the people there are the same as us, but that is not so. There is a culture gap. It is no use trying to use your own cultural context and frame of reference for the meaning it had for them in theirs. Its application twists the meaning with viewpoints and moods that are awkward in their situation. It straps the text with our logic, emotions, and cultural expectations, which we think must fit their context but are often wholly unfamiliar to them. Yes, we will have to pay attention to their cultural context for the meaning, not substitute our own.

But God has not left us with an enigma to resolve. Though reading the Bible is a cross-cultural experience, the truths of God's word are indeed clear and straightforward. His words about faith, trust, love, hope, salvation, and walking worthy of the gospel stand out flawlessly; however, we need to work on applying them in our context, in our Western day-to-day lives. I am attempting to get our attention in a day when we may have become too casual, even careless, with the Bible. In other cases, we have made his word into a puzzle so complex that only expert theologians or teachers can claim the ability to explain it, and then the next one differs from the first, and the great debate begins and divides. In some ways, we have taken it to mean what we want it to mean—made something out of it to benefit ourselves.

We are talking about *God's* message to humankind through the ages. Our informality and inattention have not given it the respect it calls for, and our cultural values on complex logic, detailed analysis, and systemization have also caused their damage. But, though knowing something about the original culture and situation is definitely helpful, we are not left alone to understand what God says to us. He speaks to us through his Spirit by his word in every age and culture and intends to be understood. Our work is to determine what trust and obedience look like in our situation. What are we to do? How are we to act today in light of his message to us?

Instead of more complexity, God constantly seeks to bring us back to simple faith, essential trust, steadfast loyalty, pure humility, the freedom he gives us in Christ, and the desire to obey him in our lives—in our twenty-first-century situation. God looks at our hearts to find faith and its outcomes regardless of our cultural values or personal habits. The ancient truths and essential virtues must be displayed in the modern world in a relevant way in every culture.

Scripture References: Ps 37:3–6 with 23–24; Prov 3:5–7; Isa 55:10–11; Mic 6:8; Matt 5:8 with Titus 1:15; Luke 10:38–42; John 8:31–32 with 36; 14:15 with 25–27; 15:5–11; 17:24–26; Acts 8:26–35; Eph 4:11–16; Phil 4:4–9; Heb 4:12.

185. Connecting with the Message of the Bible

All Scripture is God-breathed... so that the man of God may be thoroughly equipped for every good work.

—2 Tim 3:16–17

IF READING THE BIBLE is entering the world of the first century, how do we cross that cultural gap to understand what God is saying to us today? First, we must consider that, as different as we are from people in the Bible, there are also ways in which we are very much like them. Our commonality with them is that they were human as we are. They were struggling to survive in their situation according to what their culture prescribed and allowed. Not unlike today, God was the center of life for a few of them and on the edges or outside of life for most of them. Those who respected God and his ways were not perfect. Even though some are called righteous, they, too, needed God's grace and only had so much time to live their lives for him. The cultures of these people were not perfect, but they were the ones God chose to use in revealing himself. He is no less able to use his word and Spirit to reveal his will to us in ours than he was to use theirs in that day.

We must realize that we are not without help in understanding the Bible. God's desire is that we know him and understand his will for us; through his Holy Spirit, he guides us to that end, giving us sensitivity and understanding. Much of what God gives us in the Bible is plain and straightforward. The challenge for us is choosing to follow his way. The stories of the good Samaritan and that of the tax collector and Pharisee in the temple could not be clearer. He has not hidden secret "truths" from us that only "special" people can discover. But we must approach the Bible with an open mind, ready to take its teachings to heart. We must also approach it with humility, knowing that we do not know everything about God's ways, with the wisdom to know we need his help, and with patience to trust him and see his purposes worked out in our lives.

In addition, in his plan, God gave some to be pastors and teachers among us who give themselves to him in the detailed examination of his word, people who study the cultural and social boundaries within which it was given to us and those barriers of our own culture and our human situation that hinder us. These help us understand the relevancy of God's message for us in our day, not only its countercultural truths but also its message of freedom in Christ. Paul tells Timothy he and, therefore, all pastors and teachers must discipline themselves to correctly handle God's word, and Jesus promises that his Spirit will accompany their efforts. All this amounts to a call for humility and caution as we approach God's word, but also a confidence that he will work in our lives through it. We need not be theologians or scholars, but we must be humble, careful, and prayerful readers, trusting what God says and not being confused or deceived by false teachers who misuse it to gain a following and benefits for themselves.

Scripture References: Ps 25:9; Isa 46:10, 55:8–11; John 14:15–16, 25–27; 16:7–15; Acts 20:28–31; Rom 3:9–12, 12:1–2; 1 Cor 1:20–25, 2:9–15, 6:12 with 10:23–24 and 31; Eph 4:11–16; Col 1:9; 1 Tim 1:3–7, 4:4–5; 2 Tim 2:15 with 3:16–17; Titus 1:5 with 10–16.

186. Sovereignty with Grace

Yet to all who received him, . . . he gave the right to be children of God.

—*John 1:12*

THERE IS A GREAT deal in the New Testament about God's grace that has been poured out on everyone who will accept it, about our freedom in Christ when we do, and about his answers to our prayers, but we must also see there his sovereignty. It is one of our greatest comforts in life, next to his lavish grace on our behalf. It did not all just happen. He sovereignly chose to make a way open to himself through Christ and to give mankind the choice of loyalty to self or to him. His offer of grace for our forgiveness through the merits of Christ was a sovereign decree he made before the foundations of the world were in place. All who would believe in him would become his children. These he elected to know the peace of a relationship with him in this world and to possess salvation eternal. It is a universal decree that awaits the decision of each person, for he does not want any to perish. Who else than the sovereign God of the universe could justify forever those who deserve utter destruction by the death of the one who knew no sin? In his omniscience, he gave Adam and Eve the sacred and decisive gift of free will. The choice that gift set in motion showed God's grace to be crucial and fundamental for knowing his forgiveness and peace, the flourishing of life now and forever.

Adam and Eve chose not to trust God. Though we live with the consequences of their decision, you and I have the same choice to trust God for our salvation and each event of our days. Complete justice must be served in a universe created by God, and he sovereignly chooses to offer it by grace to all who believe through faith in his Son, Jesus. For those willing to receive it, there is no longer *any* condemnation. Those refusing God's offer of Christ will be separated from him forever by their own choice. These are without excuse, but anyone incapable of making this choice is in God's loving hand of perfect justice.

After people come to God through Christ and want to honor him with their lives, the mystery of his providence is at work together with them in their situation and decisions, good and bad, to guard their way to bring about his purposes. Looking back, we can see many things God has done to bring us to this day. Sometimes we trusted him and other times we were not paying attention, but he was at work, shaping us to serve him in some way and to make himself known to others (glorify himself) through us. We may not yet realize how our lives have affected others, and perhaps will not know until we get to heaven, but every thoughtful word, every act of kindness, and every encouragement to trust God touches those around us in a way God can use.

Scripture References: Gen 3:1–24; Deut 32:4; Pss 25:4–5 with 8–12; 139:1–18 with 23; Matt 18:12–14, 25:31–33 with 40; John 1:12–18; 3:16–21, 36; 5:24; 8:36; 14:6; Acts 4:12; Rom 1:18–21, 8:28–39; Gal 5:1, 13–15; Eph 1:3–6, 11–14; 2:1–10; Col 1:13–23; 1 Tim 2:1–6; Titus 2:11–12, 3:3–7; Heb 7:23–28; 1 Pet 2:16–17; 2 Pet 3:9, 15.

187. Knowing Heads and Anxious Hearts

God is our refuge and strength, an ever-present help in trouble. Therefore we will not fear, though the earth give way and the mountains fall into the heart of the sea.

—Ps 46:1–2

WHEN JESUS WALKED ON water toward the boat, Peter expressed an unusual faith and said, "Lord, if it is you, tell me to come to you on the water" (Matt 14:28). They were already afraid it was a ghost, but Peter was willing to put his life in his hands if it was Jesus. Once out on the water, however, his fear of what he was actually doing and the possible result under such turbulent conditions overcame his reason. He began to sink, but Jesus reached out and caught hold of him to save him. It is a story of our lives as Christians that what is in our heads, what we know to be true, is sometimes overcome by our fears and doubts. We have all been there. It may be concern over trouble in our lives, fear of social pressure, returning memories of childhood trauma, excessive stress, or what seems to us desperate circumstances, one thing or another that threatens to overturn our commitment to the truth. Sometimes our sins of greed or selfish desire for what is not our own push us to do the opposite of what we know to be right. Sometimes, when we are emotionally empty and don't "feel" saved, our mood takes over, and we doubt any of it is true. But our mood does not change the facts.

When Jesus got into the boat with Peter, "the wind died down" (14:32–33). On another occasion, Jesus was asleep in the boat with the disciples when a powerful storm threatened their lives. The fearful disciples woke Jesus, and he "rebuked the wind and the raging waters; the storm subsided, and all was calm" (Luke 22:24). The disciples were amazed and terrified all at once. They should have known. A thousand years before, or three different occasions, David and other psalmists spoke of God as the one who stills the roaring seas of the storm. Here he was, in their boat with them. And he is with us in ours.

We must remember that when Peter's faith weakened, Jesus reached out and saved him. He is always there and reaching out to us, whatever circumstance, temptation, or mood is trying to wedge its way between him and us. We can trust God's word when we can't trust our hearts, and life in this broken world will give us plenty of opportunities to practice grabbing his hand. He may calm the storm or help us through it as his purpose is fulfilled, but he is there, and we must be determined to trust him. When the way ahead seems dark to us, we can rely on him; even when we "walk through the valley of the shadow of death" (Ps 23:4), he is with us, and he is faithful. He understands us in our weakest moments, and he cares. "A bruised reed he will not break, and a smoldering wick he will not snuff out" (Matt 12:20). In all this, what he wants is our trust.

Scripture References: Gen 50:15–21; Exod 1:22—2:10; Pss 9:9–10; 23:4; 34:18; 37:3–6; 46:1–3; 56:3–4; 62:5–7; 65:5–7; 89:9; 91:1–4, 14–16; 93:3–4; 103:10–18; 107:23–31; Prov 3:5–7; Isa 40:31 with 41:10; 43:2; 50:10; Dan 3:15–18; Matt 12:20, 14:22–33; Mark 4:35–41 with Pss 65:7, 89:9, and 107:29; John 14:27, 16:33; Phil 4:6–7; 1 Pet 5:6–7.

188. Self-Centered

Set your mind on things above, not on earthly things.
—Col 3:2

Many have said that pride is the root of all sin. Others say it is the love of money. These indeed cause a great deal of sin. But pride and greed are symptoms of self-centeredness and selfish ambition—the actual causes. The self at the center is the root of all evil. If we give it power over us, we will seek whatever will bring some human benefit, satisfaction, pleasure, or relief from our fears, emotional pain, or insecurities. Some of us deceive ourselves with false confidence that we are better than those around us who do not know how to assert and advance themselves. The proud feel most secure when they can manipulate the situation and people around them to their benefit. If they can keep others in a position of making them look good or feel good about themselves, they consider it a success, but they are feeding the beast in them, making their need for control worse.

We may think we are above it. That, however, may only be because we have little in our lives to feel proud about. Let the least attainment come about, and we may see it in ourselves. We will want to look accomplished and secure to others in our individualist society. The church is a ready stage for the self to get this desired attention and affirmation. People there are trusting and accepting, giving the selfish person a longer leash, offering grace to those of us for whom maturity is long overdue. We will never be perfect, but we can be—and are told to discipline ourselves to be—a good deal further along than we are. Because of our weak state, Paul tells us to renew our minds and set our hearts on things above. James uses the words *submit, resist, come near, wash, purify, change,* and *humble yourselves*

(4:7–10). He tells us we need God's wisdom in trying times, and that he will give it generously if we trust him.

We criticize it when we see self-centeredness in others, but it may be a decoy to distract people from seeing *we* are selfish. Christians are not only not immune to selfishness and the pride that comes with it, they may be more vulnerable to its dangers than others. When a Christian is outspoken about some sin, it may be because it is the primary temptation of their own heart. What should produce humility and compassion produces harsh judgment. We must be on our guard. The heart is deceitful. We must set it on things above. We have the freedom, always the freedom, to choose God over self, and we will grow wise with its use.

Scripture References: Pss 10:4, 18:27; Prov 4:23, 11:2, 15:33, 16:18–19, 26:12, 28:26; Isa 13:11; Jer 17:9; Matt 6:1–8; Luke 20:45–47; 1 Cor 4:7; Gal 5:19–26; Phil 2:1–4, 3:18—4:1, 4:8–9; Col 3:1–4; 1 Thess 4:11; 1 Tim 6:10; Jas 1:4–8, 3:13–18, 4:7; 1 Pet 1:13–25; 2 Pet 1:3–11.

189. Is God Angry?

For God did not send his Son into the world to condemn the world, but to save the world through him.

—John 3:17

THERE IS A KIND of thinking among many who are not Christians that God is always angry with people. Perhaps they feel he is angry about the "unchristian" things they do. But this does not come from the New Testament. There are some notable exceptions where Jesus was angry, but he never expressed anger toward those who had no way of knowing who he was. In fact, Jewish leaders felt he was overly friendly with "sinners and tax collectors." He spent his time with ordinary and needy people, many of them stumbling along with lives falling apart. He said he had been sent for their sakes. But he was not so friendly with those leaders, for they had the truth but, through pride and greed, refused to let God have his way and led the Jewish people away from God. There were cities where people saw his miracles but refused to believe his words; for them, there were words of judgment. Others who knew God through his works and claimed to be wise above his ways are called fools. Even his chosen ones in the Old Testament, the Jews to whom God revealed himself, hardened their hearts and suffered his judgment. Surrounding peoples saw his works and still chose to worship their sticks and stones. They, too, missed his mercy, though there were exceptions like Nineveh, Nebuchadnezzar, Naaman, the widows of Shunem and Zarephath, and other foreigners among them because of their faith. These experienced God's grace, called *hesed* in the Old Testament, his mercy, lovingkindness, and compassion.

Jesus shows us God's attitude toward unbelievers. Instead of being angry, God is waiting in love and grace for people to realize who he really is. He does not expect those who do not know him to behave as if they did. This anger of God some talk about may be their own projections of an angry parent in their past on him, or an association with pastors and evangelists who try to use the idea to scare people into accepting Christ as the solution. They may have experienced angry, legalistic "Christians" who were only critical of them. They do not know God, only how others have characterized him. No. God is amazingly patient with those going the wrong way and is overjoyed when a lost person realizes and accepts his grace. He pursues the unsaved and waits for them to look in his direction. He loves the world and is not willing that anyone should perish.

Scripture References: Num 14:1–35; Deut 10:17–21; 1 Kgs 17:8–24, 19:9–18; 2 Kgs 4:8–37, 5:1–17; Prov 28:26; Isa 30:18; Dan 4:28–37; Matt 9:9–13, 11:16–24, 18:10–14; Luke 11:3–54, 15:1–31; John 3:16–18, 36; 2 Thess 1:5–10; 1 Tim 1:12–17, 2:3–4; Titus 2:11; 2 Pet 3:9.

190. Satan at Your Side in the World

"You will not surely die," the serpent said to the woman.

—*Gen 3:4*

WE KNOW THAT TEMPTATION is not a sin, for Jesus was tempted and tested in every way like we are, but it was not a sin for him. He did no wrong. We are tempted by our own weakness, selfishness, greed, or desire. Though temptation is not sin, we may stumble and give in to the deception. God is there for us when we do but warns us to guard our hearts and not to fall in love with the world and its temporary, superficial, fragile, and—regarding God's plan—counterfeit pleasures.

Sometimes corrupt people can deceive us, and sometimes we are tempted by Satan himself. He takes advantage of our weaknesses and appetites. He may fix the circumstances or provide opportunities for us to fall into sin. He may look like an "angel of light," providing the perfect solution to our needs, but he is a ravenous lion seeking to devour his prey. He makes no friends. He is the father of lies and the master of blackmail. We are told to be on our guard and to resist him. We live in a broken world, in bodies of weakness. We need God's help when we are tempted and his grace when we fall. His perfect justice in Christ gives us who come to him complete and perfect forgiveness. He has written his name on our souls and our names in his book. He will never condemn his own.

Yes, we must resist the enemy at every turn. We must seek God's solutions to our problems, his peace for our anxieties, and his strength for our insecurities. We can trust his providence for our fears, doubts, and dreads—for the unknown days ahead. He will be faithful if we will be patient. "Be still and know that I am God" (Ps 46:10) are his words to us when our world is falling apart and we don't know where to turn. "Be still before the LORD and wait patiently for him; do not fret . . . it leads only to evil" (37:7–8).

Scripture References: Gen 3:1–7; Pss 34:17–19; 37:1–8, 23–24; 46:1–11; Prov 4:20–27, 24:16a; Matt 4:1–17, 12:20; Luke 4:1–13; John 3:18, 36; 5:24; Rom 8:1, 31–39; 1 Cor 4:7, 10:12–13; 2 Cor 4:4–7, 5:21, 11:13–15; 2 Tim 4:10; Heb 2:18, 4:14–16, 9:14; Jas 1:13–18, 4:7–10; 1 Pet 3:18, 5:8–11; 2 Pet 2:1–9; 1 John 1:8–10, 2:15–17, 3:20; Rev 20:15.

191. Nature Speaks

The heavens declare the glory of God; the skies proclaim the work of his hands.

—Ps 19:1

WHAT WAS GOD'S INTENTION in creating the universe so vast and some things in nature so very small? Why did he not create every landscape the same and give every day the same weather? He often draws our attention to his creation of the world in his word. What does he intend for us to see there? The answer is that everything was created to glorify him. That means to make him and his attributes known. He created it all to tell us something about his sovereignty, wisdom, power, and creativity—something about his character. It is, of course, not permanent since humankind spoiled it, but he has plans. This world, marked by human sin, carelessness, destruction, and suffering, will be made new. It awaits his word.

There is something about creation that he values more than we allow. It tells us something about the nature of reality that we cannot learn elsewhere. The heights and depths, the heat and cold, the smallness and vastness, the stillness and raging, the soft beauty of flowers strewn among craggy granite mountains tell us something about God and ourselves. The intensity of storms and volcanos, the penetrating light of the sun, the endless universe of stars, do they not tell us of his eternal existence, power, and greatness? His attention to the smallest detail? Our petty moods and emotions that seem so enormous to us, our human losses and pain so devastating, are overshadowed by his vast greatness yet tender touch in creation. God intends we see something of him there, something overwhelming for which words are inadequate and unnecessary. He intends for us to see the incalculable consequence of his attention to us. Our Creator, who, in his majestic and unfathomable magnitude, turns his thoughts to us, even the least of us, sees us as the center of all that creation, his very own, the ones he loves.

Scripture References: Gen 1:31; 1 Chr 29:10–13; Job 38:1—39:30; Pss 8:3–4; 19:1–6; 33:6–9; 89:1–2, 5–8, 11–18; 96:11–13; 139:1–12; 146:5; Isa 40:21–28, 43:1; Matt 6:25–34; Rom 12:33–36; Titus 2:11–14; Rev 21:1.

192. To Love or Not to Love

Dear friends, let us love one another, for love comes from God. . . . If we love one another, God lives in us.

—1 John 4:7, 12

WHEN LOVE IS AUTHENTIC, it gives to the other person, but it can also be less than genuine and driven by self-centered desire. It requires a delicate balance, for what is given must be for the other's benefit, even if they do not perceive it as what they want just now. Too often we give another what *we* want, not what is best for them, but for us. It can also be a love of giving the other whatever *they* want when they want it, overindulging and enabling them in ways that ultimately bring suffering in the real world. We may think this will guarantee their love for us. But that is seldom the result. Authentic love cannot be bought. Other times, "love" is a selfish love of possession—making the other what we want them to be for us. We may be thinking, "How does giving to them satisfy my desires, accomplish my plans, and keep them under my control? What's in it for me?"

These are not at all the kinds of love God asks of us toward one another. Instead, he asks of us a love interested in giving what is best for the other, promoting their highest good, respecting them, and showing kindness, consideration, and interest in them, whether that love is returned or not. Of course, there is no more rewarding love than one that is mutual in these ways. It was God's design for marriage, family, friendship, and the church. Then there is our community, and those of other cultures, outsiders to the body of Christ. We will not be able to help the lost, serve the poor, or love our enemies until we have learned to love each other. Reaching out in love to outsiders will not be accompanied by feelings of affection but rather compassion and care. We must move away from what our culture has taught us as individualists—from competitive self-assertion for personal and social survival. Just as faith is essential to following Christ, love is necessary to living for him.

Scripture References: Matt 5:13-16, 25:40; Luke 10:25-37; John 13:34-35, 15:9-13, 17:20-23; Rom 12:1-3 with 9-13; 1 Cor 13:1-13; Gal 5:13-14, 22-23; Phil 2:1-4; Heb 11:6; Jas 3:13-18; 1 John 4:7-21.

193. Opinions or Wisdom

The fool says in his heart, "There is no God."

—Ps 14:1

DISCERNMENT IS NOT EASY to come by in our social relations. Though we are repeatedly told to seek wisdom, many ignore it. This is especially so in our me–first culture. We assert ourselves. We have opinions and the right to make them known; we are selfish enough to insist our way is the only way. How blind we are to our limitations! A person's assertion that an activity, belief, or value is good or bad, that only their view is right, does not make it so. That authority must come from somewhere else. It seems our society is full of people who claim omniscience. We are reminded in Proverbs that pride brings disgrace, but humility opens the door to wisdom.

If proud but limited humans succeed in getting their way, they may not be around to see the results. However, that will not lessen the harm and damage their ideas may cause or acquit them of the effects of the crime they have committed against their neighbors or larger community in the years that follow. Most regretful are the narcissistic, sometimes neurotic opinions of "know-it-all" celebrities, greedy politicians, and so-called experts who have no meaning and purpose in life but their self-advancement. Some who follow these influencers are innocently duped, but many are without a hint of wisdom. The book of Proverbs lists them as the simple, the fool, the mocker, the lazy, the quarrelsome gossip, and the mindless. Their own folly ruins their lives, as the blind lead the blind. We must allow wisdom from God's word to direct our way, humility to guard our path, and concern for others to guide our actions. This is discernment—wisdom—that protects its owner.

Scripture References: Ps 1:1–3; Prov 2:1–22; 3:5–10, 13–17; 4:1–27; 8:17–21; 9:6–12; 10:13–14, 21; 11:2; 12:15, 18; 14:9; 15:12, 21; 17:18; 19:3; 26:12–16, 17–22; 27:22; 28:26; Matt 7:26, 10:16, 12:35–37; Rom 12:3; Eph 5:15–17; Phil 2:3–4; Jas 1:5–8, 26; 3:1 with 13–18.

194. Mask and Ego

I tell you the truth, they have received their reward in full.

—Matt 6:16

ASIAN CULTURES HAVE SOCIAL practices that avoid revealing how one truly feels. In Japan, this is called *honne* and *tatemae*. A person's actual state of emotions (*honne*) is often contrary to the collective society's expectations or requirements and is kept hidden as much as possible. *Tatemae* is the display of emotions society expects and requires for the social harmony needed in the collective community. To save face, *tatemae* is what a person displays even at great cost to themselves. It is not seen as dishonesty if it saves face for the individual and promotes harmony in the group. But this is not only an Asian practice.

As Christians in the West, we sometimes wear masks as well. We often hide our true selves, our ego. It may be for another person's good, to show sensitivity and tactfulness, save embarrassment for ourselves or others, or intentionally mislead others to our benefit. Discretion to benefit others is understood in our society and often the better part of wisdom. However, dishonesty, hypocrisy, and misleading others to deceive them rupture the harmony we are called to foster among ourselves as evidence to the world of the truth of the gospel.

Yet the church is often known for such. Some people arrive for the service and their language changes. They talk about things they would never mention at home or at work. They want to display spiritual maturity. They talk about their spiritual gift, mention their calling, and tell us they have found God's will for their life. As they talk about their Christian achievements, other Christians of good heart but low on wisdom may feel discouraged. And people outside the church can see through this mask covering the insecurities of insincere members. Their interest in God's message is soon blunted, if not turned into disrespect. Why should they listen? It is deviant behavior for people who claim to know God but have not humbled themselves, have never learned to deal honestly with their insecurities, and have never trusted God for their reputation, or, perhaps, have never trusted him for anything. "They claim to know God, but by their actions they deny him" (Titus 1:16).

This is a call for Christians to renew their hearts, realign their allegiance, recall their humble dependence on God's grace, and recalibrate their trust in God's providence. It calls for love and loyalty to God beyond what many know. Without it, there is no example of Jesus in our lives. Our message in words is hollow and without effect. We are speaking against God's work in Christ on our behalf, denying his love for the world, and contradicting his grace for all who believe. Instead, we must be examples of the love and hope we bring to the world as light in the darkness.

Scripture References: Pss 15:1–5; 51:6, 16–17; Prov 11:3, 21:2, 26:28, 28:18; Isa 59:9–15; Jer 17:10; Matt 5:14–15; 6:1–8, 16–18; John 1:4–5, 3:16–21, 8:12, 13:34–35, 15:9–17, 17:20–23; Rom 12:3–8; Phil 1:9–11; 2:1–4, 4:4–9; Col 2:16–23, 3:9–15; 1 Thess 2:3–6; Titus 1:16, 2:11–14; Jas 1:22–25; 1 John 3:18, 4:7–12.

195. Fear of Hell

Then they will go away to eternal punishment, but the righteous to eternal life.

—*Matt 25:46*

IT IS LEGITIMATE FOR nonbelievers to fear hell as it is described in the Bible. But God did not create hell for people. He created it for the devil and his angels. It may surprise some, but God does not allow people into hell unless they insist on it by ignoring or rejecting him. Except for those unable to choose God, the decision is entirely in our hands, and avoiding it does not have to do with being good people but with our acceptance of the grace and forgiveness in Christ. God does not want *anyone* to perish in hell. He is, instead, waiting, after giving them the way to his grace and every encouragement to follow it, for them to decide not to continue on their way to eternal darkness.

When people think they are not good enough to avoid hell, they are right. None of us is good enough to avoid eternal separation from God, but he covers us with the goodness of Jesus when we accept his forgiveness through Christ's sacrifice. Our assurance of heaven is entirely based on our faith in Christ and the deep reservoirs of God's grace. That is not to say we should not be good examples as his own in the world, but that our mistakes and failures do not reverse his grace. There are more references to his grace and desire for all to know him personally than to hell and judgment in the Bible. It is simply not God's desire for us, though he will not tread on his sacred gift of free will to humankind and override our decision to refuse him.

Scripture References: Ezek 33:11; Matt 13:36-42; 18:10-14; 25:41, 46; John 1:12; 3:16-18, 36; 5:25; Rom 2:5-11; 3:21-25a; 8:1, 31-39; 2 Cor 5:14-21; Eph 2:4, 8-10; Titus 2:11-14; 2 Pet 3:7-9.

196. Blind Leaders

Leave them; they are blind guides. If a blind man leads a blind man, both will fall into a pit.

—*Matt 15:14*

HUMANITY IS OFTEN LOOKING for ways to deny God's existence. Many hope so desperately that it is not true that they convince themselves they "know" it is not. In their wish fulfillment, they are running from guilt and insecurity without knowing God's grace. If they run hard and far enough, they will find those who spew theories supporting their unbelief, however incredible. The masses will grasp at these human guesses to make them the final explanation of all reality. The human philosophers of our times offer their "enlightenment" that there is no God and, therefore, no moral law, no wrong decision, and no reason for guilt. All their bullets are shot from this gun of their human assumptions. Though their mortal thinking seems to give cool relief, it destroys all purpose and meaning in life. It is a sweet and fashionable poison coursing through the whole body with momentary feelings of release and freedom. But it is not only temporary; it is fatal. By removing the engine, they have disabled the vehicle. It can coast downhill but cannot take them to any destination worth the arrival.

There is a way that seems right to a man, but its end is not only not worth achieving, it is the bitter end of eternal death. These do not know the grace and freedom God offers them in Christ. For those running from God, the cancer of their desire to escape him spreads until the power to control their lives is in the hands of the "specialist" who knows nothing about healing their disease, knows nothing about life at all. In Jer 4:22, God calls the leaders of his people in Jerusalem, those who do not know him, fools, senseless children, and those who are only skilled in doing evil. And the people

196. BLIND LEADERS

followed them, trusted them, to the bitter end of their ruin and deportation. Indeed, the blind led the blind, and everyone following fell into the pit.

Such are the blind leaders of our society, our world, but what of those "in the church" who lead us away from God? Some there claim, for personal advantage, to know the way of God but have no idea where they are going. Yet they want to take everyone around them with them. Once they remove the truth of the Bible from their ministry, *they* are the blind leading the blind. Such were the Pharisees in Jesus' day. Such are many in our day. Either God's truth is influencing human culture, or human culture is influencing God's truth. Only those who walk in the light can show the way to others. This is how we are lights in the world.

Scripture References: Ps 146:3–10; Prov 3:7, 14:12, 19:3, 28:10; Isa 5:20–21, 50:10–11; Jer 4:22; Matt 5:14–16; 13:24–30 with 36–43; 15:12–14; 23:13–16a, 33; Luke 6:39, 17:1–2; John 1:3–5, 8:12, 12:35–36, 14:6; Acts 20:2–31; Rom 1:21–22, 2:5–11; 1 Tim 1:3–7; 2 Tim 3:7; Titus 1:10–16; 2 Pet 2:1–3, 3:3–9; 1 John 3:18, 4:1–6.

197. Human Weakness, God's Strength

My grace is sufficient for you, for my power is made perfect in weakness.

—*2 Cor 12:9*

CHRISTIANS WHO ARE POOR in spirit (humble), meek (those of patient faith instead of self-assertion), pure in heart (those of unpolluted motives)—the "foolish" and the nobodies in the world's eyes—are the people God uses to accomplish the purposes of his master plan for the world. He is interested in you and me because of our faith, regardless of our weaknesses and struggles. He looks at our hearts. As incapable as we seem at times, he shows his greatness, power, and grace in our situations. In our weakness, he shows himself strong. We can never take credit for his work in and through us, but we can have contentment in his attention to us. It is not a matter of having all the money we think we need or all the intelligence, giftedness, or abilities we admire. It is a matter of doing what we can with what we have and doing it for him.

For most of us, it is evident that our strength is from God, that what is accomplished is because he has stepped in, working in the background, providing what we need. When this is not clear in our hearts, in our "best" moments, pride is not far away. And he knows it. He knows our weaknesses, faults, and struggles, yet "a bruised reed he will not break, and a smoldering wick he will not snuff out" (Matt 12:20). Even in our weakest moments, we are his, which makes all the difference if we humbly take his hand and embrace his way in our lives, if we offer what we have and can do for his purposes.

Scripture References: 1 Sam 12:20–22; Pss 9:9–10, 34:17–19, 145:14 with 18–19 and 146:6b—147:6; Prov 11:2, 15:33; Isa 40:28–31, 43:1,

197. HUMAN WEAKNESS, GOD'S STRENGTH

57:14–15; Matt 12:15–21; Rom 7:14—8:2, 28–39; 1 Cor 1:20–31, 10:31; 2 Cor 4:7, 12:7–10; Gal 2:17–21, 6:14; Eph 4:1–7; Phil 1:27, 2:1–4, 3:7–9; Heb 4:13–16; 1 Pet 5:5–7; 2 Pet 1:3–9.

198. Loving Others

Love is patient, love is kind . . . [it] always perseveres.

—*1 Cor 13:4, 7*

BEING INDIVIDUALISTS—CONCERNED FOR OURSELVES and preoccupied with our social and emotional survival—we are not particularly good at loving others. But we must change that, especially with those closest to us. The effort may demand more determination than we think and a little more intentionality. Loving another person will involve thinking about them and valuing the relationship, especially that of a spouse and then of children, friends, those in the body of Christ, and, finally, those outside of Christ. Love is responsible for preserving the relationship, and kindness and trust will be its outward signs.

Loving another means caring, giving, and forgiving as you do for yourself: caring about their concerns and progress, giving time and effort to their well-being, and forgiving their weaknesses, mistakes, and faults. But love has a determined side, too. It does not enable lapses into hurtful and wayward behavior but helps others learn to depend on God's grace and providence so they can improve how they think about themselves, go about life, and renew their strengths and abilities. Kindness, faithfulness, patience, and trust are the rails on which love runs. This may sound like a one-way street, but relationships, by definition, are not supposed to be that way. However, in our human situation, they are often unequal in the effort and attention needed and given. It demands a great deal of patience. Imagine God's patience with you before you become impatient with someone else.

It can be a struggle to put aside critical attitudes, overreaction, and resentment to see someone else progress in their faith, and how they live it out from day to day. But being a peacemaker is critical to the process. Even

198. LOVING OTHERS

so, progress for another, as for us, may be slow and uneven. We may not see it at all for some time. Wanting the best for another and the actions needed for it may not always be welcome, but, bathed in love, our intentions must persevere. There may be situations where we will not feel affection for the other person, but it is not feelings that matter. Knowing that we are following God's purposes for us is what matters. Life is too short to neglect those he has put in the circle of our care. Faithfulness must become our priority, but it must be bathed in wisdom and not neglect the self entirely. Attending to our own needs is crucial so we do not lose our potential to help others.

Scripture References: Neh 9:16–21; Ps 86:15; Prov 3:3–4, 27–28; 17:17; 18:24; Matt 5:3–10, 7:12; John 13:34–35; Rom 12:9–13; 1 Cor 13:1–13; Gal 6:9–10; Eph 4:1–3, 32 with 5:8; Phil 2:1–11; Col 3:12–14; Heb 10:24; Jas 3:17–18; 1 John 3:16–18.

199. Impatience

Each of you should look not only to your own interests, but also to the interests of others.

—*Phil 2:4*

CRITICAL ATTITUDES OF OTHERS may indicate the need to examine ourselves. We need to inspect our impatience. What self-interest is being inconvenienced, what personal peace disturbed, what personal preference irritated? Do we have a need for control that is frustrated? Often we are the cause of our frustration and impatience revealed in our reaction toward another's activity. But there is also, at times, just cause for frustration, and sometimes it needs to be addressed with the other person. This must be ruled by patience and wisdom to do the best thing regarding our desire to influence others for Christ. The carelessness and inconsideration of others *are* frustrating. But we must know if the trigger is their selfishness or ours. Patience gives us time to weigh a matter and our heart's reaction. Solomon would tell us, "Do not be quickly provoked in your spirit, for anger resides in the lap of fools" (Eccl 7:9).

There are three responses needed on our part. First, we must learn to measure our words in response to others and allow for differences in perspective, personality, and preferences. Second, our response must include kindness combined with a desire for the best outcomes for the other person. Last, we must consider that we might be the cause, or partly the cause, of our impatience and even that of the other person. It is part of being "Quick to listen, slow to speak, and slow to become angry" (Jas 1:19).

Scripture References: 1 Sam 16:6–7; Pss 37:1–8, 42:5, 139:25; Prov 12:16; 14:29; 15:1, 28; 16:23 with 32; 17:14, 27; 18:13; 19:11; Eccl 7:8–9,

199. IMPATIENCE

9:17–18; Jer 17:9–10; Rom 12:9–19; 1 Cor 13:4a; Gal 5:22–23; Eph 4:1–7; Phil 2:1–4; Col 3:12–17; 1 Tim 1:15–16; Jas 1:19–20, 5:10–11.

200. Envy

Let us not become conceited, provoking and envying each other.
—*Gal 5:26*

IN OUR INDIVIDUALISTIC WESTERN world, we compete for resources to be at ease and avoid suffering, to achieve results that make life better, and to find ways to offset our insecurities. We see others for whom these needs seem to be met in their lives, and we may envy them. At the end of Jesus' time with them, Peter was concerned that John might have it better than he would in the days ahead. But Jesus told him that was none of his concern. Each of us will walk our own path with God, receiving what he has for us and being faithful through the ups and downs of this life. He has purposes for us that we do not know in advance, and they may be quite different for us than for others. They may be wholly unexpected to us.

We will each serve and glorify God (make his greatness, love, and providence known) differently from the next person, but it is always the way to honor him if we have given him our hearts. This life is an introduction to the next. In this broken world, we are to live out faithfulness and loyalty to God and his purposes in the situations and circumstances that are ours. We will be imperfect in expressing this faith and loyalty in our behavior, but it must be our desire and goal, for God looks at the heart. We must grow in this trust of our God and Father in the events and conditions of our lives.

To compare ourselves to others—to their achievements, situation, possessions, or ministry—is to be envious; it is an acid that eats at the soul. Could we do better? Yes, we can all do better in our lives and ministries. The fruit of his indwelling Spirit must become more and more evident in our disposition and behavior. Are we of less value or outside God's will because we are not like another in their way of serving God? No. We are to

200. ENVY

be faithful to what God has given *us* to do in our situation, not to what he has given someone else to do in theirs. Our lives and work may influence only a few or touch thousands for Christ. But that consideration is stepping into God's domain. He is at work in us to accomplish *his* purposes if we are faithful to him. It is his will for us.

In some cases, others may never know what those purposes are for us. You may be called on to trust God for something only between him and you. But the outcome of that trust in your life will affect others. Above all, do not be afraid or anxious. God is specifically interested in you and involved in the outcomes of *your* life.

Scripture References: Pss 33:11, 118:6, 138:8; Prov 14:30, 16:2B; Isa 40:28 with 41:10; Matt 20:20–23; John 21:17–22; Rom 8:28–32, 12:3–8; 1 Cor 13:4; Gal 5:22–26; Phil 1:6 with 2:12–13; 4:4–9; Heb 13:20–21; Jas 1:17, 3:13–18; 1 Pet 4:7–10.

201. Starved for Grace

For I desire mercy, not sacrifice, and acknowledgment of God rather than burnt offerings.

—Hos 6:6

And what does the Lord require of you? To act justly and to love mercy and to walk humbly with your God.

—Mic 6:8

STARVATION IS AN ENEMY of physical existence in many parts of the world. For a lot of us, our lives have been filled with plenty. But in our well-supplied physical situation, spiritual starvation is all too common. The famine of grace brought on by legalism and forced on a young person's life is one form of deprivation. Many of these young ones grow up hating the source of their hardship. Others are forever tainted by its poison. Legalism is the opposite of liberalism. It adds human limitations to God's word, while liberalism removes the boundaries of God's word. However, the effects are similar in peoples' lives. Either brings death to the soul when God offers abundant life from the wellsprings of his grace.

As I have often reminded us in these pages, "The law was given through Moses; grace and truth came through Jesus Christ" (John 1:17). God means what he says. That truth must always be mixed with the grace that came with it. It is the declaration of the New Testament, the new covenant God makes with us. It brings us forgiveness, freedom in Christ, and God's justification through his sacrifice. Insecurities cannot be resolved by taking away or adding to his will for us. Contentment and peace come only from trusting God's providence and resting in Jesus. Legalism, liberalism,

201. STARVED FOR GRACE

mysticism, and syncretism are all broken cisterns that hold no water. They promise well-being but weaken us like poison or starvation. The check for God's approval they give us is drawn on an account empty of his grace. God brings us living water of his grace in Jesus that will overflow in us if we trust him. He sends us the bread from heaven that gives life for our spiritual sustenance. These are to be the essentials of our faith.

Throughout the Old Testament, God pleads with the Jewish nation to turn from the gods of their neighbors and trust him, the one who called them his own. He is asking the same of us today. His presence and help may not always look like they could be from him, but that is because we have tilted theological positions, human cultural expectations, limited perspectives, and personal preferences telling us what it should look like. These dilute the strength and purpose of God in our lives, diminishing our part in God's work in the world. Many Jews of the later Old Testament were praying for the Messiah to come. But they missed him entirely because of the theological rules they had constructed for him to adhere to and their cultural expectations shaped by their situation. God is moving in history according to his plan, not ours. He wants to include us in that movement, but it will demand our loyalty and trust in his purposes deeply embedded in grace and truth. We must join his plan, not try to make him part of ours.

Scripture References: Pss 16:11, 62:5–8, 91:1–2, 119:43–45; Isa 26:3–4, 41:10, 43:1; Jer 2:13; Matt 11:28–30, 17:11–13; Luke 19:41–44; John 1:14–18; 4:13–14; 6:32–35, 46–51; 7:38; 14:27; Rom 4:18–25; 1 Cor 8:9; Gal 5:1–6; Eph 3:10–12, 4:14–16; Phil 4:4–9; 1 Tim 2:5–6, 4:4–5, 6:17b; Titus 2:11–14; 1 Pet 2:15–17.

202. Making Disciples

"Come, follow me," Jesus said, "I will make you fishers of men."
—Mark 1:17

MEETING THEM ON THE beach after a night of catching no fish, Jesus tells Peter and Andrew to cast their net one more time. They do, and they catch a net that is so full they can hardly get it into the boats. James and John had to help them, and all four followed Jesus. On the shore again a few years later, after his death and resurrection, when the disciples have gone back to fishing and again caught nothing all night, he tells them to cast their net, this time on the other side of the boat, and once again they have a catch too large to handle. He tells Peter in that earlier event that he will become a person who will catch men instead of fish. At his departure from Earth, Jesus told the same men to make disciples as they went about their lives. Between the two catches, the call to be fishers of men and that of making disciples, he told them the fields were ready to harvest, and they were among the few laborers. This world is his field of wheat to be harvested, his lake for bringing in the fish, and he entrusts the event's accomplishment—the harvest, the catch—to us.

Jesus, as God, wept over Jerusalem, who would not welcome him. His heart is attached to the greatness of the task. We are called to be his hands and feet in this ultimately decisive movement on earth. How will we do our part? It is not trying to get people to attend church or join our denomination. It is not about trying to trick people into saying "yes" to following Christ when they do not understand what that means. It is about God using us to change the hearts of men and women, to introduce them to the Creator-God who sent Jesus, and invite them to taste the new wine that gives life to the soul that sleeps in death. There is no secret to be discovered,

202. MAKING DISCIPLES

no unique ritual to learn, no miracle to wait for; it is a calling for us all that we cannot miss. It is about our hearts and how we live our lives for him, how we incarnate the message from God in our vocations and families, in pursuing our interests, and *as we go* about our lives in this world. Our words or ritual behavior mean little without our example of their truth.

Our faith must invade our natural behavior so that, by our example, we may affect the lives of those around us. Some will have a more public part in this plan of God, and others may help from behind the scenes—some directly, some indirectly—but all are called to be examples of his saving grace.

Scripture References: Ps 34:8; Hos 6:6; Mic 6:8; Matt 5:13-16, 9:35-38, 28:16-20; Mark 1:16-18; Luke 5:1-11, 19:41-44; John 4:25-42, 21:1-14; 1 Cor 10:31; Eph 4:1; Phil 2:14-16a; Col 3:17; 1 Thess 2:10-12; 1 Pet 2:12.

203. Fixing Things

My prayer is not that you take them out of the world but that you protect them from the evil one.

—John 17:15

WHEN WE COME TO God through Christ, we may expect that everything falling apart in the world will no longer affect us. But God does not intend to fix the world just now; he intends to fix you and me. He allows people to make their own choices in this world, and there are predictable and damaging results for those who choose against God. That damage will touch our lives in various ways, but he does not intend to mend broken people without their permission. We will go on living in this world of suffering and injustice, but with confidence in his purposes and providence, as salt and light, and with a heart for the salvation of those who walk in darkness.

Difficult things will still happen. There will be illness, suffering, loss, and death in a world spoiled by sin. But we are not the same. The new wine of his grace has been poured into new wineskins. The mystery of his powerful providence is at work. We have a different perspective. We now have meaning and purpose. His way for our lives is stamped on our hearts, even in our weakest moments. Our trust in God's divine purpose and plan gives us confidence in the uncertain events of this life. He wants us to remain here for a while—to have a part in his workings and help others find his grace and help while there is still time. When this comes about, his will is being done on earth (in us and through us) as it is in heaven. His kingdom, which is not of this physical world, is being sought and found; it is then to be proclaimed by our lives. One day, not far off now, he will do away with evil and fix this damaged world with the reign of Christ, followed by a new heaven and a new earth. He is coming.

203. FIXING THINGS

Scripture References: Pss 20:7, 146:3–6; Isa 55:8–9, 65:17; Lam 3:33; Matt 5:16; 6:9–13, 33; 13:44–46; John 15:18–21, 16:33, 17:13–19, 18:38; Titus 2:11–14; 2 Pet 3:8–11 with 15a; 1 John 4:1–6, 5:10–11; Rev 21:1–4; 22:7, 20.

204. The Paradox of God's Ways

As the heavens are higher than the earth, so are my ways higher than your ways and my thoughts than your thoughts.

—Isa 55:9

GOD'S APPROACH TO HIS creation differs from what we expect in our human, culture-bound experience. Over the centuries, many have had difficulties with the Bible because it does not fit their social values or personal expectations. God seems to have little respect for political correctness and social sensibilities. There is paradox in his ways that only those who trust him recognize and appreciate. Poor, young, rural, and unknown, Mary is chosen to give birth to his Son instead of an elegant queen. Jesus' bed is a feeding trough instead of a silk pillow in a palace. He eats with sinners and tax collectors, is concerned about the poor, and criticizes the religious. He dies leaving Israel under the occupation of Rome. The religious leaders of the day did not expect these activities of the Messiah sent by the God of the universe even though he had been telling them all about it for centuries. People do not think God would do things in such a way or say things in such a manner.

Then there is God's justice that many do not like about him. These do not accept that God can do as he chooses and be just, but he can and is. His grace moves mountains of guilt and sin into the sea for those who trust him, but though he deeply regrets their choice, judgment awaits those who reject him. He is a God of love but also a consuming fire. No one who reads the Bible with an open mind can deny it. How is it that we insist on our preferences instead of letting God be God?

Only insiders understand this mystery of the universe—the inescapable providence of God and the paradox of his grace. Anyone who denies

204. THE PARADOX OF GOD'S WAYS

Christ, we are told by Jesus, he will deny before God the Father and the angels of heaven, yet there is forgiveness for Peter. David should be stoned but is declared a man after God's heart. Though none could be righteous by law, we find a list of those who, though not perfect, were righteous by their faith, even under the law of Moses, even outside Judaism, like Cornelius. God uses paradox and parable in a Middle Eastern context such that it calls on the eyes of faith instead of Western logic to see his intentions. Few things are considered cultural treason for the Western scholar as much as allowing the biblical text to speak for itself without boxing it up and strapping it down with our rational preferences for categorization, order, and logic. Some of this may help the Western mind, but God does not give it to us that way. It will take faith—eyes that see and ears that hear that the natural man or woman does not have—a sensitivity given by the indwelling Holy Spirit to understand God's purposes.

This is God's grace in the world. Today, he makes people righteous, not in the sense of perfect but in their position in Christ, completely forgiven, transformed in their desires. It is a matter of faith in Jesus' sacrifice in our place. Your good behavior cannot add to it, nor can your sin detract from it. It is God's grace in action. However we may falter in trust and good works, his approval rests on Christ's righteousness, which he has attributed to us by our faith. Some Christians have a weak view of this grace God has shown. They try to add works to maintain that approval and apply reasoning and propositional statements to lock him into their airtight system. But he refuses their box, stepping outside the boundaries they draw for him. He intends to speak for himself.

There is only one God and one Savior, one faith, a truth that cuts across all denominational lines and styles of churches. He speaks, and we must listen. Neither our personal and ecclesiastical preferences nor our theological systems put us in the body of the true church. We will have to submit to him on his terms, humble ourselves, and enter a relationship of love, trust, and loyalty with the God of the universe through the sacrifice of Christ.

Scripture References: Deut 32:4; 1 Sam 2:3-9; Ps 103:10-18; Isa 46:10, 55:8-9; Matt 10:33, 25:41; Luke 12:9, 13:22-30; John 1:10-17, 21:1-19; Acts 4:12, 10:22, 13:22; Rom 3:9-26, 11:33-36; 1 Cor 2:12-16; Eph 2:1-10, 4:1-7; 1 Tim 2:1-6; 2 Tim 4:1-4; Heb 4:14-16, 11:1-40, 12:28-29; Jas 2:20-24; 2 Pet 3:9; 1 John 1:5-10; Rev 22:21.

205. The Irony of God

Indeed there are those who are last who will be first, and first who will be last.

—*Luke 13:30*

WHEN WE READ THE New Testament, we are jarred to see that God makes the first last and the last first. In Jesus' day, under the law of Moses, the Jews were considered first and the rest of humanity last, if of any importance at all to God. Jesus came to open the way to God for all. The Jews would resent it, but many gentiles became people of faith—those first in the kingdom of God. It is God's ironic movement throughout history against people's cultural demands and expectations to carry out his plan. Mary and Joseph are reduced to outcasts of their social world to parent God's Son. Jesus is born in the worst of conditions to be the Savior and ruler of the world. He who would live must die; to be great in God's eyes, a person must become a servant. Honor comes only with humility before God, not achievements before men. We must reach the end of ourselves to find the beginning of his intentions for us.

"With God, all things are possible" (Matt 19:26); however, in our various situations, despite the deteriorating world around us, many individualists think that all things are possible in our own strength. But God says that being and doing what he wants begins with faith, and that his grace is not based on our works but is his gift. It is only with God that "all things are possible." Others may think nothing is possible in their lives. But God says his grace is sufficient even in, especially in, our weakness. He reminds us that he is at work in us for his good purposes. We are at a loss without God. But we must remember that his ways are not our ways. They will often seem

205. THE IRONY OF GOD

ironic and opposite our expectations. For Christians to live in their cultures as honorable people, they must, to some extent, become countercultural.

As individualists, we have yet to learn how to be servants among others or what humility is in our churches. We still have trouble seeing Christianity as a relationship with God, not an institution. Being a Christian leader is the role of a humble servant, regardless of "notable professional achievements." It should not be I, but we, not me, but him, her, and them. We individualists will struggle to know God, for he is in the opposite direction of our human trajectory. Many try to make him part of their plan, but he waits for them to become part of his. Mortal flesh meets infinite God on his terms only. But meet him, we must, or perish.

Scripture References: Ps 51:16–17; Prov 28:26, 29:23; Mic 6:8; Matt 5:3–10, 7:15–23, 19:16–26; Mark 10:42–45, 14:35 with Matt 19:26; Luke 4:24–28; 9:23; 13:22–30; 18:9–14; 22:24–27, 13; John 3:36; Rom 11:33–36, 12:9–10; 1 Cor 1:18–31; 2 Cor 4:6–7, 12:7–10; Eph 2:8–10, 4:1–7; Phil 2:1–4; Col 3:12–14; Heb 13:20–21; Jas 2:5; 1 Pet 3:8–12, 5:5–6.

206. Seeing God

Who may stand in his holy place? He who has clean hands and a pure heart.

—*Ps 24:3-4*

WE MUST KEEP THE lens of our mind clear of the smudges of our human perspectives and preferences. If we do not, our ideas of God will be muddled and vague, blurred by human expectations. The only way to stay sharp is to meet with God as often as possible, bathe in his love, bask in his grace, and wonder at his greatness, power, and mystery. Acknowledging him in everything we do and say helps keep our minds focused on him, not ourselves. Reading, praying, and journaling our way through time with God renews our minds to think on him and the things above while occupied with things below. Like anything else, it will take practice until it becomes habitual—until we know no other way to live for him. So it is that we will see and know him as he is instead of how our human inclinations would prefer.

Though it may seem highly unnecessary, it is at this point that we also need a word of caution about our spiritual disciplines mentioned here. Being known as a spiritual person is a coveted status among many Christians. The appearance of seeking God is often used to seek a reputation for self. Do not be drawn into such an individualist lust for recognition. Go into your room and close the door. God, who looks at the heart, will meet you there. The kingdom of heaven belongs to the humble, and it is the pure in heart who will see God.

Scripture References: Pss 19:12–14, 24:3–4, 28:6–9, 51:10, 63:1–8, 91:14–16, 139:1–18; Prov 3:5–7, 15:26 with 16:2 and 17:3; Matt 5:3 and 8; 6:1–8; Luke 18:9–14; Rom 8:5–8 with 12:1–2; 11:33–36; Eph 4:22–24; Phil

4:8–9; Col 3:1–4; Titus 1:15; 1 Pet 1:13; 1 John 1:1–5 with 10–14; 2:15–17; 4:4–6.

207. God Among Gods

For the Lord is the great God, the great King above all gods.
—Ps 95:3

THE VIRTUES GOD WOULD have us pattern ourselves after are not about personal advancement but the love of those around us, integrity of heart, humility, God-centered perspective, gratefulness for his grace, and acknowledgment of his sufficiency. To the person who seeks him, he gives more longing to know him; he gives more grace to the humble. If we worship him alone, he, in his providence, helps us become what he desires in his plan for the world. It may not be what we expect since our expectations come from human and cultural perspectives and preferences. He does not make us into perfect people or do for us all he asks us to do for him, but, though imperfectly, we become those who can harmonize with his purposes and move in his direction with the motive to honor him. He, on his part, providentially shapes our circumstances and opportunities, our situation, giving us all we need to fulfill his purposes for our lives.

From this relationship with God comes wisdom. But if we turn to the god of personal achievement, and by it try to control our surroundings to serve our ends, we will follow that god to our great disappointment. The gains of money, celebrity, power, or human pleasure that are the rewards of this god are thin and temporary. They cannot result in ultimate peace and happiness. Founded on insecurities, what comes of them melts in the heat of time and selfishness and eventually hardens into cold, sterile emptiness. The final consequence is of eternal significance. The individual perishes alone, without God, without anything. The self-made person will be undone. Personal achievement must be under God's hand to accomplish his ends. The Christian is not immune to this deception of Satan. We can

207. GOD AMONG GODS

commit spiritual adultery, allowing a love affair with the rival god of self and the illusions of the world. The LORD is indeed God among gods, and we must decide our loyalties.

Scripture References: Pss 33:16–22, 91:14–16, 95:1–7, 135:5; Prov 3:5–7, 11:28, 28:26; Hos 4:12b; Matt 16:25–26; Luke 12:15–21 with Prov 3:9–10; Rom 5:1–2; 8:1, 28–39; 12:9–21; 1 Cor 10:31, 13:1–13; Gal 5:16–25; Phil 2:1–4, 4:4–9; Col 3:12–17; 2 Tim 4:9–10; Jas 3:13–18, 4:4, 6; 2 Pet 1:3–4; 1 John 2:15–17, 3:16–20.

208. Risking the Local Church

If anyone is in Christ, he is a new creation; the old has gone, the new has come!

—*2 Cor 5:17*

THE LOCAL CHURCH CAN have an essential part in our Christian lives— a place to learn about God's great acts, his profound grace, his constant presence, the peace and contentedness that can be ours, and to do so with others who seek the same. At church, we learn together, express our gratefulness to him, praise his goodness, and pray together. However, when attending church becomes an end in itself, a social expectation, a place of human achievement and celebrity, a place of competition, personal pride, and entertainment, it is no longer Christian. Unfortunately, our inclination is to return to the old ways of survival for the security we seek, if we ever left them behind. It is syncretism. We are inclined to step away from the simplicity of enduring faith and, once again, allow the self and our culture to have their way. It is just so that the church becomes an instrument to turn others away from God rather than a place for them to meet him. In its essence, it serves a great and God-given purpose, but it is a place shaped by humans and never loses its potential to go wrong unless we stay alert, humble ourselves, and submit to the Lord of our salvation. Faith is a matter of the heart. It must be nourished and grow to motivate and rule each believer's behavior and aspirations. We are to serve and encourage one another while allowing each to be different from ourselves. The church may help or hinder this purpose of God in our lives.

We see it in the New Testament. The people in Corinth hindered the purpose of the church; the churches in Rome and Galatia had difficulties with true worship and encouraging the faith. The church at Ephesus lost

208. RISKING THE LOCAL CHURCH

its first love; in Pergamum, it allowed false teaching; at Thyatira, it allowed immorality. The church at Sardis was dead, and that at Laodicea loved this present world more than God. But somehow we think we are immune to the pride and problems of our humanity, that we can outwit Satan's strategy for us. We do not see that selfish and controlling attitudes are the greatest evil in the church. But we are not impervious to sin; if we allow it, it will destroy the Christian community. No. We must humble ourselves before God, calibrate our motives to his word, nurture our trust in him alone, and encourage the faith and good works of Christians around us wherever we meet each other.

Scripture References: Ps 25:9; Matt 5:3–10; Rom 12:3–21, 14:1—15:7; 1 Cor 3:1, 5:1, 6:5–8, 11:17; 2 Cor 12:20–21; Gal 1:6–9, 4:8–11, 5:7–10, 6:9–10; Eph 4:1–6; 5:1, 8–10, 15–17; Phil 2:1–4, 4:8–9; Col 3:1–4, 12–17; 2 Tim 4:9–10a; Heb 10:24–25; 1 Pet 5:6–7; 2 Pet 1:3–10; Rev 2:1—3:22.

209. The Sweet Poison of Legalism

For everything God created is good, and nothing is to be rejected if it is received with thanksgiving, because it is consecrated by the word of God and prayer.

—*1 Tim 4:4–5*

INDIVIDUALISTS ARE ACHIEVERS AT heart and compete with others and themselves to arrive at their goals, whatever they may be. If we bring this cultural frame of reference into the church, we turn Christianity into a standard of performance, a list of behaviors, the execution of which is considered "success." Everyone is to achieve a reputation for being "spiritual," each must be a leader at some level or become a Christian celebrity in the eyes of others in the church. For these, at its basic level, spirituality is about church attendance, giving, using "spiritual" vocabulary, knowing your spiritual gift, leading a ministry, or being an extrovert. But it is not God's way. It never has been.

Individualists can too easily become legalists who believe that obedience to their interpretation of biblical behavior makes people acceptable to God, obliterating God's grace and our freedom in Christ with a jolting black-and-white simplicity. This puts them in control. It gives them, finally, the basis for judging others, but it does not earn them God's approval, and it often covers its followers with false guilt. God looks at the heart to see if we long to honor him in all we do, if we love and worship him in honesty and humility, and if we strive to be loyal, however imperfectly, in our relationship with him. We cannot, must not, trust in our own righteousness, for it leads away from his. We must trust in his and honor him with our loyalty, simple though it may be.

209. THE SWEET POISON OF LEGALISM

Scripture References: Gen 1:31; Pss 33:18; 91:14–16; 139:1–4, 23–24; 145:17–19; Prov 3:5–7, 16:2, 17:3, 20:27, 28:26; Ezek 33:13; Matt 5:8, 6:1–8, 7:15–23; Luke 16:14–15; John 4:23–24, 5:44; Rom 8:26–27, 14:1—15:5; 1 Cor 6:12, 10:23–24 and 31; Col 3:17 with 1 Tim 4:4–5 and Titus 1:15–16; Heb 4:12.

210. The Other Side of the Door

But small is the gate and narrow the road that leads to life, and only a few find it.

—Matt 7:14

GOD DOES NOT SEE our lives in this world the way we do. In this life, we practice exercising faith that is preliminary to another life. It is similar to the time of Israel in the wilderness, which was to prepare them to enter the promised land. God is concerned about our hearts while we are in this world. He is not looking for performance but for faith that will motivate what we do. And he has prepared a place for us on the other side of a door that cannot be opened except by that faith in this world. The door will be open for those who trust him and, finished with this life, step into the next. He stands there, ready to receive us.

We take ourselves and our circumstances here too seriously if we truly believe in heaven. Life in this world will not be perfect; it will not always be what we want it to be, but there is someone at work in us during this time for his purposes. In his good providence, he uses our situation to accomplish his intention for us to become people who trust him and fit in his plan in a particular way. His activity in our lives does not always look like what we might expect from God. Our cultural or personal expectations may blind us, and he has purposes we may not notice or understand at the time. This life is not all there is, and things are not always what they seem. His greatest desire for us is that we trust him.

Perhaps a legalistic persuasion or our delicate sensitivities get in the way. But we must let God be God. His ways are not ours; why would we think they should seem natural? His concern is with our trust in him and our entrance through the door between here and heaven. He will look at

210. THE OTHER SIDE OF THE DOOR

our hearts, and many will be on the other side that we do not expect would get through that door. Others who seemed so "spiritual" here will nct be found there. We must not be concerned with how others see us here but with whether he sees trust and our intentions to honor him in our hearts.

Honoring him will not bring us the applause of men; it is not God's intention that it should. From the days of creation, loyalty, worship, and obedience to God in the Old Testament was a matter of faith. And from the day Jesus was born among us, only the lowly in heart, whatever their past sins and current struggles may have been, truly followed him. The key to the door before us is faith, shaped by trust on one edge and humility on the other. Perfection is on the other side of that door.

Scripture References: 1 Sam 16:7; Prov 3:5–7, 21:2–3; Isa 55:8–9, 66:2b; Hos 6:6; Mic 6:8; Matt 5:3, 8; 6:25–34; 7:13–23; Luke 13:22–30; Rom 1:17, 3:21–24, 11:33–36; Phil 2:12–13; 3:13–14; 4:4–7, 12–13; Heb 4:13, 11:1–16, 13:20–21; 1 Pet 3:18, 5:6–7.

211. The Nature of God's Word

For the word of God is living and active. Sharper than any double-edged sword, it penetrates even to dividing soul and spirit. . . . It judges the thoughts and attitudes of the heart.

—Heb 4:12

IF THE WORD OF God is "living and active," penetrating our inward being and shining its light on the thoughts and intentions of our hearts, then we should expect it to be different from any human communication. If we allow it, its truth reaches subtle depths in our being, displaying its infinite and ongoing meaning for our lives. For those who know God and respect the mystery of his being, it vibrates in their inmost self with ultimate and active truth, giving wisdom and revealing treasures from a God whose ways are not ours. But for those who reject God and his Son, it is a fire at the edges of the dry grass of their lives. As it was for the people of Judah who called "evil good and good evil" (Isa 5:20), so it will be for them unless they turn to him.

The Bible is full of irony and paradoxes. There are opposing truths, both operational in God's perspective and indicating the weakness of our own reasoning. It speaks to us using symbols and types, allegory, parables, prophecy, poetry, and prose. Deep in wisdom for the heart, dividing between inclination and duty, using reason outside our logic, and upsetting our impatient sense of time, the Bible reveals God and his will for humankind. It gives us the experiences of real people in history who knew him or refused him in enduring examples of faith or falsehood, perception or blindness. It comes to us, and we embrace it or reject it. Some may try to change or fashion it into what they want it to say, even cheapen it as irrelevant in our day, but it stands as God has given it, a two-edged sword, an intense light on the dark way.

211. THE NATURE OF GOD'S WORD

God's word will not let go of our hearts in the difficulties of life, but rather he will use it to carry us through the discouragements, dark valleys, disappointments, and troubles of this world. He will not leave us alone in them. Trusting him in his word leads us to confidence, wonder, peace, and contentment, though we may know trials that test our patience for the present and strengthen our trust for the future.

Scripture References: Job 11:7–9; Pss 9:9–10, 23:4, 25:12, 46:1–3, 119:103–5; Prov 3:5–7, 20:27; Isa 5:20–25; 30:15 a and b; 46:10; 55:10–11; Luke 1:53; John 16:33; Rom 5:1–5, 11:33–36; 1 Cor 1:27–31, 2:6–16; 2 Tim 3:16–17; Heb 4:12, 12:28–29; Jas 1:2–8; 1 Pet 1:3–7 with 13; 4:12–13; 2 Pet 1:20–21.

212. The Church Today

Yet I hold this against you: You have forsaken your first love.
—*Rev 2:4*

Wake up! Strengthen what remains and is about to die, for I have not found your deeds complete in the sight of my God.
—*Rev 3:2*

I RECENTLY READ SOMEONE who said the church's primary purpose is to draw people to Christ. But it is primarily the gathering of those who have already come to Christ for worship, encouragement, and training in godliness and service. Then, through their love, unity, and good works, the gospel becomes incarnate in their lives as part of their message for outsiders in need. This is seen clearly in Paul's letters to the young pastors he mentored, Timothy and Titus. It should be pointed out, as well, that the institutional aspect of the church does not enter into this witness to the truth about God and his Son; it too easily does the opposite. In our institutionalization of the body of Christ and desire to be important and popular in its organization, we often mistake cultural absolutes for biblical absolutes and syncretize the church with cultural preferences not in alignment with God's word. Somehow we think bigger is always better, cultural relevancy is more important than truth, or truth is more important than grace. But we forget: only a few enter by the small gate, cultural relevancy can mask a love for the world, and grace and truth came to us together in Christ, never to be separated.

Our gatherings should bring us to maturity in Christ and prepare us to serve God. Then we become witnesses of God's love and grace to the world around us. When this is not the purpose, the world disdains the church.

212. THE CHURCH TODAY

Disillusioned by the human additions to God's purpose, people otherwise interested in him leave the church or avoid ever entering its doors. They see pride, professionalism, entertainment, and materialism—all the things that enter when it becomes a human institution. For them, it has become a religion, among others. The light has gone out; the salt has lost its savor.

Outsiders often consider Christianity a matter of going to church, but, in many cases, that may be the last thing a person needs to cultivate a life of faith. Attending church is often for the mature in faith and stout of heart. It can be as discouraging as it can be helpful. Its leaders' constant call for support and loyalty to the organization can stand in the way of loyalty to God himself. It has a natural tendency to encourage popular Christianity, especially in an affluent, individualist society. Knowing, trusting, and serving God must be the first priority; attending church should encourage that. Those who lead us in the church must have wisdom about the inclinations of institutions, culture's influence on people, and the wheat mixed with weeds in the field of organized Christianity. Only then can they encourage our faith, hope, and love in a broken world.

Scripture References: Prov 9:10, 30:7–9; Matt 5:13–16, 6:1–8, 7:13–14, 13:24–30 with 36–43; John 1:14 with 17; 13:34–35; 15:12; 17:3, 15–23; Acts 1:8; Eph 4:11–16 with Phil 2:12–16a and 3:12—4:1; 1 Thess 4:11–12; 1 Tim 2:1–4, 6:18–19; Titus 2:4–5; Heb 13:15 with Ps 91:14–16; 1 Pet 2:12–17; Rev 2:4–5, 3:2–3.

213. Time on Our Hands

Teach us to number our days aright, that we may gain a heart of wisdom.

—Ps 90:12

THIS MOMENT AND THIS moment only is ours to choose what we will do with the life God has given us and with his purpose for our part in his work. We cannot undo the past or guess the future. This day, this hour, may be in our hands now, but it will be gone, never to be retrieved, and we will be grateful or regretful. We will never be perfect in our loyalties to God and others, but there are some things to keep before us to make the best use of the time we have.

Never neglect the people you love; be attentive and sensitive to them, for God has put them in your life. Keep your marriage romantic, your parenting encouraging, and your friendships loyal, warm, and helpful. Remember the power of words and use them carefully and thoughtfully. Let them be meaningful and for the good of those around you, not expressions of self-assertion or impatience. Monitor your emotions so that anger or frustration does not get out of hand. Do not let kindness and truth leave you—love and faithfulness fade. "Be quick to listen, slow to speak, and slow to become angry" (Jas 1:19). Keep wisdom "that comes from heaven" (Jas 3:13–18) as your friend. Remember that God's purpose for your life is to keep the big picture, even eternity, in your perspective. Rest will be necessary, and leisure activity will be restorative, but let vocation be productive and an opportunity to attract the attention of those on the outside to the treasures on the inside of a relationship with God. Enjoy your work and leisure, and be diligent but also understanding.

213. TIME ON OUR HANDS

We need to be people of loyalty, integrity, and trust. But we must also realize and never be overly discouraged that we are not always perfect in expressing these values. We must recognize that our feelings will come and go like fair-weather friends. Though duty often means doing what we should, whether we feel like it or not, we are frequently reminded that we are human with limitations and weaknesses, and must remember that God knows it. We are imperfect and, at the same time, the only kind of people God entrusts with his message and purposes. He understands the creatures he has created and has provided for our human needs and for us to meet those of others around us. He provides an abundance of the best wine for the wedding. We must accept his blessings in this life as we concentrate on his purposes that affect the next, for ourselves and those around us. We have been given this moment as a gift of his grace. We don't know how many more he will give us.

Scripture References: Pss 90:10–12, 100:3, 103:6–18, 127:1–2; Prov 3:3–4, 13–35; 4:5–9; 27:23–27; Eccl 7:8–9; Matt 6:33–34; John 2:1–11; Rom 12:3–8; 1 Cor 13:1–13; Phil 2:3–4; Col 3:12–17; 1 Thess 4:11–12; Titus 2:1–8; Heb 10:23–35; 1 Pet 2:11–17, 4:10; 2 Pet 1:3–9.

214. Unreasoned Death

I know where you live—where Satan has his throne.
—*Rev 2:13*

MANY WANT A WORLD headed toward a destiny they have chosen, using their own solutions to mental and emotional survival. To accomplish this, they must do away with God to be free of guilt and fear. Then they must trust their own judgment to lead them to happiness. Every way to know God is barricaded, every weapon of destruction leveled at him. But by removing God from the hearts and minds of the people, a monster is created that no one can feed. It then turns on its creators and devours them. Such is the mental and emotional condition of many in our times. It is human nature out of control, angry at the world for not giving them what previous God-haters could not supply: love, security, forgiveness, and meaning in life. Their atheistic teachings bring cool relief to those who do not want there to be a God. They seem to soothe but turn out to be a slow poison.

Each generation gets weaker, programming the minds of the young with ideas that remove meaning, purpose, value, and virtue from life. The atheist may not have seen God's love and grace in Christianity and are now bent on its destruction. Yes, superficial and liberal Christians are part of their problem, but even more grave, the minds of unbelievers are blinded by Satan himself, the enemy of God. Their way separates them from all that is good and the Giver of life, ending in disaster. The answer to their madness is before them, but they refuse its cure in Christ just as Israel refused the blessings of God before them. But the fact of God remains. G. K. Chesterton once said that if God did not exist, there would be no atheists.

But all is not lost. God is not silent. He continues to work in the world broken by every form of rejection of truth and trust. He has a remnant of

214. UNREASONED DEATH

people bathed in his grace, working for his purposes, and bringing the message of his kindness and mercy to the lost world. They talk of fullness of life and freedom in Christ for any who acknowledge God and his way. Many of those who seek to eliminate him are not beyond the reach of his grace. But others have made a final choice. They have closed and bolted that door, and God has granted their wish and given them over to their love of the dark side. Though he is patient with all who may yet turn to him because he desires their repentance, he will not wait forever. He is coming.

Scripture References: Deut 32:3–6; Pss 10:4, 14:1; Prov 3:5–8, 28:26; Isa 5:20–24, 10:1–4; Ezek 33:11; Zech 7:8–12; John 1:1–5 with 10–14; 3:16–21, 36; 5:24; 8:12; 17:15–19; Rom 1:18–32, 2:5–11, 3:21–24; 2 Cor 4:1–7; Eph 2:1–10; Phil 1:3–6, 2:12–13, 3:17–21; 1 Thess 5:1–11; 1 Tim 1:15–16; 1 Pet 1:3–11, 4:7–13; 2 Pet 2:1–3; 3:10, 17–19; 1 John 2:17; Rev 1:1–4 with 27; 2:12–17.

215. Unending Hope

Yet to all who received him, to those who believed in his name, he gave the right to become the children of God.

—*John 1:12*

I HEARD OF A man who once asked if God was still here watching his creation and deciding who lives and dies or if he was gone now and all was a wasteland. How cruel can God be to allow good people to die? It is amazingly common for people to blame God for the mess humankind has made of a perfect creation—the very ones who invited death to be part of it and gallivanted off into the darkness they had chosen. Those who question God today are also given the gift of life, and they greedily squeeze all *they* want out of it without ever reading a page of the user manual. True life is reserved for those who acknowledge him.

The degeneration of the world around us should not cause despair but a deeper involvement. The lawlessness, paganism, immorality, and murder of the ages are still with us. Suffering and death remain as evidence of the rebellion. The world has always needed God, and most have always refused him. Fire, water, gaping holes in the earth, the death of a generation in the wilderness, invasions, and deportations to foreign lands—God tries in vain to remind us that he does indeed have his eye on his creation. We cannot deny him his place as ruler of the universe, ban all consideration of his crucial mercy, and avoid disaster. But all is not lost. There are blessings scattered among the curses, grace, where least expected, held out to those who acknowledge him. Despite all man's rejection, God still holds out his grace. We own that grace by his blessing, and we have the message of this hope for the soul of each man and woman. He keeps us in this damaged world to be lights in the darkness.

215. UNENDING HOPE

An intervening love in the universe reaches out to all. It can redeem men and women from self-destruction and meaninglessness. The human heart can be restored, the mind know truth again, and the soul experience peace and freedom in this world when we receive the grace of God in Christ. Many will continue in their chosen way, rejecting God out of an unreasoned love for self, resentment of traumatic experiences and abuse, or because of hypocrisy they have seen. But others, though fewer, will humble themselves and choose his road. They will come to him and discover life; though they were blind, they will finally see. God is moving in our world; nothing is outside his control. He will bring about his plan for all who choose to be rescued, and no adversary, no weapon used against him, can stop his hand.

God's goodness to those who see and his desire to heal the blind are offset, however, by an intense severity toward those who say they know the truth yet, in their pride, refuse God's grace and lead others away from him. Only his grace in Christ can remove the chains of their obstinate, self-centered rejection and lift the condemnation, opening the door to him. Some have opened it a crack and are terrified of who they see there. But they must let the full light of his grace shine in. If they are willing and open the door of their lives wide to the truth in Christ, no amount of sin can hold him back from saving them, and they will know true freedom in Christ.

This unending hope for us who are awake carries us through a world of misery and rebellion where many sleep. Those who create increasingly more evil ways to reject the truth try to force their ways on us. But the Creator-God of the universe is with us. We are his. Hope is a choice of light in a dark and lost world. The message of that hope is urgent, for God is both a God of grace and a consuming fire.

Scripture References: Gen 6:11–14 with 7:1–4 and 8:15–17; 19:15–17 with 23–29; Num 16:28–35, 27:63–65 with 32:13; Pss 145:13–14 with 146:5–6 and 147:11; Prov 3:5–7 with Ps 91:14–16; Prov 21:30; Isa 5:20–30 with 11–13; Lam 3:22–26; Matt 5:14–16, 7:13–14; Mark 10:24–25; Luke 9:23–25, 17:2; John 1:1–18, 3:16–21, 5:24, 8:12, 9:25, 17:15; Rom 1:18–25, 3:21–26, 5:1–6; 2 Cor 4:6; Titus 1:16; Heb 11:1–39, 12:28–29; Jas 4:4; 2 Pet 3:8–10; 1 John 1:5–10 with 2:9–11 and 15–17; Rev 21:1–4.

216. Poor in Spirit and Pure in Heart

The sacrifices of God are a broken spirit; a broken and contrite heart, O God, you will not despise.

—*Ps 51:17*

IN THE WESTERN WORLD, most of us are far removed from the conditions of life that prompted much of the language used in the Gospels. The Beatitudes in Jesus' Sermon on the Mount are given to the disadvantaged, the farmers and herders of a poor and agrarian society. Their land was their only meaningful possession, but it was frequently taken from them by the unscrupulous wealthy who had the judges in their pockets. In addition, their country was occupied by a foreign power, and they were oppressed by religious leaders. Their attitudes of helplessness in this situation were increased by a low life expectancy because of illness, poor diet, and physical deformities. But these conditions brought the people to Jesus in search of hope. Very few of them were wealthy or powerful who heard Jesus, and the message they heard was to believe in him, a peasant-born, wandering preacher of little social consequence. It was a call for humility, justice, and mercy. A deep change of heart that many were unwilling to accept.

Most religious people of the day did not hear the message they wanted from a conquering Messiah, but some had ears to hear the real message. He tells them that the poor in spirit and the pure in heart, the humble but spiritually alert people who listen to him, can be happy because they belong to the kingdom of heaven. No one can take that away from them. It would not be theirs if they were distracted by the wealth and status of the world. The dishonest power brokers of their day were men of ease. They had large homes and servants at their call, enough to eat, and fine clothes to wear, but they forfeited their souls and gave up the kingdom for a few days of

216. POOR IN SPIRIT AND PURE IN HEART

comfort and ease. So blessed are the humble, "the poor in spirit," and the "broken and contrite [in] heart" (Matt 5:3; Ps 51:17). Though their days on earth may be fewer and a struggle for physical survival, theirs is the eternal kingdom of heaven where every tear will be dried and all suffering will cease. Those who have taken their ease here by dishonest gain, by taking advantage of the poor, even thinking they have special status with God will only know eternal darkness.

The conditions of the original audience for Jesus' words do not make his message less applicable to us in our situation today. It is a stark warning to our Western culture, where individualism has us searching for personal survival, wealth, and social success when the kingdom lies in another direction. We, too, need the attitudes Jesus listed in his sermon in our day-to-day lives, for only the humble with pure motives can know God.

Scripture References: Pss 25:9, 40:4, 51:16–17, 146:8b and 147:3 and 6; Prov 11:28, 14:20–21, 16:2, 21:13, 28:26–27; Isa 42:3, 66:2b; Jer 9:23–24; Mic 6:8; Matt 5:3–10, 22:13 with 25:30 and 41; Luke 12:13–21 and 22–34; 16:19–31; 18:9–14; Titus 1:15 with 1 Pet 5:6 and Matt 7:13–14 with 21; Rev 21:1–4.

217. Obedience

For I desire mercy, not sacrifice, and acknowledgment of God rather than burnt offerings.

—Hos 6:6

WHEN MANY TODAY LOOK back at God's law in the Old Testament, they see nothing but stern commands for submission and obedience. Indeed, no one can perfectly obey the 613 commandments. Even many people of the New Testament days, under the teaching of the Pharisees, saw their relationship with God as obedience to a distant ruler over them. So strong was their human disposition to see the Old Testament as only law and compliance that the Jewish leaders added a myriad of details for the people to observe—the Oral Torah, the traditions. They policed their enforcement and blackmailed the people with the shame of being put out of the synagogues to ensure they did not ignore even the smallest requirement. These leaders were blinded by their theological preferences for objective, outward behavior and the control this gave them over the people.

But it was not reality. All the while, God wanted mercy, not sacrifice, acknowledgment of him, not burnt offerings, the rending of their hearts, not their clothes. He wanted justice, compassion, and humility as the outcome of fasting and sackcloth. The example of the Pharisee and the tax collector in the temple shows us the stark difference between the pride of the Jewish teachers and the humility God sought. The Jewish leaders would not see obedience to God as always being a matter of the heart, not perfection in outward activity. They were blind to the lovingkindness of God throughout the Old Testament days.

Just as their theology disallowed the prophecies of the true nature of the coming Messiah, they ignored passages where God was asking for their

217. OBEDIENCE

hearts instead of their empty rituals—for grateful obedience and loyalty to the one who had brought them out of Egypt. A pure heart must always come before clean hands. Their theology limited God to their human definitions of what he wanted and what he could do. While God wanted them to order their lives around the need for justice, a love of kindness, and personal humility, they continued to enforce strict conformity to a religious code. Into this situation, he sent the Messiah, who came with grace *and* truth, and the two were never to be separated. Jesus upset their theology and social status as religious leaders. They wanted neither his grace nor his truth. They were in charge and sought to eliminate his influence over the people.

Jesus told the people that the greatest of the commandments were to love God with all our being and our neighbor as ourselves. All obedience was to follow and be infected with this attitude of love—not a feeling, but trust, loyalty, humility, and kindness that orders one's life. Jesus shows the law to always have been a matter of the heart in the Sermon on the Mount. That is why legalism in the church today is the greater sin. When we ignore God's grace, we turn his word into ritual laws that are empty of relationship and love. Our response to God's grace is the theme of both the Old and New Testaments. We know the truth, which sets us free to live lives bathed in that grace in a lost world.

Scripture References: 1 Sam 16:7; 1 Chr 29:17a and 18; Job 29:14-16; Pss 24:3-4; 51:6, 16-17; Prov 15:26, 16:2, 17:3, 21:2-3, 22:4; Isa 10:1-3, 58:6-12; Hos 6:6; Joel 2:12-13; Mic 6:8; Mal 1:10-14; Matt 5:1—7:29, 15:8-9, 22:34-40, 25:34-40; Mark 12:32-34; Luke 18:9-14; John 1:14-18, 8:31 and 36; Heb 13:15-16.

218. A Selfless Person Who Can Find?

But a Samaritan, as he traveled, came to where the man was; and when he saw him, he took pity on him.

—Luke 10:33

THE GOAL OF SELF-SURVIVAL is a strong motive for the independent Western person, and it often comes between us and loving others. Individualism is the core of our cultural values, and we struggle with it every day. We not only know no other way to survive, we have few contrasting examples to follow. Many of us grow up without love and have no idea how to love others. Though it is true in different ways in other cultures, Western people are experts at putting themselves first. Pure motives are hard to come by as we naturally look for what we can get from each encounter to help us survive. When we come to Christ in faith, he asks the opposite, that we love others and put their needs first. It demands trust in him, which individualists also find difficult to express. It is a perceived risk to our personal survival we are often unwilling to take.

Even as Christians, greed and selfish ambition for personal gain, recognition, and reputation are just below the surface. The heart is indeed deceitful, and old habits hard to break. We must practice self-awareness and caution so that the old man inside us does not come back to control us in our relationships and damage our churches. It is at the heart of a relationship with God to love those around us with *agape* love. In the logical and objective West, we emphasize justification by faith in Christ, which is essential. But the underlying thrust of the New Testament is on loving others, doing good works, being humble, and trusting God's grace and providence, which should be the fruit of that justification. We tend to minimize or gloss

218. A SELFLESS PERSON WHO CAN FIND?

over the passages on selflessness. But Jesus makes it central to knowing and serving him.

Scripture References: Ps 112:4–7; Prov 4:23; 11:25; 22:4, 9; 23:6–8; 28:22; Jer 17:9; Matt 5:3–10, 25:40; Luke 6:37–38, 10:25–37, 12:13–21; John 13:34–35, 15:12; Rom 12:10; Gal 6:9–10; Phil 2:1–4; 1 Thess 3:12; 1 Tim 6:17–19; 2 Tim 3:2; Titus 2:11–14; Heb 10:24, 13:15–16; Jas 3:13–18; 1 Pet 1:22, 4:8; 1 John 2:9–11; 3:16–20, 23; 4:7, 11–12.

219. Forgiving Others

Forgive us our sins, for we also forgive everyone who sins against us.
—Luke 11:4

GOD'S FORGIVENESS OF PEOPLE has both absolute assurances he has given us and areas of understanding he has reserved for himself. It is, once again, not always a black-and-white issue in the Gospels. Some take Jesus' words on the cross when he requests that God forgive those who carried out his execution, saying, "for they know not what they do" (Matt 27:54), as the model for forgiveness between people. However, we must consider that, though the Romans did not know what they were doing, the Jewish leaders knew full well what they were doing and received no such words from Jesus. They had the Torah, the Prophets, and the Writings, but they still rejected the truth that Jesus was the one God sent, that he was God himself. Their Oral Torah and Pharisaical theology did not allow God to send the Messiah in such a way. They refused him from the beginning, seated in their high positions of social control, filled with selfish ambition and envy, blackmailing the people with threats of expulsion from among "God's people." So they did not receive his forgiving words (while the criminal on the cross next to Jesus did). The money changers gouged the people coming to the temple to worship God in his house, and Jesus drove them out. Even the rich young ruler did not get words of forgiveness from Jesus when he came asking for benefits. He wanted God to bless the life he had achieved and to be part of *his* plan, but Jesus showed him it was about becoming a part of God's plan.

Many others in the Gospels received forgiveness from Jesus based on their faith. But when actions are against God or his people, it seems to matter if they are done innocently or intentionally for personal benefit. And it seems to matter if they had an opportunity to know God's will but rejected it

219. FORGIVING OTHERS

all the same. We must remember that while God waits for sinners to confess and repent, not all who call Jesus Lord will enter heaven; only those who humble their hearts and realize their dependence on his grace are doing his will. He does not trump our choices with forgiveness—we must come to him. His comment on the cross was in a context where the soldiers could not have known they were executing an innocent man. Pilate carries the entire blame for carrying out the evil of the Jewish leaders. Only when Jesus died and the earth shook under the darkened sky did a centurion realize he must be the Son of God. The Jewish leaders had God's word and a history of his lovingkindness and yet led the people away from him to maintain their control. Those who said they knew God's ways and led people away from him, as Jesus said, were better off tied to a millstone and thrown into the sea.

Our intentions and agendas concerning God and others affect his grace in our lives. He looks at the heart of each person. Humility recognizes we often fall short and need his forgiveness. And we are to make room for others who fall short. We must forgive their sin against us when we do not know their hearts. But leading God's people away from him is a matter between God and the offender that we must leave in his hands. We cannot step into his territory. The examples in the Bible are not encouraging for the unrepentant soul.

Scripture References: Prov 15:26, 16:2, 17:3, 20:27, 22:4; Matt 6:14; 7:13–23; 13:24–30; 18:6; 19:16–24; 23:13–15; 25:41–46; 26:3–5; 27:15–26, 54; Luke 6:37–38; 10:13–15; 17:1–3a; 23:34, 47; John 2:12–17, 13:8–10; Eph 4:1–7 with 32; Col 3:12–17; 1 John 2:8–9.

220. Trouble in the Church

Keep watch.... Savage wolves will come in among you and will not spare the flock.

—*Acts 20:28–29*

FROM THE DAY JESUS was born, proud enemies have been nearby. But, as Mary tells us, God scatters the proud and lifts up the humble. Self-righteous Christians do not exist, and if those who use the church to gain personal wealth, position, control, or reputation say they are Christians, the evidence is against them. It is the poor in spirit for whom heaven is reserved, the meek who inherit the earth, the pure in heart who see God.

Conservative Christians have long stressed the need for faith in Christ for salvation and a life of good works as evidence. But we have neglected to emphasize humility. Without humility, there can be no saving faith. Humility is built into the word *trust*. It is not just a shuffling of beliefs, the reallocating of a piece of information in the mind. It is a transformation of our understanding of reality—God is in control, we are not, and nothing can stop him. It is a realization of our desperate need for his grace. This humility is the soil that produces faith that saves and starts the process of a profound change deep in the heart and intentions, a shifting of loyalty from self to God. People in the church without this saving faith bring destruction instead of peace, tear down instead of build up. They are often the weeds among the wheat, choking its growth. Proud church leaders are the enemies, the wolves among us. The more they succeed, the less the church serves its purpose, and the blind lead the blind.

We should not be surprised by such disparity among "Christians." For we have tried to make a broad road of a narrow way. Though we welcome any and all to the banquet, each must choose a humble faith in Christ to enter the kingdom. We must be patient and long-suffering, but we do them no good and the church a good deal of harm if our message is empty of the humility of true faith. It may begin quite small in its development toward maturity, but it is not the quantity or size of that faith that matters. It is rather its genuineness that opens the way to know God. It is like the small key that opens a huge door, and once we enter we realize we are in a sacred space that God has reserved for us to meet with him. Life cannot go on the same for the one who turns that key. Some find the door but their keys of self-assertion or achievement do not fit the lock, or, looking in the window, they decide not to take the risk. It doesn't look like their church. The stairs are too steep, the hallway too long. But those who enter, tattered and weary though they are, see—beyond the entryway—the grace and goodness of God.

Scripture References: 2 Kgs 6:15–17; Pss 34:18, 145:13b–14a, 146:8b, 147:6; Prov 16:18, 22:4; Mic 6:8; Matt 5:3–10; 7:15–23; 13:1–9 with 18–30 and 36–43, 44–46; 15:10–14; 19:16–26; Luke 1:46–55, 6:39–42, 18:9–14; John 14:6 with 17:3; Acts 5:1–11, 20:28–31; Eph 2:10; Phil 2:1–8, 3:17–19; 2 Tim 3:1–5, 4:1–5; Jas 3:13–18, 4:1–10; 1 Pet 5:6.

221. Jesus and Social Justice

Put your sword back in its place, for all who draw the sword will die by the sword.

—Matt 26:52

MANY TODAY THINK THAT Jesus is telling us to fight for social justice. We can do many things to promote social justice, especially in a democratic society, but Jesus never said we should use violence and hostility to attain it. That is the way of the world. Many take his description of his God-given role as the Messiah to proclaim good news for the poor, freedom for the prisoners, and release for the oppressed as a message to us to aggressively fight for people's "rights" to this freedom and release. But he was describing what he was sent to do. To best understand what he meant by it, we must look at what he did to fulfill that role.

The government that wields the sword given to it by God must indeed fight oppression and unjust imprisonment. But unless we are in law enforcement or the military to fulfill that God-given role, we are to follow Jesus' example. We can see his example throughout the Gospels, and he describes it in his parable of the sheep and the goats in Matt 25:31–46. Those in authority who fulfill God's role given to them for justice in society who are Christians are not to hate or abuse those they put behind bars. They may yet come to Christ for forgiveness. Many have.

Jesus told Peter to put away his sword because his kingdom was not about fighting; his kingdom was not of this world. He showed compassion as he healed the blind and lame, raised the dead, and fed the hungry. He taught the crowds about the kingdom of heaven and the essentials of choosing and trusting him as the Messiah who would die and rise again. Jesus taught people to pay their taxes to Caesar during Rome's occupation of Palestine,

221. JESUS AND SOCIAL JUSTICE

but to avoid the leaven of the Pharisees—to avoid spiritual pride and hypocrisy and to submit, as far as possible, to the political leaders of the occupying forces. He prayed that God would not take us out of this world but protect us from the evil one while we are in it amid hatred and persecution. We are not told to expect good things from society but to be misunderstood, even mistreated, and respond with grace, compassion, patience, and endurance.

This is not a message Western individualist Christians want to hear or non-Western oppressed societies want to espouse. But are we to make the Scriptures say what we want them to say or let God speak for himself? In his commentary on the passage from Isaiah in the synagogue, Jesus stresses God's love and attention to gentiles in the Old Testament, while the Jews, under Roman oppression, thought of gentiles as their enemies. We cannot mirror God's love with a violent resistance toward those who oppress us. When we were his enemies, he responded with grace and offered his own Son's life to save us.

Scripture References: Matt 5:3-12, 22:15-22, 26:52-54 with John 18:36; Luke 4:16-30 with Isa 58:6-8 and 61:1-2 and Matt 5:10 and 25:31-40; Luke 12:1-2; John 16:33 with 17:15; 18:10-11 with 36; Rom 5:6-11, 13:1-7; 2 Cor 10:3-4; Eph 2:1-5; 2 Tim 4:1-4; Jas 1:2-8; 1 Pet 3:14-16, 4:12-19; 1 John 3:11-13.

222. Biblical Thinking

Do not conform any longer to the pattern of this world, but be transformed by renewing your mind.

—*Rom 12:2*

As we think, so we live our lives. Paul tells us that instead of following the values and ways of the world (or the valueless way of the world), we are to be transformed by a renewal of our minds so we will know God's will. He would tell the Corinthians that if we are in Christ, we have the mind of Christ by his Spirit. He told the Colossians to set their minds on things above and the Philippians to think about godly virtues. It does indeed matter how we think. We must let God have his way in our minds, setting them on things above, not earthly things. We are to prepare our minds for action, persistently bringing our thoughts under the control of loyalty to Christ. But many are deceived. Their minds are blinded by the god of this age. They live and walk in darkness.

Though the mind and the ability to reason are gifts of God from being created in his image, our mind can be used to think of ways to deny his existence and, therefore, his moral code for social survival. But even in refusing him, people must use the minds he has given them. Humankind has limited reasoning without God's frame of reference and cannot create values that lead to ultimate survival. Outside a mind transformed by faith in Christ, the blind lead the blind on a path away from God, away from the light, the source of life. It is treason in the kingdom for which the gravest penalty is reserved.

We must think biblically, look into what God says in his word, and trust him. We must allow it to shape our minds so that we walk in the light, and even though we occasionally stumble, taking our eyes off him, we come

222. BIBLICAL THINKING

back to his grace over and over. Thus, one brick at a time, we build our lives and well-being on the rock. Then what we think will become wisdom for the days ahead—the survival of our souls during the storms of life in a broken world and an eternity with God when we leave here.

Scripture References: Pss 1:1–3, 34:19 with 37:23–24; Prov 3:5–7, 13–18 with 4:23–27; Isa 50:10–11; Matt 7:21–29; John 1:12, 14:6; Rom 8:5–8, 12:2; 1 Cor 2:6–16; 2 Cor 4:4–6 with John 1:4–5, 3:19–21, 8:12, and 12:36; 2 Cor 10:5; Eph 4:20–24, 5:17; Phil 4:4–9; Col 3:1–4; 1 Tim 2:5–6, 6:3–10; 1 Pet 1:13–21; 1 John 1:5–10 with 2:9–11, 15–17.

223. To Forget God

My people have committed two sins: They have forsaken me, the spring of living water, and have dug their own cisterns, broken cisterns that cannot hold water.

—Jer 2:13

In the book of Ecclesiastes, Solomon (I still believe him to be the author) reminds us to remember our Creator: "Before the silver cord is severed . . . the dust returns to the ground it came from" (Eccl 12:1–7). In the ease and leisure of Western culture, it is easy to forget our God and go after the gods of this world, listen to the tales of men, follow the trends of our times, and leave justice and humility behind. What is the end of those who forget God? It was the story of the people of the divided kingdom of Israel and Judah, and it is ours. They faced terrible judgment in their day, but we think we will not. Our people follow the deception of those who claim to know the best way of life but are blinded by their destructive cravings. They lead others astray and give them false hope, but the Lord knows. Better a millstone for them. God sent the prophets to Israel and Judah, one after another, to tell them of their blindness and turn them back to him. But they resisted the message of the prophets in their love for the foreign gods of their neighbors and their lack of justice, humility, and compassion. Rebellion may be among us now, but in the kingdom it will not be so. All who turn their backs on God will be absent.

The church must consider if it, too, has grown cold. What are we blind to in our day? Many assumptions about the church's purposes and functions develop over time. Each generation adopts changes from cultural demands and trends that seem okay. We do not measure them by God's word because they seem natural. But we can be blind to our motives and ignorant of their

223. TO FORGET GOD

influence. If a prophet were to speak today, we, too, may reject his message. We are loath to admit it, but many churches have become addicted to the rewards of their culture, a sweet poison. For many, there may be too much at risk to turn back; the prophet's message will go unheeded, and God will remain forgotten. Time is not on our side. We must wake up to the urgency of a return to pure and humble faith. The King is coming.

Scripture References: Deut 8:1–20; Judg 10:6–8, 21:25; Pss 51:6, 16–17; 146:3–4; Prov 21:3, 22:4; Eccl 12:1–7; Isa 32:5, 55:8–9; Jer 2:13 with 3:21–22; 17:5–10; 23:9–40; Hos 6:6; Mic 6:8; Matt 5:8; 7:21–23; 13:36–42, 47–50; 23:37–38 with Luke 19:41–44 and 20:9–19; Luke 17:1–2; John 4:13–14 with 17:37–38; 2 Cor 4:4–6; 1 Pet 5:5b–7; 1 John 2:15–17; Rev 3:1–3, 14–20.

224. Freedom in Christ That Honors God

For everything God created is good, and nothing is to be rejected if it is received with thanksgiving, because it is consecrated by the word of God and prayer.

—*1 Tim 4:4–5*

SOMETIMES, WHEN WE FIND something we like or that helps us, we think more is better. But those of us who have tried to get more out of a good thing find it is not always the case. Whether medicine, apple pie, or money, more is not necessarily better. Our freedom in Christ is one of those things. It is a costly gift from God that can be abused. As Paul said, "Everything is permissible, but not everything is beneficial" (1 Cor 10:23). He goes on to say, "Nobody should seek his own good, but the good of others" (10:24). Our freedom in Christ is a precious gift of rightly understanding God's intention in creation and the nature of grace.

What we eat or drink, what we wear, where we go, or how we spend our money are matters of freedom and conscience given to us by our understanding of God's word and the Holy Spirit. But to enjoy this freedom without thinking about how we affect others in the body of Christ is to go beyond the limit of love he has set for that freedom. If your medical prescription says one pill three times a day, two pills three times a day goes beyond the limit of its helpfulness and can cause a good deal of harm to your health. Just so, living out your freedom in Christ, as much a blessing as it is in its recommended dose, can harm other Christians who have yet to understand the freedom God has given them. Consideration and love must take over. Our freedom is given to us so that we might have a voluntary love and loyalty for God and a voluntary commitment to our neighbor's welfare.

224. FREEDOM IN CHRIST THAT HONORS GOD

In the true body of Christ, love, unity, and truth are equally important. "Blessed are the peacemakers" (Matt 5:9).

This truth about freedom in Christ does come, however, with the warning that legalism cannot be tolerated, for it is the obliteration of the sacred gift God has given us. It is a denial of the grace of God, the very heart of the gospel. There is a principle to keep in mind about nonessentials in the expression of our faith: each believer "should be fully convinced in his own mind" (Rom 14:5) about the practices they find good and helpful that are not moral or ethical issues for us under grace. But sometimes it is better to keep what we believe about these nonessentials between ourselves and God (14:22) if it will spoil harmony in the body of Christ. We do not need to let what we "consider good to be spoken of as evil" (14:16). We must "make every effort to do what leads to peace and to mutual edification" (14:19) in the body, even when it is not wrong for us to do otherwise. "If it is possible, as far as it depends on you, live at peace with everyone" (12:18). Of course, it may become impossible. When the issue borders on legalism, we cannot deny the grace of God for adherence to nonessential practices made into exclusive ways to maintain God's approval. The solution is to teach about our grace-filled freedom in Christ, its boundaries of love for God and others, and the deadly consequences of legalism in the church.

Scripture References: Gen 1:31; Matt 5:9; Luke 18:9–14; John 17:20–23; Rom 12:18, 14:1—15:7; 1 Cor 6:12; 10:23–24 with 31; 13:1–13; Gal 5:13–14; Phil 2:1–4, 12–13; Col 3:17 with 1 Tim 4:4–5 and Titus 1:15–16 and Matt 5:8; Jas 4:17; 1 Pet 2:16–17.

225. Religion Is Not the Cure

For it is by grace you have been saved, through faith . . . not by works.
—Eph 2:8–9

RELIGION MAY BE A salve for the moment, but it is comfortless over time. However, it is the only path many know, even some who call themselves Christians. Religious works and rituals must be left behind for God himself. There is no true comfort, no rest for the soul in working to seek approval from him. That approval is not accomplished by religious acts but only found in trusting God's grace, as, by faith, we are covered with the righteousness of Christ. Those without Christ are constantly fighting for survival—social, physical, and emotional survival. It is an uphill battle until the person finds Christ—not religion, not Christianity, but Christ himself. The grace of God can be found nowhere else. Our fighting is futile. It is time we laid down our weapons and surrendered to his intervening love.

We have forsaken trust. Should we, by great human effort, meet every outward expectation of religious behavior, it cannot procure what we, as pilgrims, seek. We will have struggled in vain for peace with God while passing by the simplicity of humble trust. A personal experience of trusting God's unmerited favor in Christ reveals religious activity to be a thin veneer over a desperate lostness of the soul. Christ is the victor. Loyalty to him alone brings unconditional acceptance, complete forgiveness, flourishing hope, and, in the coming days, the ultimate survival of the soul.

So beware of falling in love with religion. It is spiritual adultery. It tells us that the rituals we follow earn us God's favor, but we worship in vain. His word tells us that he looks at our hearts. There, acknowledgment of his providence and gratefulness for his grace motivate us to love and good

225. RELIGION IS NOT THE CURE

deeds that honor him, move us to help and encourage those around us, and give credibility to our words about him.

Scripture References: Ps 91:1-2, 14-16; Prov 3:5-7, 21:3; Lam 3:25; Hos 6:6; Mic 6:8; Matt 5:14-16, 15:8-9; Luke 9:23-25, 12:13-21; John 10:22-30, 12:24-26, 13:35, 14:6, 16:33, 17:3; Acts 4:12; 2 Cor 4:4; Gal 6:7-10; Eph 1:18-23, 2:4-5; Heb 10:24, 11:6 with Jas 2:14-17.

226. God's Great Disappointment

But small is the gate and narrow the road that leads to life, and only a few find it.

—Matt 7:14

People often misunderstand Jesus when he says the gate is small, the way that leads to life narrow, and there are few who find it. It seems like God's purpose is to make it difficult to get to heaven; there appears to be an unwillingness to let very many in. But this small gate is a statement of both God's plentiful grace and his great disappointment, another paradox of that grace. It is both God's plan and man's choice in action. Humans want to be in control, to decide their own destiny. God wants them to flourish and enjoy greater good than they can ever find on their own. He does not make people love or choose him. That they must do for themselves. And there is a way, though it seems opposite our human preferences.

The gate to this narrow way is not hidden; it is hard to find because it takes eyes of faith born of humility. The world's way, full of the glitz and glitter for some, looks to meet our desires for personal gain and pleasure and the recognition of our achievements, cheap and temporary as these social rewards are in this world. So human self-assertion, achievements, wealth, and power block God's way from the vision of many, blind their minds "so they cannot see the light of the gospel" (2 Cor 4:4). For others, the tragedies and challenges for emotional and even physical well-being get in the way; the anxious and exhausting fight for survival, "the worries of this life" (Matt 13:22) distract them. People do not stumble into the narrow way by accident. It takes humility and faith, an intentional choice of Christ. One must die to live, and few are willing to step down from their status, to take the risk, to pay the price.

226. GOD'S GREAT DISAPPOINTMENT

People who choose the narrow way become those awake among others who sleep. They walk along in life knowing something the other people do not know: the purpose and meaning of it all, and their desperate need for God's grace satisfied in the work of Christ. God's love has intervened in their lives. Others not only miss the way but try to get as many as possible to follow them in their choice. They may have no meaningful values, no moral boundaries, virtues, or valor, yet they claim to be leaders who know where to go and what to do with life. Having no wisdom, they wreak havoc everywhere they go with a destructive, selfish drivenness that our age has come to look up to as an ideal: "I am the master of my fate: I am the captain of my soul," in the words of William Ernest Henley.[1]

So while they are saying "to hell with heaven," God is longing for them to turn to him, waiting for them to humble themselves, realize their need for him, and decide to take the narrow way. It is only hard to find for the proud and self-sufficient who think the broad way of the world with its pleasures and promises, however short lived, meets their self-centered needs. But God waits. In a deep and sometimes severe way, he desires they look in his direction and longs for their spiritual well-being—for the flourishing of their souls.

Scripture References: Josh 24:14–15; 2 Chr 7:14; Ps 146:1–10; Jer 9:23–24; Matt 7:13–14, 24–29; 13:18–23; 19:16–24; Luke 13:22–30, 34–35 with 19:41–44; 12:13–21; John 1:1–5 with 10–13; 4:13–14; 10:10; 2 Cor 4:1–6; Heb 11:6; Jas 1:16–18, 4:4–10; 1 Pet 5:6–9; 1 John 2:15–17, 4:1–6.

---

1. William Ernest Henley, "Invictus: The Unconquerable," All Poetry, https://allpoetry.com/Invictus:-The-Unconquerable.

227. Those Who Are Well

It is not the healthy who need a doctor, but the sick. I have not come to call the righteous, but sinners to repentance.

—Luke 5:31–32

JESUS SAID THAT THOSE who (think they) are well do not need a doctor. He was speaking to the Pharisees and other Jewish leaders of his day, who held the prescription to heal their spiritual blindness in their hands. It was filled before their eyes, but they refused to take the life-giving medicine. Their social positions were at stake. They told the people they needed to drink *their* concoction of Oral Torah to correct their sinfulness. The Pharisees, whose greatest sin was their pride, said the people could not please God without their interpretation of his will for them, their theology.

Jesus went to those whose hearts were not proud, those who were honest and knew they were sinners. Some were not yet believers, as we would call them today, but their hearts were open to God. Others believed Jesus was indeed the Messiah. What they did not need in their lives was the Pharisees. In fact, they needed to avoid them. It may best be illustrated by his parable of the Pharisee and the tax collector in the temple. The tax collector knew he was a sinner; the Pharisee not only thought he was not, he thought he was an example for all of one who follows God. Humility is part of the gospel message as the way to faith. Those without it cannot be saved. The expression "a proud Christian" is an oxymoron. Those of us who know God's grace know only too well that pride is a sin we must deal with each day. We know that Satan wants to contaminate the new wine of our faith with doubts about God's goodness, self-assertion, and the desire for self-advancement. The Physician has healed us of the guilt of our sins. Now, with God's help, we can gain ground in the fight for our spiritual health; we

227. THOSE WHO ARE WELL

can take the hill in the battle with selfish ambition that wants to reoccupy the land now owned by Christ.

Scripture References: 1 Sam 2:3; Pss 10:4, 20:7; Prov 11:2; 15:25, 33; 16:18; 28:26; Isa 14:12–14; Ezek 28:17; Matt 5:20, 7:15–23, 23:11–15; Mark 8:15; Luke 1:51, 5:27–32, 8:11–15, 12:1–2, 18:9–14; John 8:42–47; Rom 16:17–18; Jas 4:6–10; 1 Pet 5:6–9; 1 John 2:15–17.

228. Years Go By

A righteous man may have troubles, but the LORD delivers him from them all.

—Ps 34:19

GOD'S PROVIDENCE IS NOT without mystery, his grace not without paradox. The work of his Spirit is subtle, mostly without sensation, mostly outside our awareness. But it is God at work. We may learn many things about our life's events when we get to heaven that we are ignorant of here. Our past has its ups and downs, difficulties, and sometimes tragedies, but it is also often punctuated with happy occasions. Whatever is in our past and its residual effects on us today are not outside God's awareness or his ability to use them for our good and in his plan for us when we come to him. He is at work in us, however brutal or adverse some events may seem, contrasting that experience with his overwhelming grace. He does not bring bad things our way to hurt us; they are part of our context in a broken world caused by human choices, sometimes our own, not to trust him. However, he allows them to shape us to trust him, though, for some of us, the learning process will be difficult. And if we are not spiritually alert, most of his work in and around us escapes our awareness. We must live by faith, trusting him in *all* things to be at work for our good and his plan in the world.

The memories of past events—fearful, hurtful, and even traumatic—can remain vivid. The insecurities of not having someone to trust as a child make it difficult to trust and love others later in life. Sometimes the memories and insecurities come back, ripping through our lives like roaring tornados or bringing despair. The patterns for coping with harsh events in childhood follow us into adulthood. And we may keep returning to them for survival or comfort when God is waiting for us to trust him. Broken

228. YEARS GO BY

trust in the past may make this hard for us, but in the end we have nothing to lose and everything to gain in acknowledging God's grace and trusting his providence.

Yes, God wants to replace the devastating memories of these experiences with peace beyond understanding and the calm confidence that comes with trusting him with all of it. People like you and me are the reason he came. We are like the bruised reeds and smoldering wicks he cares about, the "crushed in spirit" (Ps 34:18) he saves. God sympathizes with our weaknesses; he "remembers that we are dust" (103:14). But his plan is for the well-being and the flourishing of our souls in this broken world and, over the years, to use our testimony of his love and grace in his plan for that world. In our early days, we could not see very far down that path, but it leads to where he says it does, and he makes the journey possible.

Years go by, and we all one day find ourselves in the autumn of our lives. Much has happened, a good deal has changed, and we may not feel like we fit in today's world. But from this perspective we look back on his providence in our lives, remembering his hand on us over the years. It makes these the best years of our lives. Yes, we will grow weaker in our bodies and abilities, but God is not absent as our age creeps up on us. There are now other things, such as wisdom from recalling his providence and faithfulness, his untiring patience with us, our accumulated experience of trusting him, and the wonderful people he put in our lives that strengthen us in our remaining days. Though sometimes our faith was weak, we fought to maintain our trust in him, who is always faithful, to stay on the road he set before us when things looked least likely to turn out for his purposes. Though we stumbled at times, here we are, by his strong grace and steadfast love, writing or reading this paragraph.

Now, we must offer to him these last years and allow him to use us as we seek to serve him however we can. Our faith may still be weak sometimes, as ridiculous as that may sound, but he knows and cares, and until he takes us, we are here for him. He is faithful. The boundaries of his blessings have fallen to us in pleasant places even through the hard times of life. And now, in the days left to us, we know peace and are filled with gratefulness.

Scripture References: Gen 37:14c-28 with 45:4-7 with 50:19-20; Deut 4:9; Pss 1:1-3; 9:9-10; 16:1-11; 34:17-19 with 22; 37:1-6 with 16-19 and 23-24; 46:1-3 with 7 and 10; 73:23-28; 90:4 with 10 and 12; 91:14-16; 103:10-18; 119:71 with 92-93; 145:13-19; 147:3; Isa 26:3-4; 55:8-9; Matt 5:3-10, 12:15-21; John 14:27 with 16:33; 1 Cor 1:9; 2 Cor 1:18-22; Phil 1:6 with 2:12-13; 4:4-9; Heb 4:14-16, 10:23-25, 13:20-21; Jas 3:2a; 1 Pet 1:22-25; 1 John 5:4-5.

229. God's Providence Matters

Work out your salvation with fear and trembling, for it is God who works in you to will and to act according to his good purpose.

—*Phil 2:12–13*

WE ALL HAVE GOOD and bad events and experiences in our pasts. We often glorify the good things in our earlier days until anyone else present at the time would not now recognize them, and we allow the disagreeable, offensive, and upsetting events to control our attitudes and outlook for years afterward. We may try to get the good things back, to get them to repeat themselves. Then we attempt to forget or compensate for regrettable things by sometimes unconsciously trying to fill our lives with what we missed. We strive to make up for what we lacked, substitute the loss of emotional fulfillment with temporary fixes, earn the approval we never felt, or prove someone who hurt us wrong. These efforts can take over our lives.

We must turn from longing for the good or trying to fix the bad in the past to God's grace, work, and provisions in the present. Though we live in a world scarred by the selfish hearts of mankind, he has never been absent. He can use all that has happened to us in the past to shape us for his purposes today when we open ourselves to his work in us. He never wanted those things for us; they would never have happened if humankind had not distrusted his goodness. But God, in his power, *can* change, and, in his providence, *will* change the scars that regrettable events and situations of the past have wrought in our lives into that which shapes us for today, for his purposes, and for our good. He can and will meet every need, but it will demand trust in God, violated in Eden, rekindled in our hearts.

We must seek and then trust him for our daily bread—that God will meet the needs of today—and we must trust him for the days ahead. He is

229. GOD'S PROVIDENCE MATTERS

not far off; we are. And it is up to us to come near him, open and vulnerable, humble and grateful. He offers forgiveness when we seek him in spirit and in truth, that is, in our inmost being and with honesty. We must let go of regrets and vengeful thoughts, let go of feeling sorry for ourselves. The blessings of today are enough, even overwhelming, if we allow them to fill our longings. If not, we will be ruled by selfish ambition or live with unsatisfied anger and resentment.

Many lead lives characterized by the possession and control of material things in this life, impatience and insistence when others get in their way, grasping for what cannot be found here, or arrogantly denying the past that is eating away at their souls. They are trying to fix their problems while the only real solution is outside them. We must let go of it all and trust God, taking hold of his purposes for our lives. We must relax in God's goodness and, as Joseph did in Egypt, acknowledge his providence, which brings us to this moment. Then we can welcome today's blessings from his hand.

Scripture References: Gen 45:4-7 with 50:19-21; Pss 84:4-5 with 10-12; 145:18-19; Jer 23:23-24; Matt 6:9-15, 11:28-30; John 4:23-24; 5:24 with 12:35-36; 8:12; 13:6-11; 14:21-27; Rom 8:28-39; Eph 4:22-24, 5:8; Phil 1:6 with 2:12-13 and Eph 2:10 and 2 Tim 3:17; Col 3:1-17; 1 John 1:8-10.

230. Dread and Anxiety

Trust in the LORD with all your heart and lean not on your own understanding.

—*Prov 3:5*

Do not be anxious about anything. . . . And the peace of God, which transcends all understanding, will guard your hearts and minds in Christ Jesus.

—*Phil 4:6–7*

ANXIETY IS A NORMAL human response when we face uncertainty. Sometimes our fears are unfounded, but that does not make them any easier to overcome. Other times we know exactly what we don't want to happen—what we dread. We fear the suffering or loss that may come to us and deeply want to avoid it. A relationship that brought warmth and encouragement, like that of Lazarus to Mary and Martha, may end. Jesus himself wept at Lazarus's tomb. Death is not what God wanted for people; it was their foolish choice in the garden. Jesus brought Lazarus back to life. But Lazarus died again, for death is part of life on earth since the first couple did not trust God, even in a perfect world. That is the essential truth to realize—it is still all about trusting God in our broken world.

Jesus, in his humanity, would become anxious about his own suffering in Gethsemane, though he knew what his death would accomplish. He prayed three times that God might, if possible, find another way as he did for Abraham, when God told him to sacrifice his son Isaac. Jesus would not have shared humanity's stresses and anxiety if he did not want to avoid the suffering of a torturing death on a criminal's cross. Though he was God, he

230. DREAD AND ANXIETY

was also fully human. We would find it difficult to identify with and trust Jesus in our own situations if he had allowed his divinity to take over at that moment. It was not a sin for him to ask God to remove the suffering even though he told us not to worry. He spoke to us as God; he lived among us as a human. Ultimately, he trusted God's will with his human life, which changed the world forever.

Paul was also unsettled by his suffering and anxious for relief. He asked God three times to remove it. Yet he told us to be anxious for nothing. He also worried about the faith among the churches he had started. Would they be strong enough for the challenges of the world and false teachers? He prayed for God to help them constantly. Peter regretted his denial of Jesus and later was anxious about his future at the end of the Gospel of John. But in his letter to Asian Christians, he says to cast all our anxiety on God because he cares for us. It was a letter from Rome in the early days of Emperor Nero's persecution of Christians. These men knew about stress and anxiety, but God chose them to write his words of trust and comfort for us.

We will not realize the importance of trusting God entirely unless we experience the need to do so. The anxiety that comes with life's insecurity, ambiguity, and unpredictability hovers over us and creates that need. Jesus, Peter, Paul, and many others in the Bible (think of Abraham, Joseph, Moses, Esther, Daniel, and the many prophets such as Habakkuk) felt that anxiety. It is not sinful to feel that anxious sense of fight or flight; it is part of our limited humanity. The essential thing to remember is that it puts the choice to trust God before us, and that is where we find the peace he gives. The suffering in life and death itself will be conquered by Christ in the days ahead. But for now we must seek to trust him with a resolute heart and unbending determination. Do not forget his faithfulness. His good providence is at work in you.

Scripture References: Deut 31:8; Josh 1:9; 1 Kgs 19:13–14 with 18; Pss 22:1–31, 23:4, 37:1–11, 55:22, 56:3–4, 84:10–12; Prov 3:5–7; Lam 3:22–26 and 3:33 but also Ps 119:67 and 71; Hab 1:6–11 with 3:16–19; Matt 6:25–34, 26:36–46; John 11:11–44; 14:27 with 15:33; 21:17–21; Rom 5:1–6, 8:28–39; 1 Cor 15:24–28, 50–57; 2 Cor 12:7–10; Phil 1:6, 2:13, 4:6–9; 1 Thess 5:24; Heb 2:14–18, 4:14–16, 5:7–10; 1 Pet 5:6–7; Rev 20:14, 21:1–5.

231. The Disintegration of a Culture

They are from the world and therefore speak from the viewpoint of the world, and the world listens to them.

—1 John 4:5

CULTURES ARE HUMAN SYSTEMS. Because humankind was created in God's image, there are traces of his hand, more evident in some cultures than others, in how people have organized themselves to live as a group. Unless they degrade themselves, people in all cultures can reason, have a conscience, and value relationships. God planned these and other aspects of cultures for our good, and people of genuine faith know these gifts are necessary for social survival. Cultural values are qualitative descriptions of attitudes that drive our decisions and quantitative behaviors. They are built on beliefs, assumptions, and understandings as part of a cultural system that is complex and integrated. In a healthy society, these values are considered ideals for virtuous behavior, personal well-being, and community cohesion. As such, these ideals become traditions, and people either desire and feel compelled to express and use them to guide behavior or substitute them for human ideals of self-advancement. Whatever the values of a healthy culture, they are hard won, and it is considered an important responsibility to pass them on to the next generation. Though Christianity is rapidly decreasing in Western society, many Western ideals had their roots in the Bible in earlier days. From these values come the laws and functioning of a judicial system to protect society from the danger of disintegration. Yet law and justice are some of the first biblically based values to disappear as societies weaken.

Over time, cultures move from qualitative to quantitative considerations of value. They decline in their desire for the original, often biblical, values and ideals and begin leaning toward self-centered behavior to gain

231. THE DISINTEGRATION OF A CULTURE

feelings of worth, a social identity, pleasure, material wealth, and power to control others that give them a thin sense of security. Many will join those leading the society in this direction, or at least not hinder their efforts to take it captive to their "progressive," often hedonistic, ideology. The consciousness of right and wrong, good and bad, that God gifted to them has intentionally been pushed aside for the freedom to live their lives without God. This effort inevitably becomes one of erasing God from life in every possible way—the beginning of the end. I, who write, and you, who read, have lived through one of the darkest decades of our own culture. I have reflected that in many places in this book. Except for God's grace, you would not be reading it here. Perhaps today he is giving our society a little longer to change its ways, a little longer for we who know him to light up the way out.

At the bottom of this downward spiral, people measure life in terms of quantity instead of quality to the point of extinguishing the values that provide for survival. Valor and virtue are left behind for corruption, and selfish motives for power, wealth, and celebrity status take over. Justice is perverted for personal and political gain. But God sees and knows the hearts of people as they "call evil good and good evil" (Isa 5:20).

As a remnant of those still faithful, we who know him must remain loyal to him and live in the freedom he gives us in Christ in a very broken world. He knows the struggles we face in that world and asks us to trust him and seek to be his light in dark places. We are his instruments to bring hope to that world, living water to those in the desert; we show the way back to God in Christ, who the world has rejected. He is the fountain of the only hope for mankind.

Scripture References: Gen 1:28 with Mic 6:8; Ps 37:1–11; Isa 5:20–23, 10:1–3, 53:1–6; Matt 5:14–16; 24:4–14 with 25:31–34 and 41; John 4:1–26, 14:6, 16:33, 17:13–19; Acts 4:12; Rom 1:18–25, 3:22–24; 1 Cor 8:5–6; Phil 4:4–9; 1 Thess 5:1–11; 1 Tim 2:1–6, 4:1–10; 2 Tim 3:1–5; Titus 2:11–12; 2 Pet 3:1–15; 1 John 2:15–17, 4:4–6.

232. The Power of God Today and Tomorrow

Behold, I am coming soon! My reward is with me, and I will give to everyone according to what he has done.

—*Rev 22:12*

EVEN THOUGH WE KNOW we are to acknowledge God in all our ways, it is hard to keep in mind, in our day-to-day activities, that we who know him are of another kingdom and surrounded by a spiritual universe. But that does not change the fact that we are and that God is at work. Moving in the background, he controls the course of the universe and providentially guides our lives toward his purposes. When the people of God left Egypt, they were attacked by the Amalekites in the desert. God said he would erase the memory of Amalek from the earth for their murderous treachery against his people. Four hundred years after those who left Egypt were gone, and new generations took their place in the promised land, God fulfilled that promise. God will do all he has promised whether we are there to see it or not.

God's powerful presence on our behalf is revealed to us in explicit terms when he shows the servant of Elisha, threatened by the massive army of the Arameans, his horses and chariots of fire in the mountains around them. That same power is at work in our lives. We live as if God were often distant from us, perhaps even distracted, but his horses and chariots of fire are still there. He is powerfully present in all of creation. No one moves, no one thinks, without God knowing it. Though he has given humans free will and lets many things take their natural course in the world mankind has twisted and spoiled, he is ultimately in absolute control and will bring about his purposes and its consummation.

232. THE POWER OF GOD TODAY AND TOMORROW

He will come. Just as no one could stop him in his judgment of the nations around Israel in the Old Testament, no one can stop him now. True believers will be removed from his wrath, and he will come. He will judge the world justly, vindicate his own, and, ultimately, set up an eternal kingdom without sin and suffering after the ultimate enemies are cast into hell. He is never distracted, does not sleep, never forgets. Though he moves in the background of the world around us now, one day he will openly act in ultimate authority, and the whole world will see. All will stand before the God they have denied, stripped of their achievements and pride, with nothing to defend them from the terrible light of his penetrating eye, piercing their souls and revealing all. For those who have refused his grace and chosen their own way, God will regretfully honor their wish; they will inherit its consequences.

Scripture References: Exod 17:8–16 with 1 Sam 15:2–3 and 32–33; 2 Kgs 6:15–17; Pss 37:1–11, 91:14–16; Prov 3:6a; Isa 14:26–27, 40:28–31 with 41:10–13; 50:10–11; 1 Thess 4:13—5:11; Heb 11:1 with 6 and 13; 12:22–29; 2 Pet 3:1–18; Rev 20:7–10, 21:1–4, 22:7 with 12–13.

233. Adam, Eve, and Sin Today

Each one is tempted when, by his own evil desire, he is dragged away and enticed. Then, after desire has conceived, it gives birth to sin.

—Jas 1:14–15

IN THE MANY THEORIES concerning the original sin of Adam and Eve, there is a theme of an inherited inclination to sin for all people who followed them. It is clear enough that we do not inherit their guilt. Our guilt is ours alone. If humans inherited guilt, Jesus would have had it in his human nature. But what about the inclination to sin? Theologians often see a need to blame Adam and Eve for this weakness toward sin in all who followed them. Some seem to ignore the question of where Adam and Eve inherited their inclination to sin. They were not created with it. Adam and Eve *were* created with the sacred gift of free will to choose to trust God or to try to satisfy their needs and desires in their own ways. Choosing their own way was accelerated by Satan when he tempted them to go against God's provisions and desire what he made them feel God was withholding from them. We were born with the same free will, a gift from God in the midst of our own, often selfish, desires and the temptations Satan puts in our path. Free will has the potential for enormous good or evil, which the couple realized only after eating the forbidden fruit, though they had been told of its dangers.

Satan tempted Adam and Eve directly as there were no social influences of others who lived in sin to draw them away from God. We, too, choose God's ways and provisions or seek our fulfillment in our own ways. Many of us do not do so well. Yes, Christians fall short and need God's forgiveness. We sin, often in the same way and for the same reasons Adam and Eve sinned. We do not need to inherit this inclination. Satan opened the door to ignore God's word; they were enticed and then willingly chose

233. ADAM, EVE, AND SIN TODAY

against God's way. God's sacred gift of free will also keeps that choice before us. Selfishness is awakened by opportunity. With Satan's help, unbelievers continue to surround believers with the temptation to choose their ways of fulfilling our needs for survival and fulfillment. It is always before us, and we are responsible for our choices. We cannot be too careful.

Adam and Eve were each created with a soul and a consciousness of self with needs for survival that God met for them until, with the free will he gave them, they chose their own ways of "survival." God provides solutions for our survival today in our broken world. He uses social, personal, and spiritual means within the boundaries he has set. But people have invented, with Satan's help, illicit ways of satisfying these needs. These solutions are often more immediate and are perceived to bring greater gratification than God's intended ways. Some Christians have tried to reign in free will with legalism, creating their own boundaries to keep people from "sin." This was the approach of the Pharisees and their Oral Torah in Jesus' day; he did not have kind words for them. God intended that we choose to live in the freedom he gives us in Christ.

Nevertheless, even as believers (Adam and Eve were), we can choose, by the free will he gave us, a shortcut to fulfillment or wait for God's provision and purposes in our lives. We neither inherit Adam and Eve's guilt nor their inclination to sin. We have our own inclinations and guilt as well as God's solution for us in Christ.

Scripture References: Gen 3:1–7; Ps 127:1; Isa 3:18; Lam 3:25–26; Dan 3:16–18; Luke 4:1–13; Rom 3:23, 5:12–19, 10:9–10; 1 Cor 7:1–5, 10:13; Col 3:1–17; Jas 1:13–15, 22–25; 3:2a; 1 Pet 3:18; 1 John 1:5–10.

234. Doing Good and Evil

Our people must learn to devote themselves to doing what is good
—*Titus 3:14*

Faith without deeds is dead.
—*Jas 2:20*

I OFTEN CALL THE gift of free will God gave us a sacred gift—one that God will not tread upon, though he seeks to influence and help us choose good over evil. That gift does not override human depravity, but it does undo any idea of *total* depravity—a doctrine teaching that humans cannot do anything good, including being unable to repent and turn to God to receive his grace. It is said that we inherited this depravity from Adam and Eve. Adam and Eve chose to disobey God. They decided to go against his provisions for them, for which they were punished, and the creation was tarnished. But their actions did not lock us forever into an inability to do anything good. The Bible records hundreds of examples of people doing good and a great many exhortations that we should do the same. This is usually treated by those who say we cannot do good with comments like "You cannot do it; you must let God do it through you." But these words are not found in the Bible. We have to take responsibility for the good or bad things we do, for our choice to honor or dishonor God, for keeping or disregarding his boundaries for our freedom in Christ.

People can accept God's grace in Christ and are urged to do so. But they can also turn away just as the Israelites in the wilderness could look on the bronze serpent to be healed or refuse and die. The rich young man who came to Jesus turned away. During Paul's ministry while in prison, Demas chose to love the world more than serve God. What we have inherited from

234. DOING GOOD AND EVIL

Adam and Eve are the results of their sin and the sins of all those after them. People, societies, cultures, countries, and civilizations have all been affected and pay a heavy price for the sins of humankind. Egged on by Satan and each other, they continue to destroy creation and human societies, which has an influence on unbelievers and Christians alike.

Yes, we sin as Christians. We do not have to sin, but we do. When we bring our sins before him, he forgives us and exhorts us to do good works as a witness to the world of his work of grace in us. The choice is truly ours; it always has been.

Scripture References: Gen 3:1–24; Ps 113:10–18; Mic 6:8; Matt 5:14–16, 7:15–20; John 1:10–13, 3:16–17, 4:10–14, 5:24, 8:12; Acts 16:31; Rom 3:23, 10:9–10; 1 Cor 3:10–15, 10:23–24 with 31 and Phil 2:1–4; Gal 6:9–10; Eph 2:8–10; 1 Tim 6:17–19; 2 Tim 3:16–17; Titus 2:7, 14; 3:1, 8, 14; Heb 6:10, 13:15–16; Jas 1:13–18, 3:2a, 4:7; 1 Pet 2:9–12, 5:6–11; 1 John 1:5–10.

235. The Ordinary

Here is a boy with five small barley loaves and two small fish.
—John 6:9

A DEAD STICK, a common stone, ordinary water, a crust of bread. What could be more commonplace, more unexceptional than these kinds of everyday things in our world? But God uses the ordinary to do the extraordinary, the unremarkable to accomplish remarkable events in his plan for the world. A dead stick is used in Pharaoh's court and to part the Red Sea as God's people flee slavery just ahead of the well-armed military of Egypt. A common stone is used to slay a giant threatening the people of Israel, ordinary water, to make the best wine people at a wedding had ever tasted, and a couple of small barley loaves and two fish, to feed five thousand people weak with hunger.

In each case, there were different levels of faith and courage: a tested and questioning Moses; a young, enthusiastic David; an unassuming mother, Mary, believing in her son; and tired disciples handing out bread and fish. We must become used to God using the common to accomplish the uncommon and the ordinary to fulfill his extraordinary purposes. That familiar wine would come to symbolize the blood of Jesus shed for us, that crust of bread, his broken body on the rough timbers of the cross. God uses the unrefined to undo the sophisticated, the mundane to produce the impossible, the weak to defeat the strong, and the simple to bring down the powerful strongholds of Satan. In the process, he makes the first last and the last first.

We must not let our cultural expectations or personal preferences get in the way of God's work in our lives and the world around us. If God chose a young peasant girl burdened with the mundane chores of first-century

235. THE ORDINARY

life and of no particular social status to give birth to the Messiah, he can use us. If he used a feeding trough amid the straw and smells of a stable to cradle the King of the universe come to his own, what might he use in our lives? For we are his workmanship, his project, and work in us for his purposes, he will. Expect the unexpected to matter; consider the extraordinary dimension of the ordinary in his ways. The word for it all is *trust*—trust the God of the universe with all life brings to us, for his providence is in it, and "nothing is impossible with God" (Luke 1:37).

Scripture References: Exod 4:1–5, 13:15–31; 1 Sam 17:8–11 with 32 and 37–40 and 45–49; Matt 19:30, 26:26–30; Mark 9:33–37; Luke 1:26–38, 46–55; 2:4–7; 9:10–17; John 2:1–11, 6:1–15; 1 Cor 1:18–31, 11:23–26; Eph 2:10, 3:20; Phil 2:12–13.

236. The Cross

> For the message of the cross is foolishness to those who are perishing, but to us who are being saved it is the power of God.
>
> —*1 Cor 1:18*

JESUS, AFTER ALL HIS works of love and compassion for people and his revealing of God in his teachings, would die the shameful death of a criminal on a cross. A couple of coarse timbers and three or four rusty spikes would accomplish God's purpose of giving him up for us. He would suffer extreme agony for six hours and die to meet the requirement of a perfect sacrifice for our sins. The sun was hidden as the sky darkened, the earth shuddered, and the veil in the temple was torn from top to bottom. Something of enormous importance for the world had taken place, though few noticed its significance at the time. A few loyal ones stood in tears at the foot of the cross. One of the thieves being executed beside him recognized him, and a few soldiers in charge of the awful deed realized he was more than a man, but most that day were either glad he was finally gone or did not have any idea why he died or did not save himself. His followers were simply in shock. We are only told of two Jewish leaders who knew who Jesus was. Joseph of Arimathea, a wealthy member of the ruling council of the Jews, and Nicodemus, a wealthy Pharisee, had the courage, means, and humility to bury Jesus in Joseph's new tomb that day. So ended another Friday for most, but it was a bitter day for the few who knew him.

Discouraged disciples met in the morning on the first day of the next week, wondering what to make of it all. Why did it happen? What would they do next? Where would they go? For them, their world was at an end, but for God, their task was only beginning. The women who had followed Jesus had gone to the tomb earlier and now returned to say they had found

236. THE CROSS

it empty, and two angels told them he had risen from the dead. He who had predicted his death for our sins and his resurrection as the promise of eternal life for his followers had risen in victory over sin and death. The greatest, most significant event in history had been accomplished.

The world's people would be saved by trusting this work of Christ on their behalf. We were not there, have not seen him, heard his voice, or touched him, but we have believed through the message of those who were and did (1 John 1:1-4). We are people of faith—"Blessed are those who have not seen and yet have believed" (John 20:29)—as were those on the far side of the cross in the Old Testament. Without that faith, it is "impossible to please God" (Heb 11:6), for he looks at the heart, and through that faith come the works that fulfill his purposes. Because of the cross and our faith, we are his, and we are his hands and feet in the world today. The next time you see an old, weather-worn wooden beam, think of all it meant that day.

Scripture References: Ps 22:6-8, 16-18; Isa 53:1-11; Matt 27:27—28:10; Mark 15:21—16:7; Luke 23:26—24:14; John 17:15-21, 19:17—20:31; Acts 1:8; Rom 8:31-39; 2 Cor 5:14-17; Heb 7:23-28, 11:1-40; 1 Pet 2:22-25, 3:18; 1 John 1:1-4.

237. Jesus Gives Hope

Faith is being sure of what we hope for and certain of what we do not see.

—*Heb 11:1*

THERE ARE SEVERAL IMPORTANT outcomes of Jesus' death and resurrection for us. One is that life is never useless for the believer. Even on our worst days, it is full of meaning and purpose. Jesus died for us to intentionally make himself our Savior and us his children. Adopted into his family, we are now important parts of his kingdom and his plan for the world. So life is no longer hopeless; we can trust his love, grace, providence, and purposes. They are always in our favor. Though we may not understand all he is doing, it may not look like his work at the time, and it may not be what we would choose, he will *never* leave us or forget us.

Our hope gives us peace and contentment as we trust him and walk in his way. Though most of his followers in that day and on into ours are not often known for their accomplishments or influence, he chose them and us—elected all who believe—to be his representatives in the world until he returns. One day, those who trust in their wealth, influence over others, or reputation will be gone, but the meek will inherit the earth, the faithful will rule the world, and the pure in heart will see God. For the veil was torn to welcome everyone of humble faith into God's presence, to know him personally and trust him completely.

We also have hope for our weaknesses, for our sins are always forgiven in him. The disciples deserted him and ran; Peter denied he knew him three times. But Jesus' first words to them afterward were the familiar words "Peace be with you" (John 29:19–21, 26). When we come to God with our sins, his forgiveness is immediate and sealed permanently by Jesus' death

237. JESUS GIVES HOPE

as payment. Though it comes with great sacrifice for God, his forgiveness is free to us, is ongoing in our lives, and endures forever. Though we fail him, he never fails us.

Yet one more treasured result of what Jesus did is our hope in his victory over death. He guaranteed it for us by his resurrection. We live our lives now in view of an eternity with God. We see this world differently, live for a different purpose than others, and know our final destination will be a better place without suffering, sorrow, or death. We are his now and will be for eternity.

Scripture References: Ps 20:7–8; Prov 3:1–7 with 28:26 and 11:28; Lam 3:22–26; Matt 5:3–10; Mark 15:37–39; John 14:27 with 16:33; 20:19–31; Acts 1:8; Rom 5:1–6, 8:22–25; 1 Cor 15:50–58; 2 Cor 5:15–17; Eph 3:20; 1 Thess 4:13–18; Titus 2:11–15; Heb 13:5–6; 1 John 1:9; Rev 21:1–4.

238. Suffering, Difficulties, and Sorrows

I sought the LORD, and he answered me; he delivered me from all my fears.

—Ps 34:4

ONE OF THE GREAT paradoxes of God's way with us is that, though he is a God of lovingkindness, that love can seem severe and even absent in our human experience, perhaps most in times of suffering and need. Though many ignore or deny it, we all suffer in one way or another. When we realize or experience it, we do not often see the hand of God in it to serve his purposes in us or those around us. Though he never wanted it for us, he is with us in the difficulties and suffering that mankind has chosen instead of the treasures and delights of knowing him. He can use that suffering to serve his intentions, though we often do not understand those intentions until later, sometimes much later. These times draw us near to him, create a longing for intimacy with him, and give us another opportunity to trust him. Paul prayed over and over for God to relieve him of suffering. God said his grace was sufficient for him, and in the end Paul became grateful for his physical weaknesses that demonstrated the power of God in his ministry to others.

God may allow the wilderness of loneliness, a crushing awareness of our selfishness and failures, a prolonged illness, or a deep sorrow from a tragic loss, things that come to us in a sinful world, to serve his purposes. No matter our goal, we would never choose these devastating feelings and events, but God can use them to create a longing for or a deepening of an innermost, intimate relationship with him. In our desperation, we may try to deal with suffering in human and selfish ways, but trusting God can end these efforts at emotional survival as we become sensitive to him and turn

238. SUFFERING, DIFFICULTIES, AND SORROWS

to his purposes in our lives. He longs for a deep-rooted relationship with us built on our trust and his lovingkindness.

Again, we would never choose his way, and it may seem to us that he is ignoring our situation. This feeling is normal. David thought God had abandoned him in his struggle to survive. Job asked God why he hid his face from him in his extreme suffering. He felt God considered him his enemy. Even Jesus prayed that God would change the course of his coming agony if possible. He, too, asked God why he turned his face away. But as agonizing as each situation was, God was *not* absent. In each case, he was very present and showed faithfulness in *his* time and *his* way, bringing about *his* purposes.

It was a forty-year test for Israel in the wilderness; we should not be surprised if our lives should also know a wilderness from time to time or even for an extended time. Later, they went through captivity in a foreign land for seventy years and suffered so that they might recognize their straying from God, and he might show his faithfulness in returning them to the land promised to them through Abraham. We, too, may feel like we are in a "foreign land" sometimes, distant from what we think would meet our desperate needs, but God has purpose in his ways for us. After his anointing to be the king of Israel, David waited and suffered for twenty years before the throne was his. In the wilderness and lonely places in our lives, he has prepared a path to him if we will choose it. We may not see his purposes in it for years, but they are at work in us the moment we first come to him in humble faith.

Scripture References: Gen 2:15–17 with 3:4–19; Deut 29:5–6; 1 Sam 16:6–13 with 2 Sam 5:4; Job 30:20; Pss 22:1; 24:4; 59:1–9; 119:67 with 71 with 92 and 93; 146:1–11; Prov 3:5–7; Matt 26:36–46, 27:46; Phil 2:13; Heb 13:20–21.

239. Better for Having Suffered

The LORD is close to the brokenhearted and saves those who are crushed in spirit.

—Ps 34:18

SOMETIMES GOD USES DIFFICULT times, physical suffering, deep sorrows, hurtful emotional attachments, deep gouges in our feelings of self-worth, and temptations to show us his faithfulness and, often, our unfaithfulness. Sometimes it is both, and sometimes it is just part of living in a broken world that causes us to long for our destination. Yes, there is mystery. Though we prefer a God we can explain, he often moves in the world and our lives in ways we cannot fathom. Our expectations must sometimes be set aside and our preferences put on hold to have his purposes fulfilled in our lives in his way. But he is worthy of our deepest trust, for he is at work in us for our good and that he may fulfill his plan and purposes in us and through us.

It comes in many ways and has various effects on us. Though forgiven sin is *never* held against us, Satan will use it to accuse us before God and to try to discourage us. And God may remind us of it to show us how great his grace has been in our lives. The experience humbles us, as well it should. Other times, hurt and sorrow come our way, and our emotions are stretched to the last degree. We are spent, empty. It can be a dry wilderness to go through. The laments of David in the Psalms and those of Job take on personal meaning. We may think it will never end. But it does. It ends in the one who quenches our desert thirst with the water of life.

But, though we are slow to realize it, we are better people for having suffered, better people for having realized anew his lovingkindness in our lives. We must learn to trust the purposes of God that are beyond our understanding. For the battle goes on in the spiritual universe over every soul

239. BETTER FOR HAVING SUFFERED

as it did for Job. Though he never knew the answer to "why," his response is one of immense trust in God's providence: "The LORD gave, and the LORD has taken away; blessed be the name of the LORD" (Job 1:21). "Shall we accept good from God and not trouble?" (2:10). "I know my Redeemer lives" (19:25). David said, "I will always have hope" (Ps 71:14). "My soul finds rest in God alone" (62:1). "I will yet praise him, my Savior and my God" (42:5). God's ways are very different from ours. His reasons are beyond our preferences or expectations. His providence is for our ultimate good and the fulfillment of his purposes, though we may desire, as Jesus did, another way. But God's wisdom, goodness, and love are always ours, even in times of difficulty, suffering, and sorrow, and this world, though an important experience for us, is not his destination for those who trust him.

Scripture References: Job 1:1—2:10; 19:25–27; 23:10 with 17; 42:1–6; Pss 9:9–10; 13:1–6; 34:1–22; 42:5; 62:1–2; 71:14; 88:14; 102:1–11; 119:67 and 71; 137:1–6; 143:7; Prov 3:5–7 with 20:24 and 28:26; Isa 1:2 with 16b–19; 44:24–28; 55:8–11; Jer 31:1–17; Matt 4:1–11; John 14:1–4, 16:33; Rom 5:1–6, 16:20; 2 Cor 11:13–15; Eph 6:10–18; Phil 2:12–13; Heb 13:5b–6, 20–21; Jas 1:2–8; 1 Pet 5:8–11; Rev 12:10–12.

240. The End of All Things

The end of all things is near.

—*1 Pet 4:7*

IN HIS WORD, WE see God moving in the universe to accomplish his purposes. He is bringing the world and all of his creation to its consummation in his plan, but he is patient, allowing people outside of Christ time to realize who he is and how desperately they need his grace to avoid the coming "day of the Lord" (2 Pet 3:10). Suffering is not what God wants for them, but the free will he gave them is a sacred honor on which he will not tread. The decision is entirely theirs, though he deeply regrets anyone turning away from his grace. He waits for each soul to look his way. But make no mistake, the purposes of God in the world are undeniable, particular, and unstoppable. Those who trust him will be gathered into his eternal kingdom; those who do not will be left outside.

But though he comes in judgment, the grace of God is incredibly deep and exceedingly broad. Patient and understanding, knowing the hearts of men and women, he still desires to save them from the spiritual disaster of their rejection of him and their love of the world. But though many are overwhelmed by arrogant self-interest, greed, hatred, and hedonism around us, all is not lost, far from it. He has sought us and opened a way to him. All is made new for those who turn to him. Hearts and minds begin to trust him in this life while they are on their way to eternal life. The world we know will be made over to perfection. We who know him are known by him. He has his mark on our souls, our name in his book. There is no condemnation for us who are his, and no one can take us from his hand. In his presence, every need will be met, every sorrow comforted. By his grace

240. THE END OF ALL THINGS

and mercy, the kingdom of heaven will be ours. We, not perfect but pure in heart, shall soon see God.

Scripture References: Job 19:25-27; Ps 91:1-16; Lam 3:33; Ezek 33:10-11; Matt 5:3-10, 25:41; Luke 13:22-30; John 1:12; 3:16-18, 36; 5:24; 10:28-30; 14:6; Rom 5:1 and 8:1; Eph 2:1-10; 1 Tim 1:12-17, 2:5; Titus 2:11-14; 1 Pet 3:1-18a, 4:7-11; 2 Pet 3:1-15; 1 John 2:15-17; Rev 22:7.

241. God's Message and Human Culture

Do your best to present yourself to God as one approved . . . who correctly handles the word of truth.

—*2 Tim 2:15*

WORDS HAVE MEANING, AND God's are filled with his intentions for them. As complicated as communication theory is, there is still a fixed meaning in the speaker's mind that they seek to create in the listener. However, what happens in the listener's mind when a message is heard can be affected by many factors. Experiences of the listener give them positive or negative associations with the words used. They may prefer to listen to what they want to hear instead of what is actually said. Fear, unbelief, or proud self-assertion may inhibit the reception of the intended message. In communication theory, more than ten factors can keep communication from accomplishing the speaker's intention.

Of the various factors affecting reliable communication, a primary one is the cultural frames of reference used by the speaker and listener. This becomes important when the message is from God for us, and we want to pass it on to others. Words and actions belong to and have specific meanings in one social situation that do not exist or have those meanings in the next. We must not let our cultural values, personal preferences, or negative associations distort the meaning of God's words. The original cultural context of the message and that of the listener today are frameworks for meaning that must not be ignored.

So reading the Bible, as we have said, is a cross-cultural experience. We must use caution and be intentional to see the original meaning of a text as it is framed by God's deliberate use of its own cultural context. He is not limited by the forms, social relations, and values of that culture but uses

241. GOD'S MESSAGE AND HUMAN CULTURE

them and the messengers shaped by them to give meaning to the words he chose in formulating his inspired message to us. It was a countercultural message for them as it is for us. Nonetheless, God used the human frame of reference of that day while intending it to be meaningful in every culture with the help of his Spirit. We typically pay little attention to the social values of people in the biblical culture, seeing this message from God through the filter of our own cultural context and language. We are blind to this shortcoming. And we may take the message we get from the Bible to a third cultural context, paying little attention to that new framework for meaning because we are blinded by our own. Some questions are in order. Where is the concern for the original message? Do we understand its intended meaning in our own context? Whose message are we teaching in other cultures?

It's time to get serious in ministry training and church teaching about the intended message of God. The cultural values and trends of our society today must not influence it for us; they should only shape the context within which it must be applied. His words must be given their full intended meaning in our lives and in the lives of those to whom we minister. This involves contextualization of the meaning of the words from the original language and cultural frame of reference to ours today with the absolute intention of maintaining that original meaning. We must then be intent on its relevant application in our own situation and then to that of others.

Scripture References: Pss 12:6; 56:3-4 and 10-11; 78:1-2; 119:103, 105, 130; Prov 4:20; Isa 40:13-14, 55:8-11; Jer 29:18-19; John 1:1 with 14; 12:47-50; 14:23-24; 1 Cor 2:13; 1 Thess 2:13; 2 Tim 2:2 and 15; 3:16-17; Heb 4:12; 1 Pet 1:22-25.

242. The Way of Wisdom

Blessed is the man who finds wisdom, the man who gains understanding, for she is more profitable than silver and yields better returns than gold.

—*Prov 3:13–14*

IN THE BOOK OF Proverbs, wisdom is the highest attainment for the human being. Yet it is an elusive subject in our Western, logical, direct, quantitative, and informational culture. What may be confusing to our Western minds is how God uses the Middle Eastern mind of that day to describe it. Using five main Hebrew words, most of them with companion synonyms, Proverbs gives a multifaceted mosaic of wisdom without the linear style and organization we expect. The holistic, sometimes indirect, style of the colored tiles in the Psalms, Proverbs, and Ecclesiastes fashion the artistic mosaic of a person of wisdom in contrast to those without it. It does this in the expected style of wisdom literature in that day and part of the world. Depending on the translation, *training, understanding, skillfulness* in practical endeavors, *discretion* in social interactions, and the *knowledge and fear* of God are all part of this medley of colors the generalizations give us. Odd as this presentation may seem, wisdom puts our relationship with God at the center, and is given the highest order for our lives. However difficult it may be for us to grasp in our day, it is our profound loss to overlook it.

Worth any price, wisdom brings life, honor, influence, and peace to its upright owner. To hate it is to be a fool and love death. Wisdom comprises several aspects of life and comes out of their combination. It incorporates, first, the essential element of our view of God and the spiritual universe, then goes on to reasoning and decisions, character and motivations, desires, self-control, humility, and, finally, actions based on these components of our being. The Bible reminds us that the fear of the LORD is the beginning of wisdom. The verses of Prov 3:5–7 anchor this truth in all of life. However, we overlook much of this extensive value because of the cultural gap that separates us from the Proverbs in our Western thinking and values. Yet, there, the sensitive person gains sustenance and understanding, finds the essentials for life, and avoids the fate of the fool.

But we dare not overspiritualize this wisdom (or the Christian life, for that matter). This wisdom is to be connected to the ordinary things of life where it becomes decisive in relationships as it influences the commonplace, mundane, and dreary events and activities as much as noble events. The Proverbs, with their many principles and generalizations, are like an owner's manual telling us how the designer intended us to use our life in this world. They show us that living our lives in other ways ends in ruin and death. The main thing God did not intend was for us to try to live life without him. Discerning what honors God enriches our relationship with him and encourages others. Applying that understanding to everyday life is to live with the meaning and purpose God planned for us in creation.

Wise people are known for helping, encouraging, and training others in everyday events of life as we control our anger and tongues and avoid tempting but irrational inclinations. These boundaries require a certain amount of self-regulation, determination, and patience that can accept delayed gratification for the greater good. But he or she must also have the humility to be open to, even search for, instruction and correction. So the wise person knows better than others how imperfect they are, that they are inclined to error, and therefore need to keep learning.

There are results of wisdom in the lives of its owners. As James tells us, the wise person is known by his or her good works and humility. Led by the hand of God, James makes the characteristics of that wisdom from God clear when he lists virtues and values not as commonly known among Christians as they should be. Much of this depends on one's motives, as the first characteristic he gives us is purity, and Jesus tells us the pure in heart shall see God.

Wisdom is practical and deals with the realities of life in our world, including its competition for our loyalties, alternatives to personal happiness, and substitutes for trusting God. It is in this context that we are given the choice to live for God or not, to be shaped by him or left to ourselves. As steel is tempered by a heating and cooling process to be tougher, more flexible, or stronger to fit its application, we who choose God are shaped and tempered in this life to fit God's purposes for us. It is not possible to use steel to its full capacity in a particular use without heat treatment. In the same way, our journey in the world is a preparation stage of accumulating wisdom and applying that changed character in God's work according to his plan for us in that world. The analogy continues. The treatment for us to have wisdom may take some heat.

Scripture References: Job 28:28; Ps 91:14–16; Prov 1:7; 3:13–17; 8:1–21; 9:1–12; 11:2; 12:15; 13:10, 14, 18, 20; 14:1, 3, 8, 16, 33; 15:7, 33; 16:23; 19:11; 22:4; 23:9, 24–25; 24:3–4; 31:10–31 note 26; Eccl 7:8–9 and 19 with Prov 29:11; Eccl 7:11–12, 19; 8:1; 12:9–11; Matt 5:8 with Titus 1:15; Eph 2:8–10; 2 Tim 3:14–17; Titus 2:11–14; 3:1–2, 8, 14; Jas 3:13–18.

243. Achieving Wisdom

Wisdom is supreme; therefore get wisdom. Though it cost all you have, get understanding.

—*Prov 4:7*

PEOPLE ARE CAPABLE OF attaining wisdom by being created in God's image. However, it is not developed in them automatically; it takes desire and intention to gain its advantages and is a process of continual growth. Though accessible to all, wisdom is costly in terms of the attention and effort needed to take hold of it. Though Christians usually consider their motives and courses of action at some level, they can get into ruts of habitual behavior and patterns of thought that are difficult to break and not helpful for them or the people around them. Trusting God and keeping the goal of wisdom before us help us shape our behavior in ways that honor him. We must remember that a flourishing tree of wisdom grows in the soil of humility near the stream of God's word.

We need wisdom to order our lives around God's desires for us and for the best outcomes in relationships. We probably all know people who go through life without thinking at all. Though there are respectful people among them, those who do not know God are repeatedly described in Proverbs as going the wrong way. The worst of them are portrayed as simpleminded, lazy sluggards, stubborn fools, and arrogant scoffers/mockers. These descriptions show the disaster of scorning wisdom altogether.

However, as we said, there are people without Christ who are respectable, knowledgeable, and considerate. Some are just clever, but others have a human understanding of survival and success in life, even if their hearts are empty of purpose and meaning for it all. They have human wisdom but with the critical limitation of not knowing their Creator. Wisdom does not save; it enriches.

Through God's word, we can have the perspective that sets us apart from those with only human judgment or those without any wisdom. It is not that we live a life so different from theirs; we buy our groceries at the same store, do the laundry, sweep the house, go to work, and mow our grass as they do. But we live life with a different perspective and frame of reference, doing most of the same things but with different meanings and purposes, with God and his grace and providence at the center. Though some may think much of the wisdom literature in the Bible is unspiritual, there is no secular life and sacred life separation—only ordinary life lived well to honor God or lived without thought for him. It is not about being religious but living this ordinary life with a particular perception and understanding that puts God at the center and lives out our freedom in Christ. Religious people often do the opposite—put their achievements and performance at the center, living in bondage to the rules they have made. Religious ritual does not impress God; it is our hearts that he wants.

However, though Christians should have more wisdom than others, the fact remains that becoming a Christian does not remove our humanness. Not all Christians live life with wisdom. It is learned, not discovered. It is something to attain as one grows in their relationship with God. Each person is at a different stage in their journey, and, unfortunately, some have stalled out along the way. They still have Bibles and attend church, but it makes little difference in their lives. We really must trust in the LORD with all our hearts, learn the limits of our own understanding, and acknowledge him and his providence in all our experiences in this life to know the peace of his care for us.

In summary, true wisdom begins with knowing God and the humility that comes with it. Wisdom from God has particular functions and meanings for the believer as it generates good works that bear testimony of our faith and his work in a broken world. We do not trust ourselves or social celebrities but God's good providence as he rules over everything.

Scripture References: Gen 1:26–27; Job 28:20–28; Pss 1:1–6; 90:4 with 10 and 12; 91:14–16; 111:10 with 14:1; 146:1–10; Prov 1:1–7, 22–33; 2:1–6; 3:5–6; 4:5–13; 8:34–36; 9:9–10; 11:2; 13:4, 20; 14:7; 15:33; 16:16; 17:24; 18:15; 21:3; 22:4; 23:22–23; 26:12; 28:26; Eccl 7:2–4; Isa 26:3–4; Hos 6:6; Mic 6:8; John 16:33 with 14:27; Eph 5:15–17; Phil 4:6–7; Jas 1:2–8; 1 Pet 2:11–17.

244. Unsettling Change

We are the clay; you are the potter; we are all the work of your hand.
—Isa 64:8

AS MUCH AS WE might like it on a certain level, change can also be difficult, complicated, and unsettling. It might be a slight change in the ordinary course of events, the irritation of a different way of doing something we see as simply unnecessary. But it might also be an extensive change in how we live our lives in a new context. As we get older, we regret these interferences in our lives more and more. Why change things that were working just fine the way they were? Where are the days when a new computer, television, or car were simply shiny, clean, fresh editions of the old ones instead of complex products of creative nerds in office cubicles with fifty options you'll never use but have to manage anyway to get a simple job done? My older readers will understand.

Yes, there is frustration, but change is a normal part of life in many ways, and we benefit from much that is discovered, invented, or developed, even though there are also times when change is not for the best. Different does not always mean better. At its worst, change can be thrust upon us in a tumultuous, stressful, unexpected event or crisis. Readjustment can seem to take forever. Things will never be the same. Our mind goes back to how it was before. We may think those days were without stress and that we will never get used to the new "normal" of our lives.

But God knows. He is not unaware of the changes in our lives or the stress that they bring. His key word for the Israelites was to *remember*. They were to remember how he brought them out of Egypt and how he had saved them over and over in the wilderness when they turned to him. He wanted them to remember his faithfulness and gave them the feast of the Passover to bring it to their hearts and minds year after year. In a broken world where humankind has free will, many things will go wrong that God never wanted for his creation; his creatures chose to go their own way, and all mankind feels the results of that sin. He keeps us, for now, in that world, but he wants us to know his grace, rest in his providence, and remember his faithfulness.

If we have chosen to live for God in this world damaged by sin, remembering God's providence in our lives and the lives of others is of great importance in the stress of its adversities. He has been faithful in bringing each of us to this day, and he will continue to be faithful even if we do not recognize his hand in the events of our lives. Times and circumstances change, but we must trust his work in us and in the world, for we are his, the work of his hands, and he is with us even when we least recognize his presence. His faithfulness is timeless and never changes.

We might ask, "Why does he not just keep stressful circumstances and change from happening?" But we must consider how we would trust him—what he desires most—if there is nothing to trust him for. Where would the humility of submission and trust be found if we could handle every circumstance in our favor? Trusting him is not a real choice unless there are other options, other things to trust, bad choices we could make. We all suffer from worries that upset us, anxiety that threatens us, suffering that debilitates us, and from change. These things are common in our shattered world and naturally bring disappointment, pain, grief, and emotional upheaval. We should not deny that these emotions are part of our experience. Everyone has them, sometimes with disorienting frequency, but we must see them as signals or reminders to trust the one who cares and can use them to shape us into people who can best reflect his love and grace in this world. He knows and cares and will use them for his purposes in and through us. He is the potter; the clay cannot mold itself. Remember his love, grace, faithfulness, and good providence in days of unsettling change and upheaval.

Scripture References: Exod 12:27, 13:3–4, 18:7–12; Num 21:4–9; 1 Sam 12:22 with 24; Pss 9:9–10, 23:4, 89:33; Prov 3:5–7; Isa 64:8; Matt 28:20b; John 14:1 with 27 and 16:33; Rom 5:1–6, 12:1–2; Eph 2:4; Phil 1:6 and 2:12–13; 4:4–9; Col 3:1–4; Titus 2:11–14; Heb 13:1–8; Jas 1:2–8; 1 Pet 1:3–7, 4:12–16 with 5:6–11.

245. The Dull Ache of Conscience

If God is for us, who can be against us?

—*Rom 8:31*

FEELINGS OF GUILT COME in all shapes and sizes. Sometimes we feel guilt because we have done something wrong that we need to fix with another person, admit to God, and feel the assurance of his ongoing grace in forgiveness. But sometimes we feel false guilt because, in our legalism, we do not think we have done well enough to earn God's approval (a highly unbiblical concept) even though our sins are forgiven. Other times, we feel it when we can't think of anything offensive in our behavior or thoughts. Then there is the dull ache of conscience over past sins, long confessed and forgiven, which may disguise itself as anxiety without cause. The accuser wants us to feel guilty of sins forgiven and completely removed, and he's pretty good at it. Of course, sometimes we *should* feel guilty when we are oblivious to our offensive behavior. Conscience should be there for us, but we may have rationalized uncharitable things in our hearts as maybe not so bad after all. Proverbs says, "guard your heart" (Prov 4:23). That is, to watch over it with self-awareness and be aware of its inclinations.

It is much better to know, confess, and fix the wrongs than to become numb or allow them to eat away at us. But most important to our discussion here is the false guilt that may linger after we have come to terms with our faults and failings and acknowledged them in God's presence, after God's strong grace has covered them. If you still think you are likely to fail again after dealing with some besetting sin, you are right. If you think God has not completely forgiven you of your sinful behaviors after coming to him with them, you are dead wrong. We are the unworthy recipients of God's enduring mercy and untiring grace, a love that escapes human words. No one and nothing can pry us out of his hand, pull us away from the costly grace given freely to us in his Son.

We must never be insensitive to our sinful inclinations but never doubtful of God's enormous grace and complete forgiveness. False guilt—that feeling that may linger after going to God with our sin—is worse than whatever we have done wrong. It denies the worthiness of his greatest gift to us in Christ; it devalues his suffering on our behalf. His righteousness is more than sufficient to remove our sin, but we are holding out, saying it is not. But *nothing* can cancel the enduring work of Christ on our behalf. We have had our bath and need only to have our feet washed. And when washed, we can never doubt the job was well done.

Forgiven sin should remind us of God's grace, humble our hearts before him, fill us with gratitude, and energize us to live for him. The closer we are to him, the more aware we are of our shortcomings and our continued need for that grace. But we also realize that forgiven sin will *never* be brought up against us, ever. We are truly free from its power over us. We can no longer be blackmailed by the accuser.

Scripture References: Ps 103:6–18; Prov 4:20–27; Isa 53:4–6; John 13:6–11; Rom 3:22–24, 5:1 with 8:1–2, 28–39; 2 Cor 5:21 with 1 Pet 3:18; Eph 2:8–10; Col 1:13–14, 21–22; 1 Tim 4:1–5; Titus 2:11–13, 3:3–8; 1 John 1:5–10; Rev 12:7–10.

246. Choosing God's Way in a Broken World

Enter by the narrow gate. For wide is the gate and broad is the road that leads to destruction, and many enter through it.

—Matt 7:13

YES, GOD IS LOVE, but before we get carried away with emotional sentimentalism, we must also remember that he is a consuming fire. He cannot be domesticated to live in our world according to our rules, but he also plunges those who have embraced his Son into deep, far-reaching, and unlimited grace. He makes them his own, attends to their needs, and makes his way known to them. The way of popular Christianity—of cheap trinkets, giddy emotions, and deceptive gimmicks—does not lead to him. Church marquees with snappy rhymes are not enough. A love for sentimental Christianity is the opposite of his way. Spiritual reputations, celebrity leaders, or megabudgets in the local church will not do. The God of the universe is beyond all this. He is known by those who have acknowledged his grace in the shadow of his greatness and power.

We must welcome his ownership and hold on to his purposes with deeply rooted humility and gratitude while respecting his independence from our designs and accepting his mystery. We must allow his word to be the surgeon's scalpel, his compassion to comfort our souls, and his glory—the expression of the significance of his being and works—to be the purpose of our lives. We must live each day conscious of his greatness, aware of his careful providence, acknowledging his lordship, and grateful for his grace. We are utterly dependent on him, who rules the universe with penetrating love, unfathomable power, and infinite wisdom. Though covering believers with grace, he cares for the world with sorrowful regret for all who reject him. He does not want anyone to perish in their lostness, but if they choose to ignore his grace, he will not keep them from the destination they have chosen. They have opted for their own way with the sacred freedom he granted them. He will not violate his gift to mankind.

Some belonging to a widespread popular level of Christianity may turn back. But we who are humbled to know God cannot. The way is not open to us. We are not our own but have been purchased with the greatest sacrifice. His protection is around us when we acknowledge his name, the "Most High," the "Almighty" (Ps 91:1, 14-16). He will not let go whatever may come to pass. From here, we go forward in the stillness of worship, in humble acts of faith and goodness, and with a message of hope and grace in our broken world. There *will* be trouble. In these last days, some of us may pay a price for our loyalty to God, but we are still his, and, in his purposes and providence, "all things work for the good of those who love him" (Rom 8:28). Nothing can separate us from his love. We have his name stamped on us; he has ours in his book.

Everyone has a need for survival, but we who know God go beyond mere survival to a relationship with God himself and to the significance this gives to life, significance even in a damaged world. We want our lives to count for him. It is a journey of courage combined with faith, resulting in hope. Don't let anyone or any setback frustrate that outcome for you. Instead, as you bend every effort to realize it, trust God's omnipotent providence to bring it about in his time. "Trust in the Lord. . . . Delight yourself in the Lord. . . . Commit your way to the Lord" (Ps 37:3-5), and he will make it happen. But be still before the Lord and wait patiently for him (v. 7); his ways are not our ways, but his providence is perfect.

Scripture References: Num 16:7; Pss 25:4-5, 8-9; 37:1-11; 40:31; 46:1-11; 68:32-35; 90:17; 91:1-2, 14-16; 139:1-12; Prov 3:5-7; Isa 6:1-5, 43:1-3, 55:8-11; Lam 3:25-26; Matt 5:10; 13:36-42, 47-50; 25:41; John 14:6; Rom 8:28-39 with John 14:27 and 16:33; 1 Cor 6:19-20; Titus 2:11-14; Heb 11:1 with 6 and 13; 12:28-29; 1 Pet 1:17-21; Rev 2:1—3:22, 20:11-15 with 21:1-4.

247. Responding to an Intervening Love

Oh, the depth of the riches of the wisdom and knowledge of God! How unsearchable his judgments, and his paths beyond tracing out!
—*Rom 11:33*

WHO INDEED HAS KNOWN the mind of the Lord? He has intervened with his love, but there is mystery in his providence and paradox in his grace; his ways are past finding out. It leaves to us . . . trust. We conclude our journey in this volume with a medley of paraphrased verses on the strong theme of the Bible, trust in God built on humility.

Trust in the Lord with all your heart, and do not lean on your own understanding and logic. In all your ways, acknowledge his providence, and he will make your path known. Trust in the LORD and do good; delight yourself in him, and he will give you the desires of your heart. Commit your way to him, and he will make the path you have chosen—and others have criticized—known to the world as God's way.

Do not be anxious or angry when evil men carry out their schemes against the faith. Instead, be still before the LORD and wait patiently for him. He will deal with his enemies in his own time, and you will inherit his blessings. Even if the mountains fall into the sea and it rises, shaking the earth, be still. He is God, and he will carry out his plan for the world to its very end. Do not be anxious; only trust God in all things. Give them to him in prayer and wait on him; though none understand it, he will give you peace that will protect you.

Humble yourself before God, and he will lift you up. He will be your refuge and strength, always with you in the events and experiences of life, even in the shadow of death. Taste and see that the LORD is good and gracious toward those who trust him. God has unexpectedly intervened with his love for mankind and waits for us to turn to him. We may have made him wait for a long time. He has always wanted us in his arms, and today, here we are, unworthy but bathed in his grace. Now, we must trust that mystery of his providence and the paradox of his grace as we go forward for him.

Scripture References: 2 Chr 16:9a; Pss 4:5 with 51:17; 20:7; 23:4; 26:3–4; 32:10; 33:11; 34:8; 37:1–11; 40:4; 46:1–3 with 10; 84:11–12; 91:1–2 with 14–16; 112:7; 118:6–9; 125:1–2; 143:8–10; 147:11; Prov 3:5–7 with 28:26; Isa 50:10; Jer 17:5–8; Lam 3:22–26; Mic 6:8; Nah 1:7; Rom 11:33–36; Jas 4:10; 1 Pet 5:5–6.

www.ingramcontent.com/pod-product-compliance
Lightning Source LLC
Chambersburg PA
CBHW052045290426

44111CB00011B/1627